...eneration

...di, Girolamo
...1605
...me of wife illegible ── 2nd Generation

... (first name illegible)
...of Girolamo
...32 ── 3rd Generation

...h Generation

Lombardi, Marcantonio
d. Sant' Agata
Great Great Great
Grandfather of
Composer G. Verdi ── 5th Generation

Lombardi, Barbara
d. Sant' Agata
daughter of
Marcantonio Lombardi ── 6th Generation

Bianchi, Giovanni
m. Lombardi, Barbara ── 7th Generation

Bianchi, Francesca
(paternal grandmother
of the composer)
b. Sant' Agata 1747
d. 1807 at Madonna dei Prati ── 8th Generation

The Family tree of Giuseppe Verdi

This family tree was prepared
by Mary Jane Matz, with the help
of Gabriella Carrara-Verdi,
Don Sisto Bonelli,
Don Adolfo Rossi,
Romano Galti and the
Ufficio Anagrafe of Busseto,
as realized by Rus Anderson.

..., Maria Teresa
...ant' Agata
...ivelli, Giulio
...oncole 4/26/1793 │ Verdi, Maria Domenica
b. Sant' Agata 1775
m. Pedretti, Costantino
at Roncole 2/11/1795 │ Verdi, Maria Rosa
b. Sant' Agata 1773
m. Demaldè │ Verdi, Pietro Antonio
b. Sant' Agata 1771 │ Verdi, Marcantonio
b. Sant' Agata 1769 ── 9th Generation

...poni, Giuseppina
...15
...97 ── 10th Generation

...en

Barezzi Family of Verdi's First Wife

7th Generation Great Grandparents
Barezzi, Carlo Antonio

8th Generation Grandparents
Barezzi, Giovanni
m. Carrara, Giuseppa*

9th Generation Parents
Barezzi, Antonio
m. Demaldè, Maria
Uncles
Barezzi, Stefano**
map maker in Napoleon's army
Barezzi, Orlando

10th Generation
Barezzi, Margherita
b. 1814 **Wife of the Composer** d. 1840, in Milan

* Carrara, Giuseppa

Her sister was Donna Margherita Carrara,
godmother of Antonio Barezzi, all his
brothers and sisters, and of Margherita
Barezzi, Verdi's wife and Margherita Uttini,
Verdi's first Cousin.

**Barezzi, Stefano

As the restorer of Leonardo Da Vinci's The
Last Supper he invented the process of
removing frescoes from the wall and res-
toring them without using paint or brush.

Brothers
Barezzi, Giovannino
Barezzi, Demetrio
Barezzi, Marianna
also 3 other children

The Verdi Companion

The *Verdi* *Companion*

EDITED BY

William Weaver
AND
Martin Chusid

W · W · Norton & Company   NEW YORK   LONDON

Library of Congress Cataloging in Publication Data
Main entry under title:

A Verdi companion.

  Bibliography: p.
  Includes index.
  1. Verdi, Giuseppe, 1813–1901. I. Weaver, William,
1923–   II. Chusid, Martin.
ML410.V4V295   782.1′092′4   79–14793
ISBN 0–393–01215–8

Isaiah Berlin, "The Naiveté of Verdi," reprinted by permission of the author.
Originally published in the *Hudson Review,* Spring. 1968.

Maps on pages 32–33 reprinted from *The Red Shirt and the Cross of Savoy, the
Story of Italy's Risorgimento, 1748–1871,* by George Martin, © 1969. By permission
of the publisher, Dodd, Mead & Company.

Luigi Dallapiccola, "Words and Music in Italian Nineteenth Century Opera,"
reprinted by permission of the publisher, Il Saggiatore, Milan.

Designed by Mary A. Brown

1 2 3 4 5 6 7 8 9 0

Contents

Preface

*U*ntil recently few people read books about Verdi. For that matter, books on his life or on his music were not numerous, and—with rare exceptions—they were unhelpful and even inaccurate. But over the past two decades a double Verdi renaissance has taken place. On the one hand, performances and recordings of his less-known operas have led to a more nearly complete understanding of his development as an artist; and, with this greatly increased first-hand knowledge of his music, critical attention to the works has also broadened and deepened. Performers, scholars, critics, and audiences have joined forces, and a new, more interesting, sometimes unexpected picture of Verdi is emerging.

For a long time we knew surprisingly little about Verdi, and, still worse, we were not even aware of our ignorance. The simplest facts of his life—even his birth-date—were incorrectly reported, and there were no reliable editions of his music. Now a critical edition of his scores is being prepared; long-forgotten documents are coming to light; and two centers for Verdi research—the Istituto di Studi Verdiani in Parma, Italy, and the American Institute for Verdi Studies at New York University—now exist to provide materials and guidance for investigators, students, and performers.

We can see Verdi now in a new, brighter light; and as we come to know more of the man, of his passions and his manner of composing the operas, we also hear them—even the most perennially popular—with new ears.

This *Companion* is also a result of the new approach to Verdi; the Editors hope that its contents will stimulate further interest in the composer and his music. Its chief aim is to bring together, to synthesize and make easily accessible some of the results of the continuing investigation of Verdi's personality, both musical and human.

Verdi did not spring from nowhere; he developed as part of a strong musical tradition, as the chapter on Verdi and the Contemporary Italian Scene clearly shows. In thinking about any composer's development, it is important to know what music he heard, his cultural context. We know what was being performed in the Vienna of Beethoven and Schubert, in the Paris of Debussy, Ravel, Stravinsky; but the operatic world of early nineteenth-century Italy is relatively unknown, except for a handful of surviving popular works. Verdi grew up in that world, soon dominated it, and over a number of years changed it, not only musically but also—as another chapter of this *Companion* indicates—economically and socially.

One chapter of the volume is rightly devoted to Verdi's special use of the voice, his vocal tastes; and several chapters examine Verdi's literary texts. Rather than discuss individual works, the editors felt it was fruitful to see Verdi whole, from different points of view.

One of those points of view, inevitably, is the political. More than many other artists, Verdi was a man of his time: a time for Italy of crucial political change and violent upheaval. The events of the Risorgimento deeply affected the composer, and it is not going too far to say that Verdi's music undoubtedly had its effect on the Risorgimento.

The *Companion* is also meant as a handbook, a manual. Though the facts—dates, names, places—of Verdi's life are gradually being established, many are now available only in specialized publications, often out of print. For the Verdian who wants to go more deeply into a particular opera or an aspect of the composer's history, the *Companion* provides a bibliographical guide. The book also includes, for handy reference, a documented chronology of Verdi's life. This extensive section locates, insofar as possible, the composer's whereabouts at any given time and indicates where works were conceived, worked on, completed, performed, and, in the case of the elusive songs, published. There is also a *Dramatis personae,* a brief guide to the people whose lives touched or influenced Verdi's in some way. The Verdi family tree, in the book's endpapers, illustrates the ramifications of the family and their long ties with the land of Sant'Agata, to which the composer returned in his middle years to spend the remainder of his life.

Though the book bears our names as editors, it is the work of many hands. Several of the contributors, besides writing their own essays, gave valuable advice about the book as a whole. Our editor Claire Brook was a tireless and patient collaborator from the *Companion*'s inception. Our heartfelt thanks also to Amy Aaron, Barbara Fischer-Williams, Neil Ratliff, and especially to Tom Kaufman, who helped in the compilation of the *Dramatis personae* section.

William /Martin
Weaver/ Chusid

List of Abbreviations

ABBIATI	Franco Abbiati, *Giuseppe Verdi*. 4 Vols. (Milan, 1959).
ALBERTI	Annibale Alberti, *Verdi intimo: Carteggio di Giuseppe Verdi con il Conte Opprandino Arrivabene (1861–1886)* (Verona, 1931).
ARDITI	Luigi Arditi, *My Reminiscences* (New York, 1896).
ATTI	*Atti del Congressi Internazionali di Studi Verdiani* (Parma).
BARILLI	Anton Giulio Barilli, *Giuseppe Verdi: Vita e opera*. 3rd ed. (Genoa, 1892).
BRAGAGNOLO-BERTAZZI	G. Bragagnolo and E. Bettazzi, *La vita di Giuseppe Verdi narrata al popolo* (Milan, 1905).
BUSCH	Hans Busch, *Verdi's Aida: The History of an Opera in Letters and Documents* (Minneapolis, 1978).
CAPPELLI	A. Cappelli, *Cronologia, cronografia e calendario perpetuo*. 3rd ed. (Milan, 1969).
CARTEGGI I–IV	Alessandro Luzio, ed., *Carteggi verdiani*. 4 vols. (Rome, 1935, 1947).

CHUSID	Martin Chusid, *A Catalog of Verdi's Operas* (Hackensack, New Jersey, 1974).
CONATI	Marcello Conati, "Bibliografia verdiana: Aspetti, problemi, criteri per la sistemazione della letteratura verdiana," *Atti* 3 (1974), 546–63.
CONATIC	Marcello Conati, "Cronologia delle prime rappresentazioni dal 1871–1881," *Genesi dell' Aida, Quaderno* 4 (Parma, 1971), 156–77, 186–87.
COPIAL.	Gaetano Cesari and Alessandro Luzio, eds., *I Copialettere di Giuseppe Verdi* (Milan, 1913).
DAMERINI	Anselmo Damerini, "Sei lettere inedite di Verdi," *Il Pianoforte* 7 (Aug.–Sept. 1926), 221–26.
DE BELLIS	Frank V. de Bellis and Federico Ghisi, "Alcune lettere inedite sul *Don Carlos* dal carteggio Verdi-Mazzucato," *Atti* 2 (1972), 531–41.
DE RENSIS	Raffaello de Rensis, *Franco Faccio e Verdi: Carteggi e documenti inediti* (Milan, 1934).
FURLOTTI	Arnaldo Furlotti, "Una musica inedita di Giuseppe Verdi," *Scenario* X (1941), 83–84.
GARIBALDI	Luigi Agostino Garibaldi, *Giuseppe Verdi nelle lettere di Emanuele Muzio ad Antonio Barezzi* (Milan, 1931).
GARZANTI	*Atlante storico Garzanti: Cronologia della storia universale.* 3rd ed. (Milan, 1969).
GATTI	Carlo Gatti, *Verdi.* 2nd rev. ed. (Verona, 1951).
GHISI	Federico Ghisi, "Lettere inedite dall'epistolario Verdi-Mazzucato appartenete a Frank V. De Bellis," *Associazione Amici della Scala. Conferenze, 1968–1970* (Milan, c. 1970), 151–76.

GOSSETT

Philip Gossett, "Verdi, Ghislanzoni, and *Aida*: The Uses of Convention," *Critical Inquiry* I/2 (Dec. 1974), 291–334.

GUALERZI

Giorgio Gualerzi, "Un secolo di *Don Carlos*," *Atti* 2 (1972), 494–504.

GÜNTHER A

Ursula Günther, "Zur Entstehung von Verdis *Aida*," *"Studi musicali* 2 (1973), 15–69.

GÜNTHER B

———, "Der Briefwechsel Verdi– Nuitter–Du Locle zur Revision des *Don Carlos*," *Analecta Musicologica* 14 (1974), 414–44.

GÜNTHER D

———, "Documents inconnus concernant les relations de Verdi avec l'Opéra de Paris," *Atti* 3 (1974), 564–83.

GÜNTHER E

———, "Zur Entstehung der zweiten französischen Fassung von Verdi's *Don Carlos*," *International Musicological Society. Report of the Eleventh Congress Copenhagen 1972* (Copenhagen, 1974), 1, 396–402.

GÜNTHER G

——— "La Genèse de *Don Carlos*, opéra en cinq actes de Giuseppe Verdi, représentée pour la première fois à Paris le 11 mars 1867," *Revue de musicologie* 58 (1972), 16–64; 60 (1974), 87–158.

HUSSEY

Dyneley Hussey, *Verdi* (London, 1940; New York, 1962).

KIMBELL

David R. B. Kimbell, "Poi . . . diventò 'L'Oberto,'" *Music and Letters* 52 (1971), 1–7.

LA FENICE

Verdi e La Fenice. Ente Autonomo del Teatro La Fenice nel Cinquantenario della morte del Maestro (Venice, 1951).

LAWTON

David Lawton, "Tonality and Drama in the Early Verdi Operas," Ph.D. dissertation, University of California, Berkeley, 1973.

LAWTON-ROSEN

David Lawton and David Rosen, "Verdi's Non-Definitive Revisions: The Early Operas," *Atti* 3 (1974), 189–237.

MARCHESI F

Gustavo Marchesi, "Gli anni della 'Forza del destino,' " *Verdi: Bollettino dell'Istituto di Studi Verdiani* II/4 (1961), 17–42; II/5 (1962), 713–44; II/6 (1966), 1505–42.

MARCHESI R

————, "Gli anni del Rigoletto,' " *Verdi: Bollettino dell'Istituto di Studi Verdiani* III/7 (1969), 1–26; III/8 (1973), 849–75.

MATZ

Mary Jane Matz, "Verdi: The Roots of the Tree. An Examination of the Unexplored Verdi Documents of the Bassa Parmense," *Verdi: Bollettino dell'Istituto di Studi Verdiani* III/7 (1969), 333–64.

MILA

Massimo Mila, *La giovinezza di Verdi* (Turin, 1974).

MONALDI

Gino Monaldi, *Verdi: 1839–1898.* 4th ed. (Milan, 1951).

MONLEONE

Giovanni Monleone, *Le dimore genovesi di Giuseppe Verdi e la creazione dell' 'Aida' "* (Genoa, 1941).

MORAZZONI

G. Morazzoni, *Verdi: Lettere inedite.* Printed with G. M. Ciampelli, *Le Opere Verdiane al'Teatro alla Scala* (Milan, 1929).

NOSKE

Frits Noske, "The *Boccanegra* Revision: Correspondence between Verdi and Boito," *The Signifier and the Signified* (The Hague, 1977), 335–413.

OBERDORFER

Aldo Oberdorfer, ed., *Giuseppe Verdi. Autobiografia dalle lettere,* 2nd ed. (Milan, 1951).

OSBORNE

Charles Osborne, *The Complete Operas of Verdi* (New York, 1970).

PASCOLATO

Alessandro Pascolato, *Re Lear e Ballo in maschera. Lettere di Giuseppe Verdi ad Antonio Somma* (Città di Castello, 1902).

PORTER   Andrew Porter, "The Making of *Don Carlos*," *Proceedings of the Royal Musical Association* 98 (1971–72), 73–88.

PROD'HOMME   Jacques-Gabriel Prod'homme, "Lettres inédites de G. Verdi à Léon Escudier," *Rivista musicale italiana* 35 (1928), 1–28, 171–97, 519–52.

RADICIOTTI   Giuseppe Radiciotti, *Teatro, musica e musicisti in Sinigaglia. Notizie e documenti* (Milan, 1893).

REDLICH   Hans F. Redlich and Frank Walker, " 'Gesù morì.' An Unknown Early Verdi Manuscript," *The Music Review* 20 (1959), 233–43.

RESASCO   Ferdinando Resasco, *Verdi a Genova: Ricordi, aneddoti ed episodi* (Genoa, 1901).

RINALDI   Mario Rinaldi, *Le opere meno note di Giuseppe Verdi* (Florence, 1975).

RONCAGLIA   Gino Roncaglia, *Galleria verdiana (studi e figure)* (Milan, 1959).

ROSENL   David Rosen, "Verdi's 'Liber scriptus' Rewritten," *The Musical Quarterly* 55 (1969), 151–69.

ROSENM   ———, "La *Messa* a Rossini e il *Requiem* per Manzoni," *Rivista italiana di musicologia* 4 (1969), 127–37; 5 (1970), 216–33.

ROSENQ   ———, "Le quattro stesure del duetto Filippo-Posa," *Atti* 2 (1971), 368–88.

ROSENS   ———, "The Staging of Verdi's Operas: An Introduction to the Ricordi *Disposizioni Sceniche*," *Proceedings of the XII Congress of the International Musicological Society (Berkeley, 1977)*, in preparation.

SARTORI   Claudio Sartori, " 'Rocester' la prima opera di Verdi," *Rivista musicale italiana* 43 (1939), 97–104.

STEFANI

Giuseppe Stefani, *Verdi e Trieste* (Trieste, 1951).

TEBALDINI

Giovanni Tebaldini, "Il Conservatorio di Milano. Francesco Basilj e Giuseppe Verdi," *L'Archivio musicale della Cappella Laurentana* (Loreto, 1921), 144–53.

WALKERA

Frank Walker, *"L'Abandonée:* A Forgotten Song," *Verdi: Bollettino Quadrimestrale dell'Istituto di Studi Verdiani* I/2 (1960), 785–89.

WALKERB

———, "Introduction to a Biographical Study (Parliamentary Deputy at Turin, Opera Composer at St. Petersburg)," *Verdi: Bollettino dell'Istituto di Studi Verdiani* II/4 (1961), 1–16.

WALKERI

———, "Verdi's Ideas on the Production of His Operas," *Proceedings of the Royal Musical Association* (1949), 11–21.

WALKERL

———, "Unpublished Letters: A Contribution to the History of *Un ballo in maschera,"* *Verdi: Bollettino dell'Istituto di Studi Verdiani* I/1 (1960), 28–43.

WALKERV

———, *The Man Verdi* (London, 1962).

WALKER VIENNA

———, "Verdi and Vienna," *Musical Times* 92 (1951), 403–5, 451–53.

WEAVER

William Weaver, *Verdi: A Documentary Study* (London, 1977).

ZOPPI

Umberto Zoppi, *Angelo Mariani, Giuseppe Verdi e Teresa Stolz in un carteggio inedito* (Milan, 1947).

The Verdi Companion

The Naïveté of Verdi

Isaiah Berlin

for W. H. Auden

SIR ISAIAH BERLIN, O.M., Kt., C.B.E., M.A., F.B.A., was educated at Oxford and has been associated with the University for
most of his life. He has also lectured and taught at Harvard,
Princeton, and the City University of New York. He was director
of the Royal Opera House, Covent Garden, 1954–56, and is now
a member of its board. His publications include *Karl Marx, The
Hedgehog and the Fox,* and *Four Essays on Liberty.* His collection of
essays, *Russian Thinkers,* edited by Hardy Henry, was published
recently.

My topic is Verdi's "naiveté." I hope that this phrase
will not be misunderstood. To say that Verdi was naive in
any ordinary sense is an absurd suggestion. But it seems to
me that he was so in a very special—now forgotten—sense,
in which this term was once used by Friedrich Schiller.
Verdi greatly admired Schiller's dramatic works, which
inspired four of his operas. But it is not this—the affinity
of Verdi and Schiller which has often been remarked—
that I wish to discuss. My thesis is concerned with a different link between them.

In his once celebrated essay, published in 1796, which
he called *Ueber naive und sentimentalische Dichtung,* Schiller
distinguished two types of poets: those who are not con-

I

scious of any rift between themselves and their milieu, or within themselves; and those who are so conscious. For the first, art is a natural form of expression; they see what they see directly, and seek to articulate it for its own sake, not for any ulterior purpose, however sublime. Let me quote his own words:

> Such poets occur in the youth of the world and later: they are severe and chaste, like the virgin goddess Diana in her woods. . . . The dry, truthful way in which such a poet treats his material often resembles lack of feeling. The object possesses him entirely. His heart does not, like a cheap metal, lie on the very surface, but, like gold, must be sought in depths. He is concealed by his works like God by the world He has created. He is his work, for the work is himself. Only someone who is unworthy of a work, or does not understand it, or is satiated by it, will look in it only for the creator.

Homer, Aeschylus, Shakespeare, even Goethe, are poets of this kind. They are not, as poets, self-conscious. They do not, like Vergil or Ariosto, stand aside to contemplate their creations and express their own feelings. They are at peace with themselves. Their aim is limited, and they are able, if they have genius, to embody their vision fully. These Schiller calls *naiv*. With them he contrasts those poets who come after the Fall. Let me quote again: "When man enters the stage of culture, and art has laid its hand on him . . . the primordial, sensuous unity is gone . . . and the harmony between sense and thinking, which in the earlier state was *real*, now exists only as an *ideal*. It is not *in* a man, as a fact of his life, but outside him, as an ideal to be realized." The unity has been broken. The poet seeks to restore it. He looks for the vanished, harmonious world which some call Nature, and builds it from his imagination, and his poetry is his attempt to return to it, to an imagined childhood, and he conveys his sense of the chasm which divides the day-to-day world which is no longer his home, from the lost paradise which is conceived only ideally, only in reflection. Hence this ideal realm is bounded by nothing; it is in its very essence indefinable, unattainable, incapable of being embraced by means of any finite medium, no matter how great the poet's capacity for finding, molding, transforming his material. Let me quote Schiller again: "Visual art reaches its goal in the finite: that of the imagination, in infinity." And again, "The poet is either himself nature: or he seeks her." The first of these, Schiller calls *naiv,* the second, *sentimentalisch.*

For Schiller as for Rousseau, once ideas enter, peace, harmony, joy, are gone forever. The artist becomes conscious of himself, of his ideal aims, of their infinite distance from his own divided nature, that is, of the estrangement of his society and himself from the original and unbroken whole of thought and action, feeling and expression. The characteristic poetry of the "sentimental" is satire, that is, negation, an attack on that which calls itself real life but is in fact a degradation of it (what is now called alienation from it), artificial, ugly, and unnatural; or it is elegy—the affirmation of the lost world, the unrealizable ideal. This distinction is not at all the same as that between the classical and the romantic (whatever that may be), if only because it is not concerned with the presence or absence of objective rules, universal standards, fixed criteria, or an eternal ideal order. Aeschylus, Cervantes, Shakespeare, Ossian, the heroes of Romanticism, condemned by the Classical school as undisciplined and wild, are *naiv;* the models of Classicism—the authors of dramatic, or idyllic, or satirical, or epic poetry—Euripides, Vergil, Horace, Propertius, the neoclassical poets of the Renaissance, are nostalgic, self-conscious, deeply *sentimentalisch.*

The naive artist is happily married to his Muse. He takes rules and conventions for granted, uses them freely and harmoniously, and the effect of his art is, in Schiller's words, "tranquil, pure, joyous." The sentimental artist is in a turbulent relationship to his Muse: married to her unhappily. Conventions irk him, although he may defend them fanatically. He is Amfortas and seeks peace, salvation, the healing of his own or his society's secret and patent wounds. He cannot be at rest. Of him Schiller says:

> His observation is forcibly pushed aside by fancy, his sensibility by ideas, he closes his eyes and ears so that nothing may disturb his self-absorption in his own thoughts . . . his soul is fascinated by its own play . . . he never sees the object, only its transformation by his own reflective thought. . . . We cannot apprehend his feelings directly, at first hand, only their reflection in him . . . as he contemplates himself from outside, as a spectator.

Hence the effect of the sentimental artist is not joy and peace, but tension, conflict with nature or society, insatiable craving, the notorious neuroses of the modern age, with its troubled spirits, its martyrs, fanatics, and rebels, and its angry, bullying subversive preachers, Rousseau, Byron, Schopenhauer, Carlyle, Dostoevsky, Flaubert, Wagner, Marx, Nietzsche, offering not peace, but a sword.

Schiller's distinction, like all dichotomies, can, if taken literally, be carried much too far. But it is very original and very suggestive. If we ask whether in modern times there are artists who in Schiller's sense are naive—at peace with their medium—integral as men and artists, as tranquil and solid and free from self-consciousness or obsession and fulfilled artistically as, say, Cervantes, Bach, Handel, Rubens, Haydn, men whose art culminates in its object and is not used for some spiritual end beyond itself—to reach out for some unattainable ideal, or as a weapon in a war against philistines and traitors, we could answer, "Yes, indeed: Goethe, Pushkin, Dickens, at times Tolstoy (when he forgets his doctrine and his guilt), certainly these, Rossini and Verdi. Among composers of genius, Verdi is perhaps the last complete, self-fulfilled creator, absorbed in his art; at one with it; seeking to use it for no ulterior purpose, the god wholly concealed by his works, severe farouche, like Schiller's Diana, suspicious of anyone curious about his inner life, wholly, even grimly, impersonal, drily objective, at one with his music. A man who dissolved everything in his art, with no more personal residue than Shakespeare or Tintoretto. In Schiller's sense, the last great naive poet of our time."

Of course, anyone who has any knowledge of Verdi's life knows that it was intertwined with that of his country: that his name became the very symbol of the Risorgimento, that *Viva Verdi* (not for political or monarchist reasons alone) was the most famous revolutionary and patriotic cry in Italy: that he admired both Mazzini and Cavour, both the revolutionary democrats and the king, and in his way, united in his person the diverse strands which made the Italian nation. He always (to use Herder's simile) lived near the center of gravity of his nation, and spoke to his countrymen and for them, as no one else did, not even Manzoni or Garibaldi, to both of whom he was close. His convictions, whether they moved to the right or the left, moved with those of popular feeling; he responded deeply and personally to every twist and turn in the Italian struggle for unity and freedom. The Hebrews of *Nabucco* were Italians in captivity. "Va, pensiero" was the national prayer for resurrection. The performance of *Battaglia di Legnano* evoked scenes of indescribable popular excitement in the revolutionary Rome of 1849. *Rigoletto,* no less than *Don Carlo, Forza del destino,* and *Aida,* is inspired by a hatred of oppression, inequality, fanaticism, and human degradation. The hymn which Verdi wrote for Mazzini is only an episode in a single great campaign. For half a century he was the living symbol of all that was most generous and universal in Italian national feeling.

All this is so. Nevertheless, it is not at the center of Verdi's art. Insight into his music does not require us to know all, or any, of this. Of course all knowledge of what a man of genius was and felt is interesting, but it is not always essential. The point is, however, that it is essential in the case of the great "sentimental" masters: no one who does not realize what Beethoven felt about tyranny can fully understand the *Eroica,* or *Fidelio,* the first great political opera; no one who is ignorant of the relevant social movements in Russia can understand the significance of *Boris Godunov,* or *Khovanshchina.* Schumann's aesthetic outlook, Wagner's mythology, the Romantic theories that dominated Berlioz, are indispensable to the understanding of their masterpieces; but it is not necessary to know Shakespeare's political views to understand his historical plays; it might help, but it is not required. It is so with Verdi. Anyone who is acquainted with primary human passions—paternal love, and the full horror of the humiliation of men by other men in a dehumanized society—will understand *Rigoletto;* insight into a hero destroyed by jealousy is sufficient for understanding *Otello.* Knowledge of basic human emotions is virtually all the extramusical equipment that is needed to understand Verdi's works, early or late, great or small, *Suona la tromba* as much as *La traviata; Attila* or *Luisa Miller* no less than *Forza del destino* or *Aida; Il corsaro* or *Ernani* as much as *Il trovatore,* the *Requiem* or *Otello,* or even *Falstaff. Falstaff* is musically and artistically absolutely unique. Nevertheless the requirements needed to do it justice do not include, as indispensable *sine quibus non,* knowledge of the personal views or attributes of the composer, or the historical circumstances of his life or those of his society. This is not needed in his case any more than in those of Bach or Mozart or Rossini, of Shakespeare or Goethe or Dickens. From *Oberto, Conte di San Bonifacio* to the *Quattro pezzi sacri,* the character of Verdi's creations is, in Schiller's special sense, wholly *naiv:* they spring from a direct vision of the object. There is no effort to reach beyond, to an infinite and unattainable empyrean, and lose oneself in it, no ulterior aim, no impossible attempt to fuse antagonistic worlds —music and literature, the personal and the public, concrete reality and a transcendent myth. Verdi never seeks to close a breach, to compensate for the imperfections of human life, or heal his own wounds or overcome his society's inner cracks, its alienation from a common culture or from the ancient faith, by using magical means, by conjuring up an infernal, or a celestial, vision as a means of escape or revenge or salvation. This is as true of *Falstaff* as it is of *Un giorno di regno* or the *String Quartet.* "Desire," said a British philosopher in the eighteenth century, "culminates in its object." Verdi belongs to this tradition, and represents its finest flowering. Verdi's art, like that of Bach, is objective, direct, and in harmony with the conventions which govern it. It springs from an unbroken inner unity, a sense of belonging to its own time and society and milieu, which precludes the *nostalgie de l'infini,* the conception of art as therapy which lies at the heart of what Schiller calls *sentimentalisch.* In this sense Vergil, Propertius, and Horace were *sentimentalisch:* "sentimental" and also models of Classicism; while the *Song of the Niebelungs* or *Don Quixote,* idealized by the Romantics, are *naiv.*

Verdi was the last of the great naive masters of Western music, in an age given over to the *Sentimentalisches.* He remained scarcely affected by it. He may have been interested in, or even influenced by, Wagner or Liszt or Meyerbeer; but the influence was confined to method, technical innovations. Their worlds and their doctrines remained alien to him. After him naiveté is to be found, in the West at any rate, only in the borderlands, outside the central movement—among the composers of the Slav countries, Spain, perhaps Norway, where social conditions resemble an earlier Europe.

Verdi is, of course, not without an ideology. But it is that of vast numbers of mankind across large stretches of history: this is, indeed, one of the central meanings of the term *humanism.* Alberto Moravia traces it to his peasant origin and upbringing, which triumphed over the bourgeois society of his time. Peasants are an ancient and universal social class, and if it is this that worked in Verdi, it is not irrelevant to what Rousseau and Schiller meant by relatively uncorrupted relationship with nature.

The attacks on Verdi are notorious. They came from many quarters. In England, Mr. Chorley found him too noisy, that is, too vulgar, compared to Rossini, Boieldieu, etc. Nor was the wish to return to Rossini and Bellini confined to the conservatives of the north—it came from Italians too; least of all, let it be noted, from Rossini himself. Naturally the principal onslaught came from the champions of the new music: the Wagnerians and the Lisztians, the protagonists of all that was most self-conscious, extramusical, "sentimental," from faith in music as a messianic rebirth of the spirit. Boito, who was later to denounce Wagner as a false prophet, was in his day deeply caught by this. His explosion against Verdi is too well known to cite.

This is as it should be. Verdi was indeed the greatest, most triumphant obstacle to the new aesthetic religion: it was not worth wasting powder and shot on Pacini or Mercadante, even on Meyerbeer, Auber, or Halévy, while Verdi was dominant: he was the archenemy, the traditionalist of power and genius. Still more violent were the attacks from the East, delivered by the great new national school of the Slav world, in particular the Russians. Balakirev and Borodin, Musorgsky and Stassov, detested Verdi: not for his occasional platitudes and vulgarities— not for "Questa o quella" or "O tu Palermo," but for the very qualities in which his strength resided, his acceptance of, and his identification with, the hateful *formula*—the conventions of opera. The Russians, inspired by populist ideals, disciples of the unknown master Dargomyzhsky (whom they regarded as a genius of the first order), believed in musical realism, in the most intimate interrelation of words, plot, expression, music, historical and social consciousness. They virtually invented the expressive semi-recitative to convey the finest psychological nuances of the "real" inner and outer life of both individuals and masses. When Busoni declared that love scenes should not occur on the stage—because what is intimate should not take place in public—this most sophisticated man echoed, however unconsciously (he would have been horrified to be told this), this literal realism. The Russians were in open revolt against the Italian opera of Paisiello, Cherubini, Rossini, Donizetti, Bellini. At long last the miserable crew of operatic purveyors showed signs of going under; but Verdi had breathed new life into the tradition and reconquered the musical public for the beastly *formula,* the mechanical succession of detachable operatic "numbers," the bits and pieces which could be performed in any order, from, for example, the *Requiem,* with which Verdi and his singers toured Europe. They denounced all those self-contained arias, duets, trios, quintets, choruses, the inevitable appoggiaturas and artificially stuck-on cabalettas and cavatinas, the mechanism of the all too predictable orchestral accompaniment, the terrible hurdy-gurdy that killed the living expression of real experience. *Prince Igor* seemed to them spontaneous and "real," whereas *Don Carlo* and *La traviata* were Christmas trees decked out with meretricious baubles. Not that they liked Wagner any better—he seemed to them "a pompous disseminator of clamorous confusion," to use Boito's phrase. Serov, their colleague who admired and imitated this master, was duly drummed out of the nationalist regiment. Their gods were Liszt and Berlioz. The greatest enemy was always Verdi, upon whom they looked as the early German Romantics looked on the French arbiters of taste in the eighteenth century: shallow, pompous, stilted, artificial, utterly predictable, utterly worthless. Liszt and Berlioz were Rousseau—the return to the colors and sounds of nature, to real individual feeling from the corrupt, commercialized sophistication of the standardized authors, Marivaux, Crébillon, Marmontel, above all, Voltaire, the dancing masters, with their powdered wigs and rhymed couplets and carefully contrived epigrams amid the bric-a-brac of the trivial and heartless salons.

This (as in the case of the Germans and the French a century earlier) was the attack of the *sentimentalisch* on the *naiv:* equally inevitable, perhaps, and equally exaggerated and wrongheaded. Verdi went his way, wounded, but ultimately serene and unperturbed. Doubtless he did not belong to the new world of Baudelaire, Flaubert, Liszt, Wagner, Nietzsche, Dostoevsky, Musorgsky. There is no reason to think that he was aware of this, or would have cared if he had been. He was the last great voice of humanism not at war with itself, at any rate in music.

No matter how sophisticated his scores, there is no trace, right to the end, of self-consciousness, neurosis, decadence. For that, in Italian music, we must wait for Boito, Puccini, and their followers. He was the last master to paint with positive, clear, primary colors, to give direct expression to the eternal, major human emotions: love and hate, jealousy and fear, indignation and passion; grief, fury, mockery, cruelty, irony, fanaticism, faith, the passions that all men know. After him, this is much more rare. From Debussy onward, whether music is impressionist or expressionist, neoclassical or neoromantic, diatonic or chromatic, dodecaphonic, aleatoric, or concrete, or a syncretism of these, innocence is gone.[1]

To escape from the inflation and the appalling elephantiasis of late German Romanticism, a variety of astringent, deflationary styles came into being. But the return to Bach or to Pergolesi, or to Gesualdo, or to Machaut, is a conscious attempt to look for antidotes. This has indeed generated much original and fascinating music, anti-*sentimentalisch*, and thereby itself *sentimentalisch*, inasmuch as it is self-regarding, self-conscious, doctrine-influenced music, accompanied by theories and manifestoes, neo-Catholic (Solesmes), atonal, surrealist, socialist-realist (neo-diatonic), etc., to justify it. We expect ideological declarations, programmatic statements, anathemas from Wagner or Berlioz or Debussy or the Russian composers in the twentieth century. But just as we should have regarded a

1. There is a sense in which, for instance, Bruckner can be called naive. But that is the ordinary, not Schiller's, sense. In Schiller's sense of the word, Bruckner's visionary mysticism, the combination of sensuousness and effort at self-transcendence (as in the even acuter case of César Franck and the Schola Cantorum) is the deepest imaginable *Sentimentalität*. So is the very notion of the *Gesamtkunstwerk*, with its striving for an unattainable integration of all the elements.

manifesto on the function of literature signed by Dickens or Dumas *père* as almost inconceivable, so a *profession de foi* by Verdi on the aesthetic or social significance of Italian opera or its relation to the *commedia dell' arte* (of the kind to be found in the writings of, say, Boito or Busoni) would rightly be suspected of being an exceptionally unplausible forgery. Manifestos are a symptom of revolt or reaction, personal or collective; that is to say, of an acute phase of "sentimentality." The remoteness of Verdi, who is so often and, in a sense, so justly described as one of the most deeply characteristic and representative artists of the nine-teenth century, from this particular condition, which is usually held to be a central feature of that period—its typical malaise—is, perhaps, what is most arresting in his personality, both as an artist and as a man. In this respect he has no successors. In music at least, he is the last "naive" artist of genius. The desire to "go back" to Verdi itself becomes a form of incurable nostalgia, of acutely non-Verdian "sentimentality," from which he was himself wholly and peacefully free.

It is natural enough that what during the high tide of the *sentimentalisch* movement, from, say, the 1870s to the 1930s, was looked upon both by the German and the anti-German (i.e. Franco-Russian) musical public (and its critics) as Verdi's popular, vulgar style, should have re-emerged during the last quarter-century, as the last direct voice of the great tradition. It is felt to be so in conscious contrast with the quest for the remote and the exotic—symptoms of recession, the desire to obtain comfort or derive new life from traditions remote in space and time—the music of the Middle Ages or of the Age of Reason, or the relics of the folk tradition in Eastern Europe, Asia, Africa, and the islands of the Pacific.

Noble, simple, with a degree of unbroken vitality and vast natural power of creation and organization, Verdi is the voice of a world which is no more. His enormous popularity among the most sophisticated as well as the most ordinary listeners today is due to the fact that he expressed permanent states of consciousness in the most direct terms, as Homer, Shakespeare, Ibsen, and Tolstoy have done. This is what Schiller called *naiv*. After Verdi this is not heard in music again. Verdi's assured place, in the high canon of the musical art, which nobody now disputes, is a symptom of sanity in our time. The sociology of this phenomenon, like that of Verdi's own position in his own time, is itself a fascinating topic, but not one with which I am qualified to deal.

Verdi and the Risorgimento
George Martin

GEORGE MARTIN is the author of *The Opera Companion: a Guide for the Casual Operagoer* and *Verdi, His Music, Life and Times.* He has lectured both here and abroad on operatic subjects and has conducted a seminar at Yale on Verdi. Among his other books is a history of Italy in the nineteenth century, *Red Shirt and the Cross of Savoy.*

Great men sometimes can put a personal stamp on an event or episode; besides articulating it, they can help to shape it. Winston Churchill, after the fall of France in World War II, so well expressed Britain's lonely defiance of Nazi Germany that its spirit not only rang round the world but helped to forge the ultimate victory.

Such identification or stamping is easier perhaps for heads of state than for artists, for the events with which the former are associated are often greater or at least more particular. Artists, however, have an advantage in another way. If they live long enough and are great enough, they can articulate not just an event or moment in time but an entire era, a civilization with all its social customs and attitudes. Who can watch Molière's plays without feeling the currents that disturbed life in mid-seventeenth-century France? Or hear Bach's cantatas without sensing the spirit of early-eighteenth-century Lutheran Germany?

But such stamping, of course, is reciprocal: the man affects the era, and the era, the man. With Verdi the era was the Risorgimento, a period in Italian political and social history that roughly spans the nineteenth century. At its start, Italy, in a phrase of the day, was only "a geographical expression," for the Po valley, peninsula, and islands were divided into more than ten political units, none of them powerful, most of them dominated by foreign powers. At its end these states were united in a Kingdom of Italy, moderately powerful, truly independent, and with its capital at Rome. And socially the people were beginning to feel themselves a nation: what divided them was less important then what they had in common. In place of French, German, Latin, or local dialect, Italian increasingly was spoken, and in place of Neapolitan, Venetian, or Roman music, an Italian style emerged.

Verdi was the greatest artist of this movement. Throughout his work its values, its issues recur constantly, and he expressed them with great power. In a country divided by local dialects, customs, and governments, his music provided a bond for all sorts of men. In his person—starting life humbly, living it honestly, even nobly— he became for many a symbol of what was best in the period. If he and his art were partly shaped by the Risorgimento, they also in part shaped it.

Verdi was born, on October 9, 1813, into a world turned upside down by the French exuberantly exporting their Revolution. Starting in 1796 a succession of French armies crossed the Alps to bring Liberty, Equality, and Fraternity to the Italians and also to rob, tax, and conscript them into the French armies. In the confusion the ten chief Italian states—a theocracy (the Papal State), two kingdoms (Sardinia-Piedmont, Naples-Sicily), three republics (Genoa, Venice, Lucca), and four duchies (Tuscany, Parma, Modena, Milan)—were continually reorganized by the French into new entities, and by 1813, for easier administration, Napoleon had absorbed the greater part of six of them directly into France. Among these was the former Duchy of Parma, in which Verdi was born, so that technically he was born a Frenchman.

Within two years, however, the British, Russians, and Austrians had defeated Napoleon and at the Congress of Vienna assigned the Italian states to the Austrians to reorganize as they wished. In the subsequent shuffle only three of the former states—the theocracy and the two kingdoms—were powerful enough to regain any independence. The pope was able to reconstitute his Papal State across the center of the peninsula. The Bourbons of Naples regained their dual kingdom of Sicily and Naples, ruling all of Italy south of Rome. And in the northwest the House of Savoy returned from its island of Sardinia to its capital on the mainland, Turin. In addition, because the Kingdom of Sardinia could serve as a buffer between France and Austria, Vittorio Emanuele I was allowed to add to his mainland province of Piedmont the former Republic of Genoa. The rest of Italy, chiefly the rich Po valley and Tuscany, was divided into a kingdom and four duchies, with the Austrian emperor ruling the Kingdom of Lombardy-Venetia and obedient relatives placed in the duchies. The new order reduced the former ten states to eight and eliminated the three republics. The Viennese Habsburgs believed in government by absolute monarchy, and in their Italian possessions wherever possible they rooted out any traditions or new French ideas about self-government.

Among the obedient relatives given an Italian throne was the emperor's daughter, Marie Louise, whom in 1810 he had married to Napoleon in an effort to secure peace. After Napoleon's defeat and her refusal to accompany him into exile she became as Maria Luigia the figurehead of Austrian rule in the reconstituted Duchy of Parma, a small state between the Po and the Apennines. One of her new subjects was the infant Verdi. Twenty-eight years later, when still a somewhat rough, country musician, he would dedicate to her, his sovereign, his revolutionary opera *I lombardi,* and she, an Austrian archduchess and former empress of France, would present him a jewelled pin. At their meeting with its exchange of incongruous gifts two extremes of experience briefly touched.

The town in which Verdi grew up, Busseto, sits in flat farm country midway between the cities of Parma and Piacenza. In his youth it was a small market town of about 2,000 persons, a neat rectangle of buildings still tightly girdled by medieval walls. At one corner looking out over the tilled fields was the "Rocca," a small castle, and at each of the others, a squat tower. Not far to the north was the Po. In summer the weather was hot and dry, and in winter, cold and damp. Farming was the district's chief activity and source of wealth.

Verdi lived in Busseto until 1832, when he went to Milan to study music, and again from 1836–38, while he held the town post of *maestro di musica:* organist, choirmaster, director of the local orchestra, band, and music school. During these years he married the daughter of his patron and had two children. Tragically, within a three-year period the entire family died, and for a decade in a desolate, desperate manner he pursued his career elsewhere while establishing himself as a European composer. Then he returned (with the woman he later married), bought land, began to farm it, built a large, comfortable house, and—with only occasional interruptions to travel, compose, or produce an opera—personally managed the farm until his death on January 27, 1901.

Verdi's youth in a farming community and his return to it helped to keep his role in the Risorgimento primarily artistic. Busseto served as a base from which to follow the issues and events of the day while avoiding the activism of the large cities. Even in the decade that he lived in Milan, his constant travels to other cities to stage or conduct an opera insured his position as a spectator. In Milan he had friends who wanted to expel the Austrians from Lombardy and who were, in Austrian eyes, revolutionaries. Verdi was sympathetic to his friends' aims, but was too often absent to join their conspiracies. When in 1848 the city rose and in five days of street fighting drove the Austrian army out, Verdi was in Paris. He hurried back but was too late for the fighting and, when the Austrians retook the city, was not included in their reprisals.

He was fortunate, too, to be a citizen of Parma. Of all the Italian states it was the most lightly governed and, probably as a result, the most peaceful. Where rulers of neighboring states seemed often to seek confrontations with their subjects, Maria Luigia and her successors avoided them. Though Verdi frequently had difficulties with censors elsewhere, he had few in Parma; nor was he ever fined for his opinions, or his land expropriated for his actions, as happened to many in Milan. For an outspoken Italian patriot in the mid-nineteenth century, Parma was the easiest state in which to live.

The Risorgimento, like many political and social movements that continue for several generations, began obscurely, passed through several phases, and ended by fading imperceptibly into something quite different. Historians do not agree on the date at which a sense of nationality first appeared among the people of Italy, the moment at which Venetians, Romans, Neapolitans began to think of themselves as Italians. It is clear, however, that the sense was greatly stimulated by the French invasions following the Revolution.

The French not only talked endlessly about "We, the French," exciting those they harangued to think of "We, the Italians," but in the name of their Revolution they swept away the remains of Italian feudalism, reorganized the states on a more rational basis, and staffed them with skilled administrators—thereby greatly increasing trade— and ruled, at least at the start, through assemblies to which the Italians sent delegates. The memory of those constituent assemblies survived the later imperialism of Napoleon and clashed, after the Congress of Vienna, with Austria's desire to impose an absolute monarchy on every Italian state.

The first revolution to shake the peninsula occurred in

Naples in 1820. It was the work of a secret society whose members were known as the Carbonari, or Charcoal Burners, because the society was organized by *vendite,* or "shops," for the ostensible sale of charcoal. There were "shops" or clubs in every Italian state, but they varied greatly and lacked cohesion. Those in the south had a wide membership and much sociability in the meetings; in the north they tended to be restricted to the educated, to be more purely political in aim and more conspiratorial.

The Neapolitan clubs had members in every branch of the government, including the army, and their revolution consisted simply of declaring themselves and staging an enormous parade through Naples. They demanded a constitution, requesting the king to continue as a constitutional monarch. Faced with a government at a standstill, he agreed. But eight months later, after secret negotiations with the Austrians, he called in an Austrian army that swept the constitution aside and reimposed an absolute monarchy.

A revolution with a similar aim started in Turin but was more quickly crushed, again by an Austrian army called in by the king. And still another revolution planned in Milan was prevented by the arrest of its leaders. Everywhere men went to prison or into exile, and Austria was clearly recognized as the chief obstacle to independence for any Italian state. For many, too, the belief increased that no trust should be placed in kings.

Ten years later, in 1831, there was another Carbonaro revolution. This time the conspirators planned to combine Parma, Modena, and as much of the Papal State as lay east of the Apennines into a constitutional Kingdom of Central Italy. By offering the throne to the Duke of Modena they hoped to persuade Austria to acquiesce, and they looked to France, at the time a constitutional monarchy, for diplomatic and even military support.

Though the duke of Modena had agreed to accept the throne, on the eve of the revolution he betrayed many of its leaders to the Austrians. The remainder, nevertheless, met in an assembly at Bologna and formed a provisional government. But the French did nothing, while the pope, the duke, and Maria Luigia called in the Austrian army stationed in Lombardy. The revolution, the first to aim at uniting several Italian states under one ruler, collapsed. It was the last effort of the Carbonaro societies, and a new phase of the Risorgimento emerged.

Its leader was Giuseppe Mazzini, a tall, thin, passionate young man from Genoa who could write with the fervor of an Old Testament prophet. Believing that the Carbonaro societies had been too limited in their aim of constitutional monarchy, too ready to accept the existing Italian states as permanent, and too inclined to rely on France or Britain for support, Mazzini founded a new secret society, La Giovine Italia, or Young Italy, whose purpose was to unite all the Italian states in one republic without foreign help. The Italians were to do it alone by putting aside all pettiness and thoughts of self and, through moral regeneration, becoming a people ready to work and die to achieve a better world. The start would be Italy, free, united, and a republic.

From exile in Marseille and later Geneva, Mazzini spread his ideas throughout Italy by a journal, *La Giovine Italia,* that was banned in every state. Yet copies were well distributed, travelling frequently in trunks with false bottoms or crates of fish or pumice. Once through customs they passed from hand to hand, circulating often for years. Some articles proposed in detail how town uprisings might be organized; others described how guerilla bands could fight from the hills; still another argued that a federation of states was more suitable for Italy than a republic. But as most of the journal was written by Mazzini, his views predominated, and they were presented with mystical authority.

As an active revolutionary, however, he soon proved himself incompetent. In 1834 he attempted to spark an uprising in the Kingdom of Sardinia by leading a small army into Piedmont from Switzerland. For months he and his men gathered in Swiss hotels, posing as tourists and imagining they were undetected. The expedition when it finally crossed the border was a complete failure. Without meeting any military opposition it simply disintegrated; its only accomplishments were the temporary capture of a customs station, the burning of some customs uniforms, and the planting of a Tree of Liberty. But over the years Mazzini's ideas, which he continued to propagate, had a powerful effect. Always he urged a united Italy, for only so could freedom from foreign domination be maintained. Always, as a first step to unity, he urged Venetians, Romans, Neapolitans, and others to substitute for their traditional loyalties to towns or districts a new loyalty to the Italian nation. And always, he insisted, Rome must be the capital of that new nation. There had been classical Rome and then medieval or papal Rome; there must now be Italian Rome.

To these political and even religious ideas of Mazzini there was a literary counterpart. The poet Leopardi wrote verses of aching beauty about the ruin that was Italy and the cause of it that was Austria. Less direct but more influential, because more widely read, was Manzoni's novel, *I promessi sposi*, the story of a peasant marriage long prevented by evil men and circumstances. The novel's political and social significance, however, lay less in its story than in its language. When Manzoni first published it in 1827, its descriptive passages were in the current literary style, an eighteenth-century leftover that no one talked; and its dialogue was in the current slang of Milanese dialect that almost no one wrote. Then as the book sped through edition after edition, he constantly revised it to include more and more Italian words and constructions— essentially the Tuscan dialect—and where no words or constructions existed, he made them up. By the definitive edition of 1840 the language was entirely Italian, and for many the novel was also a primer and dictionary. It, and the many lesser works it inspired, in effect created a serviceable, modern language for an emerging nation.

And then in music there was Verdi. There were others before him, of course. Rossini's *William Tell* (1829) has a strong dose of anti-Austrian feeling, and near Naples in 1844 a group of Mazzini's followers faced a firing squad while singing a patriotic chorus by Mercadante. But with Verdi the nationalistic feeling was not incidental to one opera or even two, but an integral part of his career.

His third opera, *Nabucco* (1842), and the first to make him famous, is a story of Nebuchadnezzar's pride, downfall, and subsequent acceptance of Jehovah, whose people he has taken captive. The music is rough, vigorous, exciting, and, at times, beautiful, but its chief glory is a long, slow chorus for the Israelites, captive in Babylon, yearning for their homeland: "Va, pensiero, sull'ali dorate . . ." (Go, thought, on golden wings . . .).

All over Italy, as the opera passed from town to town, Italian patriots heard in that chorus their own emotions after failing so often to end their Austrian captivity.

. . . Oh, mia patria sì bella e perduta!	. . . Oh, my country so beautiful and lost!
Oh, membranza sì cara e fatal! . . .	Oh, memory so dear and fatal! . . .

At the premiere at La Scala, and at most performances later and elsewhere, despite police prohibitions against repeats, the audiences demanded the chorus be sung again. The police disliked repeats, for they were apt to become demonstrations against the Austrian officials in the boxes, but if the audience insisted, what could the conductor do? Generally he shrugged his shoulders and later pled that it seemed more dangerous to balk the audience than to satisfy it. In any event, why not repeat a chorus that was based on the Bible? The operas were difficult to censor because the texts became offensive only by allusion.

Verdi followed *Nabucco* with *I lombardi alla prima crociata* (1843), *The Lombards on the First Crusade.* The opera is based on a narrative poem of Tomasso Grossi in which a family feud in Milan, arising from the love of two brothers for the same woman, is finally resolved years later on a crusade to the Holy Land. At the premiere the audience cast itself as the Lombards and the Austrians as the Saracens defiling the Holy Land; it put the crusade into the future and greeted with frenzy a chorus calling the Lombards from despair to battle. The tenor cries, "La Santa Terra oggi nostra sarà" (The Holy Land today will be ours), to which the chorus—and audience—replied, "Sì! . . . Guerra! Guerra!" (Yes! . . . War! War!). Pandemonium followed, and the police were unable to stop a repeat.

Such scenes were not accidental. Verdi and his librettists deliberately wrote as close to sedition as the censors might be persuaded to allow. In *Attila* (1846), in which the audience was invited to equate the Habsburgs with the Huns, the electrifying lines were sung by a Roman general to Attila: "Avrai tu l'universo, Resti l'Italia a me" (You may have the universe, but leave Italy to me). The lines quickly became an anti-Austrian slogan, and if on police order they were dropped from a performance, then that, too, produced a demonstration in the theater.

The impact of such scenes at the time was very great partly because of the role of the opera house in the daily life of the towns. It was the principal center of recreation. Performances began generally at nine in the evening, and, with the house lit chiefly by chandeliers of candles, the house lights were not dimmed. Except at an opera's most exquisite or exciting passages, members of the audience constantly entered or left their boxes, waved and whispered to each other around the auditorium, conducted business in the halls and foyers, and made the evening as much a social as musical event. Even the wholly unmusical went to the opera constantly. In both Milan and Parma *Nabucco* was played so often in its first full season that more seats were sold to it than the town had inhabitants.

In the decade of the 1840s, after his success with *Nabucco*, Verdi composed an average of two operas a year, and most of them had at least one scene or chorus that struck a patriotic response. Even in *Macbeth* (1847), seemingly an

unlikely opera for Italian patriotism, he inserted a chorus
for Scottish exiles, "O patria oppressa" (O fatherland oppressed). At the performances in Venice, the audiences
took to throwing onto the stage bouquets of red and
green, the Italian colors, which provoked demonstrations.
When the police forbad red and green, the audience threw
bouquets of yellow and black, the Austrian colors, for the
pleasure of watching the singers refuse to pick them up.

Nevertheless, Verdi's choice of *Macbeth* for an opera is
an indication that he wanted to do more than compose patriotic pot-boilers. The play had never been performed in
Italy. Shakespeare was read and admired by an educated
few, and for Verdi to have found his way to *Macbeth* was an
example of his natural good taste and wide reading.

The play was also an odd choice for an opera in its lack
of love interest. There had been operas before without
young lovers: Donizetti's *Lucrezia Borgia* was one, though
even it had scenes of affection between a mother and son.
In *Macbeth* there is only the disintegration of two adults destroyed by illegitimately held power. For all of its Scottish
setting it was a natural subject for a Risorgimento audience, if the composer could make the public see it. Verdi
did, and the opera, though revolutionary in its musical
style, had a popular success.

Verdi's interest in statecraft, government, and the effect
on men of the exercise of power is a recurring theme in his
operas. It is prominent in *Nabucco, Ernani, Macbeth, Simon
Boccanegra,* and *Don Carlos,* and not far from the center of
I due Foscari, Giovanna d'Arco, Un ballo in maschera, and
Otello. Even in the triumphal scene of *Aida* it appears
briefly in the clash between the priests and the king over
the fate of the Ethiopians. The interest was lifelong and
deep—Verdi's letters are full of it—and is perhaps a reason he had such success in putting political and patriotic
ideas onto the stage. Certainly it is a reason that his operas
seem to many to offer a wider range of experience than,
say, those of Puccini, which tend to focus on young lovers.

The very lack of love interest in *Macbeth,* however, played to Verdi's strength. He plainly had no difficulty in putting his patriotic feelings onto the stage for all to share, but he seems for many years to have been shy about exhibiting his personal emotions. Not until *Un ballo in maschera* (1859), when he was forty-six, did he compose an extended love duet for passionate adults, and even after that he did not do it often. Typically before then, he would have a third person present, such as the hermit in the *I lombari* trio; or he would hasten almost ludicrously through the scene, as in *Giovanna d'Arco;* or as in Act II of *La traviata*, the tenor did not respond because he was unaware of the reason for Violetta's great outburst. Or, most often, the tenor-soprano love duet would be the most conventional music in the opera, as in *Rigoletto* or *Il trovatore*.

Why? The reason was not a failure of emotion within him, for as *Un ballo in maschera* demonstrated and *La traviata* and others hinted, he could write powerful music for love duets. And as his wife's letters to him suggest, his love was passionate. Rather, he was reticent. It is extraordinary that among the thousands of his letters that have survived, there is not one that can be called a love letter. He simply did not put such thoughts on paper or, for the most part, onto the stage. They were private. He is the opposite of those artists of today who cannot say "my country" without embarrassment yet will recount their love life on television.

In his attitude there was a message for the audience: that fighting to create a free and united Italy was more important than personal happiness. His operas are filled with lovers torn apart by the call of duty. Never for a moment did Verdi suggest that the choice presented was easy, but he left no doubt how it should be made.

For many in Italy the choice became real in 1848, "the mad and holy year," because of the number of revolutions. Within the triangle of Paris, Warsaw, and Palermo, in almost every city of more than a hundred thousand, the people suddenly demanded reforms and generally won them, sometimes peacefully, sometimes by force. Almost everywhere they asked for a free press and a constitution or, if one existed, an extension of the franchise.

In Milan and in Venice, quite independently, the people expelled the Austrian garrisons. The Venetians promptly proclaimed a republic, but the Milanesi hesitated, hoping to persuade the king of Sardinia to support them with his army. Verdi, who had hastened to Milan from Paris, urged a republic, but others, not necessarily monarchists, argued that help from Sardinia was vital: the Austrian army had only withdrawn, not surrendered.

When that view began to prevail, Verdi returned to Paris. He wrote a patriotic hymn, *Suona la tromba* (Sound the Trumpet), that he sent to Mazzini—"Do with it what you wish. Burn it if it doesn't seem good enough"—and started work on a patriotic opera, *La battaglia di Legnano.* The hymn had little success; the opera, more.

In January 1849, when Verdi went to Rome to conduct its premiere, the city was convulsed with excitement. The pope, who had been liberalizing his government, had suddenly been deposed as the political head of the Papal State and held prisoner by the most extreme republicans. Escaping, he and many conservatives had fled the city. Those leaders remaining, mostly republicans, announced that a Constituent Assembly with representatives elected by direct and universal suffrage would meet on February 5 to select a new form of government for the Papal State. As the eyes of Catholics everywhere focused on the Eternal City, Republicans from all the Italian states began to pour into it. Among them were Mazzini, by now the most famous revolutionary of his day; Giuseppe Garibaldi, who had just returned from South America, where with his red-shirted Italian Legion he had proved himself a brilliant military leader; and Verdi, who came to conduct the premiere of *La battaglia di Legnano.*

The occasion was a "furore," which recommenced at each performance. The opera tells the story of the Lombard League defeating Frederick Barbarossa in 1176, and in addition to the usual call to place duty before happiness it also preaches the need for Italian unity. Historically members of the Lombard League were men of medieval towns and cried "Verona" or "Milano," but throughout the opera Verdi has them cry "Italia" (as in *Attila*), and loyalty is to the nation, not the town.

Probably any opera would have succeeded that waved a flag and allowed the chorus to sing of "la patria," but the opera is much more, and even today is occasionally revived. In Rome at the opening performances Verdi was called again and again to the stage and cheered as a symbol of the patriotic movement. He did not enjoy the adulation and soon left Rome for Paris, once again missing an extraordinary historical episode.

As expected, the Constituent Assembly at Rome proclaimed the Papal State a republic with a constitution and its capital at Rome. In so doing the Assembly cut through the thorny problem of the pope's temporal power—his political power as head of the Papal State as opposed to his spiritual power as head of the Church—simply by voting it out of existence. In future, priests, cardinals, and the pope himself, if he chose to return to Rome, would be citizens like all other men, each with one vote, though the pope was also offered "all the guarantees necessary to secure his independence in the exercise of his spiritual power."

From the Kingdom of Naples where he was staying the pope responded with an appeal to the nearby Catholic countries, France, Spain, Austria, and Naples, to intervene with arms and restore him to power. Not only would he not negotiate any change in his temporal power but he would now abrogate his previous reforms in his government. At issue, roughly, was whether the Papal State could be merged in a unified Italian state, whether Rome could be an Italian as well as a Catholic city.

Austria was fighting the Milanesi, Venetians, and Sardinians in the Po valley, and France, eager to reestablish its influence in Italy, responded to the pope's call. Although at the time itself a republic, it sent an army to extinguish the Roman Republic. The Romans put a band on the walls to play *La Marseillaise,* but the French guns were not spiked by the irony. The campaign, while all of Europe watched, continued for ten weeks, ending in a month-long siege of the city.

Despite a proclamation by the pope that "Rome, the principal seat of the Church, has now become, alas, a forest of roaring beasts, overflowing with men of every nation, apostates, or heretics, or leaders of communism and socialism," there was no Reign of Terror, no mass confiscation of property or persecution of priests. Five cardinals remained in the city throughout the siege, unmolested, and church services continued. Mazzini, with his sad, long face and dressed always in somber black, though the city's political leader, continued simple and democratic. He slept and worked in a small room in the Palazzo Quirinale, and anyone, official or not, could speak with him. At night he ate either in a cheap restaurant or had a supper of bread and raisins in his room. Sometimes, when alone, he would play his guitar.

Garibaldi, who commanded the city's defense, managed to hold out weeks longer than anyone had imagined possible and by inspiring his volunteers to extraordinary feats of valor gave Rome a new glory. By contrast the French seemed militarily inept and their alliance with the pope an unholy crusade to stamp out self-determination. In the coming years an increasing number of Catholics, inside Italy and out, would agree that of necessity the capital of any unified Italian state would have to be Rome.

For the moment, however, the movement for Italian unity and freedom ended in defeat and, for many, death. Among these was a young aristocrat, Luciano Manara, whom Verdi knew well. Manara had led the fighting in Milan's uprising, the Cinque Giornate, and thereafter had formed a regiment of Milanesi to continue the fight against Austria. When Austria defeated the Milanesi and proclaimed Manara and his men outlaws, he led them to Rome. Although most were not republicans but monarchists, wanting to create a kingdom of northern Italy under the House of Savoy, at least at Rome they could fight for an independent Italy.

During the siege he was killed, still only twenty-four years old and leaving a wife and sons in Milan. A member of the regiment who was with him at his death later published an account of it that stirred still greater sympathy for the Italian cause.

> After having partaken of the Sacrament, he did not speak for some time. Then once again he commended his sons to my care. "Bring them up," he said, "in love of religion, and of their country." He begged me to carry his remains into Lombardy, together with those of my brother. Seeing that I wept, he asked, "Does it grieve you so much that I die?" And when my suffocating sobs prevented my replying, he added in an undertone but with the holiest expression of resignation: "It grieves me also." . . .
>
> . . . A short time before he died he took off a ring, which he held very dear, placed it himself on my finger, and then drawing me close to him, said, "Saluterò tuo fratello per te, n'è vero?" [I will greet your brother for you.]

It reads like an opera libretto. But in these years many Italians lived and died in just this exalted fashion, and Verdi wept for more than one as a personal friend. Not long after Manara's death he received from the family a tiny statue of himself that had been found among the dead man's possessions, and years later when Verdi himself died, the statue still stood on his desk, in memory of Manara.

With the fall of Rome in July 1849 to the pope and his French allies, and of Venice in August to the Austrians, the Italian revolutions of 1848 came to an end. Their only achievement was in the Kingdom of Sardinia, where the House of Savoy, now led by twenty-nine-year-old Vittorio Emanuele II, had granted a constitution and, despite Austrian pressure, refused to retract it. Everywhere else Austria or its autocratic allies had regained control and became even more repressive in their governments, for any concession soon led to demands for greater freedom and self-government. And the Risorgimento entered still another phase.

The leadership now passed from Mazzini to Vittorio Emanuele's prime minister, Camillo Cavour. His policy, as he developed it in the 1850s, reflected the feeling of many after the failures of 1848 that Italy by itself could never expel Austria. The Austro-Hungarian Empire, with its huge land mass, millions in population, and greater wealth, would always be able to field a larger, stronger army. An ally had to be found, and the only possibility of sufficient size and strength was France. But to persuade the French government to act, obviously certain concessions would have to be made.

One was clear and touched republicans. Plainly neither the king of Sardinia, nor his chief minister, nor Napoleon III, who had recently transformed France's Second Republic into its Second Empire, would risk war with Austria to create an Italian republic. Most republicans, including Garibaldi and Verdi, saw this and gradually throughout the decade abandoned a republic as the necessary form of government for a free and united Italy. A constitutional monarchy under Vittorio Emanuele would be acceptable *provided* the new Kingdom of Italy was truly independent and united all the Italian states including the Papal State and with it, Rome.

There were many hesitations in the shifting loyalties. Cavour, by nature and need to be flexible in policy, was a devious minister who kept his plans obscure. Often to republicans he appeared to be aiming only to expand the Kingdom of Sardinia in northern Italy rather than to unite the entire peninsula. It was clear that he was courting France, but not clear what concessions he was offering. With a French army supporting the pope at Rome, how could he use a French army to divest the pope of Rome? Napoleon III would never agree to it, for the Catholic party in France was among his strongest supporters. From

London Mazzini sent agitated warnings into Italy not to put any trust in Sardinian leadership and to rely as before on direct action. But most Italians, Verdi among them, were inclined to see what diplomacy could do.

What Verdi brought from the past to his work in this decade, chiefly *Rigoletto, La traviata,* and *Il trovatore,* was the quintessence of the Risorgimento in both its quality and point of view. These by now were deep in Verdi's soul—he was thirty-seven in 1850—and remained part of his character until he died. As with most men his attitudes were formed in the years before forty.

The point of view is tragic and may be symbolized by Hector in *The Iliad*—Hector who, knowing that he will be killed by Achilles, still fights to defend his city, and dies. This, Verdi's operas suggest, is man's lot in life, yet how noble. And this view of life, hopeless but magnificent, was dominant among those who were stirred by the Risorgimento. Again and again throughout the period Italians acted in a manner that seemed to say: We know our acts will probably achieve nothing except to cause us to die, yet we must do them if we are to be men. When Verdi was criticized for having too many deaths in *Il trovatore,* he replied, "But after all, death is all there is in life. What else is there?"

He was not a fatalist in the sense of believing that nothing a man can do will affect his fate. He believed in individual action, but he was also enough of a realist, or perhaps pessimist, to know that action is often ineffective and almost always costly. Yet his operas are filled with individuals taking action against their immediate self-interest to respond to some nobler principle. Violetta in *La traviata* is one; Manrico in *Il trovatore,* another.

The quality of his point of view appears in the range of his compassion and delicacy of feeling, both matched at times by other artists and even by events of the Risorgimento. During Milan's Cinque Giornate, for example, the insurgents succeeded in capturing an Austrian barracks only when a cripple, Pasquale Sottocornola, hopped and skipped across the open street to put resin on the wooden doors and then risked his life again to ignite the resin with a torch of burning straw. Such courage and patriotism in a cripple seemed as remarkable to most Milanesi of 1848 as did the paternal love in *Rigoletto* to most of the opera's early audiences. Art and events widened the scope of men's sympathies.

This was perhaps best stated by Giuseppe Giusti in *Sant' Ambrogio*, one of the finest of Risorgimento poems. In it Giusti wanders into the church of Sant' Ambrogio in Milan, where a large detachment of Austrian soldiers is attending Mass with the Milanesi. Early in the service a band near the altar starts a song "like the pleading voice of a people who groan in hardship and remember lost possessions." It is a chorus from Verdi's *I lombardi,* and Giusti is deeply moved. At its end a German song rises from the soldiers, a prayer, a lament, and in it Giusti hears "the bitter sweetness of songs learned in childhood" and sung again in days of sorrow and exile. In his heart sympathy chases out hate, and he recognizes the Austrians as fellow men. Similarly Verdi, even in propaganda pieces such as *Attila* and *La battaglia di Legnano,* made of the enemy, Attila or Barbarossa, not a monster but a dignified warrior. At its best the Risorgimento, in its art and events, ennobled its participants.

By January 1859 it was evident that Cavour had reached some sort of understanding with Napoleon, and that war with Austria was imminent. Verdi, in Rome in February for the premiere of *Un ballo in maschera,* once again became the symbol of patriotic aspiration. Excited Italians in all cities suddenly realized that his name was an acronym of "*V*ittorio *E*manuele *R*e *D*' *I*talia" (Vittorio Emanuele King of Italy), and *Viva Verdi!* was scratched on walls and shouted in the streets. Wherever his operas were performed, the audiences called endlessly for the composer, particularly if Austrians were present. And wherever Verdi himself was discovered, crowds often gathered spontaneously and broke into cheers.

The unification of Italy, or the expansion of Sardinia, I

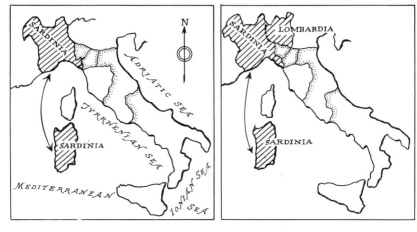

At the Beginning of 1859   **After July 1859**

Cavour meanwhile succeeded in bringing the French
army into Italy, and it with the Sardinian army greatly
enlarged by volunteers fought the Austrians to an armistice. The result after almost a year of negotiation was that
Austria retained only Venice and its mainland province of
Venetia; France received two small provinces from the
Kingdom of Sardinia, Nice and Savoy; and the remainder
of the Kingdom of Sardinia, by far the larger part, was
allowed to unite with the former duchies of Parma, Modena, and Tuscany to form a new kingdom that in population and wealth dominated the peninsula. Verdi was one
of the four delegates designated by the joint Assembly of
Parma and Modena to inform Vittorio Emanuele that the
people had voted for union.

The new Sardinian kingdom, however, stopping short
of the Papal State and the kingdoms of Naples and Sicily,
infuriated Garibaldi: it was less than a united, free Italy
and not for any such half loaf had he and many others
foresworn Mazzini's ideal of a republic. With a thousand
men, I Mille, embarked on two boats, Garibaldi one night

The unification of Italy, or the expansion of Sardinia, II

After March 1860	**After October 1860**

steamed secretly out of Genoa and headed for Sicily. Escaping the gunboats sent to intercept them, he and the Thousand landed at Marsala and announced they would fight for "Italy and Vittorio Emanuele." To the astonishment of the world, within a month they had captured Palermo, the Sicilian capital, from 24,000 troops loyal to the king of Naples but badly led. "By God," Verdi wrote of Garibaldi to a friend, "there really is a man to kneel to!"

But Garibaldi and his army, now greatly swollen with volunteers, did not stop in Sicily. By September he had crossed the Straits of Messina, marched up the peninsula, captured Naples, and penned a Neapolitan army of 50,000 between himself and the papal border. At the rate volunteers rushed to join him it seemed possible that he might soon have enough men to march on Rome, forcing the French army there either to attack him or withdraw. The situation lent itself to cartoons: Here was Garibaldi conquering half of Italy in Vittorio Emanuele's name, yet about to strike the king's best friend, Napoleon, right in the eye.

Garibaldi's success and the dangers it threatened gave Cavour the chance to present Vittorio Emanuele's government to Napoleon as the best hope for peace and order in Italy. With French connivance the Sardinian army took the two eastern provinces of the Papal State, leaving to the pope only Rome and its province, and joined Garibaldi in besieging the Neapolitan army near Gaeta. Of Garibaldi and the Sardinian generals Verdi exclaimed, "Those are composers! And what operas! What finales! To the sound of guns!" By November 1860 all of Italy except the provinces of Venetia and Rome were ready to be joined in an independent Kingdom of Italy.

Garibaldi knew that the chief reason for the presence of the Sardinian army south of Rome was to prevent him from attacking the city, and the fact angered him deeply. He was also furious that Nizza, or Nice, where he was born, had been ceded to France. Nevertheless, he had said repeatedly that he would turn over Sicily and Naples, half of Italy, to Vittorio Emanuele, and he did it, without conditions. Then in the supreme gesture of the Risorgimento, the purity of which made him the world's most popular hero of the nineteenth century, he refused any reward for his services. He would not accept from the king a title or a castle, a steamer or even a dowry for his daughter. What he had done, he had done for Italy.

The following year, on Cavour's personal insistence, Verdi stood for election as a deputy from his district to the first national parliament. Cavour was eager to have such a well-known Risorgimento figure in the government, and Verdi was easily elected. He conscientiously attended the meetings in Turin and in the voting always followed Cavour's lead, saying, "That way I can be absolutely certain of not making a mistake." But after Cavour's sudden death in June 1861, a disaster for the new kingdom, Verdi's political activity declined, and though he dutifully finished out his term, he did not stand for reelection. His allegiance to Cavour had been personal, and he did not transfer it to any other of the king's ministers.

Indeed, like many republicans, he seems to have offered

his allegiance to the constitutional monarchy with his head but to have been unable to command it from his heart. Requested in 1862 to represent the new Kingdom of Italy at the London Exhibition, he composed a cantata, the *Inno delle nazioni* (Hymn of the Nations), in the finale of which he intertwined *God Save the Queen, La Marseillaise,* and, to represent Italy, *Mameli's Hymn* or *Fratelli d'Italia.* His choice of anthems was startling, for *Partant pour la Syrie,* not *La Marseillaise,* was the national anthem of the French Empire, and *Mameli's Hymn* was simply a popular republican song particularly associated with the defense of the Roman Republic. Verdi himself seems to have had second thoughts about the fitness of his choice, for during his life he forbade any performance of the cantata in Italy. Today, when both France and Italy are republics, *La Marseillaise* and *Mameli's Hymn* are their national anthems.

In the decade of the 1860s, the last before the issues of the Risorgimento began to fade before newer problems, the conflict over Rome sharpened. In 1864 the pope issued an encyclical accompanied by a Syllabus of Errors that seemed to preclude any accommodation between the Papal and the Italian states. The Syllabus listed eighty propositions that the pope considered "the principal Errors of our times." Among them were freedom of conscience, religious toleration, freedom of discussion and the press, and, finally, the idea that "The Roman Pontiff can and should reconcile and harmonize himself with progress, liberalism, and recent civilization." To many, Catholics and non-Catholics alike, the Syllabus seemed an incredibly reactionary attack on all that was most progressive in the nineteenth century. Two years later attention focused still more powerfully on the issue of Papal or Italian Rome when the Kingdom of Italy, as its reward for supporting Prussia in the Austro-Prussian War, acquired Venice and mainland Venetia. Now only Rome and its province were not united in the Italian state.

Against the background of The Roman Question, as it was increasingly called, Verdi chose Schiller's play *Don Carlos* for an opera. The play discussed the conflict of church and state, but at the court of Spain under Philip II and the Inquisition; thus it combined topicality with the glamour of great days past. It also repeated in a new setting other Risorgimento themes that had constantly appeared in Verdi's work: the call to duty over happiness, the liberal prince of *Ernani,* the statecraft of *Boccanegra,* and, as with Rigoletto and Violetta, a character, Philip, often presented as unsympathetic, who could be exposed with sympathy. And overriding all, perhaps, there was the chance to affirm the political views which Verdi himself held: freedom of conscience, discussion, and the press, and the necessity for the Church to accommodate itself to the more liberal doctrines of the Italian state.

At the opera's premiere in Paris on March 11, 1867, aside from any difficulty the audience may have had with its music, the opera's politics spoiled its reception. At the moment in which the King tells the Grand Inquisitor "Tais-toi, prêtre"—"Hold your tongue, priest"—the Empress Eugenie, a leader of the Catholic party in France, turned her back on the stage. For some her gesture was a command to dislike the opera, and they successfully attached to it for many years the suggestion that it was anti-Catholic whereas at most it might be described as antipapal. But whatever the weight of the reasons it had only a moderate success until the next century when, following World War II, it suddenly found enthusiastic audiences everywhere.

Verdi was fifty-three when he composed *Don Carlos,* and partly because of events and his increasing age it is the last of his operas on a current political issue. Thereafter the Risorgimento themes appear in his work in forms more and more attenuated until they are absorbed almost entirely in pure art. This is often the way with artists, but few who start so topically can end so artistically. Or as Bernard Shaw said of him, "It is not often that a man's strength is so immense that he can remain an athlete after bartering half of it to old age for experience."

In July 1870, while Verdi was composing *Aida,* two extraordinary events followed in quick succession. On July

18, while the Church was meeting in Vatican Council I, the pope proclaimed the dogma of papal infallibility, and on the next day Napoleon III, egged on by Bismarck, declared war on Prussia. The new dogma irritated the governments of the great Catholic countries and cost the pope their support just when he needed it most, for Napoleon soon withdrew the French army from Rome to fight the Prussians. Then all that stood between the Italian kingdom and its desired capital was the papal army of 13,000 men. After Napoleon's defeat at Sedan the Italian army began its advance, and on September 20, following a short bombardment, it entered the city in the name of Vittorio Emanuele II, King of Italy. The pope, protesting, withdrew into the Vatican, and the Papal State, the oldest sovereignty in Europe, ceased to exist.

Only Ecuador protested the violation of the pope's territory. France, Austria, Spain, and Germany merely murmured that the pope's spiritual freedom must be preserved, and the Italian government promptly submitted to Parliament a bill that would guarantee it. Only after the passage of this Law of Guarantees, in May 1871, was the capital moved to Rome, and the Risorgimento came to as much of a formal end as such movements have.

In *Aida,* which had its premiere on December 24, 1871, all of Verdi's usual Risorgimento themes are present: the aria "O patria mia," the chorus calling for war, the antagonism between king and priests, and the oppressed people. But already they are slightly distanced by the non-European setting, and time has begun its process of eliminating topical allusion to leave a drama more purely artistic. In one of the opera's most beautiful phrases, Amonasro, after knocking Aida to the ground for refusing to put her duty to Ethiopia before her love for Radames, sings:

Pensa che un popolo, vinto, straziato	Think that a people conquered and tortured,
Per te soltanto, per te soltanto risorger può . . .	Through you alone, through you alone can rise . . .

In the 1840s and 1850s during such a scene, with the very word *risorgere*, members of the audience would have thought: yes, yes, that is how it is. In the 1870s and 1880s the older members recalled, that is how it was.

Verdi's next work, his *Messa da Requiem*, was a formal farewell to the Risorgimento. Manzoni, the author of *I promessi sposi*, died at eighty-nine on May 22, 1873, and there was an outpour of praise for him. There was criticism, too, chiefly in clerical newspapers and on the ground that he was a bad Catholic and had insulted the pope by accepting an honorary citizenship of Rome. Verdi, whose enthusiasm for Manzoni had steadily grown since first reading the novel at sixteen, was eager to honor him as one of the glories of Italy.

He did not attend the funeral, but a week later visited the grave alone. Then through his publisher he proposed to the mayor of Milan that he write a Requiem Mass to honor Manzoni on the first anniversary of his death. Verdi offered to pay the expenses of preparing and printing the music, if the city would pay the cost of its performance on the anniversary date; thereafter the Requiem would belong to Verdi.

The performance took place as scheduled in the Church of San Marco and was a success in every way: international attention was focused on Manzoni; Milan was said by everyone to have done the right thing; and for the occasion Verdi produced a masterpiece.

His Risorgimento themes are here translated into abstractions—pity, terror, conflict, joy, uncertainty—expressed in the liturgy of the Mass. Verdi himself was not a practicing Catholic: he would drive his wife to church but not accompany her inside. Like most Risorgimento figures he was an anticleric in that he opposed the organization of the Church, its financial and political power, and its priesthood. Of the love of God or even the existence of God he was in his wife's words "a very doubtful believer," and the Requiem reflects this. From the terrors of eternal death it offers no certain release. There is no sunny amen,

no vision of a kind God or promise of divine intercession—
only dwindling power and continued uncertainty. Such
apparently was Verdi's belief even in youth, and at the
time of the Requiem it also reflected the increasing uncertainty felt by many as the doctrines of Darwin and the new
sciences began to shake traditional beliefs. Thus the ancient text received a new, modern interpretation by an artist being true to himself and his time.

Verdi was sixty when he composed the Requiem, and
after it he gave every appearance of having retired. In
1880 he published a *Pater noster* and an *Ave Maria,* both on
Italian texts by Dante; the following year he staged a revision of *Boccanegra* in which a new and powerful scene once
again attacked the medieval rivalry between cities that had
betrayed Italy to foreign domination; and in 1884 he
staged a shorter version of *Don Carlos* with several scenes
rewritten and a new prelude to fill a large cut. Then, just
when these short pieces and revisions had convinced the
world that Verdi had indeed retired, he composed and
produced two new masterworks, *Otello* in 1887 and, in
1893 at age eighty, *Falstaff.* For this extraordinary append-
age to an already long career his wife, his publisher, and
his librettist deserve much credit, for they conspired to
keep him composing, but the will to work was also there.

In the past Verdi had composed operas in which Risorgimento themes had played little or no part, but these,
like *Luisa Miller, Stiffelio,* or *La traviata,* tended to be modest, domestic dramas. *Falstaff,* a comedy, is in this line.
Shakespeare's *Othello,* however, offered him a chance to
incorporate just the kind of patriotic and martial spectacle
that in the 1840s he invariably had taken. His different
approach now shows how much he and the times had
changed.

Italy in the last two decades of the century moved steadily in directions of which Verdi disapproved. The government engaged in several tariff wars with France and in
1882 joined Germany and Austria in a Triple Alliance. To
Verdi the policy was wrongheaded: France, not Germany,

was Italy's natural ally. He also opposed Italian colonial ambitions, which, like the pact with Germany, he felt was a pursuit of empty prestige. Italy, with seventeen million illiterates and as many starving peasants, had no business in Ethiopia: "We are wrong, and we will pay for it." And as in politics, so in art. German culture was increasingly admired, and the younger composer strove to imitate the symphonic and orchestral styles of Brahms and Wagner. Verdi, too, admired Wagner, but he felt Italian composers should follow Italian traditions: song, not symphony. Though perhaps right in his ideas, he felt and was out of step with the times.

None of this, even indirectly, appears in his *Otello,* and there are only a few of his old Risorgimento themes, now chiefly in abstract forms. In earlier days he might have composed an *Otello* in which Desdemona sings of Venice "O patria mia," or Otello rallies a Venetian army to drive the Moslems from Cyprus, or Christians taken prisoner by the Moslems lament their captivity. But now these earlier themes when present are only musical forms: a prayer for the soprano, a friendship duet for the tenor and baritone, or a chorus of victory. Along with Shakespeare's first act set in Venice Verdi dropped all the ephemera of politics and nationality to plumb the psychological truth of the human drama. The opera is art without topical allusion. Led by his librettist and his own taste, he concentrated with more power than he had ever brought to an opera before on the two great mysteries of existence, love and death.

Like Molière and Bach, Verdi spoke for an age but also through his art created a body of work that transcends time and place. In his operas the political issues of the Risorgimento and the social attitudes informing it are prominent—indeed, a good way to grasp the tone of the movement is through Verdi—yet the operas and the *Requiem* continue to speak to audiences who know nothing of the Risorgimento and whose problems are quite different.

What, then, remains in his work if the ephemera of time and place are drained away?

First, the potential nobility of man. In his early and middle years Verdi saw men and women risking life and personal happiness to further an ideal, and in his operas he celebrated them, holding them up as models to be copied. In *La traviata* Verdi wept for Violetta, but he presents her decision in her circumstances as right. His operas, though with artistic restraint, are didactic: they urge men and women to be noble.

As a corollary, however, throughout his work sounds a constant note of melancholy. Life, he suggests, is hard, happiness fleeting, and death the only certainty. He never pretends in his call for generous, noble actions that these do not often end in suffering, but offers them as the best response to death.

Though these themes, the potential nobility of man and the tragedy it often entails, were stimulated in Verdi by the events of the Risorgimento, they are universal, sensed by adult men and women everywhere. Though in different eras they may be more or less to the fore, they are never wholly absent from the feelings of men. They are an important reason why Verdi's operas, generations after his death, still find an audience.

Verdi in Milan

Giampiero Tintori

GIAMPIERO TINTORI, composer and musicologist, has been the director of the Museo Teatrale alla Scala since 1965. His publications include studies of Stravinsky, Marcello, and Neapolitan opera. He has also been responsible for a number of exhibitions, including the monumental Scala bicentennial in 1978.

Verdi did not come to Milan to conquer the city. His patron, the well-to-do Busseto tradesman Antonio Barezzi, had no ambitions of the sort, nor could he have the most remote notion of what lay in store for his future son-in-law. He cherished only a modest, villager's aspiration: that of seeing his protégé seated at the organ in the Duomo of Busseto, to the dismay of the clerical faction which supported a certain Ferrari's claim to the post. And Barezzi did not lose heart when young Verdi's application for admission to the Milan Conservatory was rejected. Unlike nineteenth-century music lovers, we need not reproach Professor Basily, the head of the conservatory, who was called upon to judge a country youth past the maximum age for admission and prepared by Provesi, the local bandmaster.

Barezzi then entrusted young Verdi to Lavigna, *maestro al cembalo* at the Teatro alla Scala, a sound musician. He was the composer of the opera *La muta per amore*, first performed on Paisiello's recommendation at La Scala in 1802, and with apparent success, since it was repeated the following season. His other operas include *Di posta in posta* (1808), also given its premiere at La Scala, where it received thirty-six performances, an *Orcamo* (1809), and *Chi s'è visto s'è visto* (1810). He remained at the cembalo in La Scala from 1802 to 1832, and died in 1836, too soon to enjoy his pupil's success.

In Milan, Verdi frequented musical circles and La Scala; he cannot have been enthusiastic at the idea of returning to Busseto, especially since he had friendly supporters in the larger city. He was able to hear much music that the ittle theater in Busseto could never have offered him, though in that town he had heard *Il barbiere di Siviglia* (daring to replace Rossini's overture with a composition of his own).

Upright man that he was, he was unwilling to disappoint Barezzi's village ambitions, though tempted by the adventure of Milan. The contract with the impresario Merelli was truly lucky for Verdi, since, after the failure of *Un giorno di regno*, it obligated him to write another opera, the *Nabucco* which in 1842 triumphed at La Scala and was the cornerstone of his fame as a composer.

After the unsatisfactory production of *Giovanna d'Arco*, given at La Scala on February 15, 1845, Verdi divorced himself from the Milanese theater, although he still remained bound to Milan. Among other reasons, there was the fact that his publisher Ricordi was located there.

Verdi's rapprochement with La Scala and Milan began with the revised version of *La forza del destino* (1869), the European premiere of *Aida* (1872), and the revised versions of *Simon Boccanegra* (1881) and *Don Carlos* (1884); the reconciliation was crowned with *Otello* in 1887 and *Falstaff* in 1893. Milan was also the recipient of Verdi's Casa di Riposo for aged and needy musicians.

During his visits to Milan, he lived in the Hotel Milan in Via Manzoni, formerly known as the Contrada del Giardino. The proprietor of the hotel was Commendatore

Spatz, a Swiss hotelier, whose daughter was to marry Umberto Giordano.

We have spoken with people who actually saw Verdi in the streets of Milan, the object of reverential awe, furtively pointed out by passersby. During his final illness in January, 1901, anxious crowds awaited reports on his condition daily. Outside the Hotel Milan there was silence: the street had been covered with straw to muffle the noise of the carriages.

In his old age, Count dal Verme boasted that, as a young officer, he had been part of the honor guard at Verdi's burial. The commander of the unit was a thick-headed Piedmontese captain, a career army man. When he saw a close relative of the king following the bier, he exclaimed in amazement: "What's the world come to?! A prince of the royal house at the funeral of a bandleader!"

La Scala, Milan, in a painting by Angelo Inganni (1807–80). Verdi attended many performances at La Scala during his student years in Milan, and his first operas, *Oberto, Un giorno di regno, Nabucco,* and *I lombardi,* were performed there. Dissatisfied with the poor quality of the productions, Verdi refused to have anything to do with the theater for some twenty-five years. The reconciliation occured with the revised version of *La forza del destino* in 1869. After this, the European premiere of *Aida* and the world premieres of *Otello* and *Falstaff* were held at La Scala.

The first page of the autograph of Verdi's aria for two tenors "Io la vidi," his earliest known operatic composition. This work, probably written while Verdi was studying with Lavigna in Milan, predated the premiere of Verdi's first opera *Oberto* by several years. (From the Pierpont Morgan Library, Mary Flagler Cary Collection. Reproduced by permission.)

In Milan, Verdi took part in musical activities typical of the time —performances by vocal and instrumental groups, part professional and part amateur. It was a performance of this kind—Haydn's oratorio *The Creation*—that led to Verdi's first official participation as *maestro al cembalo*. Many years later Verdi related these events to Giulio Ricordi, who promptly transcribed the reminiscences:

In 1833 or '34 [in fact *The Creation* was performed in April 1834] there existed in Milan a Società Filarmonica, made up of some good voices. It was led by Maestro Masini, a man who was dogged and patient—qualities necessary for a society of amateurs—if not greatly learned. They were organizing the performance of an oratorio by Haydn, *The Creation,* at the Teatro Filodrammatico; my teacher Lavigna asked me if, for my instruction, I wanted to attend the rehearsals, and I accepted with pleasure.

No one paid any attention to the young man modestly seated in a corner. Three maestros conducted the rehearsals: Perelli, Bonoldi, and Almasio; but one fine day, by a curious coincidence, all three conductors failed to turn up at a rehearsal. The ladies and gentlemen were growing impatient, when Maestro Masini, who did not feel able to sit at the piano and accompany with the score, turned to me and asked me to act as accompanist. Unconvinced perhaps of the abilities of the young and unknown artist, he said to me: "It will be enough to accompany only with the bass." I was then fresh from my studies, and I was certainly not in difficulties when faced by an orchestral score. I accepted, and sat at the piano to begin the rehearsal. I recall very well some little ironic smiles of the amateur ladies and gentlemen, and it seems that my youthful form, thin and not too showily dressed, was such as to inspire scant trust.

In short, the rehearsal began, and little by little, warming and growing excited, I did not confine myself to accompanying, but began also to conduct with my right hand, playing only with the left. I had a true success, all the greater because it was unexpected. At the end of the rehearsal, compliments, congratulations on all sides, and especially from Count Pompeo Belgiojoso and Count Renato Borromeo.

Finally, whether because the three maestros mentioned were too busy and could not carry out the task or for other reasons, the concert was in the end entirely entrusted to me. The public performance was given with such success that it was then repeated in the great salon of the Casino de' Nobili in the presence of the Archduke and Archduchess Raineri [actually Ranieri] and all the high society of the time.

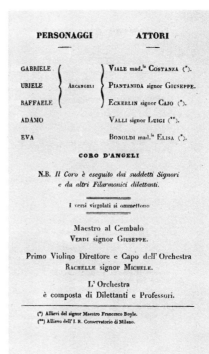

PERSONAGGI   **ATTORI**

GABRIELE			VIALE mad.ˡᵉ COSTANZA (*).
URIELE	} ARCANGELI	{	PIANTANIDA signor GIUSEPPE.
RAFFAELE			ECKERLIN signor CAJO (*).
ADAMO			VALLI signor LUIGI (**).
EVA			BONOLDI mad.ˡᵉ ELISA (*).

CORO D'ANGELI

N.B. *Il Coro è eseguito dai suddetti Signori
e da altri Filarmonici dilettanti.*

I versi virgolati si ommettono

Maestro al Cembalo
VERDI signor GIUSEPPE.

Primo Violino Direttore e Capo dell' Orchestra
RACHELLE signor MICHELE.

L' Orchestra
è composta di Dilettanti e Professori.

(*) Allievi del signor Maestro Francesco Boyle.
(**) Allievo dell' I. R. Conservatorio di Milano.

O B E R T O
CONTE DI S. BONIFACIO

DRAMMA IN DUE ATTI

DA RAPPRESENTARSI

NELL' I. R. TEATRO ALLA SCALA

L' AUTUNNO 1839.

DAMIANO MUONI
Libri, Disegni, Stampe, Ritratti
Pergamene, Manoscritti, Autografi

Milano

PER GASPARE TRUFFI

M.DCCC.XXXIX

Title page of the libretto of *Oberto, Conte di S. Bonifacio,* printed in 1839 by Gaspare Truffi for the opera's premiere at La Scala, November 17, 1839.

Giuseppe Verdi's two wives: Margherita Barezzi (UPPER RIGHT oil portrait by Augusto Mussini) and Giuseppina Strepponi (LOWER oil by an anonymous artist). The two portraits were donated to the Museo Teatrale alla Scala by the respective descendants: Demetrio Barezzi (son of Antonio) and Barberina Strepponi (sister of Giuseppina).

Verdi married Margherita Barezzi, daughter of his patron Antonio, in 1836. Two children were born of the marriage. Verdi's young family was destroyed in a brief space of time: the children died in 1838 and in 1839; Margherita died in June 1840.

Verdi's relationship with Giuseppina Strepponi (the soprano who created the role of Abigaille in *Nabucco*) probably began in Paris in 1847. They were finally married at Collanges-sous-Salève in 1859. A woman of uncommon intelligence, Giuseppina Streppini was Verdi's life-long companion. Here she is portrayed with a score of *Nabucco* on her lap.

Poster for the autumn season at La Scala in 1842, opening with the revival of *Nabucodonosor* (later known simply as *Nabucco*) by Verdi.

Nabucodonosor had been performed for the first time at the Teatro alla Scala on March 9, 1842, the last opera of the Carnival-Lent season. After the fiasco of *Un giorno di regno*, September 5, 1840, the impresario Merelli probably preferred to open the season with a new opera by Donizetti (*Maria Padilla*) and to continue it with operas certain of success: *Saffo* by Pacini, *La straniera* by Bellini, *Belisario* by Donizetti. The season included a second novelty, *Odalisa* by Nini, which failed miserably. According to Verdi, some old sets were adapted "by Perroni" for *Nabucco*. He was certainly referring to the sets by Cavallotti and Menozzi for the ballet *Nabucodonosor* by Cortesi, performed on October 27, 1838; these were then retouched by Peroni (not Perroni).

Despite the success of the opera, it was given for only eight evenings, because the season was ending. Merelli therefore decided to revive it in the Autumn season (to which this poster refers) and, beginning on August 15 of that year, *Nabucodonosor* was performed fifty-seven times with Teresa de Giuli Borsi replacing Strepponi, Amalia Zecchini instead of Bellinzaghi as Fenena, the tenor Gagliani in place of Miraglia, and the baritone Ferri in the title role instead of Ronconi. Of the principals in the original cast only Prospero Dérivis remained.

The young Verdi; lithograph by Corbetta from a drawing by Alessandro Focosi.

Countess Clara Maffei (1814–86), whose salon was a center of Milanese intellectual life for a half century. Verdi was a close friend of the countess and of her estranged husband, Andrea Maffei, the poet and librettist (of *I masnadieri*). In her old age Clara Maffei fostered the careers of the young Francesco Faccio and Arrigo Boito, whom she introduced to Verdi. Painting by Angelo Inganni (1807–80), La Scala, Milan.

OPPOSITE PAGE, ABOVE. Title page of the libretto printed by Gaspare Truffi for the premiere of *I lombardi alla prima crociata* at La Scala (1843).

BELOW. The bass Ignazio Marini (1811–73) created the title roles in Verdi's first opera, *Oberto* (1839), and in *Attila* at the Teatro La Fenice, Venice, in 1846. Sketch by Giuseppe Carnovali, known as Il Piccio.

I LOMBARDI
ALLA PRIMA CROCIATA

DRAMMA LIRICO
DI TEMISTOCLE SOLERA

POSTO IN MUSICA

DAL SIG. MAESTRO GIUSEPPE VERDI

DA RAPPRESENTARSI

NELL' I. R. TEATRO ALLA SCALA

IL CARNEVALE MDCCCXLIII.

Milano
PER GASPARE TRUFFI
MDCCCXLIII

OPPOSITE PAGE, TOP LEFT. This costume for *Giovanna d'Arco* was designed for the protagonist, soprano Erminia Frezzolini for the first performance at the Teatro alla Scala on February 15, 1845.

TOP RIGHT. *Giovanna de Guzman,* the first and censored Italian version of *Les Vêpres siciliennes,* was given at La Scala on February 4, 1856. This costume was designed for the heroine, the soprano Marianna Barbieri-Nini, who had created Verdi's Lady Macbeth at the Teatro della Pergola, Florence, on March 14, 1847.

LOWER LEFT. *La battaglia di Legnano* was written for the short-lived Roman Republic and performed at the Teatro Argentina, Rome, on January 27, 1849. It was performed at La Scala for the first time on November 23, 1851. This costume, designed for the Scala production, was for the baritone Marra, who sang the part of Rolando.

LOWER RIGHT. *La traviata,* first performed at the Teatro La Fenice, Venice, on March 6, 1853, left impresarios dubious because of its subject, unheard of on the opera stage of the time. Because Italian opera audiences were accustomed to seeing dramas of a historical nature or, at least, set in remote times, the characters were clothed in seventeenth century dress and the setting was changed to Paris and its vicinty, 1700. This practice lasted until the early years of this century. This costume was designed for Giorgio Germont in a Milanese production of *La traviata,* at the Teatro della Cannobiana in 1856.

Cover of an early piano-vocal score of *La forza del destino,* printed by Ricordi. (This is an idealized drawing. There is no such scene in the opera, although the setting suggests the last act.)

ATTO I. — Scena IV.

ELISABETTA
Possente Iddio!..

CARLO
Carlo io sono... e t'amo!

OPPOSITE, TOP. Antonio Ghislanzoni (1824–93), after a brief career as a baritone (he sang in a performance of Verdi's *Ernani* in Milan), became a popular journalist and librettist. Verdi apparently asked him to revise the text of *La forza del destino,* and Ghislanzoni was commissioned to versify and translate the French prose text of *Aida* into Italian.

OPPOSITE, BOTTOM. After its premiere in Paris, *Don Carlos* received one of its first Italian performances on December 26, 1868, and again, in the revised four-act version, on January 10, 1884. Casa Ricordi published a deluxe edition of the score with lithographs by G. Gonin (not to be confused with F. Gonin, famous illustrator of the 1840 edition of Manzoni's *I promessi sposi*). Act I, scene 4: the meeting of Don Carlos and Elisabeth in the forest of Fontainebleau.

BELOW. A page from the *disposizione scenica* (production book) for *Aida* by Guilio Ricordi. (See page 187.)

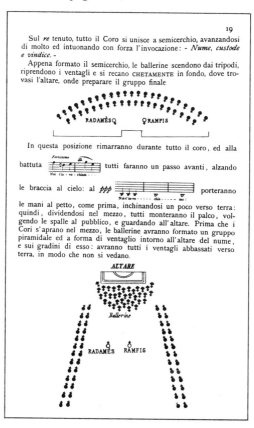

19

Sul *re* tenuto, tutto il Coro si unisce a semicerchio, avanzandosi di molto ed intuonando con forza l'invocazione: - *Nume, custode e vindice.* -

Appena formato il semicerchio, le ballerine scendono dai tripodi, riprendono i ventagli e si recano CHETAMENTE in fondo, dove trovasi l'altare, onde preparare il gruppo finale

In questa posizione rimarranno durante tutto il coro, ed alla battuta tutti faranno un passo avanti, alzando le braccia al cielo: al *ppp* porteranno le mani al petto, come prima, inchinandosi un poco verso terra: quindi, dividendosi nel mezzo, tutti monteranno il palco, volgendo le spalle al pubblico, e guardando all'altare. Prima che i Cori s'aprano nel mezzo, le ballerine avranno formato un gruppo piramidale ed a forma di ventaglio intorno all'altare del nume, e sui gradini di esso: avranno tutti i ventagli abbassati verso terra, in modo che non si vedano.

59

Teresa Stolz, in a pastel by Gariboldi. The Bohemian soprano (1834–1902) was one of the leading Verdi interpreters of her time. Famous for her performance as Elisabeth in *Don Carlos*, which she sang in Bologna in 1867 for the opera's Italian premiere, she excelled also in *La forza del destino* and *Aida*. She was the first interpreter of the soprano part in the *Messa da Requiem* (1874), whose autograph Verdi dedicated to her and which she sang under his direction in Milan, in the church of San Marco. Again with Verdi conducting, she sang the *Messa* at the Opéra-Comique in Paris, at the Albert Hall in London, and at the Vienna Opera in 1875.

Verdi conducting the *Messa da Requiem* at La Scala on May 25, 1875. This is an illustration from a popular magazine: a work of the artist's imagination in which only the features of the chief performers have some resemblance to reality. There are five rows of boxes at La Scala, in fact, not three; the orchestra and chorus could not have been placed as shown, nor would Verdi have conducted facing the audience. Verdi, Stolz, Maria Waldmann, Giuseppe Capponi (tenor), and Armando Maini (bass) are fairly convincing likenesses. The ingenuousness of the drawing is evidence of the composer's wide popularity.

ABOVE. Francesco Tamagno in the final scene of *Otello* (1887). The typical nineteenth-century furnishings and the absence of Otello's dagger on the floor suggest that the picture was taken in a photographer's studio. And the barely visible Desdemona is probably not the soprano Romilda Pantaleoni, who created the role.

LEFT. Tito Ricordi II, Giuseppe Verdi, and Giulio Ricordi (left to right).

LEFT. Arrigo Boito and Giuseppe Verdi.

BELOW. Caricature published in the periodical *Il trovatore* at the time of the premiere of Verdi's *Falstaff* February 9, 1893).

Verdi's burial on February 26, 1901. Verdi left strict instructions that his funeral be private and simple. His wishes were respected, but only for his temporary interment. A few weeks later, when his remains were moved from the Milan Cimitero Monumentale to their permanent resting place in the Casa di Riposo, an impressive, solemn ceremony took place. Toscanini conducted the orchestra and chorus of La Scala in "Va, pensiero" from *Nabucco*.

OPPOSITE. The Casa di Riposo, home for elderly musicians in Milan, which Verdi described as "my last and best work," was designed by Camillo Boito, Arrigo's brother, a successful architect.

Giuseppe Verdi's grave in the Casa di Riposo, Milan. Giuseppina Strepponi Verdi is buried beside him. The plaque on the wall commemorates Margherita Barezzi, the composer's first wife.

BELOW. A page from the autograph of *Falstaff*, Verdi's last secular composition. The illustration shows the beginning of the final fugue. The entire autograph was reproduced in facsimile in 1951. Original in the archives of the Casa Ricordi, which kindly granted permission for this reproduction.

Verdi and the Contemporary Italian Operatic Scene

Julian Budden

JULIAN BUDDEN, M.A. (Oxon.), B.Mus. (London), was for five years Chief Producer, Opera, and is now External Services Organizer for the BBC. His *The Operas of Verdi* (two volumes have so far appeared) is the most thoroughgoing study of the subject. Budden has contributed to a number of International Congresses of Verdi Studies and is a member of the editorial board of the Univerity of Chicago/Ricordi complete Verdi edition.

*I*n *The Summing Up,* Somerset Maugham stresses the advantage to an aspiring author of knowing French on the grounds that where other countries have writers, France, like England, has a literature. By the same token it could be said that until the artistic disruption of our own day Italy had an opera, where Germany, France, and Russia had opera composers. Only in Italy was there a tradition persisting across the centuries. Sometimes it seemed to falter; but at the last moment there was always a Rossini or a Mascagni to shore it up. It was a tradition that held possibilities for the foreigner no less than the native. Handel, Gluck, J. C. Bach, Haydn, and Mozart in the eighteenth century; Meyerbeer, Nicolai, Balfe in the nineteenth.

When the young Bizet offered an Italian opera, *Don Procopio,* for the Prix de Rome in 1858, he knew that his examiners would be in no doubt as to the canons by which it must be measured. Had he offered a German opera such canons would have been far harder to determine. Nevertheless, the status of Italian opera in Bizet's time had changed since the beginning of the century in one important respect. It had become local, not to say provincial. The mainstream of music had been diverted elsewhere. In the eighteenth century the princelings of Germany all aimed at securing Italians as their Kapellmeisters (one reason, this, why such men as Salieri and Paer had such an unsavory reputation among their German colleagues) at least to have their most promising native employees sent to Naples or Bologna to learn the latest secrets of their craft. By 1800 the foreigner could learn far more at the conservatoires of Paris or Leipzig than in any comparable Italian institution. Indeed the more ambitious Italians of the time—Cherubini, Spontini, and eventually Paer—all emigrated to Paris, where the atmosphere was more lively and stimulating. For the truth was that during the first decade of the century Italian opera was passing through one of its periods of crisis, and the tradition that had lasted for more than a century seemed on the point of decay.

Yet the hour produced the man. In 1813, the year of Verdi's birth, the twenty-one-year-old Rossini scored a double triumph in Venice—in comedy with *L'italiana in Algeri* and in opera seria with *Tancredi.* Of the two the latter was the more important; not only did it carry Rossini's reputation outside Italy; it laid the foundations of a style of opera that was to last beyond the middle of the century. Successive works defined a general plan which by 1820 held undisputed sway throughout the peninsula. Looking back on a career which began when Rossini's star was at its zenith, Giovanni Pacini wrote, "Everyone followed the same school, the same fashions, and in consequence were all imitators of the great luminary. But, good heavens, what else could one do, since there was no other way of making a living?"[1]

To define the precise extent of Rossini's innovations, how far he invented and how far he merely codified, would require a detailed study of the period such as no one has yet attempted. Certainly there was no question of an artistic revolution such as Wagner was to bring about; conditions in Italy made this impossible from every point of view. German audiences were prepared to be edified: Italians wanted to enjoy themselves—hence the minimal influence of Gluck in Italy and, with the exception of *Don Giovanni,* the relative unpopularity of Mozart. At the center of the scene was the star singer: any reform which aimed at diminishing his or her territory was doomed from the outset. Nor can it be said that Rossini's melodic style was entirely new. The opening of "Una voce poco fa" can be found in the same key, but in a tragic context, in Paer's *Sofonisba,* while the ditty with which Cenerentala beguiles her lonely hours by the fireside is discernible by fits and starts in Zeliska's first aria in *L'amore coniugale.* The novelty lies in his method of musical organisation. The bourgeois audiences of the postrevolutionary time wanted simple, songlike ideas. These are to be found in Paer and Mayr, certainly, but side by side with elaborate, concertolike structures more suited to the taste of the previous century. The sonata-movement-without-development characteristic of old-style opera seria Rossini confines to the overture. If his arias and duets are shorter and simpler than those of Paer they are part of a longer structural unit, the *scena,* defined by the number of characters on stage at a given time, but in Rossini's scheme including the entrance of a principal character together with the preparations for that entrance. In consequence the taste of a modern audience was met without any sacrifice of scale.

Various factors contributed to his success. A natural ex-

---

1. G. Pacini, *Le mie memorie artistiche* (Florence, 1875), p. 54.

uberance and taste for artifice enabled him to satisfy his star singers with roulades and embellishments far more ingenious than the kinds they were accustomed to impose on the works of other composers. He possessed a strength of musical personality that stamped itself on certain procedures that were not new when he first used them, but which thereafter became unmistakably his. Foremost among these is the crescendo that follows the second subject of every overture and often bridges two statements of an aria movement. Its invention has been variously ascribed to Paer, Mosca, and Generali; but in fact the listener need look no further than Mozart's *Symphony No. 32* in G to find a perfect specimen, complete with tremolando strings. Mozart's, however, is merely one variant among many of the so-called Mannheim crescendo. Rossini's is like a personal trademark; and it remains as such even when employed by a Donizetti or a Bellini. Likewise, the prismatic style of orchestration, with its abundance of contrasted wind solos, evident as early as *La scala di seta* of 1811, can be found in certain passages of Mayr. It was Rossini who made it the norm. Above all, Rossini was a master of rhythm. This is the secret of the *vis comica*, the belly laugh that he brought to the Italian opera buffa. One has only to think of the opening of *La Cenerentola*, a sequence of busy unison phrases without a vestige of melodic interest. All that matters here is rhythm and pitch. The descending pattern is like the drawing of a bow, from which the following violin melody shoots up with the force of an arrow. Through means such as these coupled with a classical instinct for form Rossini was able to devise a musical architecture, flexible and elaborate on the surface, strong and simple beneath, and ideally suited to a society that required a rapid turnover of new works.

The basis of this architecture is balance and contrast. The aria in two movements which began to replace the da capo aria during the 1770s had been, formally speaking, a fluid affair, ranging from a fast movement with a slow introduction ("Non ho colpa" from *Idomeneo*) to a slow movement with a fast coda ("Dove sono" from *Figaro*). In the "code Rossini" the two sections were in equilibrium—expressive andante or adagio, followed by a brilliant allegro to be known as the cabaletta (a term whose origins no one has yet been able to discover). Both are in simple, binary form. The first ends with a free cadenza; the second is repeated (in part during the second decade of the century and in toto thereafter), with an intervening orchestral passage and a coda to match. The single-movement romanza is also to be found, this too containing its own inbuilt contrast, especially where it begins in the minor key and ends in the major.

Duets, on the other hand, are usually in three movements—fast, slow, and fast. Of the various designs they can assume, one stands out as particularly characteristic, since it derives from Rossini's ability to blend lyricism and declamation in a formal movement. The first singer leads with a type of melody which the German musicologist Friedrich Lippmann has defined as "open"[2]—a succession of ornate flourishes interspersed with pauses that serve both to mask the basic regularity of its construction and to effect an easy transition from the preceding recitative to the strict tempo of the duet itself. An interplay of orchestral and vocal ideas follows, culminating in a series of vocal roulades which end in emphatic orchestral poundings and a full close. A parallel verse follows for the second singer. Then the music will move to a new key, with the singers in dialogue. After a half-close comes a new lyrical movement during which the voices become linked in sixths and thirds. Here the melody is smooth and regular, but with voluptuous prolongations toward the final cadence. There is a short transition, sometimes in the form of a "surprise" (entry of a messenger, hunting horns off stage) which alters the situation and with it the mood of the singers. This launches the final movement, which is fast and in the form of a double cabaletta with the melody stated by the

2. F. Lippmann, "Vincenzo Bellini und die italienische opera seria seiner Zeit," in *Analecta Musicologica 6* (Cologne, 1969), 170.

two singers in succession, then, after a ritornello, together, either in unison, in harmony, or with each phrase in dialogue. Here the pattern of repetition is designed not only to give a sense of symmetry to the whole but to ease the action to a halt and prepare for a bout of applause. Two larger and more complex designs may be mentioned: the so-called *introduzione e cavatina*, which regularly begins the opera, and the central-act finale, both of which are fully crystallized in *Tancredi*. The first starts with a choral movement in which the melodic interest is centered in the orchestra, and which may or may not include an episode with an intervention by a secondary character. A principal makes his entrance (his—*not hers*—since in general the prima donna's entrance was reserved for the second act or scene) and sings a snatch of declamatory recitative followed by a slow aria movement ending with cadenza. There is another burst of chorus, sometimes in dialogue with the principal, who then advances to the footlights and sings a cabaletta punctuated by choral comment. A long orchestral diminuendo, usually covered by applause, clears the stage. The same design, modified and rechristened *rondò finale*, may bring down the final curtain.

But to end the first-act finale (for in Rossini's day two acts were the rule), a more monumental structure was required. Even before the turn of the century the multimovement ensembles that mark the midpoint of opera buffa had begun to find their way into opera seria in more sedate form. With Rossini the basis became again one of contrast and balance—two movements in which the action moves forward, and two in which the characters are frozen in a state of wonder or despair. The first is usually based on an orchestral melody which is pursued through various keys with the characters present declaiming, in rapid dialogue, often in hurried exclamations like "Spietato!" "Orror," "Che gioia!" "Io fremo!" and so on. The action then halts and the music develops a *largo concertato*, a multiple soliloquy of complex part writing sometimes in the form of a round or false canon sometimes led by one of the principals with the rest joining in at the end of the first musical paragraph. Then the orchestral motif is resumed and with it the action. The final movement, a *stretta,* is again static in character, but noisy and brilliant where the concertato had been slow and expressive.

Yet even at its lowest ebb Italian opera possessed one notable advantage over that of other countries—a tradition of conversational recitative which carries the action forward between one formal number and the next and allows the musical attention a certain respite while preserving the sense of continuity. It derives from the special quality of the Italian language with its fluent, easy articulation and wealth of ready assonance. In English or German a rhyme is either intentional and strong or unintentional and clumsy. In Italian, an inflectional language, it is often difficult to avoid rhyming. In French the problem is a different one—that of establishing a metrical framework in a language that has no tonic accent. The outcome is the same in all three cases; neither in English, German, or French is there any natural equivalent of Italian *versi sciolti,* with their quick rhyme and free alternation of seven- and ten-syllable verses. The recitatives of Handel's oratorios, no less those of Rameau's operas, are stilted and formal. Singspiel and opéra comique preferred to make use of spoken dialogue occasionally varied with *mélodrame,* or speech over music. Only Italian opera enjoyed the benefit of recitativo secco, with its fleet movement over an unemphatic basis of harpsichord accompaniment.

During the second decade of the nineteenth century, however, a revolution in operatic thought took place in favor of the through-composed work with continuous orchestral texture. Its origins probably lie in the spectacular operas composed for the newly reopened Paris Opéra—Méhul's *Ossian,* Spontini's *La Vestale* and *Fernand Cortez.* These were imported to Naples during the reign of Murat, where at the same time examples of the older tragédie lyrique were being revived in Italian translations. All of these had orchestrally accompanied recitative, which from then on became the rule, first at the San Carlo, Naples, and within ten years in every theater in the peninsula. From Italy the vogue spread to Germany, resulting in such works as Schubert's *Alfonso und Estrella* and *Fierrabras* and Weber's *Euryanthe.* Yet only in Italy did it regularly produce happy results. Recitative in French grand opera from *La Vestale* to *Guillaume Tell* can be heavy and tedious, needing the cunning of a Meyerbeer to disguise its essential inertia. Of the Germans Weber came nearest to solving the problem; Schubert and Schumann were beset by it in varying degrees. Up to the time of *Das Rheingold* Wagner's transitions are frequently weighed down by the meter of their text.

For the Italians, however, it was a simple matter to score for strings what had originally been recitative with keyboard, adding the occasional touch of wind color where appropriate. Recitativo accompagnato had of course existed in all opera, usually by way of emphatic preparation for an aria or duet. Now the two variations were able to mingle in that synthesis of declamation and lyricism, or orchestral and vocal motifs, of strict and free time known as the *scena* (c.f. *scena ed aria, scena e duetto*) which remains a constant feature of Italian opera until well after the midcentury. Extraneous to the German ideal of total, uncompromising continuity, conversational recitative remained the lymph in the bloodstream of Italian opera.

Rossinian opera represents a moment of classicism in the country's musical history: all its elements are in perfect equilibrium. Yet it obviously could not withstand the romantic tide for ever. Nor is the disapproval of Weber, Schumann, and Berlioz due to envy alone; for all three, like true romantics, laid stress on the portrayal of individual characters and particular emotions; and there is no doubt that emotion in Rossinian opera seria is mostly generic. The Viennese critic Eduard Hanslick quotes with some approval the view of one of Gluck's contemporaries that Orpheus's famous lament would equally well fit the lines:

J'ai trouvé mon Eurydice   I have found my Eurydice
Rien n'égale à ma bonheur.[3]   Nothing equals my happiness.

Rossini would have furnished him with a more concrete
example of emotional ambivalence. The second act of his
Mosè in Egitto ends with an aria movement for the heroine
in which she laments the death of her lover, the Pharoah's
son. In the French version *Moïse*, this same piece expresses
the joy of Sinaida after hearing her son promise to marry
the princess that his father has chosen for him. Rarely, except in his choral numbers (e.g. the chorus of darkness),
does Rossini make use of romantically expressive harmony. To Wagner the clusters of fioritura that mark his
slow cantabili were like artificial flowers.[4] Even Verdi looking back at the opera of the 1820s considered that much of
it was nearer to singing exercises than to real music.[5]
     The phenomenal success of Bellini's *Il pirata* in 1827
brought about the desired change. If it created no new
forms, it established a new emotional perspective in Italian
opera, carrying it decisively into the Romantic age. The
case of Bellini has baffled many a musical historian. In
matters of technique he remained something of an amateur, not because he lacked an academic training, but
rather because that training came too late for him to put it
to the service of his creative ability. He was nineteen when
he entered the Naples Conservatory; and there is no need
to doubt the anecdote according to which his teacher
Zingarelli told him that he was not born for music.[6] In
order to bend the tradition of Italian opera to his special
talent, to precipitate his own musical personality with its
powerful melodic and harmonic intuitions that often anticipate those of Chopin, he required a basis of simplicity.
The interplay of voice and orchestra in Rossini's manner

3. E. Hanslick, *The Beautiful in Music,* English trans. G. Cohen (London, 1891),
48–49.
4. R. Wagner, *Gesammelte Schriften und Dichtungen* 3 (Leipzig, 1871–73), 250.
5. Letter to G. Piroli, May 30, 1868, in Carteggi III, 53–54.
6. See F. Pastura, *Bellini nella storia* (Parma, 1959), 60.

was quite foreign to his thinking. Even in movements launched by an orchestral theme (e.g. the duet between Pollione and Adalgisa in *Norma*) the voice superimposes a melody of its own which does not complement the original theme so much as reinforce it. The second idea ("Sol promessa a Dio") is unashamedly vocal with the most rudimentary of orchestral accompaniments. Throughout Bellini's operas vocal values are paramount. Opera for him was the difficult art of "making people weep through singing,"[7] a definition that applies to his orchestral introductions and ritornellos no less than to his vocal lines.

Likewise his declamation, to which he attached great importance, is entirely free from the exuberant rhetoric of Rossini and his followers. There are no open melodies in Bellini after his apprentice work, *Adelson e Salvini*. Everything proceeds in smooth, lyrical statements with a deliberate avoidance of artifice. The false canon in Bellini's hands is even less of a pretence at counterpoint than in Rossini's; in "O di qual sei tu vittima" (*Norma*) and "No, non ti son rivale" (*La straniera*) a melody is presented three times with faint differences in texture due to the number of singers taking part. All three movements in the duet "Serba i tuoi segreti" consist of regular themes sung by the two singers in succession and then together—but what magnificent themes!

From this it will be gathered that far from enlarging the range of procedures in the "Code Rossini" Bellini contracted it. Apart from the long, nonrepeating cantabili such as "Casta diva" (*Norma*) and "Ah non credea mirarti" (*La sonnambula*), which recall Milton's description of "Notes with many a winding bout of linked sweetness long drawn out," his themes generally run to a pattern likened by E. J. Dent to that of "The Vicar of Bray" or "The British Grenadiers"—i.e., a simple A–A–B–A.[8] This is an exaggeration, since in Bellini the first A is never quite the same as

---

7. Letter to C. Pepoli (undated), c. May 1834, in V. Bellini, *Epistolario*, ed. L. Cambi (Verona, 1942), 400.

8. E. J. Dent, *The Rise of Romantic Opera* (Cambridge, 1976), 170.

the second and third, while the B is articulated differently from either (see "Ah per sempre" from *I puritani*). But it is all very different from Rossini's way, where despite similarities of voice and content no two arias or duets will be found to have exactly the same shape. In other words, the patterns of the "code Rossini" described above have in Rossini's own hands the quality of Platonic forms—hypothetical abstractions on which each new piece of music was a variation. In the works of his immediate successors such forms became external and all too obtrusive. It is a common enough phenomenon in the early Romantic age: form in the hands of Mendelssohn and Schumann offers a far narrower range of possibilities than in Haydn, Mozart, and Beethoven. The "masculine" first subject and the "feminine" second subject became the unvarying rule.

For all that, Bellini's was the voice of the future. It was under his influence that the ideal of *canto fiorito,* of which Rossini's art was the most elaborate expression, began to give way to a style that aimed at the natural accents of human utterance. This in turn altered the traditional distribution of leading characters. The eighteenth-century castrato had become a rarity since 1810 or thereabouts. His place as *jeune premier* together with his familiar title of *musico* had been taken over by the female contralto, whose voice is particularly suited to the cool heroics of Rossinian opera seria. Tenors were reserved for villains or heavy fathers. From about 1830 on, however, the contralto became relegated to the subhero—the hero's bosom friend or the heroine's silent adorer. The tenor with his far greater resources of palpitating emotion replaced her as the juvenile lead, relinquishing his villainous functions to the *basso cantante,* soon to develop in Verdi's hands into the dramatic baritone. True, opera seria had known tenor heroes in Rossini's time, especially in those works written for the Teatro San Carlo, whose roster contained such names as David, Garcia, and Nozzari; and of course the heroes of opera buffa were rarely anything else. But their style of singing was quite different from that of the lyric tenors of today, though it can still be heard on old records of Fernando de Lucia. It is light, floated, agile; decorative rather than deeply expressive. No Rossinian tenor, with the exception of Otello, was required to sing above an A flat with full chest resonance. The prototype of the new Romantic hero (allowing for certain idiosyncrasies of register) was Giovanni Battista Rubini, who created several of Bellini's most memorable roles. From his time onward fioritura gradually disappeared from the male aria to be replaced by a simpler, more fervent lyricism and a more impassioned declamation. Not everyone considered this change to be for the better. Old-fashioned theorists and historians such as the Belgian Fétis held that Bellini and those who came after him had ruined the true art of singing[9]—an accusation that bore especially heavily upon Verdi.

In his earlier operas, in fact, Bellini was much more uncompromising in his attitude to fioritura than he later became. In both *Bianca e Fernando* (definitive version) and *La straniera* the vocal writing is almost entirely syllabic with just the occasional expressive melisma. But a passage of arms with a soprano in the first, and a newspaper polemic after the premiere of the second, caused him to alter course, so far indeed as to revert to the tradition of a florid contralto hero in *Zaira* and *I Capuleti ed i Montecchi*. His last operas include a measure of fioritura in the female roles, but with a notable change of emphasis. The roulades and gorgheggi symbolize the fragility, the unattainability of the Romantic heroine rather than the pomp and grandeur of the prima donna.

In his immediacy of expression, his awareness of his own limitations, and his consequent care in the choice of plots, Bellini stands closer to the young Verdi than do any of his contemporaries. The lacrymose Bellinian ethos pervades the whole of Verdi's first opera, *Oberto, Conte di San Bonifacio*, with its villain who bewails his own villainy and its tragedy enhanced by general sympathy and compas-

9. F. J. Fétis in *Revue et Gazette Musicale* No. 37 (Paris, Sept. 13, 1850), quoted in M. Mila, "Fétis e Verdi," in Atti 3, 312–21.

sion. Even later, when Verdi's style had taken on a more pronounced masculinity, references to Bellini abound in his letters. "Let the poet have in view the finale of *Beatrice* or *Norma*,[10] he wrote when preparing to set the abortive *Cromwell* alias *Allan Cameron* alias *Woodstock,* which was eventually shelved in favor of *Ernani.* He referred Antonio Somma, his chosen poet for a *King Lear* to "No, non ti son rivale" and "Meco tu vien, o misera" from *La straniera* as a model blend of words and music. As late as 1881, when about to start work on the revision of *Simon Boccanegra,* he allowed himself a characteristic tirade against the frills and fancies of modern harmony and scoring, adding "and I haven't such a horror of cabalettas; and if a young man of today were to come up with one like 'Meco tu vien, o misera' or 'Ah perchè non passo odiarti?' I would go and listen with the best will in the world."[11] Both cabalettas are of the moderato variety typical of Bellini, occurring respectively in *La straniera* and *La sonnambula.* For Verdi it was Bellini who more than anyone justified the *primo ottocento* tradition from which he himself sprang.

Throughout the 1830s Rossini and Bellini remained the two stars by which Italian composers took their bearings, Bellini being progressively in the ascendant. The open melody became rarer, the plain, lyrical period more common. The largo concertato, from being an imposing piece of complex tracery became a moment of melodic transfiguration gathering up the individual threads in a sad, sweet cantilena. As Rossinian Classicism retreated into the past, the prevailing style of melody became popular, the accompaniment more obvious (the bolero-like pounding that accompanies many a cabaletta seems to have arisen since Rossini's time). Yet the older procedures remained to be drawn upon where appropriate. The most accomplished practitioner of the 1830s convention was without doubt Gaetano Donizetti, who combined the formal resource of Rossini with Bellini's Romantic spirit, and at the same time

10. Letter to Count Mocenigo, Aug. 5, 1843, in Morazzoni, 20.
11. Letter to Giulio Ricordi, Nov. 20, 1880, in Copial., 559–60.

developed a dramatic momentum which provided Verdi with a valuable model. Unlike Bellini, he had been thoroughly trained in music from an early age, and so possessed a fluency of technique which the younger composer might justly envy ("with my style," Bellini wrote, "I have to spew blood"[12]). Yet it was not until after the triumph of *Il pirata* that Donizetti found his own personal voice. Less of an innovator even than Bellini, his skill lay not in inventing new forms so much as in adapting and combining the old ones to meet the demands of different dramatic situations. Certain procedures may indeed have originated with him—notably the duet movement in dialogue (e.g., "Soli noi siamo" from *Lucrezia Borgia* and "È men fiero" from *Pia de Tolomei*). But he never stamped it with his own patent as Rossini would have done. By the late 1830s it was in general use without any specifically Donizettian connotations. Another feature of his later operas is a growing tendency to allocate different themes to different characters within the same movement so as to heighten the tension between them (e.g., "Nol sai che un nume vindice" from *Roberto Devereux*), where Rossini and Bellini would have made them repeat the same melody in succession. This was a principle that Verdi was to carry still further, though as late as *Aida* (1871) he could still revert to the old pattern of threefold repetition for a duet-cabaletta.

Throughout his seventy-odd operas, Donizetti's range of expression is phenomenal; yet until the last twenty years only his two comedies, *L'elisir d'amore* and *Don Pasquale*, were permitted to rank as masterpieces, in which the spirit of Rossinian opera buffa is rekindled in a glow of Romantic sentiment. A narrow view, certainly, and largely a relic of the Wagnerian aesthetic, but it is understandable. An age which demands the single, unrepeatable masterwork will not find it in the "serious" theater of Donizetti or indeed in that of the 1830s generally, with the possible exception of *Norma*. The reason lies in the theatrical condi-

12. Letter to F. Florimo, June 14, 1828, in *Epistolario*, 109–15.

tions that obtained in Italy at the time and, in particular, the position occupied by the star singer.

According to a well-known story, the young Rossini was so incensed at the way in which the castrato Velluti persisted in smothering with meaningless embellishments the music written for him in *Aureliano in Palmira* that he decided for the future to write out all decorations himself—a resolve which he is supposed to have maintained for the rest of his career, so putting an end to singers' licence, and subjugating them once and for all to the composer's will. Nothing could be more misleading. Both during Rossini's time and long afterward singers exercised their right to decorate a melody when and where they pleased. The second statement of a cabaletta was as regularly embroidered as the reprise of a da capo aria. Mario, the most fashionable tenor of the mid-century, was famous for the taste with which he embellished. Maria Malibran, Jenny Lind, and Adelina Patti all had their own ornamented versions of well-known arias. Patti even performed her own "Una voce poco fa" to the aged Rossini, much to his whimsical dismay ("What a charming air, my dear! Pray who is the composer?"). This is the version sung by many soprano Rosinas of today. But singers' licence was not confined to matters of decoration. In the age of the prima donna the singer was more important than the song. Star performers took precedence over composers both in their fees and the order of their engagement, and they expected the composer to serve them unconditionally. If he provided an aria that did not suit their vocal means they had no scruple in replacing it with one from another source which did—no very difficult feat in the days when opera plots ran to standard patterns with stock situations. Hence every singer carried a supply of so-called *arie di baule* (literally "suitcase arias") to be drawn upon when the composer was either recalcitrant or, more frequently, not present to complain. For after he had fulfilled his contract by producing the score by the appointed time, rehearsed the singers, and attended the first three performances (seated

by the leading double-bass player and ready to acknowledge applause—and woe betide the opera whose composer failed to show himself to the public on such occasions, as Donizetti found to his cost), he had no control
over the fate of his score.

In Germany and Austria publishers such as Simrock and
Artaria brought out more or less complete vocal scores of
operas after their first production. In France operas were
engraved in full score and protected by law. In Italy such
protection was impossible to enforce so long as the peninsula remained under a multitude of different governments. No one worked harder to remedy the situation
than the publisher Giovanni Ricordi. He was the first Italian to print vocal scores under the supervision of the composer; and it was largely through his agency that in 1840
the Austrian Empire and the Kingdom of Sardinia con-
cluded a treaty for the reciprocal protection of theatrical
works—a small enough step in itself, but the first move in a
hard-fought battle that the composer was eventually to
win.

Meanwhile, the composer adapted himself to the prevailing conditions with as good a grace as possible. It was
pointless for him to choose a subject until he knew what
principals he would have at his disposal. During rehearsals
he would tailor his music to the specific abilities of each,
"concealing their natural defects," as Pacini put it, "and
showing off their good points."[13] The implications of this
are clear enough. If every principal aimed to present himself as a beautiful singer the range of negative emotion
available to him was bound to be narrow. That is why there
are no Pizzaros or Caspars in Italian opera of the period.
Up to 1830, or thereabouts, it recognized two categories of
principal bass: the basso buffo, who specialized in comic
acting, declamation, and patter, and the basso cantante,
who possessed a lyrical technique (that he was often expected to combine it with the special skills of a buffo is

13. G. Pacini, 72.

shown by the examples of Figaro, Dandini, and Dr. Malatesta). Both were associated primarily with comedy. When the basso cantante began to make his way into the serious genre it was important for him to prove his credentials—a bass who can sing. Accordingly, he required the composer to provide him with smooth, lyrical lines similar to those of a tenor or a soprano, and in the upper register of his voice. The savage snarl would not do. Therefore, the bass or baritone villains of Italian opera, beginning with Bellini's Ernesto, have to express their malevolence through a smooth, lyrical irony. No one was more aware of his inadequacy than Bellini himself; and he welcomed the subject of *I puritani* all the more for its lack of a villain.[14]

With the exception of the Teatro San Carlo, Naples, on which the Bourbons were prepared to spend large sums of money, few opera houses could afford more than three or four first-rate singers, at most, so that plots had to be modified accordingly. Happily, there existed a subcategory of singers known as comprimarii, standing between the primi, or full principals, and the secondi, who did little more than announce arrivals or happenings. The comprimario was allowed a short cantabile or romanza (add a cabaletta to it and he automatically becomes a principal), and he could even be one of the partners in a duet. More often, what appears to be a duet between principal and comprimario is really an *aria con pertichini* or aria with interventions (e.g., Leicester's "Ah, rimiro il bel sembiante" from *Maria Stuarda*). With the aid of experienced librettists such as Cammarano, Donizetti was especially skillful at suggesting a wider dramatic canvas than actually existed.

Suppose, then, that an opera composed for La Scala, Milan, has proved so successful that the management of the Teatro La Fenice, Venice, decides to mount a revival of it as soon as the term of La Scala's proprietorship has run its course. It is unlikely that the singers who created

14. Letter to Santocanale, Apr. 11, 1834, in *Epistolario*, 315.

the leading roles will be available. The new soprano may specialize in agility where the original one had been more famous for dramatic expression. The part conceived for a full bass may have to be adapted for a baritone, whose area of comfort may be a tone or so higher. If the composer had already been engaged to provide the novelty of the season (*opera di obbligo*) required of all major theaters, the problem was easily solved: his contract would be extended to enable him to take charge of the revival. He would provide alternative numbers where necessary and adapt the music already written to the company's needs by a process known as *puntatura,* whereby the vocal line is altered while the harmony remains unchanged. He might convert a comprimario into a primo or vice versa. Extra lines would be provided by the stage director, himself normally a librettist. The composer's work was thus butchered; but at least he has wielded the knife himself.

But if, as was mostly the case, he himself was not present, the work of adaptation would be left to the *maestro concertatore,* whose function was similar to that of a modern *répétiteur.* True, the composer might be commissioned personally by one of the principals to provide an alternative aria which would then become the singer's property; and if he were too busy to comply (as Donizetti usually was) he might recommend an aria from another of his operas in which the situation was similar. In most cases, however, the singer would not even seek his opinion, but merely insert an aria of his or her own choice. So it was that when, three months after its initial success at La Scala, *Oberto* was given as the season's standby opera (*opera di ripiego*) in Turin by the cast for which Nicolai had composed *Il templario,* the new Cuniza filled out her role with a cavatina from Mercadante's *Elena da Feltre.* The following autumn Verdi's new opera, *Un giorno di regno,* failed disastrously at its premiere at La Scala. All further performances of it were canceled and replaced by revivals of *Oberto,* sung by the cast who had performed it in Turin. This time Verdi not only provided the singer, Luigia Abbadia, with a new cavatina of his own; he also replaced her duet with the tenor with another of more ample design. (In Turin she had omitted the original altogether, as it lay too low for her). Neither of the later pieces appears in the published score; but both can be found in an appendix to Verdi's autograph.

For the first ten years of his career, Verdi was to supply similar substitute pieces for individual singers, though with reluctance. In the letter that accompanied a new romanza for Almerinda Granchi to sing in *Nabucco* in Venice, Verdi took care to ask for the full score of it to be returned to him, "since I want the opera to remain as written."[15]

As has been suggested, such a system presupposes a certain generic quality in operatic plots. During the 1830s and later all subjects, however diverse their origins, were quarried for stock situations; and the majority resolved themselves into simple tales of star-crossed lovers. The tragic ending, exceptional in Rossini's day, had become the rule in Donizetti's. Opera buffa retained something of its old variety, especially in the hands of librettists such as Romani or Ferretti; but here too the characters themselves ran to stereotypes—soubrette soprano, languishing tenor, intriguing basso cantante, and fussy, bumbling basso buffo. As well as that, the genre itself, which had flourished so notably at the turn of the century, had begun to lose ground to opera seria (it even retained the outdated recitativo secco). More characteristic of the time was the so-called opera semiseria, whose plots fall broadly into two categories. The first is descended from the revolutionary *pièce de sauvetage* and deals with a rescue and the overthrow of a usurper (e.g., Bellini's *Bianca e Fernando*). The second, more common variety traces its roots still further back to the French *comédie larmoyante* of the later eighteenth century ("the true sentimental," in Sheridan's words, "and nothing ridiculous in it from beginning to

---

15. Letter to Count Mocenigo, Dec. 19, 1842, in Lawton-Rosen.

end"). Examples range from Paisiello's *Nina* and Rossini's
La gazza ladra (1817) to Bellini's *La sonnambula* (1830) and
Donizetti's *Linda di Chamounix* (1842). Here comedy and
tragedy can mingle freely, and the sighs and palpitations
of a prima donna on the verge of insanity may be relieved
by the chatterings of a basso buffo. Minor composers of
the time who were unable to scale the heights of opera
seria sometimes achieved notable success in the mixed
genre—Luigi Ricci with *Chiara di Rosembergh* (1833), his
brother Federico with *La prigione di Edimburgo* (1838);
both operas left a small but distinct impression on Verdi.

From all this it will be gathered that Italian opera of the
time had a looseness of organization quite out of keeping
with the quasi-symphonic ideals that were gaining ground
in the north among a generation that had discovered Beethoven; and that the better a composer succeeded in
adapting himself to the conditions described above the
more his oeuvre resembles a fluid continuum rather than a
chain of self-sufficient, individual works of art. The fact
that from each opera only about half a dozen numbers
might be published made it easier for him to borrow and
adapt from a previous work—a practice in which Rossini,
Donizetti, and even Bellini indulged without scruple. The
idiom of the time was as narrowly defined as at any period
in the eighteenth century, so that to a casual ear all composers seem to be quoting from each other. The London
critic Henry Chorley accused Verdi of lacking originality
and proceeded to ascribe to Donizetti what he thought to
be Donizetti's, and likewise to Federico Ricci, Bellini, and
Mercadante. To the Viennese Hanslick, more knowl-
edgeable and even less sympathetic, Italian operas were
like persons from another race, distinguishable only by
each other, all looking alike to European eyes.[16]

Among Donizetti's tragic output *Lucia di Lammermoor*
has always held a special place as an archetype of Italian
Romantic opera; and archetype is precisely what it is, with

16. E. Hanslick, *Die moderne Oper*, 1 (Berlin, 1880), quoted in M. Mila, "Verdi e
Hanslick," in *La Rassegna Musicale Italiana* 21 (1951), 212–21.

numbers which were to serve as a model for later composers, Verdi included, for certain situations—the haunted vision ("Regnava nel silenzio"), the lovers' farewell ("Verranno a te sull' aure"), the concertato of confrontation sweetly transfigured ("Chi mi frena in tal momento?"), the lovers' curse ("Maledetto sia l'istante"), the soprano mad scene, the Romantic hero's death ("Tu che a Dio spiegasti l'ali"). Yet the Romantic spirit which informs the opera's best moments is by no means uniformly maintained. The soprano-baritone duet in Act II ("Il pallor, funesto, orrendo") does not even reflect the sense of the words, being cut in the most conventional of Rossinian molds. It could be said that Sir Julius Benedict did the chattering violin melody better service when he transposed it into the minor key for the duet between Eily O'Connor and Danny Man in *The Lily of Killarney.* The bass aria with *pertichini* ("Ah cedi, o più sciagura") is there merely because the Teatro San Carlo had a principal bass to sing it; and it is usually omitted in modern performances. For the Paris version of 1839 at the Théâtre de la Renaissance, Donizetti eliminated much that was inessential, but he allowed the cavatina "Regnava nel silenzio" to be replaced by the characterless, chirrupy "Perchè non ho del vento" from *Rosmonda d'Inghilterra,* written for the same soprano who had created Lucia in Naples. Even in his most famous work he was to some extent at the mercy of a florid prima donna.

It is all too easy to view this as evidence of artistic decadence, forgetting that throughout the eighteenth century the same standards, the same practices prevailed all over Europe. No one thought of giving an opera the organic form that we expect of it today. The aim was to create it anew with each revival, according to the singers available. There was no premium on originality as such. Handel, Hasse, and Gluck felt free to borrow from their contemporaries, as well as from their own earlier works. Mozart's *Idomeneo* has a tighter, more continuous construction than most opere serie of the time; yet Mozart happily rewrote the part of Idamante for a tenor, providing him with a new duet with the heroine; and one of his dearest wishes was to refashion the title role for the basso profondo Ludwig Fischer—a change which would have involved a still more radical alteration of the original score. We forget that two of the greatest operas of the century are usually heard in versions that their composers never knew: *Don Giovanni* in an amalgam of the Prague and Vienna scores, with two tenor arias where Mozart allowed for only one; *Orfeo ed Euridice* in a conflation of the Paris and Vienna versions based on the one made by Berlioz for the mezzo-soprano Pauline Viardot-Garcia in the mid-nineteenth century. In opera seria from Alessandro Scarlatti to Mozart, plot and situations all show a family likeness. In Hasse and J. C. Bach, as in Donizetti and Bellini, the tyrant reflects long and lyrically as to whether or not he should sign a death warrant. The difference is that in the eighteenth century he would pardon the accused even if proven guilty; a hundred years later he will condemn him (or more probably her) even when innocent.

Nonetheless, by the 1830s the aesthetic which had viewed opera as a series of abstract emotional states and which glorified artifice as an assertion of human dignity no longer prevailed. Contemporary taste began to demand the sculpting of individual characters who develop along with the action, while the more advanced spirits of the age such as Berlioz and the young Wagner were moving toward a view of opera as the continuation of the symphony by other means. Clearly Italian *melodramma* could not remain forever with one foot in the previous century. Yet its way forward was hampered both by the tyranny of the singers and the conservative nature of an Italian audience. By the end of the decade, however, notions of reform were in the air. Donizetti was spending most of his time in Paris and Vienna, where audiences encouraged him toward a bolder and at the same time more thoughtful approach. Otto Nicolai, in his brief but not inglorious Italian career, fortified the current Italian idiom with German

workmanship and harmonic expression. A letter written
by Mercadante to Francesco Florimo in 1838 reads like the
manifesto of a latter-day Gluck:

> I have continued the reform begun with *Il giuramento*—
> more variety to the forms, away with trivial cabalettas; con-
> cision, less repetition, more novelty in the cadences, due at-
> tention paid to the dramatic side; orchestration rich but
> without swamping the voices; long solos in the concertati
> avoided since they oblige everyone else to stand stock still
> to the detriment of the action; not much bass drum and
> very little stage band.[17]

Pacini too describes in his memoirs how, having
emerged from temporary retirement in order to write
Saffo, he first of all studied ancient Greek meters and
modes before setting to work (though no one would guess
this from looking at the score). A few years later he set out
on a revolutionary path of his own in an opera based on
Alfieri's *Merope.* "My intention was to depart completely
(so far as the Italian musical art permits it) . . . from all the
accepted forms, following the action and expressing in
music the various passions and natures of the characters.
For Merope I devised an impassioned vocal style; for
Egisto a vigorous and agitated manner; and a reserved dis-
simulating one for Polifonte."[18] But he continues sadly
that the opera failed to please and was never revived;
hence he had no alternative but to revert to the conventional forms which even by 1847 had not changed in essentials; nor were they to do so for more than ten years.

Clearly, neither Pacini nor Mercadante was the man to
bring about the needed reforms—Pacini because his invention, though fluent, was trivial, Mercadante because his
temperament was essentially neoclassical with a penchant
for the decorative and the monumental. His improve-

17. Letter to F. Florimo, Jan. 1, 1838, quoted in F. Florimo, *La scuola musicale
di Napoli* 3 (Naples, 1880), 115.
18. Pacini, pp. 102–3.

ments were all on the side of musical craftsmanship and of a somewhat academic cast. Dramatically they were negative. In works such as *Il giuramento* and *Il bravo* (arguably his masterpiece) he did indeed reduce the number of trivial cabalettas, molding the introduzione of the first into a scheme that curiously anticipates Verdi's in *Un ballo in maschera* with three one-movement cavatinas placed between the opening and closing choruses. But the problem of dramatic pace eluded him; and far from trimming the conventional forms to suit the action, he became increasingly disposed to expand and elaborate them. The 1840s was the decade of the Risorgimento, whose spirit found expression in opera through an abundant use of the patriotic chorus. The pattern had already been hinted at in Bellini's *I puritani* (written, significantly, in collaboration with the exiled Italian patriot, Count Pepoli), where there is hardly a number in which the chorus does not intervene. In Vaccai's *Virginia* (1845) and Mercadante's *Orazi e Curiazi* (1846) the chorus is in the forefront of the action; but the effect is to slow up the dramatic pace. The later works of Mercadante are weighed down with irrelevancies, of futile displays of science, by a style of scoring that is an exaggeration of Rossini's, and in general by that disproportion of means to end which is the unfailing sign of a decaying tradition.

By now, however, Verdi had arrived on the scene and was moving in a different direction. Where others enlarged and embroidered, he shortened and simplified. The contrasted movements of the Rossinian grand duet, already modified by Donizetti to fit the requirements of a faster-moving action, were further dissolved by Verdi into a dialectic of short, interlocking movements, each of which carries the dramatic argument a stage further. Recitative is cut to a minimum; likewise ornament, where it serves no expressive purpose. In matters of scoring Verdi never beautifies; his instrumental style is plain, blunt, and strictly functional. To the cautious reformers of an earlier generation his music often appeared coarse, even downright ugly

(Nicolai declared in his memoirs that Verdi must have the heart of a donkey); but his was the way forward.

Of his first sixteen operas, four may be singled out as marking the most important steps in his progress from the general cut of *primo ottocento* melodrama to the unique masterworks of his maturity. The first is *Nabucco* (1842), from which Verdi himself dated the start of his career. It was in this opera that his voice first emerges in all its clarity. The slow, swinging melody of the chorus "Va, pensiero," from which the opera takes its tone, owes something to Bellini (again the example of "O di qual sei tu vittima" comes to mind) just as the general plan and plain, massive proportions can be traced to Rossini's grand operas such as *Le Siège de Corinth* and *Moïse*, which were already current in Italy in translation. But the synthesis is wholly original! With the simple, unison chorus developed on a grand scale, Verdi made his own terms with the *Zeitgeist* in a way that Mercadante and his generation had failed to do, and without loss of dramatic impetus. According to his pupil, Muzio, it was *Nabucco* that earned Verdi the nickname "Papà dei cori."

In *Ernani* (1844) the broad, rather posterish technique of *Nabucco* is applied successfully to a drama of individuals who, though still to some extent generic in their emotions, are portrayed as archetypes of their voice categories (soprano, tenor, baritone, and bass) and thus in their ensembles define each other by contrast. This too was the opera that marked the first of Verdi's triumphs over the censorship and a demanding prima donna. Victor Hugo's *Hernani* was a perilous subject in a Europe dominated by Prince Metternich. Bellini and Romani considered it, then dropped it for fear of trouble with the authorities. Verdi carried it through with only the slightest of modifications, resisting the management's demands that the title role should be cast as a contralto *en travesti* and insisting that the nobleman Don Ruy Gomez de Silva should be allowed to play the horn on stage. The prima donna, Sofia Loewe, had demanded a rondò finale for herself to close the opera. Donizetti, faced with a similar request from Henriette Méric-Lalande in *Lucrezia Borgia*, complied against his better judgement and waited for a revival elsewhere to rewrite the ending. Verdi held out for a final terzetto and won. Most important of all, *Ernani* was Verdi's first collaboration with the hitherto unknown and inexperienced librettist Francesco Maria Piave. If by the mid-1850s Piave had become the most sought-after theatrical poet in Italy, it was because Verdi had created him. In those days librettists, like composers, all spoke the same language, drawing upon a common stock of artificial phrases; but inevitably some spoke it better than others. In the days when the theater lights were never lowered and each member of the audience had a printed libretto which he could follow during the performance, poets such as Romani and Cammarano were inclined to be touchy about their work, knowing well enough that the journalist who had insufficient knowledge to criticise the music could make fair game of the text and frequently did. Giovanni Ruffini refused to acknowledge paternity of the libretto of *Don Pasquale* after Donizetti had finished altering it, so providing Cammarano with a problem of authorship which has only recently been solved. The experienced librettist could in fact make a very valuable contribution to the musical structure of an opera. Pacini was not mistaken in emphasizing Rossini's share in the formal equilibrium of *Norma* and *La sonnambula*. *I puritani* shows only too well what can happen to the proportions of a Bellinian opera in Rossini's absence. Quite different were the relations of Piave and Verdi. Here it was the composer who took the lead from the start, prescribing the lengths of the scenes and the ratio of *versi sciolti* to lyrical lines, and never resting content until he had got the poet to provide him with exactly what he wanted. As the years went by he demanded an increasingly terse style of poetry in which the traditional circumlocutions give way to the *parola scenica* (Verdi's phrase) which "sculpts the situation." The result is often clumsy, if not bizarre, when seen on the printed page, divorced from the music; and Piave often suffered the scorn of critics and literary cognoscenti. "A libretto that bears Piave's name is condemned in advance," Verdi complained apropos of *Simon Boccanegra* in 1857[19] but the despised hack remained Verdi's partner for all the composer's most daring operatic ventures.

Prominent among these is *Macbeth* (1847), in which for the first time Verdi attempted the portrayal of an entirely individual character. This was possible only with the collaboration of the singer concerned (the baritone Felice Varesi) at a very early stage. Having made sure that he was available for the premiere, Verdi sent him the music number by number in draft form, with detailed instructions for its interpretation and occasionally asking his advice about the scoring. He persuaded him to do without the traditional two-movement cavatina, since he would obtain ("cavare") a far greater effect from the duettino with Banquo.[20] (Even so must Bellini have convinced Rubini to accept the quartet of *I puritani* in place of an entrance aria). The death scene was not to be played in the manner of Gennaro (*Lucrezia Borgia*) or Edgardo (*Lucia di Lammermoor*), and so on. *Macbeth* was Verdi's first contact with Shakespeare, and, as he wrote to Piave, "if we cannot make it a masterpiece, let us at least do something out of the ordinary."[21] Nowadays we hear it in the 1865 version written for the Théâtre Lyrique, which differs from the original by roughly a third. Even without the improvements brought about by eighteen years' experience, it must have sounded very startling to an audience of 1847: the opening scene on the blasted heath, based on a pattern of threefold repetition in rising sequences (derived from the presence of three covens of witches), the dagger soliloquy, the scene of Banquo's ghost, the prophecies and the "show of kings,"

19. Letter to C. Vigna, Apr. 11, 1857, Copial. 553.
20. Letter to F. Varesi written between January and March 1847, G. C. Varesi, "L'interpretazione di Macbeth," in *Nuova antologia* (FLorence, Nov.–Dec. 1932), anno 67, fasc. 1458, pp. 433–40.
21. Letter to Piave, Sept. 4, 1846, in Abbiati I, 643.

the sleepwalking of Lady Macbeth, the final death scene ("Mal per me che m'affidai"), in all of which the traditional forms are broken down and reassembled in a new continuity. Never had the minor key been used so tellingly—or so abundantly. There was much shaking of heads; and not a few were found to declare that the cheers that greeted Verdi after the final curtain were for the composer of *Attila*. Nonetheless, the opera circulated satisfactorily enough, though not without causing Verdi some concern about its interpretation; and he never ceased to insist that this was not an opera like any other. In his preoccupation with details of decor and staging he seemed to anticipate the concept of a *Gesamtkunstwerk*. Significantly, it was after the premiere of *Macbeth* that he wrote to his publisher requesting that in his contracts with the impresarios who wished to mount his works a clause should be inserted forbidding all cuts and transpositions. Needless to say, his demand was not met.

After two years spent in Paris with only the briefest excursion to Italy, Verdi returned finally to his native Emilia in 1849 to work on his fifteenth opera, *Luisa Miller*, in which commentators beginning with the contemporary Abramo Basevi discerned a new manner, more intimate and refined, less obviously grandiose than in the previous works. The long-limbed, somewhat inflexible melodies descended from "Va, pensiero," with their elaborately throbbing accompaniments, gave way to simpler ideas articulated in shorter phrases, more lightly and variously scored. It was not a sudden transformation. The so-called second manner had been anticipated in parts of *Il corsaro* (1848), even in isolated moments in *I due Foscari;* nor is it maintained throughout *Luisa Miller* (indeed the heroine's second-act aria is uncomfortably grandiose for a village girl), but it dominates the entire last act, aided by the special nature of the subject—Schiller's bürgerliches Trauerspiel *Kabale und Liebe.* How far the experience of Paris contributed to this new turn in Verdi's style is discussed elsewhere. But the effect in *Luisa Miller* is wholly Italian, sensitized by a new poetic intuition. With it comes a subtler harmonic sense and the consequent ability to depict shades of emotion and character unknown to the broader frescoes of his early years. Above all, the shorter phrases permitted thematic development and hence the possibility of musical transition from one idea to the next, which was to culminate in the seamless continuity of *Falstaff*. Like its immediate successors, *Luisa Miller* remains an opera of separate numbers, each marked off by an emphatic cadence point and a full stop for applause. But from now on the stop becomes more of a semicolon.

With the triple achievement of *Rigoletto* (1851), *Il trovatore,* and *La traviata* (1853), Verdi might well be supposed to have closed the chapter of *primo ottocento* opera. The first of these most obviously points to the future with its wealth of arioso declamation, its freely organized opening scene, its lack of a conventional concertato finale, its intricate pattern of duet movements in which the orchestra takes an unusually prominent part, and above all its stupendous final act built round one of the most original storm pictures in all Italian opera. *Il trovatore,* on the other hand, directs a backward glance on the world of Donizetti, lighting it up in a fiercer glow and a new spirit of rhythmic dynamism. Here for the first time is an opera based on the polarity of two prima donnas—a dramatic mezzo-soprano (new to Verdi's gallery) and a lyrical soprano. *La traviata* seemed to penetrate to the distilled essence of Italian Romantic melody almost so as to suggest that further progress upon this road was impossible. True it is that from that time onward Verdi derives his musical stimulus more and more from across the Alps and from his own study of the classics. But he continued to write mostly for Italy (even for the Parisian *Les Vêpres siciliennes* and *Don Carlos* he counted on an Italian circulation); therefore he could not afford to lose contact with the tastes and traditions of his fellow countrymen, though he came dangerously near to doing so with *Simon Boccanegra* (1857). The story of Italian opera after the mid-century, however unedifying, is still relevant to a study of Verdi.

The 1850s were a period of stagnation. After the abortive uprising of 1848 Austrian and papal authority tightened over the peninsula; and operatic subjects hitherto regarded as innocuous were now viewed with suspicion and prohibited. The operatic chorus of the 1840s was banned even in the most blameless of contexts. Alfieri's *Virginia* had furnished opera fodder for three-quarters of a century. Yet Mercadante had to wait fifteen years for a production of his *Virginia* of 1851. There was more safety in comedy, which consequently enjoyed a revival, beginning with the pretty little opera comica-fantastica, *Crispino e la comare*, by the brothers Ricci. It was in opera buffa too that Petrella first made his name with *Le precauzioni*. Opera semiseria likewise flourished. In his *Violetta* (1853), Mercadante threw up yet another pastoral heroine, who, calumniated by a buffo bass, brings down the final curtain with a coloratura rondò finale of triumph. All such operas, however tuneful, merely elaborated an antiquated tradition in which, incredibly, recitativo secco still connects the formal numbers as if *Don Pasquale* had never existed. Orchestral melodies with the voices *parlanti* are rather more plentiful than before; otherwise the basso buffo still chatters, the soprano still carols and chirps, and in general the situations and emotions remain those of fifty years ago. It was a tradition that had nothing to offer to Verdi, and it finds no echo in the operas that he wrote at the time. The humor in *Un ballo in maschera* has its roots in *opéra comique*.

Meanwhile, *melodramma tragico* remained frozen in a Donizettian mold; only at the end of the decade did a thaw set in. This was partly due to a cautious revival of instrumental music, and more particularly to the rise of the professional conductor, who would eventually dislodge the prima donna from her long-held pride of place. Previously the musical direction of an opera had been divided between the *maestro concertatore,* who taught the singers their notes and rehearsed them at the piano, and the primo violino, who conducted the performances with his bow from a violin part. Angelo Mariani, himself a violinist, was the first to adopt the practice (universal north of the Alps) of conducting with a baton and taking charge of every detail of the performance, so making possible a precision and refinement of execution unimaginable before. The first fruits of his collaboration with Verdi can be seen in the final act of *Aroldo*, where the complexity of choral and orchestral writing is of the kind that could only be realized under an authoritative baton. From then on, Verdi was to insist on the need for a professional conductor for his own works. Yet it was some time before Mariani's example took effect throughout Italy. His counterpart at La Scala, Alberto Mazzucato, had many a running battle with the leader of the violins—so at least it would appear from the memoirs of Sir Charles Santley, who sang there at the time. Not until the succession of Franco Faccio was the conductor's authority unchallenged. In Naples the old dispensation remained in force as late as the 1870s; consequently, Verdi pronounced the theater as unsuitable for modern opera despite its abundance of good singers and players.

An important result of the foundation of the Italian state (1861) was the explosion of intellectual activity in the north, all the more violent for having been so long repressed. Of the avant-garde movement known as the *scapigliatura*, whose members read Baudelaire, drank absinthe, and blasphemed against all received values and beliefs, the musical spokesman was the young Arrigo Boito, determined to forge Italian opera anew through closer ties with literature and the abolition of conventional forms. His reviews in his own *Figaro* and the *Giornale della società del quartetto* are the equivalent of Schumann's in the *Allgemeine musikalische Zeitung* of the 1830s; and like Schumann he found heroes and villains all too easily. After the premiere of Faccio's *I profughi fiamminghi* (1863) he hailed its composer as the man born to cleanse the altar of Italian opera, "befouled like the walls of a brothel," so making an enemy of Verdi for the next sixteen years. Boito's credibility as a prophet received a severe check with the fiasco of his own *Mefistofele* in 1868. The musical ideas are striking enough, but the ability to weld them into an organic whole is lacking—a fault palliated rather than remedied by the revision of 1875, which resulted in the work we know today. A worthier specimen of his talent is the libretto he wrote for Faccio's *Amleto* (1865), with its verbal ingenuity and new diversity of meters. The opera itself was received with cautious respect as its premiere. "Faccio is a good musician," Mariani, the conductor, wrote to Verdi. "It's a pity that what's good in his score isn't new; and what's new is rather boring."[22] A revival in Milan in 1871 failed utterly, after which Faccio devoted himself entirely to his true métier, that of the conductor.

Nonetheless, whether due to the clarion call of Boito, or to the example of Gounod and Meyerbeer (favorites of the epoch) and indeed of Verdi himself, the walls of the post-Rossinian Jericho were certainly beginning to crumble. Even before 1860 the stretta finale had ceased to be obligatory, though it could always be drawn upon where the situation made it appropriate. Most central finales now finished with the concertato followed by the briefest of rapid codas. By the same token the cantabile-cabaletta pairing began to dissolve; and it was the cabaletta that withered, largely because interest in vocal acrobatics waned rapidly during the 1860s. A soprano with a florid technique might safely be accommodated with a coloratura coda to her opening cantabile, as in Petrella's *La contessa d'Amalfi* (1864), or indeed be given a brilliant genre piece like the bolero in the same composer's *Giovanna di Napoli* (1869). Another solution is the single movement that combines the lyricism of a cantabile with something of the pace of the cabaletta. Yet once again, the aria in two movements is still valid if the situation calls for it, as with the soprano cava-

22. Letter from A. Mariani, May 20, 1865, Abbiati III, 17–18.

tina in Petrella's *Caterina Howard* (1866). But the second movement is rarely an old-style cabaletta with melodic repeat and intervening ritornello; usually it has a simple ternary design with the voice singing throughout.

Duets too begin to show a new variety of structure. The old pattern of three contrasted movements is now obsolete. The preferred scheme is one of alternating solos varied by *parlanti* and free *scena* material, and ending in a fast movement which again has the pace of a cabaletta without its form. The influence of France is evident in the number of ternary arias with a freely modulating central episode and full reprise. Strophic song, couplets, picturesque chorus, and genre pieces of all kinds proliferate during the 1860s, evincing a tendency toward a belated grand opera. Verdi's own *La forza del destino* reflects in its own more purposeful way the chaotic diversity of the Italian scene.

The last five years of the decade saw the disappearance of the solo cadenza and with it one of the last remaining devices specifically designed to interrupt the act for applause. Operas continued to be written in separate numbers, but with a decreasing stress on the final cadence of each. In the conservative south Petrella continued to write works that fell into self-contained units, whereas for the theaters of Milan and Turin Cagnoni experimented with a more continuous style, which involved a discreet use of instrumental leitmotiv (in the manner of Meyerbeer, rather than Wagner, needless to say). All without exception show a tendency to retreat from time to time into the melodic commonplaces of fifty years ago. The opening solo of an 1860s duet sometimes recalls the rhetorical manner of Rossini, without the fioritura; but in its new context it has lost its architectural function to become no more than a hackneyed gesture. Apart from the occasional, inept experiment, the harmonic style of the time remains curiously impoverished.

Verdi had no radical solution to offer. He himself was no revolutionary. Indeed Camillo Boito, Arrigo's brother, classed him with Petrella as a cabaletta monger. If he had begun to diversify his idiom with Parisian elements in the 1850s, its basis remained the musical language of his Italian contemporaries. He too continued to avail himself of the traditional stock-in-trade; but unlike his colleagues, he knew how to present it in a fresh, dramatic light. Above all, he knew how to condense, to burn away the dead wood. Where the conventional Italian cantabile has four limbs, his own has three, the third doing duty for two. His progressions are often elliptical, presupposing the hearer's ability mentally to bridge the missing chord. He will give a new yet perfectly logical twist to an orthodox melody by displacing the bass note of common chords, as in "Il lacerato spirito" (*Simon Boccanegra*), or color time-honoured cadences with nonfunctional harmony, as in the Marchese di Calatrava's duettino with his daughter in *La forza del destino*. He never shrinks from an audacity where the situation requires it. The discordant counterpoint of motifs which move on two different planes of sonority in the first act of *Un ballo in maschera* sounds startlingly modern even today. How far Verdi himself was a pioneer in the developments described above is hard to assess. Certainly *Macbeth* seems to have been the first opera to dispense with the stretta, if we except Bellini's *La straniera* of 1829. He wrote his last brilliant cabaletta for soprano in 1857 for the heroine of *Aroldo;* and in Riccardo's "La rivedrà nell' estasi" and Renato's "Alla vita che t'arride," both from *Un ballo in maschera,* he provided early examples of cantabili which have the pace and character of cabalette. Carlo's "Urna fatal" and Alvaro's "Qual sangue sparsi" from *La forza del destino* (1862) (the latter expunged from the revision) typify the double aria, with the second movement in modified cabaletta form.

A fully fledged instance of the French ternary aria is found as early as *Simon Boccanegra* (a still earlier example in *La battaglia di Legnano* [1849] is on too small a scale to count). Again it seems to have been Verdi himself who broke the taboo whereby minor-key movements, however sorrowful, were supposed to come to rest in the major. True, Donizetti partly forestalled him in the exceptional "Havvi un Dio" in *Maria di Rohan*, written significantly for Vienna; but there was a major-key cabaletta to provide the necessary relief. In both her arias in *Un ballo in maschera* Amelia begins and ends in the minor key, while in the second she scarcely grazes the major mode at all. Not until Faccio's *I profughi fiamminghi* (1863) does this example appear to have been followed up. For the duet-cabaletta Verdi found a special use in the 1860s in situations in which lovers delay their parting until too late. The movement begins in orthodox fashion with successive statements by each character, but the third is either avoided or cut short by the catastrophe which we have all been expecting. Here the repetitions, instead of slowing down the dramatic pace, increase the tension. There is no full stop for applause. Only once in those years does Verdi write a cabaletta whose melody is given three times as in Bellini's day: "O terra addio" from the final scene of *Aida* (1871); and the character of the music makes it unrecognizable as such.

Aida itself remains a remarkable synthesis of old and new, in which tradition plays a larger role than might be supposed. The cut of the choral scenes derives, like so much Italian music of the time, from French grand opera. Yet the choral march ("Gloria all' Egitto") which opens the finale of Act II is already hinted at in Donizetti's *Poliuto*. Models for the two-part texture of the prelude can be found in Cagnoni's works, notably in *Un capriccio di donna* (1870). Nor would Verdi have ventured his splashes of Egyptian local color if the huge popularity of *L'Africaine* over the previous five years had not pointed the way. With its Metastasio-like plot and generic characters, *Aida* marks another moment of classicism in the Italian tradition, this time an isolated one. For it had no progeny worthy of the name; and though it never lacked performances it was never appreciated in the way Verdi had hoped for. The influential critic Filippo Filippi considered it inferior to *Don*

Carlos. For some years to come Italians continued to write grand opera with or without ballet; but always in the high sensational Romantic vein, of which Ponchielli's *La gioconda* (1876) is one of the worthier specimens. During the 1870s the reform of the conservatories, the new emphasis on instrumental music, the interest in German culture which was the psychological result of Prussia's victory over France and which came to be reflected in the Triple Alliance of 1882, all combined to sweep away the last remnants of the post-Rossinian tradition. Much nonsense was talked about Wagner at that time. Even the intelligent Filippi had remarked that to deny his influence upon Verdi both in *Aida* and *Don Carlos* was like denying light to the sun. The truth was that Wagner's writings had been known for some time, but not the works which embodied his theories. The first of his operas to be given in Italy was *Lohengrin,* performed at Bologna in 1870 and followed the next year by *Tannhäuser.* Both are nearer to French grand opera than to the "artwork of the future." To a generation that had not yet heard *The Ring* anything pretentious or experimental was dubbed Wagnerian, from Gobatti's incompetent *I Goti* (1873) to Boito's *Mefistofele,* which in its revised form at last obtained a sympathetic hearing. Of greater moment was the Italian premiere of Massenet's *Le Roi de Lehore* in 1878. From then on Massenet became the chief guide to young composers in the formation of a style in which the act finally replaced the *scena* as the structural unit, the cabaletta, largo concertato, and stretta had no place, and the orchestra played a more prominent role than ever before in the thematic organization. During the 1880s his influence was supplemented by that of the mature Wagner, until in 1890 a new synthesis was reached in Mascagni's *Cavalleria rusticana,* with which the Italian opera tradition was reborn. With this crude but confident work before them, Mascagni's slightly older contemporaries, Leoncavallo and Puccini, found their own voice, as did a handful of minor composers who if they had lived twenty years earlier might have suffered the obscurity of a Cagnoni or a Lauro Rossi. As it is, such operas as *Andrea Chénier* or *Adriana Lecouvreur* are unlikely to relinquish their hold on the polular repertory.

None of these developments has much relevance to the final works of Verdi; *Otello* and *Falstaff* have no more to do with the contemporary Italian scene than have the last quartets of Beethoven with Schubert's Vienna. True, Verdi ruthlessly and with apparent reluctance "de-cabalettized" the original *Simon Boccanegra* in his revision of 1881. Yet both here and in *Otello* and *Falstaff*, not to mention the definitive *Don Carlos*, he retained the grand concertato as essential to the musical arthitecture. The continuity of *Falstaff* is at least as unbroken as in any work of Puccini, but it is achieved by quite different means—by the transformation of one idea into another, by a network of tiny developing motifs, some of which derive from the rhythm of a verbal phrase ("Dalle due alle tre," "Te lo cornefico," etc.). Of the younger composers he spoke well of Catalani, though he considered him to have an exaggerated idea of the importance of the orchestra. (The canard of the forged letters to Perosio pouring scorn on the "maestrino lucchese" has been thoroughly scotched by Frank Walker,[23] yet evidently not killed, since credulous commentators continue to bring it out). But the higher norm of dissonance of the "giovane scuola" was alien to him. His comments on Mascagni's *L'amico Fritz* are typical. After condemning the libretto as the worst he had ever read, he added

> As for the music I got some way ahead with it but I soon became wearied with so many discords, and all those false relations, and those interrupted cadences and side-slips . . . and then so many changes of tempo, practically at every bar—all very piquant but they offend one's ear and one's sense of rhythm. The verbal accentuation is on the whole good; but it never really "sculpts" the dramatic situation. . . . No doubt the music is very fine; I just look at it from my

23. F. Walker, "Verdian forgeries: Letters hostile to Catalani," in *The Music Review* 20 (Feb. 1959), 28–37.

point of view. But then I'm an old die-hard ... well old, certainly, but not so much of a die-hard as all that.[24]

In Bruneau's *La Rêve* he found himself longing for the vent-hole of a concord (the reference is of course to Falstaff's desperate cry from the buck-basket). He had spoken in much the same terms of the prologue to *Mefistofele,* which sounds fairly bland to modern ears. The truth is that, though Verdi was capable of far greater tonal and harmonic unorthodoxy than the "veristi," he demanded a basis of limpid consonance such as was no longer fashionable in the 1890s. In his old age he drew more sustenance from the classical tradition of the eighteenth century than from the works of his younger compatriots; Domenico Scarlatti and Clementi lurk behind the handkerchief trio in *Otello.* The tempo di minuetto and final fugue from *Falstaff* have their roots in Boccherini and Mozart. True, there are traces of the Flower Song from *Carmen* in Fenton's sonetto; likewise the disposition of forces and combination of ideas at the end of Act I of *Falstaff* suggest that Verdi must have been present at the Milanese premiere of *Die Meistersinger* in 1890. But it is not difficult to imagine how he would have detested Wagner's overture with its chains of suspensions resolving upon one another.

If Verdi's two final masterpieces can be said to stand outside their time their example was not lost on a subsequent generation of Italians. The pretty, puppetlike operas of Wolf-Ferrari stand in much the same relation to *Falstaff* as the symphonies of Mendelssohn to those of Beethoven. From the opening scene of *Falstaff* Puccini learned that almost sonata-like organization of motifs which marks the beginning of so many of his operas from *La bohème* onward. The love duet from *Madama Butterfly* would never have come into being without the model—however freely followed—of that in Act I of *Otello.* Above all, Puccini learned from Verdi the use of nonfunctional harmony

24. Letter to Giulio Ricordi, Nov. 6, 1892, Abbiati IV, 426–27.

and the displaced bass line. It is understandable that Giulio Ricordi should have called him "the successor." The truth is that no real succession was possible. Like all the great classical composers, Verdi brought an era to an end by summing up all that was best in it.

Verdi and the Business of Writing Operas

Bruno Cagli

BRUNO CAGLI, a graduate of the University of Rome, has published numerous articles and essays dealing with early nineteenth-century Italian opera. Since 1971 he has been director of the Fondazione Rossini, Pesaro. In May 1978, he became artistic director of the Accademia Filarmonica Romana. He has staged operas and is a critic of *Paese-sera* in Rome; he teaches at the University of Urbino.

In December 1871, Verdi received a letter from the important critic Filippo Filippi, saying that the Khedive of Egypt had invited him to Cairo for the premiere of *Aida*. Former editor of the *Gazzetta musicale di Milano*, Filippi was writing at this time for *La Perseveranza*. Announcing his departure, Filippi volunteered to perform any errand the composer might wish to entrust to him and also offered to inform Verdi about the progress of rehearsals.[1] This offer was a formality, since any information would have reached Italy after the opera's opening. In any case, Verdi's reaction to the unctuous letter was certainly not what Filippi had anticipated. The idea of a propaganda barrage for the

1. Copial., 271 ff.

opera's launching aroused "disgust" in the composer, who
did not mince words:[2]

> You in Cairo? This is the most powerful publicity that
> could be imagined for *Aida!* To me it seems that, in this
> way, art is no longer art, but a trade, a pleasure excursion,
> a hunting party, a commonplace pursuit, which must at all
> costs have notoriety, if not success. The feeling it arouses in
> me is disgust, humiliation!—I always recall with joy my
> early days when, virtually friendless, with no one to speak
> about me, with no advance conditioning, with no influence
> of any sort, I came before the public with my operas, ready
> to receive its salvos, and very happy if I managed to arouse
> some favorable impression. Now, what an array for an
> opera! ... Journalists, artists, chorus members, conduc-
> tors, musicians, etc., etc., all must contribute their stone to
> the edifice of publicity, thus to construct a frame of triviali-
> ties that add nothing to the merit of the work, but rather
> obscure its real value. This is deplorable, profoundly de-
> plorable!!

There is something forced about the violence of Verdi's
outburst, and also something disingenuous about its closing, in which he claims to yearn for the innocence of his
early professional life: "*à la grâce de Dieu*, for that is how I
began, and how I wish to end my career."[3] The first to
doubt the possibility of such a return must have been
Verdi himself, who knew very well that the days when audiences judged operas unaffected by publicity and critics
and fashion were long past. By this time, Verdi had
worked for decades with impresarios and publishers, unwilling to risk their investment without a carefully calcu-

2. In Copial. Filippi's letter is headed "Milan, December 8, 1871," while
Verdi's reply, from Genoa, is dated the same day. Also on December 8, Verdi
wrote to Giulio Ricordi, copying out both Filippi's letter and the reply, inviting
Ricordi to publish them at the opportune moment.
3. Verdi's ill-tempered reaction may have been caused partly by his knowledge
of Filippi's encouragement, in the past, of anti-Verdi musical factions, including
Italian Wagnerism.

lated possibility of profit. And Verdi himself had made a decisive contribution to changing the relationship between composer and the outside world, especially from the social and economic point of view.

In his letter to Filippi, Verdi was actually measuring the distance that separated the profession of opera composer in the second half of the century from that same profession in the "age of innocence," the period of his debut. Perhaps in looking back over the changes, in which he had been protagonist, Verdi felt a certain responsibility.

In Verdi's boyhood during years dominated by Rossini, the job of opera composer in Italy still remained rooted in the eighteenth-century artisan tradition. In his later years of residence in France, Rossini was inevitably affected by the quite different situation there. As Verdi said in a letter to Camille Du Locle,

> Surely no one will deny Rossini's genius! And yet, despite all that genius, in *Guillaume Tell* you can perceive that fatal atmosphere of the [Paris] Opéra, and sometimes—though far less often than in other composers—you hear there is something superfluous, something lacking, and the musical procedure is not as straightforward and confident as in the *Barber*.[4]

Here Verdi really touches on the eternal conflict between a new form struggling to impose itself and the more casual product of older times, the times of the confidently written *Barber*. But the reasons for the change also lay in the fact that in Paris the first formula of the state theater had been promulgated: a theater financed from above, its production controlled by the ministry and its spokesmen, its theorists, the critics and journalists. This was a species quite unknown to Italy in the first decades of the nineteenth century.

In those decades, the Italian opera composer was a mu-

4. Copial., 219 ff. See also Abbiati III, 324.

sical journeyman. He signed a contract with an impresario to write a new opera for a certain fee, then traveled to the city where the opera was to be performed. The contract gave the impresario complete freedom to select the opera's subject and the poet to versify it (though the composer was sometimes able to voice an opinion on the matter). The librettist was usually some local man of letters, who acted as regular poet for the theater or for the impresario. The composer had to supervise the preparation of the opera and, according to a rule that remained in force for decades, he had to be present at the first three performances. If the opera was a success, the impresario could lend or rent the music to other cities or could himself assume the responsibility of mounting it elsewhere. Thus a successful opera remained in the repertory for five or six years, ten at most, after which it was abandoned. Even legendary, triumphant works like Cimarosa's *Il matrimonio segreto* were unlikely to be seen in the theater fifteen years after their premiere.

The impresario, who retained ownership of the opera, generally retained the autograph also. This explains how almost all the autographs of operas performed at La Scala came into possession of the firm of Ricordi, when Giovanni Ricordi purchased the theater's archives.[5] Thefts of scores and pirate performances by unscrupulous impresarios, who had someone orchestrate the piano-vocal score (the only score published in most cases), were the order of the day. The composer's position was unprotected, and we find constant complaints on this subject in the letters of Bellini and Donizetti. There was also the custom of inserting into one opera a number from another opera by the same composer, or even by someone else. Vocal parts were frequently and freely adapted.

Much as he may have disliked the idea, the Italian composer, in the time of Verdi's boyhood, knew he had two masters: the impresario and the performer. They, in turn,

---

5. In 1825. Since 1814 Giovanni Ricordi had been the theater's copyist.

were conditioned by the necessity of making money at the box office. In those years, the prestige of some composers could moderate certain excesses; and often the composer was called to supervise personally revivals of his most successful operas. In these cases, he himself would frequently add new arias, replace numbers, adapt the parts to the new cast. Thus there exist various, equally authentic versions of most operas by Mayr, Rossini, Donizetti, Pacini, Mercadante. But many others also exist and are not authentic, since the composer had no control over the revisions.

In his early years, Verdi occasionally composed a new number for a singer; but this was a practice he disliked, and he was soon able to refuse such requests. Before him, Rossini had succeeded in tempering some singers' license, writing out his own *abbellimenti* and arranging for full scores to be printed, to establish definitive texts. Rossini also retained ownership of some autographs, and—contrary to tradition—he did take some interest in the selection and writing of his librettos.

In the 1830s Donizetti and Bellini firmly claimed such rights as had been won. The composer derived a greater awareness of his own role from the new ideas of Romanticism, which especially influenced Bellini. Bellini was the first Italian composer who insisted on writing no more than one opera a year and, at the same time, on earning enough from it to live comfortably.[6] Bellini's letters show the care he took in choosing a subject and in signing a contract, in which—for the first time—economic demands were based on the impresario's earnings.[7]

A typical aspect of the Italian operatic world of the early

6. See Francesco Pastura, *Bellini secondo la storia* (Parma, 1959), *passim,* and in particular Chapter IX, 545 ff.

7. In a letter from Puteaux of July 24, 1834, written to Francesco Florimo, Bellini copied out for his friend the words he had already written to the impresario Lanari: "I presume you will find all my demands quite justified, for in sacrificing the entire ownership, which for *La sonnambula* alone earned us so far 14 thousand Austrian lire including the published edition . . . I find this demand honest . . ." These words (even though, in Luisa Cambi's transcription, they are not quite clear) indicate Bellini's careful checking of accounts and impresarios' earnings. See Bellini, *Epistolario,* edited by Luisa Cambi (Milan, 1943), 414 ff.

nineteenth century—reflected also in Verdi's life—was the ease with which young composers could make their debut; and subsequently they found the doors of even the greatest theaters open to them. Failures, which no one could escape, did not prevent their rapid rise. In the Italy of that time, a young composer found countless opera houses, large and small, prepared to accept new works or to have new music written to old subjects, bringing them musically up to date.

Even as students, the young had opportunities to present their compositions. Sometimes a singer might commission an added aria for an old opera, or a student might be asked to write music for the ballet that always accompanied a certain opera. But the big theaters also welcomed conservatory graduates. In Naples, if a professor spotted a talented youth, the *maestrino* would have the chance of presenting a one-act opera or a cantata at the Teatro del Fondo or the Teatro San Carlo, on a gala night and with first-rank performers.[8]

Credit for the rapid recognition of the young composer must be given chiefly to the much-maligned impresarios. Described as unscrupulous, crude, ignorant men, they were nevertheless genuine talent scouts. In this respect, the activity of the prince of impresarios, Domenico Barbaja, is legendary. But other impresarios of the time, men like Alessandro Lanari, Giuseppe Paterni, Vincenzo Jacovacci, and Bartolomeo Merelli, also encouraged the creation of an enormous number of new operas, including many masterpieces.

This was the world of the Italian theater when Verdi decided to become an opera composer, and his debut was largely the work of Merelli, who offered the twenty-six-year-old composer the opportunity of presenting his first

8. See Pastura, 71 ff. and 83 ff. It should be borne in mind that Donizetti made his professional debut at the age of twenty-one; Bellini when he was not yet twenty-three; Mercadante, at twenty-four; and Pacini, when he was a mere seventeen. Rossini, who made his debut at eighteen, in the space of three years and one month had already had thirteen operas performed, two of them at La Scala, one at the Fenice, one at the Valle in Rome.

work, *Oberto,* at La Scala. Verdi's first four operas were given in the space of a few years in Italy's leading opera house and with choice singers. With the decline of Mercadante and Pacini, and the illness of Donizetti, Verdi was soon the undisputed master of the world of Italian opera, able to impose his will on it.

The relationship between Verdi and his librettists has been widely examined. Characteristically, he was quick to lay down the law in the choice of subjects and in the actual writing of the librettos. Having won these rights, Verdi went on to claim others, ultimately placing future composers on a completely different level from that of their predecessors. As the Italian nation achieved unity through the efforts of its patriots, the Italian opera world also reached a kind of unity thanks to two forces: Verdi and Casa Ricordi. In spite of various vicissitudes, they remained allied, even after Italian unification was a reality, when Verdi sat on the committee appointed to draft the national law on literary and artistic property.

Relations between Verdi and impresarios and between Verdi and publishers—for which we have a rich documentation, only partially studied—indicate Verdi's progressive domination and vigorous defense of hard-won rights. Even before the premiere of *I lombardi,* he and Giovanni Ricordi debated a publishing contract, actually intended to be for life.[9] After that opera's success, Verdi gained greater self-confidence. In the negotiations for his next opera, which was to be *Ernani,* the first written for a theater other than La Scala, the composer proved exceptionally tough. He had plenty to say about the subject of the opera, the cast, the date of the premiere, and, naturally, the fee. After having received a draft contract from the Teatro La Fenice in Venice, Verdi wrote the theater's president, Count Nani Mocenigo, an enlightening letter, dated from Parma, May 25, 1843:

9. The life contract was apparently proposed by Verdi himself and rejected by Giovanni Ricordi, whose famous commercial flair for once failed him. See Abbiati, I, 419.

I have received the contract. I seem to find in it some points that could raise questions, and since surely neither you nor I wants to quarrel, I am thus making some changes which, of course, you may accept or reject.

I cannot agree to article 2 of the contract, because the Presidenza might reject the first and the second libretto, etc., and thus we would never reach an end. The Presidenza can rest assured that I will try to have a libretto written for me that I can feel, and hence set to music in the best possible way. If the Presidenza does not have faith in me, then it can have the libretto written at my expense: provided always that this expense is within my possibilities.

I cannot agree to article 3 because (as I wrote in my letter from Udine), it is my rule to make the orchestration during the piano rehearsals, and the score is never entirely finished until the rehearsal before the dress rehearsal.

In the 7th article the words "after the 3rd performance has taken place" must be removed, because the third performance might not take place for a thousand reasons to which I must not be subject.

It is necessary to add a 10th article, as below.

2nd: the relative libretto will be at the composer's expense.

3rd: Maestro Verdi is required to be ready to produce the new opera about a month after the premiere of *I lombardi*, always provided that there have been all the rehearsals necessary for a good performance.

4th: . . . he will be given 12,000 (twelve thousand) Austrian lire in three equal instalments. The first on his arrival in the city, the second at the first orchestral rehearsal, the third after the dress rehearsal.

10th: the artists who are to perform the new opera of Maestro Verdi will be chosen by the Maestro himself from the list of the company . . .[10]

Franco Abbiati has called this letter an "essay in accountancy," but it is far more than that. In the first place, Verdi

10. Abbiati I, 465–66.

does not agree that the Fenice may have final say on the choice of libretto. He prefers—as he was always to prefer afterward—to commission the libretto at his own expense, thus guaranteeing himself the opportunity of supervising the writing.

Another fundamental clause is Verdi's refusal to deliver the orchestral score by a set date. Thus he reserved the right to revise it up to the predress rehearsal.[11] He also eliminated the old obligation which held the composer at the theater through the third performance, and finally he insisted on choosing his singers personally, with the right to refuse to open if rehearsals were unsstisfactory. If one compares this draft contract with the surviving one for Rossini's *Il barbiere di Siviglia,* one has an idea of the change which had taken place in the composer-impresario relationship.[12]

But Verdi was soon to make even greater gains. They were determined by the rapid decline of the impresario, who was replaced, as far as the rental of operas was con-

11. Obviously, in the hasty preparation of operas composed and staged in a very short time, composers like Rossini or Donizetti might deliver some numbers at the last moment. But it is clear that Verdi means to reserve the right to judge the effect of certain pages and, especially, of the orchestration.

12. The contract is quoted in Radiciotti, *Gioacchino Rossini, Vita documentata ed influenza sull'arte* (Tivoli 1928), 178 ff. Between the Duke Sforza Cesarini, impresario of the Teatro Argentina, and Rossini it was agreed, among other things, that:

> Rossini promises and commits himself to compose and stage the second opera (buffa), which will be presented in the above-mentioned season in the theater indicated, and on the libretto, whether new or old, that will be given him by the aforenamed duke, the impresario.
>
> Maestro Rossini commits himself to deliver the score by the middle of January and to adapt it to the voices of the singers; he further commits himself to make all those changes that may be deemed necessary both to the success of the music and to the convenience of the singers . . .
>
> Maestro Rossini will be further obligated to conduct his opera, according to the custom, and to be personally present at all the rehearsals with piano and with orchestra whenever it is necessary, and he commits himself also to be present at the first performances, which will be given consecutively, and to conduct the performance at the cembalo . . .
>
> In compensation for his work the Duke Sforza Cesarini agrees to pay him the sum of four hundred Roman *scudi,* after the first three performances, which he must conduct at the cembalo."

cerned, by the publisher. Again Verdi was instrumental in this shift. Rather than deal with impresarios himself, he preferred to sell his operas directly to the publisher, perhaps with a clause committing the latter to have the works first performed in a major theater.[13]

In the course of the nineteenth century, Casa Ricordi gradually took over almost all Italian music publishing and acted as Verdi's agent for Italy. In France, Verdi dealt chiefly with Léon Escudier. The publisher leased the opera to the various theaters and the various impresarios, paying the composer a percentage of these rental fees. Verdi made careful provisions for operas written for certain countries, especially those where legislation was beginning to control authors' rights.

Abundant documentation allows us to observe the progressive decline of the impresarios of individual theaters. Verdi's *Copialettere* opens, in fact, with a series of documents dealing mostly with contractual demands. His discussions with Lanari for the Florence production of *Macbeth* are significant; here Verdi also fussed about details of the staging of his opera, which he knew was unusual and difficult. A little later, Verdi promised Lanari a new work for the autumn of 1851, but insisted on retaining rights to the score—that is, rental rights for other theaters—which he obviously planned to sell to Ricordi. Old Lanari, once called the "Napoleon of impresarios," had to give up the idea of presenting the new opera. He wrote to Verdi, with regret: "My aim, in dealing with you, was to honor my archive with the ownership of a score of your composition; for I too, though not to a great extent, engage in business of this sort. But I see that you have other aims, and so I am forced to renounce a project I greatly desired."[14] There

13. As a rule Verdi proceeded in this way: he would establish contact with the management of a theater and, at the same time, would offer the opera to a publisher, who would then take over the negotiations. At the end of Verdi's life, Casa Ricordi took the initiative, urging Verdi to write new works.

14. See Abbiati II, 119–20. Also in 1851, an attempt made by Solera to give an opera in Madrid ended in failure because, requesting a sum of one thousand gold napoleons, Verdi would grant only the rights for Spain and Portugal (ibid., 139).

was no room, in other words, for small-time, adventurous impresarios any more.

But relations with publishers were not simple either. Some negotiations with the firm of Lucca, also eager to have a Verdi opera, were dragged out endlessly. Nor was it all smooth sailing with Ricordi. Casa Ricordi is the subject of frequent complaints from Verdi about the scant attention it paid to supervising performances, about its typographical errors in the printed piano-vocal scores, and, finally, about the lack of precision in its accounts. There is, for example, a long series of recriminations in Verdi's letter of October 24, 1855 to Tito Ricordi: here the composer discusses the problem of relations with foreign countries and the devices that, with the excuse of various clauses and items besides the simple rental of the score, finally subtracted income from the author. Verdi bluntly reminds the publisher that the true architect of the Ricordi fortune is Verdi: "I had hoped you would not adopt these tricks with me, who am to a large extent the source of your colossal fortune."[15]

Verdi's sensitivity to his own artistic and economic rights is also shown by the numerous embargos he placed on theaters, including La Scala itself, when they did not offer sufficient guarantees of serious purpose. He made various attempts to overcome the difficulties he suffered from the fact that he was a subject of the Duchy of Parma (before unification). As English publishers were accustomed to printing his operas without paying royalties, some friends suggested Verdi change his citizenship. Verdi was unwilling to go this far, but he carefully examined the idea of having Parma negotiate a special agreement with England; and he asked his friend, the notary Balestra, to test the terrain:

> A recent law of the House of Lords deprives any foreign author of his rights if he does not belong to a nation that has an international treaty with England. So those pub-

15. Ibid. II, 310 ff.

lishers find it more convenient to appropriate our works without buying them from the author. This is natural. In my two journeys to London I was advised to apply for English or French citizenship, or even Piedmontese (for France and Piedmont have international treaties with England); but I, who wish to remain what I am, namely a villager of Roncole, prefer to ask my government to make a treaty with England. The Parma government has nothing to lose by this agreement, which is purely artistic and literary: it would have only the nuisance of requesting it through Parma's representative in England, who is, I believe, either the Austrian or Spanish Ambassador.[16]

England was not the only foreign country that gave Verdi trouble. He quarreled frequently with Escudier and with the managements of the various Paris theaters. In 1856 he had to sue Calzado, impresario of the Théâtre-Italien, for staging *Il trovatore* without the composer's consent. Verdi lost the suit.

In Italy, meanwhile, the political situation was changing, and the problem of authors' rights was eventually regulated. Once again, Verdi was in the front line. As deputy to the Italian Parliament in the 1860s, he made a valuable contribution to the deliberations of the special committee formed to draft the new law on artistic property. The correspondence with Tito Ricordi about this law shows that Verdi was concerned with safeguarding not only the composer's rights but also the librettist's. Previously librettists had been paid a flat fee, and some of them—including Solera and Piave—had ended their lives in poverty. To protect composers' rights, Verdi made a less happy suggestion, advising the postponement of the publication of full scores for several years after the work's premiere. He wrote to Tito Ricordi:

If, without the composer's consent, an impresario really cannot stage an opera until after its publication, it seems to

16. Ibid. II, 313 ff.

me there is no great inconvenience in waiting four or five or ten years after the premiere before printing an opera. By then its success has been assured in various theaters. For that matter, full scores are hardly ever printed in our country . . .[17]

This proposal, supported by Casa Ricordi, indicates the lack of sensitivity to the demands of musicology which was to perpetuate the inferiority of Italian musical publishing down to our own time. It is partly Verdi's own fault that even today a number of his (and other Italian composers') operas have never been printed in full score. The new law was passed on June 25, 1865. Ricordi immediately secured the rights to the operas of Rossini as well.

Verdi recognized the gradual change in the opera composer's position. On December 25, 1882, he wrote to Giulio Ricordi about some newspaper gossip concerning a hospital being constructed at Verdi's expense. After pointing out the exaggerations of the press, Verdi said: "the papers are making an atrocious joke when they speak of my immense wealth! Immense?!! How could it be so? You know better than anyone else that when I wrote many operas, operas were badly paid; now that they are paid well and produce good income, I hardly compose any more."[18]

A study of the documents, with their protracted negotiations of contracts and with Verdi's frequent stubbornness, should not, however, lead one to believe that Verdi thought only of economic advantages. He was just as stubborn in his battle for artistic values. After Verdi, Italian composers were granted, as a normal right, the possibility of composing an opera over a period of time sufficient for reflecting on the details. The era of the opera written in two weeks was past and forgotten. Along with the speed of composing, the atmosphere of composition also changed. In earlier times, composers wrote in the city of the opera's

17. Ibid. II, 820–21.
18. Ibid. IV, 204.

performance. Verdi, from his middle years on, worked at the Villa Sant'Agata and often summoned his librettists there.[19] Composers were able to control productions and also singers, whose whims now went unheeded. To be sure, mistakes in editions and less than ideal performances continued, but Verdi managed to obviate these as much as possible, at least in the two countries that mattered most to him, Italy and France. Before Verdi's time, it would have been inconceivable for a composer to make details of stage production a matter for contractual discussion. But Verdi gradually developed the modern concept of stage direction, and in the *Otello* contract between Casa Ricordi and La Scala he had the following clauses inserted:

> 3rd . . . I have complete authority to suspend rehearsals and forbid the performance, even after the dress rehearsal, if either the musical performance or the *mise-en-scène*, or any other thing, does not satisfy me . . .
>
> 4th The staff assigned to *Otello* will answer directly to me . . . Conductor, chorus master, director, etc. etc. . . .[20]

Furthermore, if Verdi's veto of the performance were to be ignored, Casa Ricordi was bound to pay him a fine of one hundred thousand lire. Was this the Verdi who, to Filippi, could express yearning for the simple and more hazardous ways of the early nineteenth century?

Romanticism had given the composer an immense mission, had exalted his individuality. At Bayreuth Wagner had a special theater built for his works: an enterprise unthinkable a century before. But, on close inspection, Verdi's achievement proves equal to Wagner's. From the moment he abandoned the ungrateful life of a village

19. Rossini had established a grand precedent when, finally free from his contract with Barbaja, he wrote his last Italian opera, *Semiramide*, in the peaceful surroundings of the Villa of Castenaso, to which he bade the librettist Gaetano Rossi. But to achieve this freedom Rossini had had to become the most famous musician of Europe and the husband of Isabella Colbran, who owned the villa.

20. All this was contained in a memorandum for Casa Ricordi, which was then to work out the contract with La Scala. See Abbiati IV, 305–6.

music master, he defied conventions, singers, impresarios, critics, and audiences, to build his own immense, invisible construction: the relationship with the theater, the world, and his fellowman, unparallelled in history. Like the King Philip in his *Don Carlos,* Verdi could say that he had come to know the human spirit profoundly. He had, in consequence, behaved with extreme practicality, but also with generosity. At the time of *Falstaff,* he wrote Boito, "Thieving world, scoundrel world, evil world! . . . I know it, and unfortunately I have known it thirty years longer than you have."[21]

And with this profound, long knowledge, Verdi had escaped being mocked by the world, like his final protagonist. Verdi had taken the job of writing operas terribly seriously, though he never stopped complaining about it and criticizing it. The grand old man of Sant'Agata, a national monument in his old age, could never be compared with the composer-drudge of decades before. The transformation from the trade of opera composer to the profession of genius—thanks to Verdi—had worked perfectly.

21. The letter is dated October 6, 1890. See Abbiati IV, 405.

Verdi and His Librettists

William Weaver

WILLIAM WEAVER's *Verdi: A Documentary Study,* was published in 1977, several years after the appearance of his *Seven Verdi Librettos,* a collection of translations. He has read papers at several international Verdi conferences and has contributed to the forthcoming *Verdi's Macbeth: A Sourcebook.* In 1969 he won the National Book Award for translation; he has twice been the winner of the John Florio Prize for translation in Great Britain.

Discussing Verdi's librettists, the late Gabriele Baldini once said they were not so much creative collaborators as secretaries. And it is certainly true that with most of them Verdi was very much the senior member in an unequal partnership. We know very little about Antonio Piazza, the author of *Oberto.* He was a government employee, an amateur poet, an occasional journalist. He must also have been on good terms with the management of La Scala, for two years before *Oberto*'s premiere, the name of Piazza appeared on La Scala's poster, as poet of a cantata, *In morte di Maria Malibran,* performed on March 17, 1837, with music by Donizetti, Pacini, Mercadante, Vaccai, and Coppola, and with an impressive array of singers, including the bass Ignazio Marini, later to create the role of Oberto.

The libretto of Verdi's first opera, as it was finally performed in 1839, was also to a large extent by Temistocle Solera, called upon to revise it. Solera was Verdi's first real librettist. Young as he was, Solera (1815–78) must have been a fairly well known figure in the Milan of the 1830s. Son of a patriot (who had been confined in the notorious Austrian Spielberg prison), he was a musician as well as a poet. Eight days after *Oberto*'s premiere, in fact, two members of that opera's cast—Marini and the tenor Salvi—joined the soprano Mazzarelli at La Scala to perform a "hymn" entitled *La melodia,* words and music both by Solera, whose opera *Ildegonda* was given at La Scala in 1840 with a stellar cast (it survived only three performances), followed in 1841 by his *Il contadino d'Agliate.* In those years, then, the careers of Verdi and his librettist were moving at an almost equal pace. If anything, Solera was somewhat ahead.

The libretto of Verdi's second opera, *Un giorno di regno,* was handed to the composer ready-made. Felice Romani (1788–1865) had originally written the text for Adalbert Gyrowetz in 1818. There is no evidence that Verdi and the eminent poet ever discussed the libretto, and it is unlikely that the perennially overworked Romani made any revisions for this new setting.

Solera had also originally written the text of *Nabucco* for another composer, Otto Nicolai (later to remain famous as the composer of *Die lustige Weibe von Windsor*). Nicolai rejected the libretto, which then captivated Verdi. But, though still hardly more than a novice, Verdi already had firm ideas about the shaping of a theatrical piece, and he was not shy about expressing them. Years later, in some reminiscences which were carefully written down by his publisher Giulio Ricordi, Verdi said:

> I remember a comic scene I had with Solera a short time before. In the third act he had made a love duet between Fenena and Ismaele. I did not like it, because it cooled the action, and it seemed to me to detract somewhat from the biblical grandeur that characterized the drama. One morning, when Solera was at my house, I made this observation to him, but he would not consider it, not because he did not

find it right, but because it irked him to make revisions. We both argued our positions. I held firm, and so did he. He asked me what I wanted in place of the duet, and I then suggested he write a prophecy for the High Priest Zaccaria. He did not find the idea bad, and, with ifs and buts, he said he would think about it and write it later. That was not what I wanted, because I knew many days would go by before Solera would make up his mind to write a verse. I locked the door, put the key in my pocket, and half-serious, half in jest, I said to Solera: "You will not leave here until you have written the prophecy. Here is the Bible. The words are there already." Solera, who had a furious character, did not take this remark of mine in good part. A flash of wrath flared in his eyes. I had a nasty moment, because the poet was a huge man and could easily have got the better of the stubborn composer; but suddenly he sat down at the desk and a quarter of an hour later the prophecy was written!

After the success of *Nabucco,* Solera was the logical choice to write Verdi's next libretto, again for La Scala; and *I lombardi* was an obvious story: patriotic, vast, with splendid opportunities for great choruses, exotic color, dramatic confrontations. Solera wrote two other librettos for Verdi; or rather one and three-quarters. After *Giovanna d'Arco,* he was to write *Attila,* but because of his chronically tumultuous private life, he could not finish the last act of the libretto in time. Verdi had to call on Francesco Maria Piave to complete the text. Solera wrote the composer an indignant letter, and their relationship came to an end. But, if Verdi disliked the man, he still admired the writer. Years later, when Solera was down on his luck and a friend suggested to Verdi that he help him, the composer wrote, "If you mean to do something for Solera, I praise your kind heart; but you would be acting in vain. In a week's time he would be back where he was. . . . It is his own fault if he did not have a brilliant career, if he did not become the leading operatic poet of our time." Despite his rancor, the composer did make a contribution, requiring that it be anonymous.

If Solera was fiery, brilliant, and difficult, Piave (1810–76) was exactly the opposite, and thus was much better suited to get along with the increasingly autocratic Verdi. Born on the island of Murano, near Venice, Piave had grown up in cultivated idleness; then the failure of the family business obliged him suddenly to earn his living, and as a theater lover and dilettante poet, he immediately thought of writing librettos. Thanks to the recommendation of Guglielmo Brenna, secretary of the Teatro La Fenice, Piave was given a chance by Verdi; but the composer immediately made his position clear. Writing to Brenna on November 15, 1843, he said:

> In your letter I read that Piave *would like to reach an agreement with me so as to avoid as much as possible the necessity of revisions once his work is finished.*
>
> For my part I would never like to annoy a poet by asking him to change a verse; and I have written the music for three librettos by Solera, and if you compare the original, which I have kept, with the printed librettos, you would find only a very few verses changed, and these because of Solera's own conviction. But Solera has already written five or six librettos and knows the theater, theatrical effect, and musical forms. Sig. Piave has never written [for the theater] and is naturally deficient in these things. In fact, find me a soprano willing to sing, in succession, a big cavatina, a duet that ends in a trio, and a whole finale such as [Piave has written] in this first act of *Ernani!*
>
> Sig. Piave will have his own good reasons, but I have mine, and I reply that the lungs would not stand this strain. . . .
>
> You, who have been so kind to me, please make Piave understand these things and persuade him. However little experience I may have had, I do go to the theater all year long and pay great attention. I have seen for myself that many compositions would not have failed if there had been

a better distribution of the numbers, if the effects had been better calculated, if the musical forms had been clearer . . . in short, if there had been greater experience both in the poet and in the composer. Often an overlong recitative, a phrase, a sentence which would be beautiful in a book, and even spoken in a play, makes you laugh in a sung drama.

Piave was easily persuaded, and until he was incapacitated by illness in 1867, he remained Verdi's closest collaborator. The composer often addressed him with a rudeness that, even today, makes some of his letters shocking to read; but Piave bore it all patiently. "That's how the Maestro wants it" was a recurrent remark of his; and he did his best to comply with Verdi's many demands. A few unfortunate verses have made him into a figure of fun for Italian cultural historians, but Piave had—or developed, under Verdi's tuition—a keen sense of the theater,of the "cut" of a libretto. A comparative reading of Dumas *fils*'s play, *La Dame aux camélias,* and the libretto of *La traviata* illuminates Piave's gifts.

In the early and mid-nineteenth century, Italian opera houses had their "resident poets" (Piave soon occupied this position at the Fenice, and later at La Scala), who also acted as stage directors, while supplying librettos when required. At the Teatro San Carlo in Naples, for many years the poet was Salvatore Cammarano (1801–52); and when Verdi signed a contract to compose an opera for the Neapolitan theater, it was natural that the house poet should be his librettist.

For the first time Verdi was working with a writer who was a good deal older than he, and whose practical operatic experience was considerably greater. Born into a theatrical family, Cammarano had written numerous librettos for successful composers, especially Donizetti (*Lucia di Lammermoor, Pia de' Tolomei, Roberto Devereux,* among others); he had also been the author of the then popular *Saffo* of Pacini. Cammarano's first libretto for Verdi was *Alzira.* The opera had a mixed reception, but the libretto was certainly more than adequate, and Verdi himself apparently liked it.

His first letters to Cammarano are, for him, unusually deferential. As their collaboration continued—with *La battaglia di Legnano, Luisa Miller,* and *Il trovatore* (unfinished at the poet's death)—Verdi became more outspoken about his dramatic wishes, but his respect for the poet was real, and it was to Cammarano that Verdi first broached the ambitious idea of a *King Lear* opera, a project he was to cherish for years afterwards.

In contrast to the great pageantry of the Solera operas, Cammarano's dramas, while leaving room for exoticism, were more intimate. Even *La battaglia di Legnano,* despite its heroic subject, has scenes of moving domesticity which—with others in *Luisa Miller*—point the way to *La traviata* and *Un ballo in maschera.*

Though Verdi continued collaborating with Piave and, on occasion, publicly defended the poet's verses, he harbored no illusions about Piave's lasting literary merits. When it was time to do *Macbeth,* the composer's first setting of a text drawn from his beloved Shakespeare, Verdi gave Piave an exceptionally hard time; and in the end, he turned for help to his friend, the then admired poet and translator Andrea Maffei (1789–1885).

Maffei was a pivotal figure in the Northern Italian cultural world. He was separated from Countess Clara Maffei, whose Milanese salon, for decades, attracted patriots, artists, musicians. Verdi remained friends with both the Maffeis; he and Andrea sometimes traveled together, and he relied on the older man's taste and judgement. In the case of *Macbeth,* Maffei made major contributions: the words of the sleep-walking scene, for one. But the dispassionate twentieth-century reader would be hard put to decide whether Maffei's verses—as poetry—are really superior to Piave's.

They must have pleased Verdi, in any case, since he set them, and at the same time, turned to Maffei for the libretto of *I masnadieri,* his next opera. It was based on Schil-

ler's drama *Die Räuber*, which Maffei had previously translated into Italian; and the opera was commissioned by
Benjamin Lumley for Her Majesty's Theatre, London.
This was Verdi's first foreign commission, and he was determined to put his best foot forward. Unfortunately, the
opera had only an ephemeral success and has remained
among the most infrequently performed of Verdi's works;
surely Maffei's pompous, self-consciously literary libretto
is responsible at least partly for the work's unpopularity.

From *Macbeth* on, Verdi was constantly seeking new dramatic paths; and one feels that Piave's good journeyman
work no longer satisfied him, though he fell back on Piave
often. When writing *Simon Boccanegra* (on a Piave text) in
Paris, he called on the exiled patriot and writer Giuseppe
Montanelli (1813–62) to doctor some scenes. Later, Verdi
began a collaboration with the lawyer-playwright Antonio
Somma (1809–65).

Somma is now known only as the librettist of *Un ballo in
maschera*, but, after Cammarano's death, Verdi really
meant him to be the librettist of *Re Lear*. Like Maffei, he
was probably chosen in part because of his personal likabi-
lity and in part because of his reputation as a dramatic
poet: a youthful tragedy of his had been performed by the
great Gustavo Modena, a leading Italian actor of the
1840s. Somma had also been a theaater manager; therefore he had ample practical experience. Unfortunately,
the *Lear* project never came to fruition. Verdi asked
Somma, in haste, to devise a libretto based on Scribe's *Gustave III* (which Cammarano had already exploited for Mercadante's *Il reggente*). Somma did as Verdi asked, but the
libretto was extensively altered for reasons of censorship,
and it is unfair to judge Somma's talent by the ensuing
result.

Antonio Ghislanzoni (1824–93) was not exactly a Verdi
librettist. When he was called to work on *Aida,* the libretto
virtually existed. Verdi and Camille Du Locle had written
out an elaborate prose scenario, based on the story by
Mariette Bey; and Ghislanzoni was engaged only to turn

this prose into Italian verse. But even the job of versifying had its problems and pitfalls, as Verdi's copious letters to Ghislanzoni make clear. Of all Verdi's poets, Ghislanzoni was the most professional. Though as a young man he had a patchy, brief career as a baritone (between 1846 and 1855), he supported himself for most of his life solely by writing. His output includes a vivid novel about the Italian theatrical world, *Gli artisti da teatro*, a large number of librettos (for Petrella, Ponchielli, Gomes, Catalani), and—by his own calculation—2,162 articles. He founded, edited, and largely wrote several periodicals. Issues of these are now hard to find, but they reward tracking down, for Ghislanzoni's wit is often still pungent. His *Storia di Milano dal 1836 al 1848* gives a lively picture of the city Verdi knew as a young man; and his *Libro serio* contains an affectionate and penetrating word-portrait of Verdi at the time of *Aida*.

The premier of *Aida* on December 24, 1871 took place a couple of months after Verdi's fifty-eighth birthday. For some time then, the composer seriously thought of retiring, and wrote no more operas. A period of enforced idleness in a Naples hotel led him to write a string quartet, and the death of the great writer Alessandro Manzoni, whom he idolized, inspired him to compose his *Messa da Requiem* (after an earlier plan for a *Requiem* to be written, by several composers, to commemorate Rossini, had misfired). The stage seemed to have lost its attraction. But then, in the summer of 1879, Verdi's crafty publisher Giulio Ricordi arranged for the composer to meet—or rather to renew his acquaintance with—Arrigo Boito (1842–1918), who had collaborated briefly with Verdi on the *Inno delle nazioni* (1862).

The meeting came at a crucial moment in both lives. The international success of his *Requiem* had obviously stimulated Verdi and softened his often-expressed severity towrds the public, while the gradual entry of Wagner's operas into Italian theaters had also put Italy's leading composer on his mettle. Boito, at thirty-seven, was no longer the hot-headed youth whose *Mefistofele,* over a decade earlier, had served as a rallying point for the turbulent Milanese avant-garde and a source of horror for the conservative audience of La Scala. Much revised, the opera had been presented in 1875 in Bologna with great success, and Boito was now on his way to becoming a member of the establishment. For some years he had been engaged in writing *Nerone,* his second opera, which he was never able to finish. The work eluded him always; its vast, ambitious dimensions seemed to demand more and more research, thought, labor. As the public's expectations grew, *Nerone* came to haunt Boito like an accusing specter, practically paralyzing him as a composer.

Writing librettos, besides being a welcome source of income, was also a good excuse for not composing. Boito had already provided texts for Catalani (*La falce,* 1875), Ponchielli (*La gioconda,* 1876), and others. With Ricordi's encouragement, he drafted an outline of *Otello* for Verdi, who first, as a kind of rehearsal, solicited the poet's help in revising the old Piave libretto of *Simon Boccanegra.*

Unlike most of Verdi's other librettists, Boito was an intellectual and, by the Italian cultural standards of the time, a cosmopolite. He had traveled (his mother was a Polish countess), he knew foreign literatures and languages (his English, however, was apparently poor, and he relied on the French versions of Shakespeare by François-Victor Hugo). Verdi's attitude towards Boito, initially, was suspicious, testing, but he gradually warmed to the younger man and at times even bowed to the poet's often brilliant insights and his erudition. In the end they became friends, and Boito was one of the very few people Verdi trusted. In the composer's advanced old age—after their second collaboration, *Falstaff* (1893), and after the death of Giuseppina Strepponi Verdi in 1897—Verdi clearly looked on the young man as a surrogate son. When Verdi died, Boito was at his bedside.

Boito had an alert mind and—when writing for others, to commission—a facile pen. For many years he was over-praised (especially by foreign musicologists with an inadequate grasp of Italian), considered the only Verdian librettist worthy of the composer, and used as a handy stick with which to beat Cammarano and Piave. In fact, Boito's verses are often unnecessarily elaborate, even murky; and some of his philosophical ideas—as in Iago's "Credo," which was totally his own invention—are obvious and even banal. His poetry today was a Victorian (or D'Annunzian) ring, sometimes charming (in certain pages of *Falstaff*), but—as far as quality is concerned—not very much better than the verses of Verdi's other librettists. Fortunately, in his Verdian operas, Boito had Shakespeare—and Verdi— as collaborators.

If Giulio Ricordi had not brought about the 1879 meeting of Boito with Verdi, and if Boito had not been prepared to devote himself wholeheartedly to the older composer, it is likely that we would have no *Otello* and no *Falstaff*. This fact alone is enough to win our undying gratitude toward Verdi's last librettist.

Aspects of Verdi's Dramaturgy

William Weaver

*I*n *a letter* to his French publisher Léon Escudier, Verdi once wrote; "A libretto! A libretto, and the opera is made!"[1] In another letter, to his Neapolitan friend Cesarino de Sanctis, the composer commented; "I read with reluctance librettos that are sent me. It is impossible, or almost impossible for someone else to divine what I want."[2] Because of the very importance he attached to his librettos, Verdi had a hard time finding texts that stimulated him to write music.

Now, after several decades of Verdi studies, and after the publication of a large part (but still far from all) of his correspondence, we can at least make an attempt to divine what the composer wanted in a libretto, and we can base our attempt on his own words, on his choices of works for the opera stage (for *his* opera stage), and on his rejections of works he considered unsuitable. Where a correspondence between composer and librettist survives, the Verdi scholar can now see how Verdi demanded that his poet-collaborators forge their words and their dramas to meet his requirements. As early as 1843, when he was preparing to write *Ernani*, Verdi sent letter after letter to the young, inexperienced Francesco Maria Piave, full of suggestions about the dramatic cut of the scenes, and even

1. Prod'homme, 190.
2. Carteggi I, 16.

about the verses. "Please, at the moment when Ruy [Silva] appears, leave room for a beautiful cantabile . . ." And then: "I cannot understand why you make a change of scene in the third act. I am not convinced . . . because it prolongs the action, a useless chorus has to be made in the throne room, and the scenic effect is diminished. It seems to me that the moment Carlo appears and surprises the conspirators the action must proceed rapidly to the end of the act."[3]

Verdi was equally explicit and demanding with his other poets, even when they were proven men of the theater. In the summer of 1870, while he was at work on *Aida,* Verdi wrote to the librettist Antonio Ghislanzoni, already the author of a number of librettos and, as a former professional singer, well versed in the demands of opera. In this letter, Verdi used a phrase that has since become famous, a kind of slogan now often repeated to describe Verdi's theater. The letter says, in part:

> In the duet [Act II, scene 1: Amneris and Aida] there are excellent things at the beginning and at the end, although it is too long and drawn-out. It seems to me that the recitative could be said in fewer verses. The strophes go well as far as "a te in cor destò." But afterward, when the action grows more heated, it seems to me that the *parola scenica* is lacking. I do not know if I make myself clear in saying *parola scenica,* but what I mean is the word that sculpts and makes the situation precise and evident."[4]

Since the publication of that letter, many pages have been written about the expression *parola scenica,* which is, moreover, very difficult to translate (beyond Verdi's own graphic explanation to Ghislanzoni). But here again, if we look at the words Verdi approved of and used, his meaning becomes still clearer. No composer expects the audience to understand everything that is sung on the stage,

3. Abbiati I, 474–75.
4. Copial., 641.

but it must grasp readily the essential ideas; and with Verdi, those essentials are always made evident, sculpted. The first lines of his most famous arias strike us like telegrams: "Di quella pira," "De' miei bollenti spiriti," "Eri tu," "Ritorna vincitor." It is only when Verdi was collaborating with the aesthete Arrigo Boito that the *parola* sometimes becomes less *scenica*. After the first Nannetta in *Falstaff* sang "Sul fil d'un soffio etesio," many Milanese in the audience of the premiere must have gone home to their dictionaries to discover the meaning of "etesio."

Another word that crops up again and again in Verdi's letters to his librettists is *posizione*, usually translated as "situation," as good a translation as any. But like Humpty-Dumpty in *Alice*, Verdi bent words to his will; and *posizione*, in his usuage, means a whole dramatic and emotional complexity.

The most famous and fascinating published correspondence, in this respect, is the long exchange between Verdi and Antonio Somma, the gifted dramatist who became the librettist of *Un ballo in maschera* and of the never-composed (or never-completed) *Re Lear*. Twenty-eight letters from Verdi to Somma were published by Alessandro Pascolato in 1902;[5] Alessandro Luzio, in 1935, published about twenty letters of Somma to Verdi, often, however, providing only excerpts.[6] This correspondence extended over a decade, between 1853 and 1863, a crucial period in Verdi's career; and the letters afford an invaluable view of the composer's working methods. In the very first known letter (of April 22, 1853), Verdi sums up for the poet his professional convictions and indicates their development.

> Long experience has confirmed the ideas I have always had as to theatrical effectiveness, though in my early days I had the courage to reveal them only in part. (For example, ten years ago I would not have risked doing *Rigoletto*). I find that our [Italian] opera is guilty of excessive monot-

5. Pascolato, *Re Lear e Ballo in maschera* (Città di Castello, 1902).
6. Carteggi II.

ony, and therefore today I would refuse to set subjects in
the genre of *Nabucco, Foscari,* etc., etc. They provide interesting scenes, but without variety. It is all on one note, lofty
if you like, but still always the same. I will make myself
clearer: the poem of Tasso [*Gerusalemme liberata*] may perhaps be superior, but I prefer Ariosto [*Orlando furioso*] a
thousand, thousand times more. For the same reason I
prefer Shakespeare to all other dramatic authors, not ex-
cepting the Greeks. It seems to me that, as far as effectiveness is concerned, the best subject I have so far set to
music (I am not speaking of literary and poetic merit in any
way) is *Rigoletto.* There are very powerful situations [*posi-
zioni*], variety, brio, pathos . . .[7]

Almost a decade earlier, on May 22, 1844, as his career,
following the successes of *Nabucco, I lombardi,* and *Ernani,*
was firmly launched, Verdi wrote to Piave about the libretto of *I due Foscari:*

In the tenor's cavatina there are two things wrong: the first
is that when the cavatina is over, Jacopo remains on stage,
and this is always bad for the effectiveness; the second is
that there is no shift of mood after the adagio. Make a very
brief dialogue between the guard and Jacopo, then an
officer who says: *bring out the prisoner,* then a cabaletta; but
make it forceful, because we are writing for [the tenor]
Roppa. Moreover, that Foscari character, I repeat, must be
more energetic. . . . Make the duet short, because it is the
finale. Put great feeling into it and write beautiful poetry.
. . . In the third act do as we agreed, and try to insert the
gondolier's song mixed with a chorus of the populace.
Couldn't it be arranged for this to happen toward evening
and thus have a sunset, which is so beautiful?[8]

This letter gives a good idea of Verdi's concerns in the
1840s: cavatina and subsequent cabaletta are laid out in

7. Pascolato, 45–46.
8. Copial., 426.

the conventional way, the opera is being tailored to the abilities of specific singers; and the composer is very interested in external, even superficial effects, like the sunset, which Piave duly provided for him ("il sole cammina all'occaso," the libretto says). The offstage gondolier's song—a tried-and-true effect borrowed from earlier operas, notably Rossini's *Otello*—is a foretaste of Verdi's recurrent and highly inventive use of offstage voices. This device, in later operas, became more and more subtle, in such instances as Manrico's haunting ballad of self-introduction in *Il trovatore* or Alfredo's distant repetition of "Di quell'amor" in *La traviata,* so apt that we can believe he is singing not offstage but in Violetta's memory or in her unconscious mind. A final use of distant voices is found in Act III, scene 1 of *Falstaff,* as the women call to one another, invisible, expanding the space of the action far beyond the confines of the stage.

Verdi's love of Shakespeare, a lasting influence on his dramaturgy, is confirmed not only in the letter to Somma quoted above but also in other letters, and by the fact that he kept two complete Italian translations of Shakespeare's plays always at his bedside in the Villa Sant'Agata. But as he said to Somma, in the 1840s he had the courage to pursue his convictions only up to a certain point. Thus in setting *Macbeth,* he eliminated the drunken porter. That same porter, perhaps not quite so drunk, was to turn up years later, however, disguised in the habit of Fra Melitone, in Verdi's most Shakespearean opera, *La forza del destino.* Shakespearean, that is, in Verdi's sense: a work of great variety, vast scope, juxtaposing comic and tragic, employing a number of unusual characters, all sharply defined, even if only briefly seen and heard. Though the opera is flawed (as Verdi himself realized), it is perhaps Verdi's boldest attempt to portray an entire, complex, contradictory world.

But even in his earliest operas, Verdi was not afraid of flouting conventions. The story of how he made *Nabucco*'s librettist cut a love duet from the opera may or may not be true, but the fact remains that *Nabucco* has a pair of lovers but has no duet for them. For that matter, in all the Verdi canon, there are surprisingly few love duets, in the traditional sense.[9] Before Verdi and Somma worked on *Re Lear* and *Un ballo in maschera,* the librettist submitted several ideas to Verdi as possible subjects for opera. Verdi rejected them with his usual frankness, though with greater courtesy than he sometimes displayed in such cases:

> . . . in the subjects you have proposed, though they are eminently dramatic, I do not find all that variety my mad brain desires. You will tell me that in *Soredello* we can introduce a ball, a banquet, even a tournament; but still the characters will retain a severe, grave hue . . .[10]

The German musicologist Karl Dietrich Gräwe, in a valuable discussion of Verdi's dramaturgy, describes the composer's use of *feste.*[11] As a rule, the festivity, the ball or banquet, is set in dramatic contrast with the state of mind of the hero or heroine. While Carnival explodes in the Paris streets, Violetta lies dying; in the greatest of Verdian *feste,* the drama of Riccardo-Renato-Amelia is played out against lighthearted dance music. The Verdi protagonist, as Gräwe says, is the outsider at the feast. Actually, in one instance which Gräwe does not underline, it is the villain who is the outsider, the intruder: Silva, at the wedding celebration of Ernani and Elvira, reverses the contrast, as he comes to remind the happy bridegroom of his fatal, ineluctable debt of honor.

Several writers—and especially the Italian Guglielmo Barblan—have discussed the importance of the concept of honor in Verdian drama.[12] And, indeed, there is hardly a Verdi libretto in which honor, in some form, does not play

9. Weaver, "Verdi and the drama of love," *Atti* 3 (1972), 523–28.
10. Pascolato, 47.
11. Gräwe, "L'uno e gli altri," *Atti* 3, 27–33.
12. Barblan, "Il sentimento dell'onore nella drammaturgia verdiana," *Atti* 3, 2–13.

a catalytic part. Honor can be male—military, patriotic, or even racial (cf. *La forza del destino*)—or female and sexual (cf. *Stiffelio, Un ballo in maschera*). Most often it is linked with patriotism, a key Verdian motive as late as *Aida,* and often with love, with family affection (as in the case of the honor of Alfredo and of his unnamed sister in *La traviata*).

If one were to read, from debut to farewell, the librettos of, say, Mercadante or Donizetti, straight through, one would encounter a remarkable variety of styles and settings, ranging from the neoclassical attitudes of Metastasio and Alfieri (or Alfieri epigones) to the arch-romanticism of Victor Hugo and Sir Walter Scott. But in neither of these typical composers does one find the unswerving fidelity to certain themes, certain emotional and dramatic situations, certain moral positions, which is to be found in Verdi.

The most evident and the most written-about of these situations is the relationship between father and daughter. From Oberto and his Leonora to Ford and his Nannetta, this relationship is the linchpin of Verdian drama. No doubt the composer rejected many of the subjects proposed to him precisely because this relationship was missing. In 1844, when his old friend Giuseppe Demaldè suggested Hugo's *Marion Delorme* as a possible libretto source, Verdi (who had set Hugo's *Hernani* only the year before) wrote a frequently quoted letter, saying, "The protagonist has a character I do not like. I do not like whores on the stage. Otherwise, if there were not this obstacle, it would be a beautiful subject."[13]

Now, only a few years later, Verdi composed, with great enthusiasm, *La traviata.* From a moral standpoint, Violetta is very similar to Hugo's Marion: a courtesan impelled by true love to renounce her past. What changed Verdi's mind? Some biographers have inferred that the new attitude toward *donne puttane* was due to the composer's love for Giuseppina Strepponi, with whom he had begun to live in the late 1840s. This notion is surely uncharitable and

13. Abbiati I, 502.

unfair both to Giuseppina and to Verdi, since the composer's future second wife had hardly been a prostitute (what little we know about her relationship with the mysterious father of her illegitimate children suggests that it was anything but mercenary). No, though Verdi himself may not have been aware of any specific reason, it seems permissible to surmise that he rejected *Marion Delorme* because of the absence in it of a father or a father figure. In his previous Hugo setting there had been the great character of Silva, whose long "je suis vieux" speech, bitter and ironic, became, in Piave's transmogrification, the more pathetic and amorous "Infelice e tuo credevi," emphasizing Silva's patriarchal—and paternal—qualities.

The relationship between Alfredo and Violetta is quite different from that between Marion Delorme and her Didier. Here Marion's guilty secret (Didier is unaware of her notorious past) is the pivot of the tragedy. Didier discovers the secret, condemns Marion, pardoning her only as he goes to his death. When Alfredo comes to Violetta's party in the first act (another great Verdian *festa*, at which Alfredo is the outsider), he knows all about her and there is no question of necessity or of forgiveness. If Violetta does have a secret, it is her capacity for true love—a secret even from herself until Alfredo penetrates it. But this is not the drama. It is Germont, the father (not only of Alfredo but also, finally, of Violetta, in spirit), who serves not so much as direct antagonist or villain, but simply as the representative of the outside world, the real world of bourgeois respectability and conventional morality.

Morality is another constant of Verdi's dramaturgy. Of course, in Donizetti and in other Verdi predecessors there are "good" and "bad" characters. But with Verdi morality is a different matter. Paradoxically, his heroes may be murderers, like Rigoletto and Macbeth, but they are rarely out-and-out villains. He wanted even his worst villains, for that matter, to be cynical, lighthearted scoundrels, not the traditional heavies. He wrote to Salvatore Cammarano, Neapolitan librettist of *Luisa Miller,* about the evil Wurm:

. . . in the second-act duet between Wurm and Eloisa [later Luisa]. There will be a fine contrast between the terror and despair of Eloisa and the infernal iciness of Wurm. Indeed, it seems to me that if you give Wurm's character a certain comic quality, the situation will become even more terrible . . .[14]

A few years later, writing to Somma on January 8, 1855, about *Lear,* Verdi returned to his idea of the smiling villain:

> For my part, I would not have Edmondo feel remorse, but would make him an outright scoundrel: not a repulsive scoundrel like Francesco in the *Masnadieri* [*Die Raüber*] of Schiller, but one who laughs to himself and mocks everything and commits the most atrocious crimes with the maximum indifference. . . . I have said to make Edmondo a mocking character, because in music he will prove more varied: making him otherwise, he would have to sing *heavy* phrases, with shouts. Mockery, irony are portrayed (and it is more novel) *a mezza voce:* it becomes more terrible . . .[15]

Cammarano did not succeed in the perhaps impossible task of giving the odious Wurm a comic aspect (though Verdi's music for the Wurm-Walter duet in Act II of the opera does have a light, almost buffo lilt). The Edmondo of Somma and Verdi never reached the stage, so it was not until Boito and Shakespeare provided him with Iago that Verdi was able to have his icy, mocking, lighthearted villain (unfortunately, baritones too often attempt to make him a much less interesting heavy).

Usually, however, Verdi does allow his malefactors to feel remorse, or, at least, he gives some excuse or explanation for their evil actions. Abigaille, wicked as she is, was driven by thwarted love, and she repents in the end. Even

14. Copial., 471.
15. Pascolato, 71–72.

the Duke of Mantua in *Rigoletto,* for an uncharacteristic moment, rues his libertinism and dreams of a true love. Filippo II—one of Verdi's richest characters—is alternately inexorable and, in his great monologue, humanly pathetic.

If Verdi's villains are rarely completely villainous, his heroes and heroines are seldom totally good. The heroines, including those who remain medically pure, are at the very least disobedient daughters: the Leonoras of *Oberto* and *Forza,* Luisa Miller, Gilda. Odabella (in *Attila*) is a would-be murderess (though she is inspired by revenge, a motive Verdi does not completely condemn, especially in this case, when she is avenging her father). Violetta is a courtesan; Mina (in *Stiffelio*), an errant wife. Manrico, Ernani, Corrado (in *Il corsaro*) are bandits, but they are good, Robin Hood–like bandits. Carlo Moor, in *I masnadieri,* is a bad bandit, but his misdeeds stem from the injustices he has suffered at home. He, too, is seeking revenge: not on an individual, however, but on the world.

In a Verdi opera, the officially correct moral line is often represented by the father. Germont is the obvious example, but he was preceded by other stern defenders of proper, righteous behavior: Francesco Foscari (standing for political morality), old Miller (social morality), and Stankar in *Stiffelio* (sexual morality). A Verdian father, in the name of morality, can condone behavior that from another point of view might seem dubious, such as Aida's tormented betrayal of Radamès, prompted by her father, Amonasro, in the name of a higher, more public duty to fatherland.

In almost every Verdi opera this official moral axis is clearly perceptible, though the positions of his characters may be eccentric to it. One thinks of Azucena and Rigoletto: felons both, but strongly sympathetic, not only to the spectator but also to Verdi. The avengers are in a similarly askew moral position: Don Alvaro, Fiesco, and Odabella, as mentioned above. Even Don Carlos, more victim than agent, is in the world's eye guilty of a sinful, illicit love for his father's wife. Whatever the world may think, however, Verdi's own attitude is always distinct and personal. He judges his characters with understanding, compassion, even indulgence; but they are still judged. His idiosyncratic moral attitude is nevertheless an anchor that holds the drama fast, a frame that gives it context.

At a Congress of Verdi Studies in Milan some years ago, the Italian literary critic Mario Lavagetto read an elaborate and informed paper, presenting a structural analysis of the Verdi libretto. "The libretto," he said,

> is the story of a "project" of varying nature common to two persons (X and Y, usually soprano and tenor), which can be achieved or cannot be achieved, and which in any case encounters the obstacles set up by an antagonist (Z, usually baritone or mezzo-soprano) or else by an opponent, in general a paternal or maternal figure (W, usually bass or mezzo-soprano).[16]

More simply, Lavagetto quotes George Bernard Shaw's definition of an opera plot as the story of a tenor and a soprano who want to make love but are prevented from doing so by the baritone.

Actually, in a Verdi opera, it is not the plot that counts. Whether X and Y manage to make love or not is secondary. What matters is character. From the characters comes the drama and, indeed, the music. In some operas—*Nabucco* for one—there are sharply defined characters in a plot that is nebulous to the point of unintelligibility. The characters, naturally, do not exist in a vacuum; the setting, the social context contribute to shaping them. Francesco Foscari is the product of the Venice of his time, its code concisely indicated by Piave and Verdi; Rigoletto was "made a base villain," as he says, by mankind and by nature, as well as by the artificial, amoral, treacherous environment of the court of his employer.

16. Lavagetto, "Ipotesi per un'analisi strutturale dei libretti verdiani," *Atti* 3, 45–54.

Verdi was perfectly willing to follow the Shaw formula as far as plots went. But often he deliberately avoided the X-Y-Z triangle, and these exceptions are of particular interest. They include a near-masterpiece like *Macbeth* and a near-failure like *Il corsaro*. In the former case, Verdi's drama has the strength of the two central Shakespearean characters, and it rests squarely on a moral foundation (rendered briefly but unforgettably visible by the mute appearance of the fatherly Duncan). But in *Il corsaro,* there is no Duncan, no old Miller, no Germont. The baritone Seid is another out-and-out villain, a man of a few basic and base emotions (his love for Gulnara, which in a more subtle Verdi opera might have partially redeemed him, here is only lust and does not prevent him from threatening her with execution). Corrado, the corsair, is one of the very few major Verdi characters without a past. In his opening aria he explains that he had a happy childhood until "inexorable fate" turned against him. But the rest is mystery: the form that fate's cruelty took is never revealed. In reality, Corrado is the archetypal tenor hero; he is X, and that is about all he is. More importantly, he is without father or mother; and so is his beloved Medora, whose background is equally blank. Compare these two characters with their counterparts of *I masnadieri:* Carlo is also an outlaw, but we know exactly why, and it is the whole tangle of family relationships—involving also Amalia—which constitutes the drama of the opera.

If *Il corsaro* has a merit—apart from its often beautiful music—that merit is its concision. It is one of Verdi's shortest operas. In another letter to Somma, written on May 22, 1853, Verdi said: "the audience is easily bored";[17] and in all his correspondence with his librettists, Verdi kept harping on the necessity to be brief. One suspects that Verdi himself was as easily bored as the audience which he kept firmly in mind. In any case, his librettos were conceived to be heard, not read (or at most to be read only as a complement to hearing the music).

17. Pascolato, 49.

Even when he was composing *Otello* and *Falstaff*—operas written for his own satisfaction and not to fulfil a commission—Verdi had the audience very much on his mind. Consideration for the public's reaction was also an ingredient in his dramaturgy. Though he constantly protested that he might not finish the opera in hand or, if he did finish it, he might not allow it to be staged, he never stopped inquiring about singers, possible interpreters. And as he wrote to Boito, they would be presenting themselves again to the audience, saying, *A noi:* here we are, have at us. The public was Verdi's old enemy, but it was an enemy for which he displayed a grudging respect.

Some Verdi commentators have considered *Falstaff* (like the early *Un giorno di regno*) a sport in Verdian dramaturgy. But the composer's final opera, different though it certainly is from its predecessors in many ways, still contains in one form or another many familiar Verdian elements. Love is there, and as so often in the other operas, that love is opposed by a hostile father. Jealousy—a Verdian emotion from the time of Abigaille to that of Otello—is also central to the action. And as Barblan has emphasized in the essay already mentioned, honor occupies a prominent position in *Falstaff*'s libretto. Sir John's monologue "Onore? Ladri!" is, to be sure, virtually a contradiction of everything the younger Verdi had to say about honor. Did Verdi agree with his fat knight? Certainly Falstaff enjoyed the composer's sympathies. Perhaps by the age of eighty, Verdi had also earned the right to change his attitude. He could have said, with Walt Whitman,

> Do I contradict myself?
> Very well then I contradict myself,
> (I am large, I contain multitudes.)

Verdi's Own Words:
His Thoughts on Performance, with Special Reference to Don Carlos, Otello, *and* Falstaff

Martin Chusid

MARTIN CHUSID is professor of music and director of the American Institute for Verdi Studies at New York University. In 1974 he published *A Catalog of Verdi's Operas;* he has read papers on Verdi at six international congresses and edited *Rigoletto,* the first opera to be published in the new complete Verdi edition. An internationally recognized Schubert authority as well, Dr. Chusid has also written on Mozart's operas and Haydn's Masses.

*T*he correspondence left by Verdi in the course of a long and successful career provides a wealth of valuable material about the way he wanted his operas performed. He and his second wife, the intelligent soprano Giuseppina Strepponi, wrote thousands of letters, including many to librettists, conductors, singers, impresarios, and publishers. Since he was as direct and concise in his letters as he was in his music, there is material of the highest interest available on all aspects of his professional activity. Furthermore, his concern for every facet of the lyric theater rivaled that of his great contemporary, Wagner.[1] All the original sources indicate that Verdi wrote, directed, or followed closely every phase of an operatic production: the choice of a subject; its condensation into a scenario or plot summary; the hammering out of the final text with the librettist, a difficult phase extending into the compositional process;[2] the composing of a sketch of the opera (usually consisting of the vocal parts or of the principal melodic line in the orchestra together with a bass part).[3] After this, he wrote out the vocal parts, together with the bass line on the full orchestral score. These vocal parts were copied for the singers (soloists and chorus), resulting in part-books. Then, while the keyboard rehearsals were under way, Verdi orchestrated the work. He usually finished this task just in time to have parts copied for the orchestral rehearsals. Finally, he directed the dress rehearsal and the first public performances. During all these activities, he was critically evaluating the scenery, staging, and acting.

1. In the course of an interview for a Viennese journal (1875), Verdi himself had made the comparison with Wagner. The interviewer reported, "When we came to talk about Wagner, Verdi remarked that that great genius had rendered incalculable services to melodramatic art because he had the courage to rid himself of the traditional decadent ('baroque') forms. 'I, too, have attempted the fusion of music and drama,' he said, '. . . in *Macbeth* but I could not write my own librettos, as Wagner does.' " As cited in Frank Walker's article "Verdi and Vienna," *Musical Times* (September 1951), 404.

2. Verdi wrote to Giulio Ricordi on February 3, [1870], "In writing an opera, it is not the labor of composition that weighs on me, but what holds me back is the difficulty of finding a subject to *my taste,* a poet to *my taste* and a performance to *my taste."* (Abbiati III, 330.) Five years earlier he had written to Léon Escudier, "In the end it all depends on a libretto. A libretto, a libretto and the opera is made!" (Abbiati III, 42.)

3. See the only available complete example, the facsimile edition of the *Rigoletto* sketches (Milan, 1941). Carlo Gatti, who edited these sketches and had some other pages from well-known operas reproduced, in *Verdi nelle immagini* (Milan, 1941), reported that he saw such sketches for all operas from *Luisa Miller* (1849) to *Falstaff* (1893) at Sant'Agata, the estate on which Verdi and Strepponi lived for about 50 years, and where his heirs still reside.

It should be borne in mind that Verdi rehearsed, directed, and sometimes conducted, almost every one of his world premieres[4]—in the case of *Aida* it was the European premiere. He was similarly responsible for numerous later performances of his operas as well as of the *Requiem*.[5]

Other practical issues concerned him as well: the establishment of a generally accepted international pitch; the seating arrangement of the orchestra in the pit; the sinking of that pit out of the sight of the audience;[6] designating the best player of each instrumental group as section leader or first chair; and the organization of the musical and staging staffs of the opera house. He strenuously and successfully fought for the overall direction of an opera by a conductor liberated from his chores as principal violinist.[7] He also had sound ideas on training, auditioning, and rehearsing singers, on the historical authenticity of costumes, scenery, and props, on the length of intermissions (not to exceed twenty minutes), and on the dramatic quality of the translations of his operas into

4. These included his major revisions (*Jérusalem* from *I lombardi*, *Aroldo* from *Stiffelio*, *La forza del destino, Simon Boccanegra*, and *Don Carlos*). There were only two premieres of thirty-two he did not supervise, *Il corsaro* (Trieste, 1848) and the revised *Macbeth* (Paris, 1865).

5. A tentative list includes *Oberto* in Genoa (1840), *Nabucco* in Vienna (1843), *I lombardi* in Venice (1843), *Ernani* in Bergamo (1844), *I due Foscari* in Venice (1845), *Macbeth* in Bologna (1850), *Il trovatore* in Paris (1854, and as *Le Trouvère*, 1857), *Simon Boccanegra* in Reggio Emilia and Naples (1858), *La forza del destino* in Madrid (1863), *Les Vêpres siciliennes*, revival in Paris (1863), *Don Carlos* in Naples (1872), *Aida* in Parma (1872), in Naples (1873), and in Vienna (1875), and in Paris (1876 and again in 1880, in French), *Otello* in Paris (1894), and numerous performances of the *Requiem* in Milan, Paris, London, Vienna (1874–75), and Cologne (1877). He also coached singers and gave advice informally on many other occasions.

6. Verdi acknowledged receiving this idea from Wagner. It was first done in Italy at La Scala for the European premiere of *Aida* (February, 1872), at Verdi's insistence.

7. Italy, lagging behind other European nations, had opera orchestras led by the first violinist into the 1860s and '70s. The first printed parts for *Un ballo in maschera* (world premiere—Rome, 1859) had instrumental cues indicating all solos in the part for *violino principale*. There was no printed orchestral score for this opera until the last decade of the century. Angelo Mariani is reported to have laid down his violin and to have conducted with a baton from the mid-1860s. See also *My Reniniscences* by Luigi Arditi (New York: Dodd Mead, 1896).

foreign languages. Verdi fought unceasingly for the integrity of the operatic score as written by the composer. In his later contracts (e.g., *Don Carlos*) he demanded a clause which provided that his publisher pay him a huge penalty in the event of performances with cuts, key transpositions, or other mutilations of the score or libretto. This was no simple matter; until 1860 (1871 in Rome) political and religious censors continually deleted "offensive" scenes and rewrote "dangerous" words, lines, scenes, or even complete librettos.[8] But the principal threat to the accurate realization of the written score was posed by performers unwilling or unable to follow the composer's directions.[9]

In all these matters it is clear that Verdi had experience, intelligence, imagination, an iron will, and the highest artistic integrity. Early in his career, however, the composer realized that in the theater, artistic integrity and drama were inextricably linked. Therefore, he had a single overriding concern to which everything else was subordinated—the dramatic impact on the audience. He knew that an audience moved by a performance would return to the theater, anticipating another such experience. Again and again, Verdi maintained that in the theater the greatest crime was boredom.

This conviction quite naturally led to others: to his belief, for example, that the second act of an opera should be better than the first, and that the last should be the best of all. He also believed that the last act should be short and the denouement of the opera followed quickly by the final curtain.

He realized that the complexity of opera in the second half of the nineteenth century required a team effort, and

8. See "Alternate Titles for the Operas," a listing, in Chusid, *A Catalog of Verdi's Operas* (Jos. Boonin: Hackensack, N.J., 1974).

9. See, for example, the letter on the changes in *Macbeth* proposed and undoubtedly carried out by the famous mezzo-soprano Pauline Viardot Garcia who sang Lady Macbeth at the premiere of that opera in the British Isles (Dublin, 1859). The letter is reproduced and translated (badly) in Arditi. Arditi conducted the performance in Dublin and was the recipient of the letter.

none of his later works (i.e. from *Les Vêpres siciliennes,* 1855) could succeed then—nor can they succeed now—without a fiery, enthusiastic, well-rehearsed, and well-disciplined performance by *le masse*—the choruses, orchestra, and stage bands. Naturally, Verdi insisted that there be excellent singing and acting on the part of the soloists as well. And he included the comprimario (secondary) as well as the primario parts. It is instructive to observe that the Italian master, whose carefully written contracts gave him considerable control over the selection of singers, invariably chose a vocalist who sang well but perhaps had a lesser natural instrument or a less spectacular vocal technique than others, if that performer had great stage presence and could interpret the drama convincingly. No greater compliment could be paid a performer by the hard-to-please composer than that he or she had, in Verdi's words, "il diavolo addosso" (the devil in him).

With respect to staging, as early as the first *Macbeth* (Florence, 1847) one finds numerous suggestions scattered throughout Verdi's letters. But there is another rich source of information providing clues for Verdi's thoughts on the subject. These are the production books or staging manuals, called in French *livrets de mise-en-scène* or in Italian *disposizioni sceniche.* The earliest of these come from Paris and exist in manuscript or printed form, sometimes in both forms for the same opera. Verdi was impressed by the attention given to staging in Paris—his *Jérusalem,* which reopened the Paris Opéra after a period of darkness, received a particularly lavish production—and beginning with his second French opera, *Les Vêpres siciliennes,* a more or less complete series of *disposizioni sceniche* was published by Ricordi, including all of Verdi's later operas.[10]

Following the discussion of the three operas that form the heart of this chapter, there are sections treating three

10. See RosenS. Copies of the Ricordi production books for *Les Vêpres siciliennes, Un ballo in maschera, La forza del destino, Don Carlos, Aïda, Simon Boccanegra,* and *Otello* are in the Archive of the American Institute for Verdi Studies, Bobst Library, New York University.

more generalized areas of performance: thoughts, mainly Verdi's, on tempo and character in his music, the composer's chief concerns with respect to conductors, singers, and choruses, and, finally, some additional information and some letters of value for the *mise-en-scène* of several later operas. A final note: all translations are by the author unless otherwise indicated. Access to copies of many of the originals in the archive of the American Institute for Verdi Studies, New York University, has allowed some corrections of the citations.

Don Carlos, Five Acts
(Paris, 1867; Revised Version in Four Acts, Milan, 1884)

This huge work, the last of Verdi's four operas for Paris, was his final attempt to surpass Meyerbeer in the genre of grand opera on the latter's home ground. After considering the unusually large number of principal parts—a feature of French grand opera—Verdi wrote to Franco Faccio

> [Genoa, January 8, 1879]
> [. . .] the part of Posa [is an] episodic and purely singing role. In *D. Carlos,* first of all the part of Philip must be successful, then Eboli, etc., etc., but for these parts you need seasoned artists who are actors above all, not novices. As for the music, neither the quartet, nor Eboli's aria, nor that of Posa are of primary importance; these too are episodic pieces, which can arouse a momentary interest but which do not leave [lasting] impressions. Applause is one thing, [lasting] impression is another, and it is the impression that fills the theater.
>
> (de Rensis, 183)

Earlier, while discussing possible singers for the Milanese premiere, Verdi had written to Giulio Ricordi (Genoa,

January 11, 1868) "Be very careful since a Philip [who is] a fool is not possible." (Abbiati III, 158.)

When Verdi first saw the scenario for the opera, probably prepared by Joseph Méry, the original librettist for the work, he wrote to Perrin (July 21, 1865) to suggest the inclusion of Schiller's magnificent confrontation between Philip and the Grand Inquisitor (Porter, 75). Prior to the premiere of the revised version, Verdi wrote to the new impresario at La Scala

> Montecatini, June 30, 1883
> You must be concerned first of all for the three basses, Philip, the Inquisitor, and the Monk [ostensibly Charles V or his ghost], all of whom have the same importance dramatically as well as musically. The only difference is in Philip's part, which is longer.
>
> (Abbiati IV, 217–18)

In view of the opera's length and complex staging, Verdi argued with Giulio Ricordi for more rehearsal time. He used as his yardstick the rehearsal schedule of the successful Italian premiere, conducted by Angelo Mariani (Bologna, 1867).

> Genoa, February 17, 1868
> [. . .] "[Don't tell me] that at Bologna 20 days sufficed [. . .] [because] at Bologna there were 2 rehearsals a day [. . .] In this way 20 days became 40; in addition the chorus had studied the opera for a month [prior] and the [principal] artists knew their parts. Despite this you yourself saw that many things on stage, indicated and required by the music, were overlooked completely or badly performed [. . .] In *D. Carlos* there are seven scenes, five of them very complicated and of the greatest importance. I repeat once more, [. . .] 40 days are needed,[11] with the entire personnel of the theater free of other tasks [. . .]
>
> (Abbiati III, 159)

11. According to GüntherG, at the Paris Opéra there were 270 rehearsals from August 1866 until the premiere on March 11, 1867.

Since Mariani was contracted for the Teatro Carlo Felice, Genoa, Alberto Mazzucato was chosen to conduct the
Milanese premiere of *Don Carlos*, and Verdi wrote the following letters on the performance of the opera for his
benefit.

Genoa, March 17, 1868[12]

Dear Maestro

The *ad libitum* in the solo passage for the violins [Ballet, Act
III][13] refers to the tempo: if, however, that tempo should
prove troublesome to perform, there would be no great
harm in making some changes, but not with many notes
and retaining the *harmonies.*

The change for La Destin [Eboli] is going well; if the
[high] B[flat] were choked or thin and the G were lyric and
full it would also be possible to do it this way [end Act IV,
Part 1],

leaning for a short time on either the G or the F, whichever
of the two notes comes out more powerfully.

Since we are discussing *D. Carlos*, let me make a point or
two about the opera [. . .] At the end of the third act
[original five-act version], when the King has his son ar-
rested, after the words "Disarmato ei sia" [Disarm him],
there are three *fortissimo* bars in the orchestra of the utmost
force, especially the final A,

12. Unless otherwise indicated, all references in this and the next letter are to
the Ricordi piano-vocal score, revised five-act version, Plate no. 51104.

13. Ricordi, n.d., Ger. ed., piano-vocal score, Plate no. 131240, 386, III, 1–2
(signifying page 386, third brace, measures 1–2). From this point all locations are
abbreviated in this fashion.

on which there is also a stroke of the bass drum and metal clapper (*Batt.*)[14]; then, after the words "a me il ferro" [give me the sword, sung by Posa], I should like a very long silence: and when the clarinets take up the motive of the duet again, I should like a very soft sound, veiled, I would say almost inside (*interno*), quiet, smooth, without stress.[15] You understand what I mean. I need not tell you that the clipped notes of the singers must be *senza voce*. If I dwell on this point it is because I think it extremely important [. . .] the situation is good, striking, and makes a great effect, if it is well done. The heavenly voice that comes a little later[16] should be quite high and quite distant so that the public understands immediately and well that it isn't something from this world. It is well understood that everyone on stage should pay attention only to the *auto-da-fé,* as if they did not hear the voice at all.

In the Inquisitor scene,[17] Act IV, after the words "l'ombra di Samuel," there is a passage for string instruments[18]

designated with a slur. At the [Paris] Opéra, where there is excellent diversity in the strings, the passage was performed completely staccato and in combination with the < which the wind instruments have, with the roll of the

14. *Batt.* is probably an abbreviation for the word *battochio* or *battaglia,* both of which can mean "metal clapper." But perhaps Verdi means the cymbals. Although not indicated on scores, until very late in the nineteenth century it appears to have been customary for the cymbals to play with the bass drum unless "cassa sola" was indicated. Berlioz, in his *Treatise on Instrumentation,* complains, "the bass drum is almost never used without the cymbals—as if these two instruments were inseparable by nature." (Ed. Richard Strauss [New York: Kalmus, 1948], p. 391.)

15. 237, I, to 237, II, 3.

16. 240, II, 2, to 243, I, 2.

17. Verdi always referred to the scene between Philip and the Grand Inquisitor as the scene of the Inquisition.

18. The passage extends from 261, III, 4, to 262, I, 1.

timpani and the bass drum alone [i.e. without the cymbals],[19] it made a very strong effect. [. . .]

P.S. In the Finale of Act III, at the funeral march,[20] the double basses are divided in three. The largest number should be on the fundamental [lowest] note. For example, if there are 14 double basses, put 6 on the fundamental note. If there are 12, still put 6 on the fundamental note.[21]

(de Bellis, 539–40)

Genoa, March 20, 1868

Dear Maestro

It won't surprise you to receive a second letter about *D. Carlos* after that of the other day [. . .]

I know that the rehearsals are going well; only there are some deficiencies which will certainly disappear with more rehearsals. [These are] in the delicacy of the [dynamic] shading [*colorito*] and some changes in the tempos [*movi-*

19. See fn. 15 above.

20. 187, II, to the end of 189, and 241, last measure, to 242, II, I.

21. Twelve or fourteen double basses is an extremely large number even for a symphony orchestra. But as this and other letters (e.g. on *Aida*) suggest, Verdi consistently expected more double basses than violas or cellos. In his scores he invariably wrote the bass part doubled by cello and double bass on the bass rather than the cello line. He also positioned the double basses in the pit in two groups, one to the right and the other to the left. The reason for both the arrangement and his fondness for the double basses is indicated in his letter to Giulio Ricordi in which he criticized their placement at the Teatro Carlo Felice, Genoa.

[Genoa, January 9, 1889]

Here in the orchestra they have placed all the double basses in one mass, like sheep; and the result is deplorable beyond belief. I will put it this way, when the double basses encircle the entire orchestra, with their dark sound they cover, or at least smother in part, the piercing sonority of the brass and the bad intonation of the woodwinds. And the sonority in the loud [passages] comes out full and imposing. Like this [i.e., as in Genoa] it is piercing and empty. Further, in the passages where the string section alone dominates, half of the spectators hear only an indistinct buzzing, and the other half hear too much.

(Abbiati IV, 368)

See also Verdi's letter (1888) to Franco Faccio (de Rensis, 253–54; Abbiati IV, 354–55). In this letter, nine double basses are specified. In a letter to Mascheroni (December 8, 1893) Verdi says "if you placed the double basses in a single row near the stage, the brasses remain too exposed and there would be [. . .] a reflection of sound from the walls of the theater." (Abbiati IV, 521–22.)

menti]. For example, if I said that the women's chorus in B major, Act II [beginning of Part 2] must be played lightly, very evanescently, you could say to me, "*Sig. Maestro, you have orchestrated it too heavily [istrumentato troppo].*" Agreed that it is heavily [*molto*] orchestrated, but observe that all those playful figures in the orchestra are not difficult to perform, and once the player has read them, he can give them all the light, evanescent [dynamic] shading the piece and the dramatic situation require. Certainly, in order to perform this kind [of composition] well, the orchestra player must have no fear of the notes, and he must have rehearsed sufficiently to know the notes almost by memory in order to apply himself completely to the expression and the dynamic shading. These are always the most difficult things to perform well. A good orchestra will perform well in two or three rehearsals the last movement of the *William Tell* Overture, and [yet] two or three rehearsals will not suffice to shade with refinement this little chorus.

I am dwelling upon this at length [. . .] [because] our rehearsals are always insufficient to perform these pieces well. What I've said of the chorus can be said of the "Dialogue *a tre*" which comes after the Song of the Veil [Act II, Part 2]. The orchestra there is richly nourished, but if the first violins have the courage to efface themselves somewhat, all the others will follow them with a pianissimo. Moreover, that violin figure cannot be effective unless performed with great lightness of the bow. Therefore, in these two pieces, I urge you, *Sig. Maestro*, mainly to watch the violins: so that the tempos may be calm, that nothing there be agitated, and that everything breathes the greatest elegance . . .

The first chorus, ⅜, Act III [original version], should not be too fast and should be uniform with Eboli's solo.

In this way there won't be movements in two tempos.

I know that the ballet [Act III, original version] goes very well, but I urge that you do the *Valzer* somewhat broadly[22] so that the clarinet solo there may come out more expressively. Even the variation in G may be rather broad and it will be more elegant. When the clarinet takes the *Valzer* the second time, all the strings should be playing *ppp* ... and they produce a distant murmuring. Here too it might be said that there are too many instruments; no, were there even a thousand strings, they would never cover the clarinet if the bow is used well.

In the duet of Eboli and Carlo in D flat [Act III, Part 1] I urge a great *sotto voce* for the orchestra up to the words "or dimentico il mondo."[23]

I know that the Finale [Act III, Part II] goes very well and I compliment you for this. However, watch that the *mis-en-scène* does not spoil things and cause confusion.

The Inquisitor scene is also going well and I renew my compliments. Don't forget the orchestral passage of which I wrote the other day.

In Act V, in the scene for Carlo and Elisabeth, I recommend to your attention two orchestral passages: the first, on the words "Sogno dorato io feci" [actually: "Vago sogno m'arride"],[24] is nothing but a crescendo, but if the gradation is done well, there is an effect. The other is between the violins and the cellos in C minor:[25]

Expression very great, but at the same time very calm and no violent accentuation.

In general I urge you to take great care with the delicate things and to perform them so that the piani should truly be piani and the tempos should be lively without being convulsed and violent, except in the situations where the action requires it. The lack of delicacy and [excessive] violence

22. Ricordi, Ger. ed. p. 388.
23. Ricordi, five-act revised version: 157, II, 1, to 158, last measure.
24. Ibid., 334, II, 2, to 375, III, 2.
25. Original version, Paris: Escudier, Plate no. L.E. 2765, 344, I, 2. In the revised version, C-sharp minor, 340, II, 2.

are the capital sins of our orchestras because our poor players always have tired arms, and they don't rehearse enough to perform well the delicate things and the things with few notes. But here is the chance, *Sig. Maestro,* to hold firm and rehearse as many times as are necessary [. . .]

(de Bellis, 540–41)

The following year Verdi complained to Giulio Ricordi that

[August 7, 1869]

[. . .] In *D. Carlos* I always hear talk about some duets or the aria in Act V ["Tu che la vanità"], but never of the third act, which is the climax and, I would say, the heart of the drama; nor ever of the Inquisitor's scene, which is elevated somewhat above the other pieces [. . .]

(Abiatti III, 290)

While preparing *Don Carlos* for Naples, Verdi wrote again to Giulio, this time with specific suggestions concerning the third-act finale:

October 10, 1872

[. . .] [For] the voice from heaven [. . .] find a good little soprano [who sings] in tune [and] whom we can send up in the *rafters* of the theater. Six [Flemish] Deputies are [too] few, find at least *2 or 4* more.

(Abbiati III, 607)

There are several French production books for *Don Carlos* in Paris, and Ricordi apparently printed three different editions in Milan, two of which have come to light:

Disposizione scenica per l'Opera Don Carlo . . . Milano, Napoli, Firenze: Regio Stabilimento Tito di Gio. Ricordi [ca. 1867], 55p. Plate no. 40699. "*Compilata e regolata secondo la mise en scène del Teatro Imperiale dell'Opéra a Parigi.*"

Disposizione scenica per l'Opera Don Carlo . . . Terza edizione. Milano, Napoli, Roma, Firenze, Londra: Regio Stabilimento Musicale Ricordi, [c. 1887]. 42p. Plate no. 51142. *"Compilata e regolata secondo la mise en scène del Teatro Imperiale dell'Opéra di Parigi."* The first performance of this edition (i.e. the revised four-act version without "Io la vidi" plus the original first act of the 1867 version) took place in Modena, 1886.

Otello (Milan, 1887)

Verdi's deep insight into his characters, especially Iago, is evident in his letters to his friend Domenico Morelli, the Neapolitan painter. At an early stage Verdi had even considered naming the opera after his most impressive villain. The first of these letters is in response to a verbal description of some projected sketches, the other to the sketches themselves.

Genoa, February 7, 1880

Good, very good, extremely good! Iago with the face of a gentleman. You've hit it. Oh I knew it, I was sure of it. I seem to see him, this *priest,* that is, this Iago with the face of a righteous man [. . .] This Iago is Shakespeare, he is humanity, that is, a part of humanity, the ugly [part].

(Copial. 693, 694; Abbiati IV, 111, 112)

St. Agata, September 24, 1881

[. . .] That Iago should be dressed in black, as black as his soul, nothing better; but I don't understand why you dressed Otello as a Venetian! I know quite well that this general in the service of the Venetian Republic with the name of Otello was none other than Giacomo Moro, a Venetian. But since Sig. Guglielmo [Shakespeare] wanted a Moor, he conceived him so. Otello dressed as a Turk would be unacceptable; but why couldn't he be dressed as an Ethiopian without the usual turban? For the type of figure of Iago, [. . .] you would like a small figure, of (you say) underdeveloped limbs, and, if I have understood correctly, one of those sly, malignant figures. I would say *pointed*. Very well: if you feel him like that, do him like that. But if I were an actor and had to play Iago, I would rather have a long and thin figure, thin lips, small eyes set close to the nose like a monkey's, broad, receding brow, and the head developed behind; an absent, *nonchalant* manner, indifferent to everything, witty, speaking good and evil almost lightheartedly, and having the air of not even thinking of what he says; so that, if someone were to reproach him: "What you say is vile!" he could answer: "Really? I didn't think so . . . we'll say no more about it! . . ."

A figure like this can deceive everyone, and even up to a point his wife. A small, malicious figure arouses everyone's suspicion and deceives nobody! *Amen.* [. . .]

(Copial. 317–18; Abbiati IV, 183; translation in part
from Weaver, 239–40)

As the composition neared completion, the date of the premiere drew closer and singers had to be chosen for the parts. Verdi's letters to Giulio Ricordi, who functioned as his liaison with the management of La Scala, began to include comments on the vocal requirements of the music.

Genoa, January 18, 1886
[. . .] In many and many a thing Tamagno [the future Otello] would do extremely well, but in a great number of others, no. There are some broad, extended, legato phrases where the words are produced *mezza voce,* a thing impossible for him. And what is worse, the first act would end coldly, and (what is even worse than that), the fourth!! There is a short but broad melody, and then (after he has stabbed himself) some very important phrases *mezza voce* . . . and we cannot do without them! [. . .]

(Abbiati IV, 273–74)

Friday [Genoa, January 22, 1886]
[. . .] There is nothing like these [high notes by Meyerbeer
and Ponchielli] in *Otello*. After he has confirmed the fact
that Desdemona was innocent [when] murdered, Otello no
longer has any strength: he's worn out, physically and mor-
ally exhausted: he is unable to nor should he sing more
than in a veiled, half-dead voice . . . this last is a certain
quality lacking in Tamagno. He must always sing with a full
voice, otherwise the sound comes out ugly, uncertain, out-
of-tune . . . This is a very serious matter, which gives me
much to think about! I prefer not to give the opera rather
than have that point in the score inadequately projected
[. . .]

(Abbiati IV, 274)

St. Agata, November 11, 1886
[. . .] Iago cannot be performed, and is not possible, without extraordinarily fine pronunciation, like Maurel's [. . .]
In that part it is necessary neither to sing, nor to raise one's
voice (with few exceptions). If, for example, I were a singing actor, I would do everything with lips pursed, *mezza
voce.* [. . .]

(Abbiati IV, 299)

After coaching Romilda Pantaleoni (Desdemona), Verdi
wrote to Franco Faccio, entrusted with conducting the
Otello premiere as he had been with the European premiere of *Aida* some fifteen years before.

St. Agata, September 2, 1886
[. . .] I've sent to Giulio [Ricordi] the fourth act, in which
Desdemona has the greatest and most difficult part. The
Willow Song presents enormous difficulties for the composer as well as for the performing artist. The latter, like
the Holy Trinity, must produce three voices, one for Desdemona, another for Barbara (the maid) and a third voice
for the "Salce, salce, salce."

Mme. Pantaleoni's voice, accustomed to violent parts, many times has high notes a bit too harsh. I would say there is something too metallic. If she could accustom herself to sing a little more with a head [voice] she would produce the [necessary] attenuation and her voice would also be more steady and more accurate.

[. . .] it is not true that her D is, as she says, a very bad note. There is a passage [*canto*] in which it comes out very well.

This phrase is repeated three times. The last time she succeeds nicely, the other two less so [. . .] They will all be very good if she will make them less biting, and all with a *head* [voice]; moreover, I've advised her to sing that way in many other places. If there is anything to criticize, it is in the [love] scene from the first act. There something lighter, more ethereal would be preferable, and, let us say it, something more voluptuous, as the situation and the poetry require. She performs [*dice*] her solo [passages] very well but with too much emphasis and too dramatically.

(Morazzoni, 44)

Verdi's attention to detail was obviously extraordinary, but always in the service of the drama. In the following letter to Giulio he objected to the publisher's German translation at two critical places in the last act.

January 22, 1888

[. . .] In the Willow Song the repetition of the word ["Salce"] neither has nor should have any meaning, it is an undefined voice that belongs neither to Desdemona nor to Barbara; it is a sound that is heard, but, let me put it this way, is not made clear [. . .] And, therefore, one should not say in that moment "Green Willow"—what difference whether green or yellow! Arrange it so that "Weide, Weide, Weide" [Willow, Willow, Willow] is always performed.

More serious yet; at the end, when Otello says "Desdemona, Desdemona, Desdemona . . . ah morta, morta,

morta!" A natural and heart-rending exclamation! The translation has produced a phrase neither beautiful nor natural . . . "Sweet dear dead one" or something like that. At this point there should be neither a poetic nor a musical phrase. I myself, even I, have had the good sense to produce only some sounds that have almost no tonality! Have the translator adjust the verse as he likes, but he should say three times only "morta, morta, morta!"

(Abbiati IV, 356)

Some months after the premiere on February 5, 1887, Verdi complained to Giulio Ricordi of Pantaleoni's failure to understand the part of Desdemona.

Genoa, April 22, 1887

[. . .] Judging the character of Desdemona *terre à terre;* a female who allows herself to be mistreated, slapped, and even strangled, forgives and entreats, she appears to be a stupid little thing! But Desdemona is not a woman, she's a type! She's the type of goodness, of resignation, of sacrifice! They are creatures born for others, unconscious of their own *ego!* Beings that exist in part, and that Shakespeare has poetized and deified, creating Desdemona, Cordelia, Juliet, etc., etc., types that have never been encountered, except perhaps in Antigone of the ancient theater [. . .]

(Abbiati IV, 332)

And again to Giulio some weeks later:

Genoa, May 11, 1887

[. . .] Desdemona is a part where the thread, the melodic line never stops from the first to the last note. Just as Iago must only declaim and sneer. Just as Otello, now warrior, now passionate lover, now cast down into the filth, now as ferocious as a savage, must sing and howl; so Desdemona must always sing.

[. . .] I repeat, Desdemona sings from the first note of the recitative, which is still a melodic phrase, until the last note,

"Otello non uccidermi . . ." . . . which is still a melodic phrase. Therefore, the most perfect Desdemona will always be the one who sings best. [. . .]

(Abbiati IV, 337)

After the premiere, Verdi also had some second thoughts about the staging and the sets. He wrote to Giulio,

Monday [Genoa, March 14, 1887]

Yesterday, in Nervi, while descending the grand staircase of the Eden Hotel with Boito and Du Locle, I said, "Here is the stage setting for the second act of *Otello*." The lobby of that hotel is imposing and very beautiful. It has three large windows; outside, a garden (still young); and beyond the garden, the sea.

Therefore, for [Act II of] *Otello,* a shallow set almost at the curtain and in the fabric many windows separated by slender columns, Moorish or Venetian, etc., etc. Beyond the windows a huge park with a large open space and a broad avenue, and others, smaller, crossing . . . and all kinds of plants, and trees; the sea, yes or no, as you please. The glass windows made with very transparant metallic cloth, without fear for the voices! Thus the desired dramatic action would take place, and the public would understand, rather would sense the fact that two events, two actions are taking place simultaneously at that moment: a *festivity* for Desdemona [and] a *conspiracy* between Iago and Otello.

Zuccarelli's set may also be beautiful, if you will, but it is still wrong. Turn back, I repeat for the thousandth time [. . .] there is nothing to be done but a large window. The great palaces still have the reception hall completely clear . . . all with large windows [. . .] In a word, that set must show to the public two well-marked and distinct locales: *a large park for Desdemona's festivity, a very large room for Otello and Iago.*

(Abbiati IV, 328)

Verdi was still not satisfied with the garden scene in Act II, and a prospective revival at La Scala caused him to write once more to Giulio Ricordi:

Genoa, January 1, 1889

[. . .] First of all the stage sets do not convince me. They may have been so many operatic masterworks, but they did not assist the development of the action of the drama. The first scene lacked space and depth, therefore cramping the action. The garden scene was too deep. I would change the third [scene] and make two: a small room inside for the first scene between Otello, Desdemona, Iago, and Cassio. Then, a set change in sight [of the audience] for the remainder [of the scene]. [. . .] Then you must find something better for that wretched bonfire scene [*fuoco di gioia,* Act I].

As far as the music goes, it isn't necessary to make corrections either in the dynamics or in the tempos [. . .]

Once more the solo for the double basses [Act IV, Sc. 2] has had an indecent performance at La Scala; and I reproach myself for not having thought of a remedy. [. . .] The task of noting the positions should have been given to the most able bass player and some rehearsals held separately. Now that the positions are notated by Bottesini, Faccio doesn't have anything to do except make [the bass players] play precisely, without paying attention to the tittle-tattle, to the observations that will be made by all those who don't know how to play well.

I would try something else with the chorus in the garden. I would have the solos performed by one voice alone.

1. a good boy for the first solo
2. a good baritone for the second
3. a good soprano for the third

Accompaniment, a single mandolin and a single guitar with only eight choristers for the notes of the accompaniment, and maybe even without these!

(Abbiati IV, 366; translation in part from
WalkerI, 18)

A single place in the opera still troubled Verdi: the finale of the third act. Here are two letters less than a week apart to Giulo Ricordi.

Genoa, February 3, 1889

[. . .] I would like to reduce the orchestra in the concerted section of the third-act finale at measure 38 in E$^{\flat}$ minor for 11 measures, then again for another 11 measures from the C minor to the *più mosso* at measure 82, using only 6 first violins, 6 seconds, 4 violas, 2 cellos, 2 basses. In the same section I would stage the choruses well grouped, very much isolated, and well back, so that Iago can dominate and attract attention with his movements, his actions, and his infamous words to Otello and Rodrigo, without being disturbed by the deep uproar in the orchestra. And here, it is really to the point to do *nothing* in the orchestra; *nothing* which would be dramatic. I seem to hear all the buts and ifs of opposition on account of the difficulties of holding rehearsals with the orchestra. But I answer: if instead of holding rehearsals with the orchestra alone, rehearsals that are always useless, damaging, rather, to the ensemble in the *concertato,* you were to hold one, two, three, four, or more rehearsals together with the stage action of these sections, you would succeed in the end in finding some effect, perhaps.

(partially in Abbiati IV, 371; partially in WalkerI, 18–19)

Genoa, February 9, 1889

[. . .] Thinking it over again, I am persuaded that the solos in the chorus of the second act must really be performed by one voice only, with a light accompaniment of voices and [instrumental] sounds. It should emerge more quietly, more modestly, more simply, more, I would put it this way, innocently, thereby reinforcing [literally, in sympathy with] the character of Desdemona. For example, one boy offering flowers performs a polite and innocent gesture; six boys become vulgar. And so on for the rest [of the scene].

I return again to the third-act finale. Here too there can be no dramatic truth, nor effect, if Iago is not completely isolated so that the eyes of the public are riveted on him alone; so that his words, not his voice, dominates everything and one hears only an indistinct and, if you will, an inexact murmuring! Inexact! This word makes a musician's hair stand on end, but that doesn't matter.

Conclusion: stage setting, wide and deep; choruses far off—very far off; Iago well in view; orchestra reduced.

(partially in Abbiati IV, 372; partially in WalkerI, 19)

With regard to costumes, there is an interesting letter from Boito to Verdi:

Quinto, May 16, 1886

[. . .] our period is set thus by [Shakespeare's source] Giraldi: *a short time before 1527.* I believe I was not mistaken in setting [. . .] the outside limit of 1525. A couple of years' margin between the event and the story of the event does not seem too many to me.

[. . .] I have advised the costume designer to study the Venetian painters of the last years of the fifteenth century and the first quarter of the sixteenth. Luckily for us, the two great documents in that space of years are Carpaccio and Gentile Bellini! From their paintings will come the costumes of our characters. [. . .]

(translation from Weaver, 242–43;
Abbiati IV, 284)

Finally, a bibliographical note on the production book for *Otello,* which is the most extensive of the eight extant *disposizioni sceniche* published by Ricordi:[26]

Ricordi, Giulio. *Disposizione scenica per l'Opera OTELLO* di Verdi. Milan: Ricordi [c.1888]. Plate no. 52159. *"compilata e regolata secondo la messa in scena del teatro alla Scala,"*

26. See also the article by Doug Coe, "The Original Production Book for *Otello," 19th Century Music* 2 (November 1978) and RosenS.

Falstaff (Milan, 1893)

A production book for *Falstaff* was assigned a plate number by the Casa Ricordi, but a copy has not yet come to light. (Was it ever printed?) However, we are fortunate in having an exchange of letters about the opera between Verdi and his librettist for the work, Arrigo Boito,[27] as well as many more letters from Verdi to Giulio Ricordi, who was to all intents and purposes the stage director for the premiere and perhaps the first stage director in the modern sense of the word. This was a function Giulio must have also fulfilled for *Aida,* and the revision of *Simon Boccanegra,* since he wrote their production books, as well as the one for *Otello.* Verdi's letters to others help provide additional information.

Perhaps the remark of most general interest on *Falstaff* is to be found in a letter to the Marquis Gino Monaldi, one of Verdi's biographers:

> December 3, 1890
>
> What can I tell you? For forty years I have wanted to write a comic opera, and for fifty years I have known *The Merry Wives of Windsor* . . .
>
> Falstaff is a scoundrel who commits all sorts of malicious deeds . . . but in an entertaining manner. He is a *type!* [And] there are so many different types! The opera is completely comic.
>
> (Copial. 712)

Early in their collaboration, Verdi and Boito, to whom the following letter is addressed, recognized the main problem with *Falstaff,* and indeed with all comic operas, namely the absence of a tension-building plot line which is

---

27. The complete Verdi-Boito correspondence has been prepared and printer's proofs corrected by the Istituto di Studi Verdiani, Parma. For that portion pertaining to the revision of *Simon Boccanegra* (Italian and English) see Noske, 215–40.

released once and for all at the denoument near the end of a tragedy.

Montecatini, July 6, 1889

Excellent! Excellent!

Before reading your sketch, I wanted to reread the *Merry Wives*, the two parts of *Henry IV*, and *Henry V*, and I can only repeat: *Excellent*, for one could not do better than you have done.

A pity that the interest (it's not your fault) does not go on increasing to the end. The climax is the finale of the second act; and the appearance of Falstaff's face amid the laundry, etc., is a true comic invention.

I'm afraid, too, that the last act, in spite of its touch of fantasy, will be trivial, with all those little pieces, songs, ariettas, etc. etc. You bring back Bardolfo—and why not Pistola, too, both of them to get up to some prank or other?

You reduce the weddings to two! All the better, for they are only loosely connected with the main plot.

The two trials by water and fire suffice to punish Falstaff: nevertheless, I should like to see him thoroughly well beaten also. [. . .]

(translation from Weaver, 245)

See also Boito's thoughtful comments on the laws of serious and comic theater (Carteggi II, 144–45).

Verdi's fondness for the character of Alice reveals itself in this excerpt from a letter to Giulio Ricordi.

St. Agata, September 2, 1893

[. . .] you must pay close attention to Alice's role . . . La Zilli, who has much talent and understanding and moves [well on stage], does not, however, have the elastic voice [necessary] for that part, nor the jaunty appearance. I repeat, she is good, but she does not render the role with that fire that it demands [. . .]. Alice is the first part after Falstaff. Don't encumber yourself with performers for *Falstaff* who want to sing too much, and effect sentiment and action by falling asleep on the notes [. . .]

(Abbiati IV, 517)

At the prospect of a revival some years later, Verdi wrote to Giulio,

Genoa, February 27, 1899

[. . .] If Toscanini is not experienced, the others are even less so. Soon the revival of *Falstaff*. Everything is in reverse. Falstaff will be good (perhaps!) but Alice no. . . . And take note, the protagonist of *Falstaff* is not Falstaff but Alice. What am I saying!

(Abbiati IV, 637–38)

Verdi explained his thinking on the relative importance of the two parts in a letter to Carvalho, director of the Opéra-Comique prior to their performance of the opera.

Genoa, February 11, 1894

[. . .] pay close attention to the role of Alice. First of all, it is understood that it requires a lovely, very agile voice; but above all an actress and a person who has the *devil inside of her* [diable au corps]. Alice's role is not as extended as Falstaff's, but theatrically she has as much [to do]. It is Alice who manages the entire intrigue of the comedy [. . .]

(Copial. 390, in French)

A long letter to Giulio includes additional comments on Alice as well as other valuable observations.

St. Agata, June 13, 1892

You talk to me of sending painters to London [. . .] of scenes, of costumes, of stage mechanics, of lighting. In order to do sets for the theater, one must have painters for the theater. Painters who would not have the vanity to value their own technical brilliance but [rather] serve the

Drama. For the love of God, let's not do as we did for *Otello*. In trying to do things well, it was overdone.

As for the mechanical aspect, there's little to do, apart from the scene of the [laundry] basket, which doesn't present difficulties, as long as [the staging staff] doesn't make pointless complications. Regarding lighting effects, there's need only of a bit of darkness in the forest scenes, but let it be well understood, a darkness that allows the faces of the actors to be seen. [. . .]

Now let's come to the most serious [matters] . . . La Fabbri[28] may have some success in her cantabiles with her beautiful voice on the basis of agility, as in Rossini's *Cenerentola,* etc., etc. But the part of Quickly is something else again. Song and action are required, great stage presence, and precise accentuation on the right syllable. She doesn't have these qualities. And we risk sacrificing the most characteristic and original of the four [women].

The part of Alice requires the same qualities, in addition a vivacity considerably greater. She must have the devil in her. It is she who leads the chase. [Virginia] Guerrini, fine in the part of Meg, and I'm sorry the role isn't more important.

Nannetta must be very young, quite sparkling on stage, and she must sing extremely well; above all, in the two small duets with the tenor, one of them quite lively and very comic.

[. . .] Pessina is a good artist,[29] but as far as I'm concerned, he is more singer than actor and a bit heavy for Ford's part. Furiously jealous, he howls, shouts, jumps, etc.; without which the effectiveness of the second-act finale would be lost. All the attention is directed at him, and only in fits and starts at Falstaff when he sticks his face outside the basket.

[. . .] Cesare is too [good] for the part of Pistola, but if he is content with it, it could be expanded, by giving him some

28. She was not given the part.
29. He was bypassed, as well as Cesare.

of Bardolfo's lines. For the part of Bardolfo, we also need an actor sufficiently self-confident, and who knows how to move [about the stage]. [. . .]

The music isn't difficult, but it must be sung differently from all the other modern comic operas, and not at all like the old opera buffa. I don't want it sung, for example, as if one were singing *Carmen*, and not at all like *Don Pasquale* [. . .] In general, our singers always use a fat tone; they neither have elasticity in their voices, nor clear and easy pronunciation, and they often lack [proper] accentuation and breath.

(Abbiati IV, 442–44; somewhat differently in Carteggi IV, 215 and WalkerI, 19–20)

Concerning Nannetta and Fenton, Boito wrote to Verdi,

July 7, 1889

[. . .] This love-making between Nannetta and Fenton must appear suddenly, frequently; in all the scenes where they are present, they will steal kisses secretly in corners, slyly, boldly, without letting themselves be seen, with fresh little phrases and brief little dialogues, rapid and clever from the beginning to the end of the play; it will be a most lively, merry love, always disturbed and interrupted and always ready to begin again . . . I should like, as one sprinkles sugar on a cake, to sprinkle the whole comedy with that gay love, not collecting it all together at any one point. [. . .]

(translation from WalkerV, 497; also in Weaver, 245)

Verdi responded, obviously with a draft of the libretto in hand.

[July 12, 1889]

All of your thinking is good [. . .] within two weeks I'll begin on our comedy [. . .] But we must have the marriage. Without the marriages there can be no contentment [. . .] and Fenton and Nannette must marry. That love of theirs pleases me, it makes the entire comedy fresher and firmer. That love must enliven everything and [be there] always, in such a way that I would *almost* eliminate the duet for the two lovers. In its own way that love is present in every ensemble. It is present in Part II of the second act [and] in Parts I and II of the third.[30] [. . .]

(Abbiati IV, 388)

On the part of Fenton itself, Verdi wrote to Giulio,

[late June or early July, 1892]

[. . .] the part [. . .] certainly does not have the importance of the parts of Falstaff, Ford, Alice, etc.

It is [however] a charming part, comic, witty, with some scenes for singing, for example the *Sonnet* [Act III, Part 2] which he sings at midnight in Windsor Forest [. . .] To sum up [. . .] a gracious, witty character who takes part in many scenes, without [his part] being exhausting. (Except for the *Sonnet*) a part for the *note,* the *word,* and the *gesture* . . .

(Abbiati IV, 445–46)

And again to Giulio:

Genoa, December 21, 1892

[. . .] I am uneasy about the *Sonnet,* not because it is particularly important to me as a piece. Strictly speaking, even as action it could be omitted; but because that fragment gives me a new color in musical composition and it completes the character of Fenton . . .

(Abbiati IV, 469)

After hearing Edoardo Garbin (Fenton), Verdi complained

Genoa, November 16, 1892

[. . .] he has that cursed defect of opening the final vowels of words . . . for example . . . [in the line from the sonnet] "la nota che non è più solo" he does not at all put the accent

---

30. As well as Part 2 of Act I. Abbiati, who doesn't refer to the letter by Boito cited above, concludes this letter exactly as had Boito.

on the *o* but on the *a* in a way which ends up distorting and changing the timbre of the voice. . . . This is a serious defect and difficult to correct.

(Abbiati IV, 466)

After hearing Emma Zilli (Alice), Verdi wrote to Giulio that she must

[. . .] Keep her voice steady, loosen her tongue and pronounce clearly. . . .

(Abbiati IV, 450)

In a note to Pasqua (Quickly), Verdi warned that her solo in the second part of Act II

Genoa, November 5, 1892

[. . .] must be performed *prestissimo, mezza voce,* with a single breath, each syllable clear and distinct [. . .]

(Abbiati IV, 465)

Concerning the *mise-en-scène* for the second part of the last act and the finale of Act II, Verdi wrote to Giulio,

St. Agata, September 18, 1892

[. . .] Nothing easier and simpler than this *mise-en-scène,* if the painter will make a setting as I saw it when I was writing the music. Nothing more than a large, real garden, with broad paths, groups of shrubs and trees here and there, so that one can at will hide, re-appear, disappear, as the drama and the music require. For example, [At this point in Verdi's letter, the sketch at the top of the page opposite appeared.]

In this way the men will have their place apart, and could afterwards invade also that of the women, when the latter are no longer on the stage. Thus at the end of the act the women could occupy the men's position. Don't say anything to anybody (not even to Boito) about these scrawls of mine, but see that Hohenstein's ideas are more or less in conformity with mine.

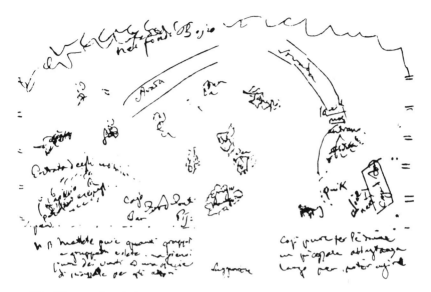

Verdi's pen sketch for Act II, Part 2

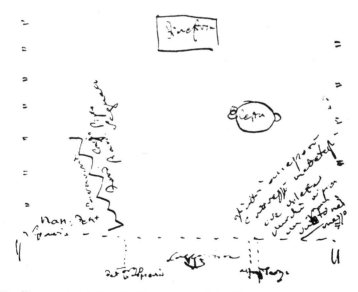

Verdi's pen sketch for the final scene of Act II

Tito told me that Hohenstein proposed to put the screen near the wings, "because it is natural and logical that a screen should lean against the wall." Not at all, here it's a matter of a screen, so to speak, in action, and it is necessary to put it wherever the action demands, all the more as Alice says at a certain point: "More this way; more that way; open a little wider;" etc., etc. The scene of the second *finale must be almost completely clear, to give room for the action and to allow the principal groups–those of the screen, of the* [laundry] basket and of the window—to be seen quite distinctly [. . .] [See Verdi's sketch, bottom of page 173.]

(translation mainly from WalkerI, 19–20, which omits the sketches; Copial. 379–81; Abbiati IV, 458–59, without sketches)

And a final bit of advice to Giulio concerning the last scene of the opera:

Wednesday [early '93, probably after January 28] [. . .] I only ask a little light for Garbin's [Fenton's] *Sonnet*. And if possible find a way to avoid the impression of *Vestals* that I get from the chorus of Fairies [. . .]

(Abbiati IV, 471)

Tempo and Character

In his article "Tempo and Character in the Music of Verdi" (*Atti* 3, 238–43), René Leibowitz says (p. 239),

[. . .] A life long preoccupation with Verdi's works has taught me that, among all of the followers of Beethoven, Verdi is certainly one of the few composers whose convictions regarding the interrelationship between tempo and character are the most profound and the most articulate. [. . .]

On the next page Leibowitz also remarks

[. . .] Generally speaking, one can say that slow movements are relatively rare in all of Verdi's operas. Such categories as: *andante, andantino, larghetto* should not, as we know, be classified among slow movements.

He then goes on to cite evidence from the scores. The Verdi correspondence provides additional support for these observations. For example, Verdi's close friend Opprandino Arrivabene wrote to him on March 17, 1870, "They say that you are the master of the quick tempos [*il maestro dei tempi celeri*]."

In explaining the lack of success of his works in Paris, Verdi several times made the point to Léon Escudier, "I am more than ever convinced that for works of music you must have first of all a musical performance: *fire, spirit, muscle,* and *enthusiasm* [emphasis Verdi's], all these [qualities] are lacking at the Opéra." (Letter of March 30, 1872, Busch, 292–93; Abbiati III, 567–68.)

Thirty years before, Verdi had written to the president of La Fenice about the Venetian premiere of *Nabucco.*

> October 19, 1842
> Here is the *Adagio* for Signora Granchi. If it is too high transpose it down a [whole] step. I ask your lordship's kindness in seeing to it that the orchestral score and parts taken from it are returned [to me as soon as they have been used] because I want the score to remain as it has been written. I also ask you to inform the maestro who will actually rehearse *Nabucco* that the tempos are not slow. They all move quickly, and especially the canon in the second finale.
> (Lawton, 360; Lawton-Rosen, 209)

A year and a half later, he wrote to Leone Herz with regard to the Viennese premiere of *Ernani.*

> Milan, April 18, 1844
> [. . .] The tempos are all marked on the score with the [greatest] possible clarity. Enough that you pay attention to the dramatic situation and the text, [and only] with difficulty can you mistake a tempo. Only I caution [you that] I

do not like slow tempos; it is better to err on the side of liveliness than to drag. Again I thank you for your attention, and because you wish to perform *Ernani* correctly. On which account I ask that the parts be entrusted to those artists best received by the public, and that the performance be accurate [. . .]

P.S. I ask that no cuts be allowed. There is nothing to remove and the smallest phrase could not be taken away without damaging the whole.[31] I want to point out that the conspiracy [scene] in the third act should be neither too slow nor too fast. The tempo is precisely like that of the Prophecy in *Nabucco* at the words "pietra ove sorge l'altro, etc." Further, I ask that you press a bit at the end. . . .

(Morazzoni, 27)

Anticipating a performance of *Don Carlos* in Parma, Verdi wrote to the conductor, Giulio Ferrarini:

March 26, 1869

It would take too long, and I would say be almost impossible to write to you all my intentions about *Don Carlos*. Besides, I believe that you and Maestro Rossi [the chorus master] have heard this opera at Bologna and Milan. At Milan the performance was limp, colorless, and almost all the tempos too slow. Without doubt at Bologna it must have been better. The only recommendation I can make is not to allow cadenzas, sleeping on notes, and to keep the tempos lively. In *La forza del destino* given just now in Milan, there were no cadenzas, no distortions, and therefore it was effective and applauded. There was an animation, a vivacity in the [orchestral and choral] groups never surpassed in Milan.

(Damerini, letter no. 3)

The poor performance of *Don Carlos* in Milan was the one about which Verdi had written in the letters to Maz-

---

31. There were in fact extensive cuts made, as Verdi's letter to Herz of June 7, 1844 indicates. See Morazzoni, 27.

zucato cited earlier. Unfortunately, Verdi's opinion of Ferrarini's performance was to be no better. (See below, "On Conductors, Singers, and Choruses.") The performance of *Forza* referred to was the premiere of the revised version, rehearsed and directed by Verdi himself.

Concerning the ballet for the revised version of *Macbeth*, Verdi wrote to Escudier early in 1865,

> [. . .] Please ask the orchestral conductor to keep an eye on the ballet rehearsals from time to time. The dancers always alter the tempos and thereby the ballet would lose all its character and fail to produce the effect of which I think it capable [. . .]
>
> (Abbiati II, 817; draft in Copial. 452–53;
> Osborne, 136)

And to Giulio Ricordi he wrote about the ballet for *Aida:*

> Genoa, August 10, 1871
> [. . .] I am very pleased that you have reached an agreement with Monplaisir about the ballet, thank him on my behalf. I would be very happy if he were willing to choreograph the little dances in *Aida.* I know he is very knowledgeable about the Orient, and he will certainly do characteristic and original things. Have the sheets of the three dances copied, and ask Monplaisir to take care that all the tempos be just as indicated by the metronome [. . .]
>
> (translation from Busch, 200; Abbiati III, 466)

Finally, an excerpt from a well-known letter by Verdi to the husband of the soprano Teresa De Giuli-Borsi about *Rigoletto:*

> [1852]
> As to the cavatina in the first act ["Caro nome"], I do not understand where there's [a problem of] agility. Perhaps you have not divined the tempo, which must be an *Allegretto molto lento*. With a moderate tempo and a perfor-

mance *sotto voce*, there can be no difficulty. But returning to
the first argument. I conceived *Rigoletto* without arias, without finales, with an interminable string of duets because
that was my conviction [. . .]

(Abbiati II, 175; Hussey, 90)

On Conductors, Singers, and Choruses

Thursday [Genoa, February 11, 1869]
[. . .] Keep well in mind, my dear Giulio, that the success of
our operas rests most of the time in the hands of the conductor. This person is as necessary as a tenor or a prima
donna[. . .]

(Abbiati III, 249)

As in this letter to Giulio Ricordi, Verdi continually
argued for a strong, lively conductor. He also realized that
this person required strong support. To Arrigo Boito he
wrote,

[Spring 1891]
[. . .] Selecting the conductor is not enough. He must be independent of the management and he must assume absolute musical responsibility in the face of the commission,
the management, and the public. More: [there must be] a
good chorus master, always subject to the musical director,
who is charged not only with the musical training [of the
choruses] but also with the staging as imposed by a *Régis-
seur* (stage director); and at performances the chorus master or the assistant chorus master should be in costume and
sing in the choruses. More: there must be a stage director,
always subordinate to the musical head [director]. [. . .]

(Abbiati IV, 420)

Earlier in the letter, Verdi had actually recommended
Edoardo Mascheroni for the position of conductor and
musical director of La Scala. But some years before he had
his doubts about the musician who was later to conduct the
premiere of *Falstaff*. In the next letter Verdi's comments to

his friend and fellow senator, Giuseppe Piroli, are very much to the point, as usual.

> Milan, June 28, 1887
>
> [. . .] [I'm told] he neglects the ensemble with the singers, the so-called *piano rehearsals,* and by preference works with the orchestra. This is a very serious mistake!! There can be no good performance if first the rehearsals with the singers are not conducted well. The players of the orchestra have the music in front of their eyes. In general they know music better than singers, and they have the conductor in their midst to guide them, etc., etc. The singer is left to himself, preoccupied with the action, the movements, the voice; and in addition, those three or four thousand eyes fixed on him. Therefore, the expert and practiced conductor must concern himself first of all with the vocal ensemble [. . .]
>
> (Carteggi III, 183–84; Abbiati IV, 342)

Verdi frequently describes singers in his letters: their strengths, weaknesses, and especially their suitability for specific roles. The precise qualities that most interested him are revealed in this excerpt from a letter to Giulio Ricordi. The opera in question is *Don Carlos.*

> Genoa, January 11, 1868
>
> [. . .] Tell me about the quality and the power of their voices, about their intonation, their style of singing, their enunciation, and above all about their acting [. . .]
>
> (Abbiati III, 158)

When called upon himself to do the auditioning, he admitted to Giulio,

> June 17, 1892
>
> [. . .] I confess that I cannot [. . .] judge a singer in a room, and not even in an empty theater, without costumes and makeup [. . .]
>
> (Abbiati IV, 444)

During a newspaper interview held in Vienna (1875), Verdi made an interesting comparison between German and Italian singers of his day. On that visit he had successfully conducted his *Requiem* and *Aida,* and had also heard *Tannhäuser.* After discussing Wagner—he praised his rival for discarding outdated and Baroque forms and for his imaginative orchestration, but felt that his music was boring in the opera house—he said:

> [Vienna, 1875]
> [. . .] There is certainly no lack of voices in Germany. They are almost more sonorous than the Italian ones; but the singers consider singing as a sort of gymnastics, trouble themselves little about the cultivation of the voice, and strive only to build up a wide repertory in the shortest possible time. They take no trouble to get fine light and shade into their singing; all their efforts are directed to bringing out this or that note with the utmost force. Hence their singing is not the poetic expression of their souls, but the physical conflict of their bodies.
> (citation from Walker Vienna, 405)

In that same interview he admired the architecture and decorations of the new Staatsoper, but thought the stage inadequately ramped for large ensemble scenes.

Verdi's choruses were always important to him; and from the time of *Nabucco* they were extremely well received by his audiences. While preparing for the premiere of the revised *Forza,* he wrote to Giulio,

> Thursday [February 11, 1869]
> [. . .] I hope the rehearsals have continued well, with those accents and dynamic shadings that I've indicated. Advise the chorus master that he must make his choristers study [i.e. rehearse] well, with precision; and above all, that he not allow an uncertain *attack* to pass. *In the* [choral and orchestral] *groups the primary thing is the attack.* Tell him to do the small fragments [in Act III] "Pane, pan, per carità" and

the other passage which follows with precision and expression.

It is necessary at any cost to adjust the voices and the effect of the women's choruses in the Encampment Scene [Act III]. The solos for the contralto, as well as those for the sopranos, are unbearable. You might consider adjusting them by adding some boys to the contraltos and by finding some good voices [for] the sopranos . . .

(Abbiati III, 249–50)

And again to Giulio in a similar vein several years later as rehearsals progressed for the Milanese premiere of *Aida:*

Genoa, December 10, 1871
[. . .] urge the chorus master[. . .] to be very, very, very alert about the *downbeat.* It is the common defect of all Italian choruses to miss the attack or to attack weakly. Even those in Bologna, who are praised so much, have the same defect. Tell him also to watch out for the *open* voices [. . .] that seem to scream "shoe laces and knitting needles" [. ..] Should the opera be a fiasco, I want it to be on my account and not because of the performance[. . .]

(translation from Busch, 263)

It will come as no surprise that Verdi's strongest feelings were aroused by performers who took liberties with his music, as the following letters to Giulio Ricordi indicate:

Genoa, April 11, 1871
. . . I believe I should comment . . . on the "intuition" of conductors and on "creation at each performance." This is a principle that leads to the decadent [*barocco*] and the false. This is the road that led music to the decadent and the false at the end of the last century and in the first five years of the present one, when singers took it upon themselves (as the French still say) to "create" their roles, consequently bungling them and producing all sorts of contra-

dictions. No: I want only one creator, and I am content to hear simply and exactly what is written. The trouble is that one never hears what is written. I often read in the papers about "effects not imagined by the author." But, on my part, I have never, never found them. I know that everything you say is directed at Mariani. We all agree on his worth; but here we are talking not about an individual, no matter how great, but about art. I cannot concede the right to "create" to singers and conductors because, as I said before, it is a principle that leads into the abyss.

Do you want an example? Once you praised an effect that Mariani got out of the overture to *La forza del destino* by having the *brass* enter in G *fortissimo*. Well I disapprove of this effect. In my conception these brass instruments—*a mezza voce*—could not express anything but the religious chant of the monk [i.e., Padre Guardiano]. Mariani's *fortissimo* completely changes the character, and that section becomes a warlike fanfare, which has nothing to do with the subject of the drama, in which war is but an episodic part. And here we are on the road to the decadent and the false.

(translation for the most part from Busch, 150–51;
Abbiati III, 447–48)

Some years later a series of performances of *Aida* in Rome occasioned the following outburst:

Genoa, March 30, 1875
[. . .] What is certain and historical is that *Aida* in Rome is a real *puppet show*. Tenors who sing baritone and sopranos who sing contralto; a conductor who lowers the notes and changes the tempos; an artist who refuses to continue singing her role: these things are intolerable. Don't speak to me about the effect, which, after all, is not what it could have been; and, above all, don't speak to me about [the effect of] the judgment scene in the fourth act, which is precisely what desolates me. When a *piece,* or even an *entire section,* stands out too much, that is harmful to the *whole.* It is no longer drama, but concert. Let the artist have his piece, if the drama calls for it; but he must be more or less consis-

tent throughout and contribute to the totality of the musical structure. For these reasons (which I have never been
able to make understood), I never wanted to write for la
Patti [. . .]

It is said that *Aida* will be done here. (I am sorry because
that banishes me from Genoa for a while.) It is also said
that they want to sign Ponchielli and Berini. No: that's impossible. They are two sopranos, and *Amneris* must have
the voice and *character* of a contralto. La Waldmann, for
example, can sing high *A's* and *B♭'s* as much as she wants,
but she will always be a contralto. [. . .]

(translation from Busch, 381; Abbiati III, 746–47)

Some days earlier Verdi had expressed himself even more
forcefully:

Genoa, March 25, 1875

[. . .] And what's more, a conductor who takes the liberty of
changing the tempos!!! [. . .] We don't need conductors
and singers to discover new effects; for my part, I declare
that no one has ever, ever, ever been able, or known how,
to draw out *all* the effects conceived by me. . . . *No one!!!*
Never, never . . . neither singers nor conductors!! But it is
fashionable now to *applaud* even conductors, and I feel
sorry for the few I esteem; even more, I feel sorry for those
who pass on indecencies in the opera house from one to
the other without end. At one time we had to endure the
tyranny of prima donnas; now we'll also have to endure
that of conductors of the orchestra! [. . .]

(translation mainly from Busch, 380; Abbiati III,
747–48, where it is dated St. Agata, April 1875)

On Staging

[1869?]

[. . .] for the person with common sense, the stage action
shows what must be done musically [. . .]

(Abbiati III, 327)

Verdi's growing interest in staging was a natural byproduct of his fundamentally dramatic orientation to composing opera. In his published correspondence this interest first surfaced during the years 1846 and 1847. In order that his opera *Macbeth* be worthy of Shakespeare, whom he revered as the master dramatist of all time, Verdi devoted much thought to the problems of staging the work. He was particularly concerned with the Banquet and Apparition scenes as well as with the acting of his principals.

Some months before the Florentine premiere, Verdi sent Felice Varesi, the carefully chosen Macbeth, his part for the first act. He included with it a fascinating letter:

January 7, 1847

[. . .] I'll never stop urging you to study closely the dramatic situation and the words; the music will come by itself. In a word, I would rather you served the *poet* than the *composer*. You will be able to derive much effect from the first short duet ["Due vaticini compiuti"] (more than if it were a *cavatina*[32]). Keep the dramatic situation well in mind: this is the moment you meet the witches who predict the throne for you. You are bewildered and terrified by that announcement; yet at the same time there is born in you the ambition to reach the throne. Therefore you will begin this short duet *sotto voce* and take care you give full importance to the lines "Ma perchè sento rizzarsi il crine?" Pay careful attention to the markings and to the words [*accenti*] to the "*pp* and *f* . . ." noted in the music. Remember that you must obtain still another [strong] effect on the notes

ah   ah   per-chè

---

32. Normally at this point in the Introduction to Act I, Varesi would expect an aria for himself. This is one of the conventions with which Verdi broke in *Macbeth* in order to stress the drama.

In the great duet ["Fatal mia donna"], the first lines of recitative, when you give orders to the servant, have little importance. But after you are left alone, gradually you are transported and seem to see a dagggger in your hands, which points out to you the way to kill Duncan. This is a most beautiful moment, both dramatically and poetically, and you must give it close attention.

Mind that it is night; everyone is asleep; the entire duet will have to be sung *sotto voce* but in a hollow voice, so as to inspire terror. Only Macbeth (as if momentarily transported) will deliver a few phrases in a loud and clear voice; but you will find all this explained in your part. So that you may understand well my ideas, I'll also tell you that the entire recitative and duet is scored for muted strings, two bassoons, two horns, and a timpani.[33] You can see that the orchestra will play extremely softly, and therefore both of you must sing with mutes as well. I implore you to emphasize strongly the following poetic ideas, which are very beautiful: "Ah, questa mano!" "Non potrebbe l'Oceano queste mani a me lavar!" Then another: "Vendetta tuonarmi come angeli d'ira Udrò di Duncano le sante virtù!" The first section of the duet, in 6/8, is rather *presto*. The second, in 3/8, is *andantino mosso*. The final section is *prestissimo, sotto voce*,[34] and upon finishing, one should barely hear the word *Lady*, spoken almost outside oneself, as if in a dream. The first finale is clear in itself. Only don't forget that after the first few measures there is a passage for [unaccompanied] solo voices, so that you and [Marianna] Barbieri [-Nini] must be quite secure to support the others [. . .]

(Nuova Antologia 281, 1932; Abbiati I, 660–61;
partially in WalkerI, 15)

33. There are other instruments in this scene, perhaps added by Verdi during the ten weeks or so between this letter and the premiere (March 14, 1847). See especially the English horn and clarinets.

34. Verdi may be referring to an early draft of the text. In both the 1847 and 1865 versions, the duet ends with Macbeth's "l'alto sonno a te spezzar" and Lady Macbeth's "non ti vinca un vil timor" sung simultaneously.

There is also a most valuable, frequently cited letter from Verdi to Escudier written shortly before the premiere of the revised version of the opera (Paris, 1865). (See Carteggi IV, 160–161 and, for the draft, Copial. 452–54.)

Together with all other important correspondence, documents, and reviews about *Macbeth*, these letters appear in the original Italian and in translation as part of the extensive documentary section of *Verdi's 'Macbeth': A Sourcebook* (New York: W. W. Norton, in preparation).

Among Verdi's concerns while mounting *Macbeth* and other operas was that of historical accuracy. To Tito Ricordi he wrote

[end February 1847]

Do me the favor of informing Perrone that the period of *Macbeth* is well after that of Ossian and the Roman Empire. Macbeth assassinated Duncan in 1040, and he was then killed in 1057. In 1039 *Harold,* called the *Harefoot King,* a king of Danish origin, ruled in England. In the same year *Hardicanute,* twin brother to *Edward the Confessor,* succeeded him. Don't fail to give this information to Perrone immediately, as I believe he is mistaken about the period.

(Copial. 448; Abbiati I, 662)[35]

In a similar vein he wrote to Giulio Ricordi prior to the Scala premiere of *Aida,*

November 28, 1871

[. . .] Keep well in mind that the ancient Egyptians (so Du Locle advises me) knew neither iron nor steel; they knew only gold, silver, and copper (brass): "All the weapons were

---

35. Without revealing his source, Abbiati adds a sentence between the last two: "It is useless to tell you that there should be neither silk nor velvet in the costumes." The sentence appears neither in the original letter (copy in the archive of the American Institute for Verdi Studies) nor in the Copial. transcriptions.

made of brass, which they tempered in a way we have lost."
[. . .]

(Busch, 257; variation in Abbiati III, 574)

The translation above is based on that of Hans Busch, whose volume *Verdi's 'Aida': The History of an Opera in Letters and Documents* contains a wealth of information on staging the work. Of particular value is a reproduction and English translation of a printed libretto of *Aida* with Verdi's own annotations and diagrams for the staging. The original of this document is at the Pierpont Morgan Library in New York. Also included is a translation of the *disposizione scenica* for *Aida*. Although Giulio Ricordi was the author of this volume, a comparison with the annotated libretto shows how many of Verdi's ideas were used by the author. This fact and the extensive correspondence between the two men suggests that the other *disposizioni* authored by Giulio, cited earlier, also contain many of Verdi's thoughts on staging.

The idea for the Ricordi series of production books undoubtedly came from the Paris Opéra, where such volumes, either in manuscript or in print, are to be found in large numbers. The first of Ricordi's series was for the Italian translation of *Les Vêpres siciliennes* (Paris, 1855). Renamed *Giovanna de Guzman,* and with the setting changed from Sicily under the French in the late middle ages to Portugal under the Spanish in the eighteenth century, the work was then acceptable to most censors in Italy.[36] If he had not himself instigated the series, Verdi certainly approved of the idea of the production books, as the following postscript of a letter to Piave indicates:

Paris, November 28, 1855

[. . .] I am sending you under [separate] cover the *mise-en-scène* of *I vespri.* It is quite fine and by reading that

36. *Disposizione scenica per l'opera Giovanna de Guzman.* Milan: Tito di Gio. Ricordi, 39 pp. Plate no. 28556. *"Compilata e regolata sulla mise en scène del Teatro Imperiale dell'Opera di Parigi."* Translation of the *livret de mise-en-scène* by Louis Palianti for *Les Vêpres siciliennes* (Paris, 1855). See RosenS.

pamphlet attentively, a child could do the staging. If *I vespri* is changed into *Giovanna de Gusman* [sic], you need only change the costumes. But the *mise-en-scène* should remain as it is.

(Abbiati II, 316)

The act of sending the staging manual to Piave, Verdi's principal librettist for almost twenty years, was more than a gesture of friendship, however. Piave was resident stage director and librettist for La Fenice in Venice, and Verdi, no doubt, expected a performance of *Giovanna de Guzman* in that theater shortly.[37] In addition to those already mentioned, two other production books for operas by Verdi were printed by Ricordi. The first is for *Un ballo in maschera* (Rome, 1859) and was written by Giuseppe Cencetti, "Poeta e Direttore di Scena" for the Teatro Apollo, Rome.[38] This volume, like those for *Les Vêpres siciliennes, Don Carlos,* and the three signed by Giulio Ricordi, is based on the premiere directed by Verdi, and therefore deserves careful attention. The other is for the original version of *La forza del destino* (St. Petersburg, 1862).[39]

Several letters by Verdi on the staging of specific operas deserve citation. While preparing for the premiere of the revised version of *Forza* (Milan, 1869), Verdi wrote to Giulio Ricordi about the scene opening Act II, the *Osteria* or Inn Scene:

[Genoa, January 15, 1869]
[. . .] The staircase landing must be small and not too high; five or six steps which lead into the room where Leonora is

37. There were, in fact, performances of *Giovanna de Guzman* at La Fenice during the Carnival season of 1855–56 and the autumn season of 1856. See Chusid, 178.

38. *Disposizione scenica per l'Opera Un Ballo in Maschera.* Milan: Stabilimento Nazionale Tito di Gio. Ricordi [c. 1860], 38 pp. Plate no. 31305, *"Compilata e regolata sulla messa in iscena del Teatro Apollo in Roma, il carnevale del 1859. Dal Direttore di scena del medesimo."*

39. *La forza del destino . . . Ordinazioni e disposizione scenica.* Milan: Regio Stabilimento Nazionale Tito di Gio. Ricordi [1863]. 44 pp. Plate no. 35120. "Probably based on the production of the Teatro Apollo, Rome (1863) . . . by Giuseppe Cencetti." RosenS, App. B.

lodged: the staircase landing on the side and not too far back. The stage setting as spacious as possible, while taking care that behind [this scene] the monastary must be prepared [for the next]. Preziosilla must sing the *Canzone* ["Al suon di tamburo"] on a rise, or at least climb there immediately afterwards to perform her sorcery. However, this shouldn't disturb the staging, because in a [military] encampment something can always be found handy at the moment, a bench, an empty barrel, etc.

(Abbiati III, 244)

Some weeks before, Verdi had written to Giulio of Carlo's "Son Pareda, son ricco d'onore" in that same scene:

Genoa, December 31, 1868
[. . .] the *ballata* in *A* in the second [act . . .] must be performed *mezza voce*, elegantly, lightly and rather quickly.

(Abbiati III, 240)

Two other letters to Giulio that same month stress the importance of the parts of the gypsy, the comic monk, and the muleteer-peddler:

December 16, [1868]
[. . .] Don't forget that in *Forza* three artists are needed with great stage presence to do Preziosilla, Melitone, and Trabucco. Their scenes are comedy, nothing but comedy, therefore good pronunciation and aplomb on stage [. . .]

(Abbiati III, 235)

Monday [December 21(?) 1868]
[. . .] [If] Melitone, Preziosilla, and Trabucco [. . .] do not perform [. . .] with the spirit and character desired, you won't have an opera but a *De profundis* [. . .]

(Abbiati III, 240)

Of *Simon Boccanegra* (Venice, 1857) Verdi wrote to Piave, who was preparing the staging,

[end 1856]

[. . .] Be especially careful with the staging. The directions
are sufficiently precise; nonetheless, allow me some observations. In the first scene [the Prologue], if the Fieschi palace is on the side, it must be clearly visible to the entire audience, because they must all see Simon when he enters,
when he comes onto the balcony, and [when he] detaches
the lantern. I believe I've created a musical effect that I
don't want lost because of the staging. Further, in front of
the Church of San Lorenzo I should like a small usable
stairway of three or four steps with some columns which
could be leaned against or could hide, one moment Paolo,
the next Fiesco etc. [. . .] *This scene must have great depth.*
The Grimaldi Palace in the first act [on the other hand]
need not have great depth. Instead of one window I should
make several down to the floor; [there should also be] a ter-
race, [and] I should put a second [painted] backdrop with a
moon whose rays would strike the sea, so that it would be
visible to the public. The sea should be a glittering, hang-
ing curtain, etc. If I were an artist, I should certainly do a
beautiful scene, simple and extremely effective.

I urge special attention to the final scene. When the
Doge orders Pietro to close the balcony [doors], the rich il-
luminations must be visible, wide so that it takes a great
space, in order that everyone can see the lights well, which
little by little are extinguished until, at the Doge's death, everything is in pitch blackness. It is, I think, an extremely effective moment and woe [to you] if the stage action is not
well carried out. It isn't necessary for the first curtain to be
very deep, but the second, the curtain with the illumina-
tions, must be extremely deep [. . .]

(Morazzoni, 38, 40; Abbiati III, 375)

Before closing, we should note another aspect of Verdi's
concern for staging: it must never be all-absorbing or
overly elaborate. To Léon Escudier he wrote,

Naples, March 20, 1873

[. . .] I do not like *mise-en-scène* that absorbs everything and
becomes the principal object. I like the *mise-en-scène* at the

[Paris] Opera House, but I wish that theater had better singing and that the choral and orchestral groups would perform with more fire [. . .] more artistically. They are tradespeople, not artists.

(Abbiati III, 622)

And again to Léon at the time of the first *Aida* in Paris:

St. Agata, March 12, 1876

[. . .] I know that now you are almost exclusively concerned with the *mise-en-scène.* That's fine, but I wouldn't want it to be too much. I am an enemy of excess, and I don't always admire your *mise-en-scène* because it can be too contrived. Quite possibly you found what was done in Milan detestable, but I would be completely satisfied with something like that.

Enough . . . do whatever you think best; but permit me to tell you that I shall not allow the stage to be cluttered by *platforms* and *machinery,* which always happens with the painters at the Opéra. The final scene should be a *subterranean chamber,* and not a *cave,* as it was in Cairo. Finally there should be a good band of musicians who do not disdain to appear before the audience. The orchestra should be complete, and pay special attention to the choristers, especially the women. All this is more necessary than a fastidious *mise-en-scène,* which, although pleasing to the eye, cannot cover the defects of a bad musical performance. [. . .]

(Translation from Busch, 390)

The following excerpts might well sum up Verdi's thoughts on performance. The first is by Giuseppina Strepponi to Cesare De Sanctis. There is no doubt that the ideas advanced are Verdi's, since they appear repeatedly in his own correspondence. The second is from Verdi to Tito Ricordi.

October 2, 1869

[. . .] A magnificent voice, a sublime artist, does not suffice to make comprehensible in all its aspects the *Opera-Poem* of our times. There must be the totality. The singing, the playing, the acting, the costumes, the scenery, everything must form this complex [. . .]

(Carteggi I, 111)

Paris, May 14, 1863

[. . .] If artists would learn to read and understand, impresarios to stage, if the [orchestral and choral] groups [*le masse*] knew how to perform *piani* and *forti* and to keep together, the effects would be different from what they are. And mind that I am not asking extraordinary, impossible things: I am simply asking for what is absolutely necessary. It is as if a painter asked for a little light to see a painting.

(Abbiati II, 733)

There can be no equivocation and there is no contradiction: a staged opera must result in an absorbing dramatic experience, and performers must realize his scores with the utmost care and vivacity. These are Verdi's messages, as valid today as they were when he wrote them.

Words and Music in Italian Nineteenth-Century Opera

Luigi Dallapiccola

LUIGI DALLAPICCOLA (1904–75), distinguished Italian composer, was also a brilliant critic, with a wide range of cultural interests. His collected essays, published in 1970 under the title *Appunti, incontri, meditazioni,* included this essay on Verdi, which appears here in its complete version for the first time in English.

A century and a half had already passed since Marco da Gagliano had defined musical drama (*dramma in musica*) as "a spectacle truly for princes." Society had completely changed; the small aristocratic audiences which had listened to the music of Peri, Caccini, Monteverdi no longer existed; the musical theater was becoming a necessity for an increasingly wide and varied public. At that very moment the melodrama burst forth. It was, indeed, an explosion.

The earliest librettists were poets, learned writers, intellectuals. The characters they created were often gods or demigods and spoke an elevated and polished language. In the period of the Italian melodrama, on the contrary, the gods and demigods are completely left aside. What happened to the language of the libretto we will see shortly. On the stage we see only men. They are often men raised to the rank of heroes, but they are always and only men. It is the melodrama that makes up for the lack of a real Romantic period in Italian literature: the melodrama, with its words and its music.

The phenomenon of a Verdi is unthinkable without the Italian Risorgimento. It matters little or nothing for our purposes whether or not he played an active part in it: he imbibed its tone and atmosphere. At that time, there is no doubt, religious feeling was at a low ebb: it was replaced by a passionate love for the fatherland, the *Patria*. It was a sincere love, without rhetoric. It was the time that saw the rise of many secret societies plotting against the Austrian oppression.

And how many conspiracies we can see in Verdi's operas! Verdi is the authentic son of the Risorgimento. The ideals absorbed in his youth influenced him throughout his whole life. Let us think of *Otello* (1887). Austria had been expelled from Lombardy three decades before, and Italy had reached its unity. But Verdi, the old man, still sings with the fire of his youth. The chorus, on the shore of the island of Cyprus, in the midst of the tempest, roars "Salva l'arca e la bandiera Della veneta fortuna" (Defend the treasure and the banner of Venetian fortune). No other period in the history of Italian music can be compared to that of the melodrama: people have never vibrated so strongly, so decidedly in unison with the composer.

Something similar had happened many centuries before in painting. Everybody has read how people knelt down when a painter was taking his newly finished altarpiece to the church. I cannot believe this was prompted by artistic understanding; the people knelt because the Mother of God was passing by. In the same way, in the nineteenth century the public was moved, delighted, and fascinated by scenes of conspiracy and conspirators, because in these it could see the sublimation of its own feelings—and because, in real life, it was on the result of such conspiracies that its own future depended. The age of the melodrama is the epic age in the history of Italian music.

It is a fact that, at the time of the Italian melodrama, the libretto developed a style which—from a literary point of view—was usually without merit: it had nothing to do with the spoken language and, confined to librettos, was brought to life only by the music with which it was associated.

From Trent, in July 1906, Busoni wrote to his wife:

> To have company for a few hours, I have bought Verdi's *Un ballo in maschera*. It is a strong work, violent, but of great power and plastic quality. Some of its moments, it seems to me, belong to the best that Verdi has written. But the libretto! And the verses!
>
> *Sento l'orma dei passi spietati. . . .*   I hear the footprints of ruthless steps. . . .
>
> Have you ever heard anything like this?

How could one fail to agree with these words? But the fact is that Verdi endeavored, above all, to make his words a springboard for a dramatic situation. When the libretto for *Aida* was in preparation, he wrote to Ghislanzoni to justify some radical changes he had made in the text: "I know that you will say: 'and what has become of verse, rhyme, and stanza?' I don't know what to answer you. I only know that whenever the action demanded it, I would at once abandon rhythm, rhyme, and stanza . . ." For Verdi, what mattered was that the syllables should be singable.

A typical example of this is found in the sketch for *Rigoletto.* Verdi had no qualms about accepting "Diana, Agnese per me pari sono." Only when laying out the orchestral score did he change this to "Questa o quella per me pari sono," and we need no demonstration to convince us that the second version is singable and the first is not.

The language of the libretto was a mixture of carelessness beyond imagination and of misplaced affection. Rarely does a librettist use the term "words" (*parole*); he prefers "accents" (*accenti*). "Bells" would have seemed to him too realistic: "sacred bronzes" sounded better. Instead of "church" he would write "temple." An expression such as "appressarsi" (a gallicism rejected by grammarians) was preferred to "avvicinarsi" (to approach). It was not "the hand" that seized the sword, but the "right." It even happened that "fire-spitting bronze" stood for "cannon," and instead of a person being "abroad," one hears he is on "foreign soil" (*in stranio suolo*).

In *Rigoletto,* it is true, the Duke of Mantua says to Maddalena "Kiss me"; but we should not forget that Maddalena, the sister of the sinister Sparafucile, is a kind of harlot. To another woman the same duke would have said "Press me to your breast." Such is the irrational fascination of the melodrama. A surrealist show, if ever there was one! Opera can sometimes be exposed to the danger of being ridiculous. We know that. But we know too that in certain cases, in art as in life, it is precisely this extreme danger that constitutes trial by fire for a sublime style. (That is just what happens with Verdi.) The word *donna* (woman) does not often appear without an adjective in librettos, and while Alfredo, in *Traviata,* addresses the guests with "Do you know this woman?" (*Questa donna conoscete?*), he refers in his irascibility, a few moments later, to the same person as *femmina* (approximately "wench"). More frequent than *donna* is *bellezza,* even *beltade* (beauty), as if the earth were populated by pretty women only. And this style was so deeply rooted in the Italian theatrical tradition that it also prevailed in the librettos translated from foreign languages. Siegmund, in the first act of *The Valkyrie,* can exclaim, "Ein Weib sah ich, wonnig und hehr" (A woman I saw, lovely and pure), but in the Italian translation, this inevitably becomes "m'è apparsa sì diva beltà"— "a divine beauty has appeared before me." When, in *William Tell,* the original reads "Nos frères sur les eaux s'ouvrent un chemin qui ne trahit pas," and in the German translation "Führt sie dem Bruderbund der stille See entgegen," nothing need have prevented the Italian translator from using *acqua* (water) or *lago* (lake)—especially since this recitative passage offered no metric problems. Nevertheless, instead of "water" or "lake" the translator chose the grotesque expression "Mobile elemento" (mobile element). This absurd language receives life by virtue of the music, and, in masterpieces, it combines with it into an inseparable whole. Furthermore, in melodramas that are good, but not masterpieces, it makes for a dramatic eloquence which is highly characteristic of and peculiar to an important period in the history of music. To me, modernization of the librettos would be as unacceptable and disrespectful as transformation of the music itself.

In order better to clarify my ideas, allow me to give an example, although I am the first to admit that it is an extreme case: I heard a performance of *Simon Boccanegra,* in which the so-called Revolt Scene takes place in the Palace of Abbots at Genoa. Simon, the first doge, is seated in the ducal chair; around him, twelve representatives of the aristocracy and the people. Peace seems to be the dominant motive of this scene, notwithstanding the sudden, horrific close.

In the libretto we read:

The same voice that thundered over Rienzi,
Message of glory and then of death,
Now over Genoa thunders.
(*Showing a paper*)
Here is a message
Of the hermit of Sorga. He begs for peace for Venice . . .
Paolo, a representative of the people, interrupts him:
Let the singer of the blond Avignonese attend to his rhymes.

It does seem, however, that the hint about the "blond Avignonese" should be enough to put the listener on the right road. But my shocked ears heard the following version:

The same voice that thundered over Rienzi,
Message of glory and then of death,
Now over Genoa thunders.
(*Showing a paper*)
Here is a message
From Francesco Petrarca: he begs for peace for Venice . . .

This is what has become of the original version, with its veiled hint: a betrayal of the spirit of melodrama. For the use of such a great name as Francesco Petrarca gives us a reality instead of the surrealism which is a fundamental condition of musical drama.

I said earlier that the language of librettos comes to life only by virtue of the music. It is now time to observe that this music, even when used for the most diverse purposes, preserves a kind of common denominator, and this precisely where the dramatic situations are similar. It is sufficient to point out that shock, terror, surprise, abduction, execration, and sometimes even desperate invocations are underlined by the diminished seventh chord; and that not only triumphs, but also the ultimate renunciation of triumphs, are underlined by trumpets and other brass instruments (I have only to remind you of the desperate "Addio vessillo trionfale e pio" in *Otello.*) Likewise, rapid, accented staccato figures are associated with persons to be expelled from human society, with conspirators, conspiracies, and surprise attacks. With all the help of this formula Italian audiences found the key to an understanding of the dramatic situation and to an emotional response to it. From hundreds of examples I will choose only five:

a. From *Nabucco:* Ishmael is expelled by the Levites (Chorus: "Il maledetto non ha fratelli").
b. From *Rigoletto:* The Courtiers decide to kidnap Rigoletto's daughter (Chorus: "Zitti, zitti moviamo a vendetta").
c. From *Trovatore:* Entry of the Count di Luna's guards.

   d. From *Un ballo in maschera:* Beginning of the trio in
   the second act; in the background, the conspiracy.
   e. From *Macbeth:* Chorus of hired murderers.

This style, which I should like to call the style of the "fixed
epithet," represented a most useful aid to the listener as
the Gregorian Chant and Protestant chorale had been, *mu-
tatis mutandis,* in other periods.
   I have spoken of a formula and fixed epithet. Homer's
commentators have said the same of such phrases as
these: Argos, breeder of horses; Achaia of the beautiful
women; swift-footed Iris; white-armed Helen; rosy-
fingered Dawn. . . . This is not the least of the reasons why
I started out by calling melodrama the epic period of Italian music. In 1939 I was asked by the great musicologist
Edward J. Dent whether I knew an Italian treatise describ-
ing the principles of the structure of arias in Italian opera.
I had to answer in the negative. But I couldn't help being
surprised that so weighty and profound a scholar as Dent
should have sought such information from me, who am no
scholar. Today, I believe I can say that a tradition of arias
existed, perpetuated by word of mouth or by example. I
should like to discuss what the poetic quatrain offered to
the composer of melodrama. I will state at once that I refer
above all to arias, ariosos, and cavatinas, to the exclusion of
other forms.

   Let us begin with a simple example, four lines from one
of the most popular scenes in *Traviata:*

Ogni suo aver tal femmina	This woman squandered
Per amor mio sperdea:	All she owned for love of me . . .
Io cieco, vile, misero,	Blind, cowardly, wretched,
Tutto accettar potea.	I could accept it all.

The widest range of the voice in the first line is a major
sixth; in the second line a minor seventh. In the music no
significant metrical differences between the two lines are
noticeable: the slight tendency to move upward, wonder-

fully emphasized by the harmony, is what strikes us most. It is in the third line that the tragedy of the action occurs: the emotional crescendo is here brought about by a discontinuous and agitated declamation that is matched by an appropriate accompaniment. The fourth line, with its emotional diminuendo (entirely independent of the dynamics of the music), brings the quatrian to an end.

Now that we have arrived at this point, it may be interesting to see how Verdi solved his structural problem when the librettist expanded a quatrain by two lines. This happens in the quartet in *Rigoletto:*

Bella figlia dell'amore	Beautiful daughter of love,
Schiavo son de'vezzi tuoi	I am the slave of your charms;
Con un detto sol tu puoi	With a single word you can
Le mie pene consolar.	Console my sufferings.

This quatrain is set to music almost exactly in accordance with the scheme just demonstrated. There is no melodic difference between the first and second line: in both the vocal line is a major sixth. The emotional crescendo is reached in the third line—where the voice spans an octave—while the emotional diminuendo follows in the fourth line. But the librettist has added two extra lines:

Vieni, e senti del mio core	Come, and feel the quick beating
Il frequente palpitar.	Of my heart . . .

Verdi accepts them, but for the sake of the musical structure he himself makes an addition by repeating lines 3 and 4 of the first stanza:

Con un detto sol tu puoi	With a single word you can
Le mie pene consolar.	Console my sufferings.

In this way the original six lines have grown to eight. Although Verdi in the first quatrain respects the traditional scheme, he now feels compelled, with eight lines at his disposal, to treat lines 5 and 6 as the climax of the two quatrains. In other words, four times a couple of lines. Thus, while the voice in the crescendo of the first quatrain goes up to A flat, it reaches B flat in the general crescendo of the quatrain-couplet. And the diminuendo is reached with the repetition of lines 3 and 4 of the first stanza.

In Leonora's cavatina in *Trovatore* the libretto contains two stanzas, each of ten lines. The same metrical pattern appears in the first two couplets, at the end of the second, a rising tendency (minor third). Lines 7 and 8 retain the same relationship as between the corresponding lines of the first quatrain: the big emotional crescendo occurs in the penultimate verse, the diminuendo in the last. Lines 5 and 6 constitute an interpolation, and that is the structural innovation of the piece. The same innovation is found in the aria "D'amor sull'ali rosee" (ten lines also), in the last act of the same opera.

Note the last two lines (sections C and D of the second quatrain), Verdi's greatest melodic miracle and so different from all the others. Where did he ever use so many remote intervals?

What I should like to emphasize again is that the emotional crescendo is always found in the third line or in the third couplet. It is brought about through rhythmic animation or through a surprise of a harmonic nature or else through an upward movement of the vocal line. It happens frequently that the final result comes about through the collaboration of two or three elements; occasionally a fourth element enters, namely an utterly unexpected piece of instrumentation. I will have occasion to return to this later on, with reference to a passage in *Otello*. A striking example of the voice's upward striving is to be found in the tenor passage "O qual soave brivido" of the duet in *Un ballo in maschera,* where the beginning of the third line contains a pause. Here we find a coda for the first time, and it may be pointed out at once that such a coda, consisting of repetition of previously heard words, is completely independent of the scheme of the aria.

Although I have limited myself up to now with quotations from operas by Verdi, the same structural scheme also exists in Rossini, Donizetti, and Bellini. In Mathilde's Air ("Selva opaca") from the second act of Rossini's *William Tell,* in the absence of a different metrical pattern in the third line, the climax of the first quatrain is underlined by the harmony. And in the classical example of Italian melody, the "Casta diva" from Bellini's *Norma,* we find the most complete confirmation of the formal principle we have been discussing. Such importance is given to the third line, indeed, that its time span is also affected; while the first consists of 16 units of three eighth notes and the second 15 (including rests), the third actually comprises 22 and the fourth only 4. We should not assume that Verdi abandoned this traditional scheme in the last period of his activities. As proof of this, we shall present a single example from the first act of *Otello.* For the climax of the so-called Tempest Scene, where chorus and orchestra are marked *ff, tutta forza,* Boito wrote the following lines:

Dio, fulgor della bufera!	God, lightning in the storm!
Dio, sorriso della duna!	God, the smile of the shore!
Salva l'arca e la bandiera	Save the vessel and the flag
Della veneta fortuna!	Of Venetian destiny!
Tu, che reggi gli astri e il Fato!	Thou, who rulest the stars and Fate!
Tu, che imperi al mondo e al ciel!	Thou, who governest world and sky!
Fa che in fondo al mar placato	Grant that the faithful anchor
Posi l'àncora fedel.	Rest on the bottom of the calmed sea.

Here, perhaps, we find a greater complexity than in the previously quoted examples. However, nobody will fail to recognize that in the third section ("Tu, che reggi gli astri e il Fato! Tu che impieri al mondo e al Ciel") the emotional crescendo is produced by harmony and by two shattering crashes of the cymbals on the weak beat of measures 4 and 8, marked *Soli* (i.e. with solo function).

At the beginning of this paper I had the occasion to quote the draft of *Rigoletto.* Let us now look at its last page. We will discover there a first rough version of the canzone "La donna è mobile"; a mere outline, obviously jotted down in haste. In its final version (the one we know and which is also contained in the sketch) the music for the first and the second lines corresponds (apart from the key) with that first scribbled notation. However, the first jotting for the third line deviates completely from the "rule." Indeed, it lacks rhythmic excitement and scope for harmonic surprises while its vocal line, instead of striving upward, descends.

etc.

As a further illustration of the fundamental importance of the third line, it may be of interest to dwell on a rather special case. We all know that most departures from the original text of an Italian opera are due to the vanity of singers. But there is one which I not only find convincing but regard as an improvement on the written version. Unfortunately I have not succeeded in discovering whether this is of remote or recent date, whether it was approved by Verdi himself or not. In the aria "Ah si, ben mio, coll'essere" from the third act of *Trovatore,* Manrico sings the same quatrain twice over. In section 1 the highest note is D flat, in section C, A flat. The second time, the top note in section 1 is E flat (though very short), to which the B flat often sung in section 3 instead of the A flat as written seems to me to correspond admirably: it is the pivot of the whole quatrain.

Regardless of whether there existed a literary tradition which, consciously or unconsciously, determined the form of arias in Italian melodrama, it is certain that, in an immense number of closed rhymed quatrains in Italian and French hendecasyllabic poetry from Dante to Baudelaire, the second line merely continues the first and emotionally goes little beyond it. The climax appears in the third line, and the last constitutes the diminuendo conclusion. I will quote only four of the innumerable examples:

From Dante:

Tanto gentile e tanto onesta pare
La donna mia, quand'ella altrui saluta,
Che ogni lingua deven tremando muta,
E gli occhi non l'ardiscon di guardare.

So sweet and so innocent appears
My lady, when she greets another,
That every tongue becomes mute, afraid,
And eyes do not dare to look.

In the following example, from Petrarch, note the past participle in the third line—*salita*—a verb meaning to ascend, rise:

La bella donna che cotanto amavi
Subitamente s'è da noi partita,
E, per quel ch'io ne speri, al ciel salita;
Sì furon gli atti suoi dolci e soavi.

The beautiful woman you so loved
Has suddenly left us
And, as I hope, ascended to heaven,
So sweet and gentle were her actions.

From Victor Hugo:

Ruth songeait et Booz dormait:
  l'herbe était noire;
Les grelots des troupeaux palpitaient
  vaguement;
Une immense bonté tombait du
  firmament;
C'était l'heure tranquille où les lions
  vont boire.

Ruth dreamt and Boaz slept: the
  grass was black;
The bells of the flocks throb vaguely;

An immense benevolence has fallen
  from heaven;
It was the peaceful hour when the
  lions go to drink.

Here the descending connotation of the verb *tomber* is cancelled by the adjective *immense* and by the noun *firmament*. Finally, in Baudelaire:

C'est la mort qui console, hélas!, et qui
  fait vivre;
C'est le but de la vie et c'est le seul
  espoir
Qui, comme un élixir, nous monte et
  nous envivre,
Et nous donne le coeur de marcher
  jusqu'au soir.

It is death which comforts us, (alas!)
  and maintains us;
It is the aim of life, its only hope;

Which, like an elixir, rises up and
  enraptures us,
Giving us courage to keep going
  until nightfall.

Note in the third line two verbs with ascending meaning—*monter* (to ascend, to rise) and *enviver* (to enrapture)—not to mention the noun *élixir*. Or has perhaps the melodrama, "popular" theater in the best sense of the word, gradually developed, unknown to its creators, from an early pristine art form? When one examines the section of the thirteenth-century mystery *Play of Daniel,* where the main character explains to the king the significance of "Mane Thekel Phares," one is struck by its structural relation to the aria in the melodrama.

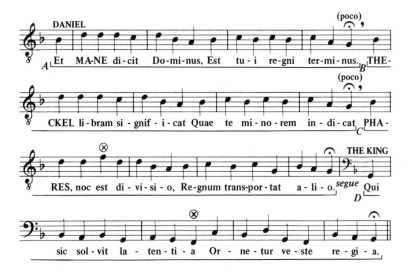

I would not want anyone to think that I regarded the emotional crescendo in the penultimate section of a musical quatrain as belonging exclusively to Italian melodrama. We can observe the same fact in other music. The first name that comes to mind is Schubert—the "folkish" Schubert in particular, certainly not that of *Nacht und Träume,* where the musical structure is totally different. At this point it is worth recalling Alban Berg's acute observation about the "instrumental" character of the voice in Schubert's lieder. In my view, the supreme originality, the uniqueness of Italian melodrama is that it entirely disregarded our instrumental tradition.

Beethoven is another name that should be mentioned, and one of the most significant cases in this connection is the *Rondo* of the *Piano Sonata* Opus 90. We have it on

Schindler's authority that Beethoven called this rondo "Conversations with the beloved"—thus a dramatic situation without the acting.

But what happens in the construction of a melodrama aria is quite different: the third section is a *gesture*. For this I could give no better proof than to quote two examples which are practically identical in melody, yet totally different in effect. The first is a passage from the second subject of the Adagio of Mozart's *Violin Concerto in A major;* the second, a passage from the sextet in Donizetti's *Lucia di Lammermoor.* In the first case, the third and fourth sections develop according to the logic and rule of instrumental writing, of instrumental civilization; in the second case they obey the demand of the stage.

While I have tried up to this point to prove that an analogy existed between the structure of the quatrain in poetry and the structure of the aria in the melodrama, I shall now expand my demonstrations and try to explain how Verdi has applied a like principle of organization to a large form such as the trio of the second act of *Un ballo in maschera.* Let us first examine the libretto. Each singer is given eight lines. In the oldest editions, which must be presumed to correspond to Antonio Somma's manuscript as well as those printed recently (see the libretto accompanying Toscanini's New York recording of 1954), the characters appear in the following order: Amelia—soprano; Riccardo—Tenor; Renato—baritone.

My first observation (and it is a fairly sensational one) is that Verdi, while setting this trio to music, reversed the order of the male voices as fixed by the librettist: the entry of the baritone was transferred from third to second place and that of the tenor from second to third. This observation should help us to realize the extraordinary lucidity with which Verdi set to work: Riccardo, the tenor, is now entrusted with the climax of the trio, and to the three stanzas written by the librettist a fourth was added as a musical recapitulation in which the three characters repeat either in full (soprano and baritone) or in part (tenor) the words they have already sung. Verdi, with his exceptionally acute feelings for the stage effect, could not fail to see that the remorse (almost a guilt complex) expressed by the tenor represented the climax of the piece. We have here a total success. The trio in *Un ballo in maschera* has been called "beautiful" and "marvelous." Many people are satisfied with such characterizations. Well, the trio will remain "beautiful" and "marvelous" even after my attempt at analysis. Analysis cannot take anything away from the aesthetically perfect, just as it cannot add anything to the artistically valueless. When, more than a hundred years after its appearance, we listen to this trio with modern ears and read it with modern eyes, we will become aware of various things which were formerly overlooked. In consequence, I

will not hesitate to speak of macrostructures and microstructures without fear of being dubbed "sophisticated."
I should like to remind you of a famous saying of the Doctor Angelicus, Saint Thomas Aquinas, on the constituents of beauty: "Ad pulchritudinem tria requiruntur: integritas, consonantia, claritas." Thus: unity—that is the overall design; consonance—that is the equilibrium of the parts; clarity—that is the significant expression of what is to be said.
We will now examine the macrostructure corresponding to the soprano's first stanza. Each of the microstructures a, b, c, d, consists of four measures; the fifth, e, corresponds to the eight measures of the codetta. A codetta of the same length will be found at the end of the second and fourth macrostructures. (One should not forget that codetta and coda have no relation to the stanza of the libretto, but are of purely musical significance—the characters only repeat words sung previously).
First microstructure:

Odi tu come fremono cupi	Do you hear how grimly resound
Per quest'aura gli accenti di morte?	In this air the accents of death?

The voice range is D–A (with B flat "di volta").
The same metrical pattern appears in the second microstructure:

Di lassù, da quei negri dirupi	From up there, from those black crags,
Il segnal de' nemici partì.	The enemies' signal was fired.

Here the melodic line begins to swing upward: in place of the fifth D–A we have the fifth F–C.
The third microstructure

Ne' lor petti scintillano d'ira	In their bosoms they flash with rage . . .
E già piomban, t'accerchiano fitti. . . .	And they already plunge down, encircle you, closely . . .

represents the climax of the first macrostructure. To this three elements contribute: the vocal range extends to the treble F; a dynamic crescendo is followed by a dynamic diminuendo; and, as if this were not enough, surprising accents are given on the weak beat of the measure by two French horns, violas, and cellos.
The fourth microstructure

Al tuo capo già volser la mira,	They have already turned their aim at your head . . .
Per pietà, va, t'invola di qui,	For pity's sake, go, flee from here.

represents the conclusion of the quatrain-couplet and, compared with the previous section, an emotional diminuendo.

Amelia's A on the word "qui" should not deceive us: it is simply a resolution note which does not weaken in the least the effect of the treble F, the vocal climax of the third microstructure. I might even say that this first A is completely independent of the three subsequent A's which are repeated almost like cries of anguish. The vocal score of the opera, even the first edition, which must be based on the original manuscript score, does not show an accent on the first A. But the three subsequent A's are accentuated.

The second macrostructure, given to the baritone, is identical with the first in construction: the variant in the final lines 7 and 8 can be ascribed only to the necessity of arriving at the dominant at the end of the stanza. In spite of this identity, I should mention that the soprano comes an octave above the baritone in the third microstructure. Then there is a double crescendo.

And now we come to the third macrostructure, the climax of the whole construction:

Traditor, congiurati son essi
Che minacciano il vivere mio?
Ah, l'amico ho tradito pur io . . .
Son colui che nel cuor lo ferì.

In contrast to the two previous macrostructures, where lines 1 and 2, as well as 3 and 4, are linked by the music, the four lines of the present stanza are separated by rests. This enables the composer to attain the emotional crescendo. Two more elements will be added: the first line is based on A, the second on C, the third on E; the fourth begins with F. As we can see, the necessary swing upward is a strictly observed triple crescendo. Note also the extremely effective interventions—"Va, fuggi; ti salva; Va, fuggi"—by soprano and baritone. Without a rest the tenor follows with lines 5 and 6, which constitute the climax of the third macrostructure and also of the entire trio. After the high A is reached on the first syllable, the vocal line gradually descends. The emotional diminuendo, both of the macrostructure and the whole piece, is introduced. When lines 5 and 6 are joined to 7 and 8, line 7 is the only passage that Verdi marked "poco allargando, col canto," although this is too often anticipated, thus breaking up the rhythmic force of the construction.

It will now be useful to count the measures of the five macrostructures, in order to clarify my ideas, arithmetically as well. The first comprises 24 measures; the second, 24; the third, for dramatic reasons the briefest, 16 (there is no codetta); the fourth, 24; and the coda, 23. On the last chord of the coda there is a pause, and it is known that it was customary in Verdi's time simply to double the value of such notes. Thus we can reckon that the coda, too, consists of 24 measures.

All told, then, there are 112 measures. The tenor's phrase "Innocente sfidati gli avrei," the climax of the composition, begins precisely at measure 56, just halfway through the piece.

To me this seems extraordinary, the more so since Verdi certainly did not count the measures. He must have conceived and carried out this miracle of proportion intuitively.

We have finally arrived at the concluding section of the

Son colui che nel cor lo ferì.

d)

Ah, l'amico tradito ho pur io . . .

c)

Che minacciano il vivere mio?

b)

Traditor, congiurati son essi
(N.B. The orchestral score reads
"sciagurati," not "congiurati.")

a)

d) *Va, ti salva, del popolo è vita*
    Questa vita che getti così.

(Baritone solo)

Climax of A and B
(Baritone and Soprano)

c) *Va, ti salva, o che il varco all'uscita*
    Qui tra poco serrarsi vedrai . . .

b) *Allo scambio dei detti esecrati*
    Ogni destra la daga brandì

a) *Fuggi fuggi, per l'orrida via*
    Sento l'orma dei passi spietati:

d) *Al tuo capo già volser la mira . . .*
    Per pietà, va, t'invola di qui.

Climax of the *first stanza*. The voice
goes up to high F; dynamic crescendo
followed by a decrescendo; accents on
the weak beat by two horns, violas,
and cellos.

c) *Nei lor petti scintillano d'ira,*
    E già piomban, t'accerchiano fitti . . .

b) *Di lassù, da quei negri dirupi*
    Il segnal dei nemici partì.

a) *Odi tu come fremono cupi*
    Per quest'aura gli accenti di morte?

Climax of the piece

Innocente, sfidati li avrei:
Or d'amore colpevole fuggo.

(M.56!)

In - no - cen - te sfi -

La pietà del Signore su lei
Posi l'ale, protegga i suoi dì.

D   Recapitulation

Soprano, Tenor, and Baritone

Soprano and Baritone *a 2*

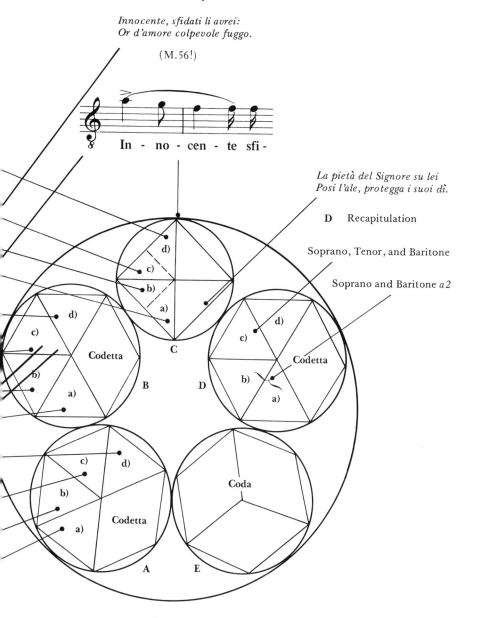

trio. The fourth macrostructure is musically similar to the first. One should observe, however, that the first eight measures of this recapitulation are now set for two voices (soprano and baritone) and not for a single voice as before, and that from the third microstructure the tenor enters also. Thus three voices appear in the fourth macrostructure and two in the parallel passage of the second.

The concluding section of the piece consists of 24 measures of coda, that is, of the sum of the measures of the three codettas previously encountered. This coda is just an ending, rather common in character. The word *common* is not meant to be derogatory: it is simply a matter of understanding, and so explaining, a local stylistic procedure that characterizes a whole period.

Everyone is free to accept or reject it; but to argue from an antihistorical position would be rather like calling the 29 measures in C major at the end of Beethoven's *Fifth Symphony* "too long," or the octaves of Ariosto's *Orlando furioso* "monotonous," or else the proportions of the Wagnerian opera "exaggerated." Particularly unjustified is a cut of eight measures in the coda—absurd, in fact, considering they do not last even ten seconds!—which is sometimes made in performances of the opera. That cut upsets the balance of the whole work.

Before concluding, I should like to ask you to listen to the *scena e terzetto* from *Un ballo in maschera*. In this excerpt, we find condensed many typical formulas and some gems of libretto language. A lonely field at night: on the stage is Amelia with her lover. A third person approaches them: the lover recognizes his closest friend; the woman, her husband. Instead of speaking of her husband, which would have been too "bourgeois," she uses the word "consort," a more refined term in the language of melodrama.

Following the recognition scene, which is underlined by a diminished seventh chord, the woman veils her face to conceal her identity from her husband. He had come to warn his friend of conspirators who—on surrounding hills—stood ready to attack him: they had seen him in the lonely field in the company of a veiled woman—a "beltade" (beauty), as the text, of course, characterizes her. Her lover could escape by a footpath, but he is not willing to leave his beloved alone with her husband. Three souls, oppressed by anxiety (each for a different reason), and, in the background, the conspiracy.

The composer's genius, the "genius of the dramatic accent," according to the happy definition given by Busoni, has surmounted the absurd situation and grotesque language, the lame syntax, the pathos of the cliché.

Translated by Alvary E. Grazebrook

On Verdi's Vocal Writing

Rodolfo Celletti

RODOLFO CELLETTI is music critic of the Italian weekly *Epoca* and a regular contributor to the monthly magazine *Discoteca*, as well as to *Opera* (London) and *Opera International* (Paris). He is the author of *Il teatro d'opera in disco*, editor of *Le grandi voci*, and has published two novels.

The first consideration in a discussion of Verdi's vocal writing is the function of each separate voice. The voices that Verdi uses are: soprano, mezzo-soprano, and contralto for his female characters; for the male characters, tenor, baritone, and bass. He utilizes them in basically the same way as did all the operatic composers of the Romantic era, from Meyerbeer to Donizetti and from Rossini to Wagner.

The characters, obviously, have a body, an age, a social position, and a moral shape; in Romantic opera there exists a kind of symbolism which associates an age, a physical appearance, a rank, and certain psychological traits with the tone quality of each voice. But it should be observed that every type of voice—soprano, tenor, contralto, baritone, etc.—is like an instrument. It is handled in a predetermined way, offers predetermined effects, and lends itself to the expression of certain aspects of human life in preference to others.

In the works of Verdi, as in those of other Romantic composers, the nucleus of the operatic plot is almost always a love story. For this reason particular importance is given to the protagonists of this story: the two lovers, or the "juvenile leads" in theatrical jargon. These roles are given, in Verdi's operas, to the soprano and the tenor, whose voices tend almost automatically to represent very young persons, whether male or female (generally between adolescence and early adulthood), physically attractive, belonging in most cases to aristocratic families and usually inspired by the loftiest sentiments: high moral, religious, and political ideals, courage, honesty, loyalty, generosity. This is because the mechanism of the Romantic opera is based on the antithesis between good and evil. The two lovers—the tenor and the soprano—personify the good and embody strongly idealized figures. Their mutual love is likewise idealized and is a pure, chaste feeling even when it is irrepressible and overwhelming.

What links two characters so conceived to the tenor and the soprano? It is simply the tonal qualities of these voices. Of the male and female vocal registers they have the lightest colored and highest voices, which are also the sweetest, the most brilliant, and, in their high notes, the most penetrating and ringing. I should add that they are also the most stylized voices, in that the others are more common, more normal, more current—even among "speaking" voices—as in the case of the mezzo-soprano and the baritone, even monochromatic in the case of the contralto and the bass. The tonal stylization corresponds exactly to the idealization, the sublimated conception of the characters embodied by the soprano and the tenor. But apart from this, operatic Romanticism physically identifies a light tone with early youth, just as it tends to link the darkest timbres (contralto, bass) with the idea of old age. In addition, the tonal characteristics of the soprano and tenor tend to express purity, chastity, delicacy, languor, melancholy, ecstasy, and, on certain occasions, enthusiasm, joy, happiness; as instruments they are also the most appropriate for singing of love.

The voice of the Romantic tenor is an androgynous

voice. It has a virile ring, for example, in high notes sung in full voice; but when the sound, produced as if barely touching the lips or in the form of a *nota filata*,[1] is reduced and shaded off, the tone acquires almost feminine sweetness, abandon, languor. Furthermore, the extent of his upper register and his greater agility in comparison with the baritone and the bass enable the tenor to execute fioriture, trills, embellishments, and to sing melodies on highlying phrases or with sudden leaps from the central to the upper range of his voice. These are the main features of the Romantic tenor and of the Verdi tenor. The latter, however, has a specific connotation. It is a voice which follows the examples of the tenors of Bellini and Donizetti, and this is particularly evident in Verdi's first operas. The point of contact, in any case, between the Bellini and Donizetti tenors and the Verdi tenor remains the ecstatic, elegiac, and nostalgic character of the love songs, whether in arias from the early operas ("Come rugiada al cespite" from *Ernani;* "La mia letizia infondere" from *I lombardi*) or from later operas ("Quando le sere al placido" from *Luisa Miller;* "Ah, sì, ben mio" from *Il trovatore;* "Je l'ai vue" from *Don Carlos;* "Celeste Aida"). It is here that Verdi takes major advantage of the light color and the soft, melancholy timbre of the tenor. It should not be forgotten that a significant part of Verdi's operatic production coincided with the historical period known as the Italian Risorgimento. Verdi's political commitment involves his tenor in the movement of national unity and makes him the voice of the generation of young men who dreamed of the liberation of their country from foreign domination. Characters like Foresto (*Attila*), Arrigo (*La battaglia di Legnano*), Henri (*Les Vêpres siciliennes*) are vocal projections of the ideals of the Risorgimento and of national union. But even in cases where there is no direct allusion to the historical situation of Italy in the

---

1. A *nota filata* ("spun-out note") is produced by gradually diminishing the volume and intensity of a sound to a point where it is almost imperceptible, like a sigh.

years between 1840 and 1860, the Verdi tenor symbolizes
noble youth in rebellion against an evil social and political
order (Ernani, Carlo di Moor in *I masnadieri*) or struggling
against class prejudices (Rodolfo in *Luisa Miller*), against
racial prejudices (Alvaro in *La forza del destino*) or against
religious constraints and obscurantism (the heretic
Manrico in *Il trovatore,* or Don Carlos).

In these cases Verdi makes frequent use of the intense
and penetrating resonance and the ringing silver tones
that characterize the tenor in his upper range. Verdi was
often reproached for this, since a voice that is frequently
obliged to produce high notes with great force is obviously
subject to strain. As a matter of fact, Donizetti and particularly Bellini, had given the tenor even higher notes than
Verdi, but in the years of Donizetti and of Bellini the very
highest notes were sung in falsetto, whereas, in Verdi's
day, they were produced with full or "chest" voice.[2] The
tessitura in Verdi's scores is often very high;[3] but this is not
the only difference. The fact is that Verdi's instrumental
fabric is more intense than that of Bellini or Donizetti and
requires a greater vocal effort.

The arias in which Verdi typically engages the tenor in
patriotic outbursts and insurrectional explosions or pro-
tests are the cabalettas: pages of rapid movement and
strongly accented, martial rhythm, with a vocal line that is
tense, vehement, incandescent. The most famous cabaletta
is "Di quella pira" from *Il trovatore,* but as an example of a
cabaletta with a patriotic and epic basis, the "Cara patria"
from *Attila* is even more typical.

The fiery "Garibaldian" climate of the Risorgimento in

---

2. In Verdi's operas, the so-called *do di petto* (chest C)—the highest note that a
tenor can usually reach in full voice—is extremely rare. The B natural is also
rare, while the A natural and B flat are more frequent.

3. By *tessitura* is meant the zone of the staff in which are found most of the
notes that the composer writes for a given voice. The Verdi tenor must often
sing in full voice, articulating syllables, in zones that range up to his highest register, while before Verdi the high notes were reserved almost exclusively for vocalized phrases. Passages containing articulated syllables in full voice almost always
fell into a lower range.

which the Verdi tenor was born and evolved provided, in the long run, a characteristic of this vocal type even in situations having no political or patriotic involvement. In other words, the vehemence of the martial cabaletta can be found in cabalettas in which the tenor is simply proclaiming his amorous ardor ("O tu che l'alma adora" from *Ernani;* "Possente amor mi chiama" from *Rigoletto*) or expressing resentment or anger for a momentary misunderstanding with his beloved ("Oh mio rimorso! Oh infamia!" from *La traviata*). We can go even further. A certain cabaletta-style ardor, a parallel aggressive and enthusiastic exuberance translated into full-voiced song, is also present in tenor extracts of a completely different type, based entirely on an amorous effusion. It is enough to recall the entrance aria of Riccardo in *Un ballo in maschera* ("La rivedrà nell'estasi") or certain phrases in famous love duets: "Adunque amiamoci, donna celeste" (*Rigoletto*), for example, or "Pur ti riveggo, mia dolce Aida."

The Verdi tenor is essentially in a state of equilibrium between lyrical ecstasy and nostalgic, elegiac abandon, on one hand, and ardent, vigorous outbursts, whether patriotic, moral, or simply amorous, on the other. These two diverse and almost opposite elements sometimes follow one another without a break, either in ensembles ("Bella figlia dell'amore" in the quartet from *Rigoletto*), in duets (a most eloquent example is the duet from *Un ballo in maschera,* "Teco io sto," sung by Riccardo and Amelia), or in the course of a single aria. Witness, again in *Un ballo in maschera,* "Ma se m'è forza perderti," and in *La forza del destino,* "O tu che in seno agli angeli."

It should also be pointed out that the ringing force of the tenor's top notes is frequently used by Verdi in ensembles (the trio from Act I of *Il trovatore,* sung by Manrico, Leonora, and Conte di Luna), in ensembles with chorus, and equally often in scenes of invective, fury, or challenge ("Oro, quant'oro ogn'avido" from *Ernani;* the "Scena della borsa" from *La traviata;* the great challenge duets of Alvaro and Carlo de Vargas in *La forza del destino*); just as some duets and trios, on the other hand, turn chiefly to account the soft, elegiac character of the tenor voice: the trio from *I lombardi* called "the baptism" ("Qui posa il fianco"), the duets from *La traviata* for Alfredo and Violetta, the duet of Manrico and Azucena in *Il trovatore,* or the final scene from *Aida.*

This being said, a final conclusion must be drawn concerning the Verdi tenor. This is a voice that Verdi did not consider in general capable of delineating great inner conflicts, deep psychological nuances, or tragic attitudes. In only three cases (Rodolfo in *Luisa Miller,* Stiffelio, and Otello) does Verdi give a complex connotation to tenor characters, in all three cases basing the character on the same element: jealousy. However, only the tragedy of Otello is seen from within, i.e., introspectively, the drama of Stiffelio is purely exterior and that of Rodolfo can be defined as half-way between the two.

With the soprano—as with the tenor—Verdi began from precedents already established by Bellini and Donizetti. For many years the type of soprano used by Verdi was what we define a *drammatico di agilità* (dramatic-coloratura), outstandingly represented in works of Bellini by Imogene (*Il pirata*), Adelaida (*La straniera*), Norma, Beatrice di Tenda; and by Donizetti's Anna Bolena, Maria Stuarda, Lucrezia Borgia, Elisabetta (*Roberto Devereaux*), and Maria di Rohan. The dramatic-coloratura soprano, as the term itself indicates, is called upon to alternate vehement, occasionally violent vocal passages with others which are of elegiac or virtuoso character. In any case, the oscillation between the opposite poles of lyrical ecstasy and impassioned exuberance that characterizes the Verdi tenor can be found in and even more marked degree in the roles for the Verdi sopranos, with the addition, at least as late as *Les Vêpres siciliennes,* of virtuoso passages (with vocalises, embellishments, rapid coloratura phrases, ornamentations, trills) which are limited, in the music for the tenor, to a few of the earliest works.

Again in comparison with the tenor, the ecstatic-elegiac

element in the music for the Verdi soprano appears more spontaneously delineated and better characterized vocally. The young Verdi—the Verdi closest to Bellini and Donizetti—can boast of good arias in ecstatic vein for the tenor, but it was not until *Luisa Miller* ("Quando le sere al placido") that he composed tenor melodies comparable to "Prendi l'anel ti dono" from *La sonnambula*, "A te o cara" from *I puritani*, "Una furtiva lagrima" from *L'elisir d'amore*, "Tu che a Dio spiegasti l'ali" from *Lucia*, or "Ange si pur" from *La favorita*. The gentle, dream-laden soprano aria appears in all its purity from the very first operas. Examples are "Se vano è il pregare" from *I lombardi*, "Non so le tetre immagini" from *Il corsaro*, "Tu del mio Carlo" from *I masnadieri*, and many others.

Another characteristic of the Verdi soprano of the first period is a marked aggressiveness that is most clearly revealed in roles of proud, willful, even warlike women. Even in the latter case the characters (Giovanna d'Arco, Odabella in *Attila*) are in revolt against a foreign yoke (typical is Odabella's martial aria, "Allor che i forti corrono"); however, even Verdi's Amazons have love songs of intense lyrical ecstasy, like Giovanna d'Arco's "O fatidica foresta" and Odabella's "Oh, nel fuggente nuvolo." But we can go even further: even a basically perverse female like Abigaille in *Nabucco* has an aria of dreamlike quality ("Anch'io dischiuso un giorno").

In the later Verdi, ecstatic arias are numerous: "Caro nome" (*Rigoletto*), "Tacea la notte placida" and "D'amor sull'ali rosee" (*Il trovoatore*), "Ah, fors'è lui" (*La traviata*), "Ami, le coeur d'Hélène" (*Les Vêpres siciliennes*). From then on, the music of the dramatic-coloratura soprano almost completely loses its vocalises, fiorituras, and ornamentation; it remains simply dramatic, but the melodic line that reveals the dreaming chastity and the heavenly abandon of Verdi's enamored heroines is even more frequent, from "Ma dall'arido stelo divulsa" (*Un ballo in maschera*) to "Me pellegrina ed orfana" and "Pace mio Dio" (*La forza del destino*) up to "O cieli azzurri" (*Aida*) and the Willow Song (*Otello*).

The fact that seems strange in some respects is that the mature Verdi's dramatic soprano, whose voice, owing to the particular nature of the musical writing, is darker, more incisive, and greater in volume than the dramatic-coloratura, appears psychologically less pugnacious, less aggressive. She does not have real outbursts of revolt against those who threaten, who betray, or who oppress her, and, in the moments of greatest tension and pathos, she looks within herself for an expression of her sorrow and her despair. The reasons are basically twofold: 1) the successful unification of Italy, which, after 1860, not only modified certain structures of the Verdi operas but also curbed that warlike vehemence which had inspired Rossini's ironic definition of Verdi as "the composer with the helmet"; and 2) the suppression of the cabaletta. The popular vogue for cabalettas, as well as the political situation, had suggested to the librettists the insertion of situations and states of mind that would justify articulated and vehement vocal lines in rapid tempos. We have already seen that even the tenor cabalettas were at a rapid tempo, as well as being articulated and vehement; in the soprano cabalettas, however (and we are referring to the dramatic-coloratura soprano), Verdi took advantage of the characteristics of this voice—the most flexible of all—to accentuate the speed and to introduce vocalises, fioriituras, and embellishments. The cabaletta thus permitted him to delineate politico-patriotic protest (again we have the example of Odabella in her aria "Da te questo or m'è concesso" in *Attila*) or moral protest (Giselda's "No, giusta causa non è di Dio" from *I lombardi*), but above all to express something that differentiates the Verdi soprano from all others. I refer to those tremulous and frequently joyous revelations of love, those enthusiastic, almost delirious outbursts of passion that follow the ecstatic arias of the dramatic-coloratura soprano. Thus, in *Ernani*, Elvira's "Tutto sprezzo che d'Ernani"; in *I masnadieri*, Amalia's "Carlo vive? Oh caro accento"; in *Il trovatore*, Leonora's "Di tale amor"; and, in *La traviata*, Violetta's "Sempre libera." All of these are vocally extremely difficult not merely because they are very high, but above all because of the way in which phrases of articulated song, fragments of vocalized melody, rapid trills and staccato notes, sudden upward leaps and unexpected drops to the lowest register follow one another with bewildering rapidity. In the duets and ensembles the Verdi soprano is treated like the tenor. In duets, ecstatic passages alternate with tense and vigorous phrases which are frequently sung, by soprano and tenor, in unison. In ensembles with chorus both voices are occasionally called upon to perform very high phrases, because the sonic effect they are expected to provide must soar above impressive choral masses and grand orchestral *pieni.*

Psychologically, the Verdi soprano is frequently more carefully delineated than the tenor and experiences inner conflicts in which the antithesis of love-duty is felt to a deeper and more lacerating degree. Hence the complexity of a person like Violetta in *La traviata,* with such extremely variegated vocal characteristics. Other complex figures are those in which Verdi, taking leave of the Romantic concept of the celestial, angel-like soprano, creates perverse female characters like Abigaille in *Nabucco* and Lady Macbeth. In both cases, but particularly the latter, the soprano vocal line is cutting, violent, and yet still marked, since this is the Verdi of the first period, by passages of brilliant singing and coloratura (e.g., in *Macbeth,* the drinking song, "Si colmi il calice"). Note, too, that in order to reveal more clearly the somber and cruel nature of Lady Macbeth, Verdi adopts a special style of composition in which extremely high passages are contrasted with others in which the soprano sings in the lowest zone of her range, producing deep sounds like those of a mezzo-soprano.

The love story of which the tenor and soprano are the protagonists is nearly always destined, in Romantic opera, to end tragically, because of the pessimistic conviction that perversity, treason, injustice, violence, social prejudices, superstition, tyranny, the interests of the state—the forces of evil, in other words—prevail in life against the forces of good. The forces of evil are embodied, in Verdi, by all the other voices (baritone, bass, mezzo-soprano, and contralto) even though some of these may, from time to time, side with the tenor and soprano. Of all the other voices, in any case, and this is typical of Verdi's operas, preeminence belongs to the baritone, who usually has the function of a true *deus ex machina* of the dramatic events.

It is impossible to give an unequivocal definition of the psychological position of the Verdi baritone, because his incarnations are extremely varied. In the general picture of Romantic opera, the primary function of the baritone would seem to be that of antagonist to the tenor. As antagonist he can be either a rival in love or a character who, as a symbol of a political force or of social or racial prejudice, opposes either or both the soprano or the tenor and plots their ruin.

The baritone as antagonist-rival is present in *Ernani* (Carlo V), *I masnadieri* (Francesco di Moor), *Il corsaro* (Seid), *La battaglia di Legnano* (Rolando), *Il trovatore* (Conte di Luna), *Un ballo in maschera* (Renato), *La forza del destino* (Carlo de Vargas). In these examples, he is not necessarily identified with blind wickedness or absolute arrogance. In *Ernani*, rancor gives way, at a certain point, to magnanimity (the real antagonist here is the bass); in *La battaglia di Legnano* and *Un ballo in maschera* the baritone plots against the tenor under the impression that he has been betrayed by him (in *Un ballo in maschera*, in fact, we have a real example of the crime of honor); and even in *La forza del destino* the rancor of the baritone is based, however mistakenly, on the guilt that Carlo de Vargas attributes to his own sister, Leonora, and to Don Alvaro. Truly wicked, then, are only Francesco di Moor, Seid, Conte di Luna (with reservations), and Iago (*Otello*), who is from many points of view an incarnation of treachery as an end in itself.

But the Verdi baritone appears almost as often in the role of father: Giacomo (*Giovanna d'Arco*), Miller (*Luisa*

Miller), Giorgio Germont (*La traviata*), Guy de Montfort (*Les Vêpres siciliennes*), Amonasro (*Aida*). In addition, even if the dramatic events place them in the role of protagonist and call for other than simply paternal qualities, those outstanding figures whom we know as Nabucco, Pietro Foscari (*I due Foscari*), Rigoletto, Simon Boccanegra, are also fathers. Add to this gallery of monumental characters Ezio (*Attila*)—a *condottiere* taken from history—Macbeth, Rodrigue (*Don Carlos*)—another instance of the noble baritone like Ezio, Pietro Foscari, or Simon Boccanegra—and, finally, Falstaff, and Verdi's predilection for the baritone register is evident.

This predilection arose, perhaps, from the fact that, in contrast to the stylized voice of the tenor, the baritone voice is realistic and, as such, more human. On the other hand, while Verdi has a relationship with all the other voices that leaves practically unaltered the fundamental characteristics already established by his predecessors (timbre, color, range, tessitura, etc.) with the baritone he takes what is in many ways an autonomous direction. In the period of Bellini and Donizetti the baritone was still considered a subspecies of bass and was even called *basso cantante* (singing bass). In some of his last operas (in particular *Linda di Chamounix, Maria di Rohan,* and the role of Abayaldos in *Dom Sebastien*), Donizetti had begun to differentiate between the baritone and the basso cantante, but this diversification was chiefly the work of Verdi. Verdi not only pushed the baritone to higher notes than Bellini or Donizetti called for, but he raised the tessitura of his roles, systematically obliging him to sing phrases in the upper reaches of his register (one of the most typical examples is the aria "Il balen del suo sorriso" in *Il trovatore*). In this way he created a voice which is halfway between the bass and the tenor and, in the upper register, brought him close to the tenor. Certain theorists of singing techniques, around 1870, defined the Verdi baritone as a "mezzotenor" and in France even today the term *baryton Verdi* designates a baritone with an extended and tenorlike high register.

The answer to the question, which might be raised at this point, as to why Verdi felt the need to have at his disposal a high baritone rather than the basso cantante of the Bellini-Donizetti era, is rather obvious. Verdi assigns to the baritone a more extended gamut of sentiments and passions than that of the basso cantante of Bellini and Donizetti and utilizes him to portray on the stage aspects of human life that had previously either been ignored or received only superficial treatment in the musical theater. He therefore required a vocal instrument different from that of the basso cantante.

Consider, for example, the first great Verdi baritone character: Nabucco. His is an exceptionally complex figure in his waverings between overweening arrogance and extreme humiliation, between ferocity and paternal affection. In vocal terms these fluctuations inspire varied and alternating musical lines which, in the first part of the opera, carry the voice to the extreme tension of selections like "Tremin gl'insani" and "Mio furor non più costretto" or, with declamatory violence, of the scene in which Nabucco proclaims himself God (Finale II). It is clear that in passages like this he is a hero, a demigod, and the fact that his voice imitates, in its upper register, the ringing silvery and quasi-epic tones of the tenor has a telling effect. But Verdi achieved the same effect, although in different dramatic situations, when, in *Ernani*, Carlo V attacks the rebellious Silva ("La vedremo, o veglio audace") or when, aware of his imperial dignity, he bursts forth, in unison with the orchestra, in the great phrase "E vincitor dei secoli il nome mio sarà!" (in the aria "O de' verd'anni miei"). Justification for raising a baritone voice into its upper range in order to display intense, ringing sounds is demonstrated in *Rigoletto* by the invective directed at the courtiers and by the cabaletta "Sì, vendetta"; in *I due Foscari* by the indignant "Questa è dunque l'iniqua mercede"; or in *Aida* by the curse hurled by Amonasro at his daughter.

This placement, as we have seen, includes the heroic phrases of the baritone (and those patriotic, Risorgimento phrases, or expressions of political passion, in *Attila, La bat-*

taglia di Legnano or *Simon Boccanegra*), as well as his out-bursts of rage, indignation or despair. It is utilized, there-fore, even when the score does not call for exalted or offended majesty or even sentiments of injured paternity (*Nabucco, Ernani, I due Foscari*), but imply for the expres-sion of antagonism toward the tenor, aroused by rivalry in love or family feuds. In many of the direct confrontations with the tenor (and on occasions even with the soprano) Verdi seems to aim at placing the baritone in a position where he can sustain the competition with vocal outbursts and ringing tones; examples include the incandescent trio in Act I of *Il trovatore*, the two vehement challenge duets in *La forza del destino,* and many other similar selections.

Back, for a moment, to Nabucco. When this character, in the Finale II, has given vent to his arrogance and, con-fused and sad, moves into the adagio "O mia figlia! e tu pur anco . . . ," we find the second explanation of the high tessitura of the Verdi baritone. When the baritone ex-presses his paternal affection—perhaps the most innate feeling for him in the Verdi operatic canon—Verdi needs a pathetic timbre and color as well as a smooth, soft vocal production; here again he finds these qualities through the partial imitation of the timbre, the color, the pathos, and the smoothness of the tenor voice. We then have the grief-stricken abandon of arias like "O vecchio cor che batti" (*I due Foscari*), "Di provenza" (*La traviata*), "Au sein de la puissance" (*Les Vêpres siciliennes*); or the melting duets for the baritone and soprano—among the most typical of Verdi's creations—like "Ella è innocente e pura" (*Giovanna d'Arco*), "Andrem, raminghi e poveri" (*Luisa Miller*), "Deh non parlare al misero" and "Veglia o donna" (*Rigoletto*), up to "Figlia! a tal nome palpito" (*Simon Boccanegra*). All of these are selections that present, in the baritone line, a tenorlike sinuosity, flexibility, and delicacy; and not only would the part have had a different sense, but it could perhaps not even have been conceived had it been written in the tessitura of Bellini's and Donizetti's basso cantante. Identical considerations arise for certain arias in which the baritone, the tenor's rival in love, sings like a veritable lover, with melancholy, nostaligia, ecstasy, or insinuating gallantry. Think of the aria of the Conte di Luna, "Il balen del suo sorriso" (*Il trovatore*), of the phrase, "O dolcezze perdute" in Renato's "Eri tu" (*Un ballo in maschera*), or, as examples of gallantry, certain phrases of Carlo V in *Ernani:* "Da quel dì che t'ho veduta" and "Vieni meco sol di rose."

Finally, to give a complete idea of the vast palette of colors and shades acquired by the Verdi baritone, I should mention the subtleties of phrasing reached in declamatory, as well as in melodic phrases, by Iago in *Otello* and by Falstaff. It should be pointed out that Verdi rarely calls for agility from the baritone. Occasionally, however, and as late as *Don Carlos* and *Otello,* he is asked to perform a trill.

The other voices, in Verdi's operas, can attain major roles, but not with any consistency. The bass represents elderly persons who can be divided into four categories: priests (Zaccaria in *Nabucco,* the Hermit in *I lombardi,* the Padre Guardiano in *La forza del destino,* the Grand Inquisitor in *Don Carlos,* Ramfis in *Aida*); sovereigns (Attila, Philip II in *Don Carlos,* the Pharaoh in *Aida*); fathers, or, more precisely, "noble fathers" (Massimiliano di Moor in *I masnadieri,* Conte di Walter in *Luisa Miller,* Monterone in *Rigoletto,* the Marchese di Calatrava in *La forza del destino,* Jacopo Fiesco in *Simon Boccanegra*); assassins, conspirators, and avengers (Silva in *Ernani,* Wurm in *Luisa Miller,* Sparafucile in *Rigoletto,* Ferrando in *Il trovatore,* Procida in *Les Vêpres siciliennes,* Tom and Sam in *Un ballo in maschera*).

In these subdivisions Verdi follows substantially the concepts shared with the other Romantic composers, all of whom tend to use the bass voice to characterize not only advanced age but regal and sacerdotal dignity, paternal authority, and even, in certain cases (like Weber's *Freischütz* and Meyerbeer's *Robert le diable*) sinister and demoniac figures. With regard to the intrinsic characteristics of the bass, the categories can be reduced basically to two.

The first includes characters for whom the solemnity of timbre—that resemblance, particularly in the lowest register, to the color and depth of certain tones of the organ—inspires mystical and sacerdotal singing (Zaccaria in "Tu sul labbro dei veggenti" from *Nabucco;* the Hermit in the trio "Qui posa il fianco" from *I lombardi;* the Padre Guardiano in the finale of *La forza del destino;* Fiesco in "Il lacerato spirito" from *Simon Boccanegra*) or regretful considerations of the sadness and loneliness of old age. In fact, when Verdi touches this theme he brings the bass voice to a unique penetration of the conditions of extreme age, as shown in Silva's "Infelice e tuo credevi" (*Ernani*) and the great aria of Philip II, "Elle ne m'aime pas" in *Don Carlos.*

The other version of the Verdi bass is evidenced more in ensembles than in arias and is based on certain sinister, somber, sepulchral qualities of the bass timbre. This is the voice with which certain characters given to the bass voice reveal downright demoniacal wickedness, a vindictive spirit, a bent for evil (Silva in *Ernani,* Sparafucile in *Rigoletto*), or a heartless, inhuman rigor in the application of certain moral or religious rules (the Grand Inquisitor in *Don Carlos,* Ramfis in *Aida*).

To what has been said up to now should be added that in the operas of Verdi—as in the rest of the operas of the Italian Romantic period—it is rare to find the voice commonly defined as *basso profondo* because of its use in a very low tessitura. Sparafucile in *Rigoletto* approaches the basso profondo, however, and there are brief but incidental passages suggesting this voice in Zaccaria (*Nabucco*), Silva (*Ernani*), Fiesco (*Simon Boccanegra*), and the Grand Inquisitor (*Don Carlos*).

The mezzo-soprano voice is hardly ever found in Verdi's youthful operas, with the possible exception of the role of Fenena in *Nabucco*—not particularly important, moreover—which, nominally written for a soprano, can also be sung by mezzo-sopranos. The first two roles of any importance that Verdi wrote for mezzo-soprano were those of Maddalena in *Rigoletto* and Preziosilla in *La forza del destino.* Preziosilla is a gay and lively young gypsy and Maddalena, equally young and beautiful, is a woman of extremely doubtful morals whom Verdi uses as a foil for Gilda, the soprano. But the really great roles written by Verdi for the mezzo-soprano as antagonist are those of Eboli in *Don Carlos* and Amneris in *Aida:* two imperious, willful female characters who, in certain respects, are also vindictive and cruel. With Maddalena, Eboli, and Amneris, Verdi introduced into his operatic repertoire, through the mezzo-soprano, a sensual note (in particular the Oriental-flavored Song of the Veil and the nocturnal encounter with the protagonist in Act III of *Don Carlos,* as well as the long phrase "Vieni, amor mio, m'inebbria" in Act II of *Aida*), anticipating an orientation that Bizet will establish in definitive fashion with *Carmen.*

The other characteristic of the mezzo-soprano is that she sings chiefly in very high tessituras (Preziosilla, Eboli, Amneris) and, at times, reaches notes that are considered very high even for a soprano. Basically, in the conflict between the mezzo-soprano and the soprano that takes place in *Don Carlos* and *Aida,* Verdi aims less at making a marked differentiation between the two timbres than at rendering the mezzo-soprano aggressive and vehement through the ringing quality and the resonance of her high notes. As far as vocal agility is concerned, Verdi's writing includes an occasional coloratura passage for the mezzo-soprano in *La forza del destino* and in *Don Carlos,* where the Song of the Veil has a definitely virtuoso structure.

The contralto is utilized by Verdi as antagonist to the soprano in *Luisa Miller* (the Duchess Federica), but in this case his choice is purely incidental. He further avails himself of the contralto as a comic figure in *Falstaff* (Quickly) and in roles of witches in *Il trovatore* (Azucena) and *Un ballo in maschera* (Ulrica), obviously associating the dark, low tones of the contralto with advanced age.

The most striking role written by Verdi in the contralto register is that of Azucena, a character who, in *Il trovatore,* shares with the baritone the function of *deus ex machina.*

The contralto—a bel canto, virtuoso voice up to Rossini and in certain operas of Donizetti, Meyerbeer, and Mercadante—is instead treated realistically by Verdi, who, nevertheless, in *Il trovatore* provided her with fiorituras and embellishments ("Stride la vampa"). Note, however, that Verdi makes Azucena sing in a markedly higher tessitura than that normally adopted by his predecessors for the contralto.

From what has been said thus far, certain characteristics of Verdi's vocal writing have already emerged. One in particular: the gradual elimination of virtuoso singing—vocalises, trills, fioritura, embellishments—which represented the heritage of the Italian opera of the seventeenth and eighteenth centuries and the very early nineteenth century, and which obeyed the rules of an abstract, allegorical vocal art deliberately detached from any realistic aspiration. The realistic elements in Romanticism led, in the opera house, to an attempt at inflections and timbres more or less closely inspired by the spoken language, or at least by that version of the language represented by the historical novel and by the dramas of Byron, Schiller, Hugo, and their contemporaries. Of the Italian opera composers, Bellini, and Donizetti to an even greater degree, had already begun to detach the male voices from the ornate and florid vocal tradition. Verdi adopted this attitude and, beginning with *Simon Boccanegra* and *Un ballo in maschera*, extended it to the female voices. But his action was not limited to the gradual suppression of vocalized, ornate singing and its replacement by syllabic singing,[4] nor to the requirement that his performers, in moments of greatest tension, give a more vigorous, stentorian, and dramatically credible vocal characterization than those of his predecessors' operas. He did not even limit himself to accentuating these moments of tension by raising the

---

4. In syllabic singing each syllable corresponds to a note, whereas in vocalized singing each syllable (or, rather, each vowel in every syllable) corresponds to several notes. Syllabic singing implies a less light and therefore a more tiring production than that required for vocalized singing.

voices further up into the higher registers and having them sing in unison with each other or in unison with the orchestra (the so-called instrumental doubling). He did more. He insisted that the vocal writing had to provide an immediate reflection of the psychology of the character, that it register feelings, conflicts, and changes of mood, with a rapidity unknown to earlier opera composers. In substance: the vocal writing of Verdi aims at establishing the supremacy of the scenic effect over the vocal or musical effect. From this emerged a type of singing that is frequently placed at the opposite pole from that of Rossini, with Bellini and Donizetti somewhere between. And hence the aversion aroused, especially in Italy and in France (Paris, where Rossini lived, was, around the middle of the nineteenth century, the last stronghold of the bel canto singing tradition), by the way in which Verdi handled the voices. But here, most definitely, lies the key to the vocal writing of Verdi.

Before Verdi, the arias usually expressed a single sentiment. The so-called cavatinas served in general to display a character through the representation of his state of mind at a particular moment; and the cabalettas that followed them were as a rule simply a more lively, more vibrant, more dramatic projection of that state of mind. Then, to depict the various transmutations of passions and sentiments, there were other types of arias: moralizing, idyllic, indignant, vindictive, prayerful, remorseful; arias of desperation, malediction, madness, agony, joy, triumph. There were analogous duets of recognition and of farewell, idyllic and furious, of challenge and of friendship. All of that ensured for each separate excerpt its unity of tone and of vocal line, gradual and carefully calibrated melodic developments, structures with a symmetry that may be called architectonic (particularly in Rossini). The urgency with which Verdi reacted to the stimulus of the scenic effect above all led him to disregard the form and the substance of these traditions, to forge ahead and to combine various styles.

This quasi-revolution is, in certain ways, more noticeable after the "romantic trilogy" (*Rigoletto, La traviata, Il trovatore*), when Verdi abandoned the use of the cabaletta. Even in his earliest operas, however, there were frequent examples, within a single aria, of psychological contrasts and, consequently, contrasts in the vocal line. Let us look, as a case in point, at Ernani's entrance aria, "Come rugiada al cespite." The movement is dream like, nostalgic—partly because it includes fiorituras—but in the central part, suddenly, it becomes even in tone (*spianato*),[5] tense, vigorous, and almost declamatory ("Il vecchio Silva stendere / osa su lei la mano. / Domani trarla al talamo / confida l'inumano"). Even more significant in this respect is the aria of Carlo V, likewise in *Ernani*, "Oh de' verd'anni miei" (Act III). It begins with languid regret and elegant fiorituras, but the second part ("E vincitor dei secoli") is vibrant, imperious, grandiose. The same takes place in Macbeth's aria "Pietà, rispetto, amore" and in many others, from "Il balen del suo sorriso" of the Conte di Luna (*Il trovatore*)—which is smooth and idyllic in the first part, ardent and vehement in the second—to Henri's "Ô jour de peine" (*Les Vêpres siciliennes*) or Riccardo's "Ma se m'è forza perderti" (*Un ballo in maschera*) and "O tu che in seno agli angeli" of Don Alvaro (*La forza del destino*). And, still on the subject of these last two operas, there are countless examples of alternation between varied and frequently opposing feelings in arias such as Amelia's "Ma dall'arido stelo divulsa," Renato's "Eri tu che macchiavi quell'anima," or Leonora's "Pace mio Dio." These are but a few cases out of the many that might be mentioned, including duets and trios. For instance, the duet of Violetta and Giorgio Germont in Act II of *La traviata* takes the soprano almost without a break from hope to despair and from collapse to resignation. And in the duet of Gilda and Rigoletto in Act II of *Rigoletto*, both singers, beginning with the andantino "Tutte le feste al tempio" and on to the so-called vengeance cabaletta, keep alternating melting and affectionate singing with harsh and incandescent outbursts.

5. Even-toned singing (*canto spianato*) is precisely a vocal style without embellishments, fioritura, and vocalization.

How does Verdi effect these sudden changes of temperature? Above all, obviously, with diverse instrumental and melodic procedures. But with specific reference to the vocal writing, a first method of depicting a sudden change of mood is to match it with a sudden leap of the voice—usually from low to high, occasionally the reverse—rather than letting the singer's voice rise—or fall—by gradual degrees. Naturally this system was in use long before Verdi, but Verdi applied it more widely than his predecessors.

Another formula is presented by the frequent contrasts of intensity and color. There is in Verdi as in no other composer before him a superabundance of dynamic markings: indications of crescendo, diminuendo, *con dolcezza, con forza, f* (forte), *ff* (fortissimo), *p* (piano), *pp* (pianissimo), and even *ppp* and *pppp*. In short, Verdi's vocal writing constitutes a continuous succession of varying gradations of tone production: vigorous, soft, and intermediate. In demanding of his interpreters this wide range of contrasts and nuances, Verdi frequently takes into account only the exigencies of the dramatic moment without evaluating the actual vocal possibilities of the average singer. It thus happens that he calls for the production of a very soft high note from characters like Radamès and Aida, Don Alvaro and Leonora—or like Otello—roles which must normally be assigned, for their intrinsic characteristics, to sopranos and tenors with full, robust, even stentorian voices, and, therefore, practically incapable of producing a soft high note. But as a matter of fact, only in exceptional cases do we hear the high note (a B flat) that closes Radamès's aria ("Celeste Aida") sung softly[6] or the high C of Aida's aria ("O cieli azzurri"), or a B flat in the aria "Pace mio Dio," which Leonora should sing *pp* after an octave leap, or an A flat in the final trio of *La forza del destino,* which Alvaro should attack *ppp,* or the other A flat, in the phrase "Venere splende," with which Otello ends the Act I love duet

6. The public is so accustomed to hearing this note blasted out at top volume that some years ago a famous tenor, Carlo Bergonzi, was booed in an Italian theater for having taken the note piano, as Verdi wrote it.

with Desdemona. These are only a few examples among the many that we could mention as evidence of the consistent failure to observe Verdi's dynamic markings. This failure reflects to a large extent the technical shortcomings of the singers or the carelessness of orchestral conductors—even the most famous, including some who are celebrated as Verdi interpreters. It also stems from the sheer physical dificulties inherent in the composer's style of writing. But Verdi's urge to achieve dramatic effect through the rapid and agitated depiction of the changing moods of a character (an urge, moreover, which—we must admit it—is one of the prime reasons for Verdi's greatness) brings in its wake the fact that the vocal writing tends toward realism, not only in the imitation of certain timbres and certain stresses of spoken or declaimed speech, but even in the imitation of normal breathing. We can offer two examples. The first is Violetta's waltz ("Sempre libera") which ends Act I of *La traviata*. The almost neurotic rhythm of this selection, even if it is justified by the state of mind of the character, obliges her to execute difficult and high-lying vocalization, often practically without time to catch her breath. The other example, perhaps still more typical, is represented by Rigoletto's great scene in Act II. From the invective of "Cortigiani vil razza dannata" to "Ebben, io piango" and "Miei signori, perdono, pietade," we have not only continuous alternations from anger to imploration—and, therefore, from full voice to the softest possible notes—but also frequent shifts in rhythm—and, therefore, of breathing—through the succession of extended, broad phrases followed by others which are broken, agitated, breathless.

These are not, of course, two isolated examples. In Verdi's vocal phrasing, the breathing rhythm is often irregular. This means that the melody is composed of phrases of unequal length which do not allow the singer to take regular and natural breaths, as was the case with earlier composers (Rossini in particular). Not infrequently, too, short phrases alternate with others where there are no markings for pauses. If we consider the duet of Giorgio Germont and Violetta in Act II of *La traviata,* the baritone should sing uninterruptedly, since there are no markings to indicate a pause, the following phrase: "Le rose dell'amor, ah non mutate in triboli le rose dell'amor . . . a' prieghi miei resistere no, no, non voglia il vostro, cor, no, no." And in *La forza del destino,* at his entrance Don Alvaro (tenor) should sing, without a single pause, twenty-two measures, albeit at a rapid tempo (Allegro): "Da lung'ora mille inciampi tua dimora m'han vietato penetrar; ma d'amor sì puro e santo, nulla opporsi può all'incanto, e Dio stesso il nostro palpito in letizia, in letizia tramutò."

It is obviously impossible to sing such phrases without a break. The singer must in such cases contrive to catch his breath in short, clandestine gulps known, in singers' jargon, as *fiati rubati* (stolen breaths). He cannot take a regular and adequate breath because it would disturb the regular flow of the music and he would lose the rhythm. But only really experienced singers succeed, by "stolen breaths" of a fraction of a second, in taking a sufficient amount of air into their lungs. The others manage, one might say, with hiccups: they have to take one "stolen breath" after another, which wearies the diaphragm (the muscle regulating the breath) and gives a sense of breathless and irregular singing. But even where Verdi does provide pauses, the succession of short and long phrases is very uncomfortable for the singer and tends to tire him.

I should say that Verdi's vocal writing is irksome above all for the irregular breathing that it imposes. Breathing is the basis of singing. Good singing consists, essentially, in taking in a certain quantity of breath and in letting it out, transformed into sound, not all at once, but gradually, continuously, reinforcing the flow—to intensify the sound—or diminishing it—to attenuate the sound— smoothly and without breaks. Otherwise the timbre of the voice becomes harsh or strident, the high notes require an enormous effort and emerge hard-sounding, the production of piano or pianissimo sounds becomes problematical, the pitch of the tone wavers and the entire vocal mechanism tends to deteriorate. What is required is a veritable breathing technique, which calls for long study and continual practice. Hence the epithet "Attila of the voice," given to Verdi between 1840 and 1860 by the followers of Rossini. Verdi, according to these followers, imposed soprano tessituras that were too high, and turned baritones into tenors and basses into baritones. Furthermore, he expected his performers to sing too often in full voice and, even more, in unison with the orchestra, a procedure which implied a continuous effort to override the sound barrier interposed by the instruments.

All of this was true, especially in comparison to the vocal writing of Rossini, who was seeking quite different effects and was not concerned with depicting psychological truth by a basically realistic imitation of human passions. Verdi and his vocal writing must be evaluated on a completely different level, just as, in theatrical practice, a great Rossini interpreter—a Marilyn Horne, for example, or a Teresa Berganza—cannot be asked to perform Verdi in the traditional manner (but by the same token Leontyne Price cannot be asked to perform a perfect Rossini role). Verdi's theatrical realism, which requires different stress from that of Rossini and Donizetti—more strongly marked, more emotional, more incandescent—does not consider the convenience of the performers, but counts on their interpretive rather than on their vocal capacities, and involves definite psychic wear (or, in any case, a corresponding expenditure of nervous energy) because of the impassioned coloring of the melodic expression. Singers who are insufficiently prepared, above all technically, to overcome these difficulties, frequently lose their voices in a few years of singing Verdi. It happens today and it happened in 1850 and in 1880. But I do not believe that this suffices to justify the nickname "Attila of the voice."

Translated by Harold Barnes

A Select Bibliography

Andrew Porter

ANDREW PORTER, M.A. (Oxon.), is music critic of *The New Yorker*. His reconstruction of the *"Ur" Don Carlos* was performed in London, Boston, and Venice. Contributor to many international Verdi congresses and author of the Verdi entry in the forthcoming (sixth) edition of *Grove's Dictionary*, he is one of the founders and a member of the Executive Board of the American Institute for Verdi Studies, whose *Newsletter* he edits.

The Verdi bibliography is immense. In the year of the composer's death, Luigi Torri attempted a "Saggio di bibliografia verdiana" in *Rivista Musicale Italiana* 8 (1901), 379–407. Twelve years later, in the centenary of Verdi's birth, C. Vanbianchi published another study with the same title (Milan, 1913). Long, uncritical bibliographies appear in Anna Amalia Abert's Verdi entry in *Die Musik in Geschichte und Gegenwart* 13 (1966), 1426–58, and in Massimo Mila's *La giovinezza di Verdi* (Turin, 1974), 507–17. David Lawton's "Per una bibliografia ragionata verdiana" in *Atti 1, 437–42*, contains a select list of thirty-seven items. Post-1974 (i.e. post-Mila) publications are listed in detail in the successive issues of the *Verdi Newsletter* of the American Institute for Verdi Studies (1976 onward); Elvidio Surian's "Lo stato attuale degli studi verdiani: appunti e bibliografia ragionata (1960–1975)" in *Rivista Italiana di Musico-*

logia 12 (1977), 305–29 also deals with more recent studies.

For the sixth edition of *Grove's Dictionary of Music and Musicians*, the present writer has prepared an extensive, classified, but, in *Grove* style, unannotated bibiography selected from publications up to October 1978. What he offers here is an informal first guide to some of the more important or interesting writings, with a few words of description or explanation when a title is not in itself self-explanatory. Sometimes, in the manner of a treasure hunt, only the first clue has been given when it leads an interested searcher to something that will in its turn direct him toward other things that he should see. When there has been simultaneous or near-simultaneous publication of a book in, say, London and New York, the "originating" city only is specified.

The widespread international attention to the study of Verdi's music—close, serious study, such as Josquin's, Mozart's, Beethoven's, and Wagner's music has long received—can probably be dated from the first International Verdi Congress organized in 1960 in Venice, by the Istituto di Studi Verdiani in Parma. Before that, there had been general studies, biographies that lifted no more than corners of the veil in which Verdi liked to wrap his life, and a few penetrating articles and dissertations. And there was a mass of material—letters, memoranda, rehearsal schedules, scores, sketches, instrumental and vocal parts, scenic designs—lying unexamined in public libraries and private collections. At that Venice congress and at its successors (in Verona, Parma, and Busseto in 1969, devoted to *Don Carlos;* in Milan in 1972; in Chicago in 1974, devoted to *Simon Boccanegra;* and in Danville, Kentucky, in 1977, devoted to *Macbeth*) the existence of this material was signaled and its importance began to be assessed. Meanwhile, keen minds played upon every aspect of Verdi's creation: his forms; his use of harmonically organized structures on scales small and large; his melodic formulae and their significance; his orchestration; the relation between verse forms and musical forms; his ideas about staging; his ideas about singing. And, as a result, Verdi study has been transformed. In the early years of this century, Alfred Noyes's line "The music's only Verdi" (he heard a *Trovatore* tune ground by a barrel-organ) reflected critical opinion in that "only." *Rigoletto, Il trovatore, La traviata,* and *Aida* were played the world over, but most serious musicians thought only *Aida, Otello, Falstaff,* and the *Requiem* worth their careful study. A Verdi renaissance began in Germany in the '20s and '30s, with performances of the lesser-known operas, and spread to Britain: Franz Werfel's novel *Verdi: Roman der Oper* appeared in English translation in 1923; Hans Gerigk's *Giuseppe Verdi* (Potsdam, 1932) treated the composer as more than a popular tunesmith; Bonavia's, Toye's, and Hussey's pioneering books are listed below.

After the 1939–45 war, *all* Verdi's operas were brought to the stage in Britain and then in Italy, while in New York Rudolf Bing made Verdi's works the cornerstone of his Metropolitan repertory. Today, they dominate the international scene more decisively than ever. With performances have come scholarly scrutiny and reassessment, and now no doctoral candidate need blushingly admit that his subject is "only" some aspect of Verdi. The composer himself might well smile at some of the studies listed below—but he would surely find this serious attention preferable to what he believed, in the 1860s and 1870s, was the attitude of Italy's young intellectuals toward his work—to dismiss it as "brothel music."

The publications of the Istituto di Studi Verdiani, whose international congresses brought so much of the new scholarship into focus, should head any list. They fall into three series: the *Bollettini,* the *Quaderni,* and the *Atti.* The *Bollettini* are fat three-volume studies, plus index, of particular operas, by various hands and on various topics related to the central subject. The texts appear in Italian, English, and German. The three volumes devoted to *Un ballo in maschera* (*Bolletino* 1) appeared in 1960. Then the pace slowed down; *Bollettino* 2, devoted to *La forza del destino*, appeared between 1961 and 1966. Of *Bolletino* 3, devoted to *Rigoletto*, the first volume appeared in 1969, and the second in 1973—and that is as far as it has gone. The *Quaderni* are slimmer volumes. The first three were published in connection with modern revivals of rarer operas. *Quaderno* 1 (1963) is devoted to *Il corsaro*, *Quaderno* 2 (1963) to *Jérusalem* (and *I lombardi*), and *Quaderno* 3 (1968) to *Stiffelio* (and *Aroldo*); they are collections, in Italian only, of essays and documents. *Quaderno* 4 (1971) is rather different; it contains an assemblage of letters about the genesis of *Aida*, a set of Mariette's costume designs for the first production, reproduced in black and white, and annals of performances in the first decade of the opera's existence. The *Atti* are the congress reports; several of the papers were revised and amplified for publication. *Atti* 1 (the Venice congress of 1966) appeared in 1969; *Atti* 2 (Verona, etc., 1969) in 1972; and *Atti* 3 (Milan, 1972) in 1974. See *Simon Boccanegra* and *Macbeth* below for the papers read in Chicago and at the Danville congress organized by the American Institute for Verdi Studies. This Institute, founded in 1976, has the most extensive collection of Verdi material in America; its archive is housed in the Bobst Library of New York University.

Catalogs

The indispensable worklist is Martin Chusid's *A Catalog of Verdi's Operas* (Hackensack, N.J., 1974). It gives dates and casts of first performances; a brief description of the autographs; a listing of how each is divided into "numbers"; details of early copies and of early scores, full and vocal (with locations); and much else that makes it an invaluable guide to Verdian textual studies and discoveries up to 1974. Cecil Hopkinson's *A Bibliography of the Works of Giuseppe Verdi*, volume 1 (New York, 1973) dealing with the nonoperatic compositions and volume 2 (New York, 1978) with the operas, is a detailed and curious publication, much of whose information will be of more concern to collectors, dealers, and librarians than to students of Verdi's music. The principal contribution lies in the information about early prints of the piano-vocal scores, and even here there are omissions. Other information must be checked against other sources. Verdi's alternative arias are discussed and cataloged in David Lawton and David Rosen, "Verdi's Non-Definitive Revisions," *Atti* 3, 189–237.

Editions

In 1977, Ricordi and the University of Chicago Press announced plans for joint publication of a critical edition of Verdi's complete works. Verdi studies—and Verdi performances—have long been hampered by the lack of an accurate text. For some of the operas, full scores are still not generally available.

Ricordi bought the rights of Verdi's first opera, *Oberto,* in 1839, and remained his principal publisher; in Italy, only *Attila, I masnadieri,* and *Il corsaro* went to the rival house of Lucca (which was taken over by Ricordi in 1888). Vocal scores were published close to the time of the premieres, the earlier works usually in oblong format. The Paris operas were published in vocal score by the Bureau Central de Musique/Escudier and almost simultaneously, in Italian translation, by Ricordi. The Italian operas up to *La forza* were also published in vocal score in Paris. Other editions proliferated, both before the establishment of copyright and after Verdi's music entered the public domain, but the "standard editions" remain those of Ricordi. Over the years they have been edited and reedited, often tacitly, and issues with the same plate number can show significant differences of phrasing and dynamics.

For hire only, Ricordi printed full scores of most of the operas, beginning with *La traviata* in about 1855. In 1912–14, study scores of *Rigoletto, Il trovatore, La traviata, Un ballo in maschera, Aida, Otello, Falstaff,* and the *Requiem* were published; these have been revised in subsequent issues. Some of the "hire only" printed scores found their way into public collections (for locations, see Chusid's *Catalog*); and E. F. Kalmus have reprinted full scores of not only the eight works listed above but also a number of other operas, including *Nabucco, Ernani, Giovanna d'Arco, Macbeth, La battaglia di Legnano, Simon Boccanegra, Luisa Miller, Aroldo, La forza del destino, Don Carlos,* and *I vespri siciliani.* Peters published a score of *La forza* (1960) and an unrecommended *Bearbeitung* of *Don Carlos* (1954). A facsimile of the *Requiem* autograph was published in 1941, and of *Falstaff* in 1951. There are Eulenburg miniature scores of the *Requiem* and of the *Quattro pezzi sacri.* Most of Verdi's songs are collected in Ricordi's *Composizioni da camera per canto e pianoforte.*

The accuracy of the printed texts is variable. See, on this subject, Dennis Vaughan's "Discordanze tra gli autografi verdiani e la loro stampa" in *La Scala* 104 (1958), 11, 71; Giandrea Gavazzeni's "Problemi di tradizione dinamico-fraseologica e critica testuale, in Verdi e in Puccini," in *Rassegna Musicale* 29 (1959), 27, 106; and the Gavazzeni-Vaughan correspondence in *Rassegna Musicale* 30 (1960), 60. An expanded version of Gavazzeni's article, together with the ensuing correspondence, was separately published in Italian, English, and German (Ricordi, 1961).

For librettos, it is best to use the Ricordi editions. The bilingual versions issued with recordings and sold in theaters, being intended chiefly to give a listener the meaning of the words sung, commonly misrepresent the lineation and verse forms of the original. *Seven Verdi Librettos,* with a literal translation by William Weaver (New York, 1974), has the same disadvantage. *Tutti i libretti di Verdi* (Milan, 1975) obscures the verse forms by setting all lines to a single margin. Edited texts of the *Ballo* and (in both languages) *Vêpres/Vespri* librettos appear in the series *Opera: Collana di guide musicali* (Turin, 1973). Production books— *disposizioni sceniche*—were published for all the operas from *Les Vêpres* to *Otello.* They became increasingly detailed:

that for *Otello* contains not only minute instructions for the staging and for every move of the singers, but also accounts of character and motivation. (See Doug Coe's "The Original Production Book for *Otello*" in *19th Century Music* 2 [1978], 148–58.) These production books are surprisingly rare, but the archive of the American Institute for Verdi Studies has a complete run of them in photostat. The *Ballo, Forza,* and *Don Carlos* books were reproduced in facsimile in the Scala program books for the 1977–78 season. For the *Aida* book in English translation, see under *Aida* below.

Biography

There is no generally recommendable, thoroughly reliable biography of Verdi. The longest and most detailed is Franco Abbiati's four-volume *Verdi,* in Italian (Milan, 1959), the first to be written with full access to the collections of documents in Sant'Agata, the Ricordi archives, and Natale Gallini's important collection. The book is unnecessarily wordy; it contains errors of fact, of transcription, and of interpretation, and what Frank Walker described as "many pages of pure fiction." The location of the documents quoted is seldom given. But for tracing in detail the history of a particular opera, recourse to the relevant chapters of Abbiati is indispensable, and he is the only source for many otherwise unpublished letters.

In English, there are several shorter biographies or life-and-works that ably marshal the facts—together with the misconceptions—about Verdi's life as they were known at the time. Ferruccio Bonavia's *Verdi* (London, 1930), Francis Toye's *Verdi* (London, 1931), Dyneley Hussey's *Verdi* in the Master Musicians series (London, 1940; a few corrections in later editions), and George Martin's *Verdi* (New York, 1963) are the best of them. Toye's book is particularly agreeable to read, and Martin's has a special value indicated by its subtitle: "His Music, Life, and Times." But new facts about Verdi's life are still being revealed almost monthly. Frank Walker's *The Man Verdi* (London, 1962), not a formal biography but a detailed study of the composer in relation to those who were closest to him, cleared up some of the legends and is written with penetrating insight into the characters of those concerned. But even Walker needs correction now.

Verdi liked to exaggerate the humbleness of his origins and even on occasion to reorder his memories, rather as he reordered the first drafts of his librettos, into more strikingly dramatic form. His father was not illiterate. His talent was recognized early and sedulously fostered. In Busseto, he received a humane classical education among schoolfellows several of whom achieved distinction in various fields. In Milan, he was soon associated with the leading Italian intellectuals and artists of his day. These things should be borne in mind when reading the earlier biographies. Two articles by Mary Jane Phillips Matz— "The Verdi Family of Roncole and Sant'Agata: Legend and Truth" in *Atti* 1, 216–21, and "Verdi: The Roots of the Tree" in *Bolletino* 3, 333–64—shed light on the composer's origins and earlier years; and she is working on a biography which in its wealth of detailed information promises to supersede all others and to produce a strikingly different picture of the composer from those previously painted.

Giuseppe Demaldè, a Bussetano who knew Verdi from the cradle and was related to Verdis, Barezzis, and Carraras, began in the early 1840s to amass facts about the composer and around 1853 drafted his "Cenni biografici del maestro Giuseppi Verdi." His barely decipherable draft and notes remained unpublished in the Busseto Monte di Pietà and are now in the Civic Library. Early biographers made some use of them, but not until 1962 were they carefully and fully transcribed, by Ernesto Macchidani. Demaldè's biographical sketch, which ends at *Nabucco*, was first published, in Italian and English, in the first three issues of the *Verdi Newsletter*. In 1867 Hercules Cavalli published his *José Verdi* (Madrid; in Spanish). The book is rare; in fact only one copy, in the Trieste Civic

Library, has so far been traced. It has the value of being written by someone who knew the composer intimately from his Busseto days. A section in Michele Lessona's *Volere è potere* (Milan, 1869) also affords a contemporary's testimony. In 1878, Gino Monaldi published *Verdi e le sue opere* (Florence), the first in his long series of gossipy, inaccurate books about the composer; Verdi himself declared that it was "filled with inexactitudes."

By this time, biographical sketches of Verdi had begun to appear in magazines all over the world. Arthur Pougin collected all the information he could find in his "vie anecdotique" published serially in *Le Ménestrel* in 1878. In 1881, this appeared in an Italian edition: *Giuseppe Verdi: vita aneddotica*, translated, annotated, and augmented by "Folchetto" (the pen name of Jacopo Caponi). It was issued by Verdi's own publisher, Ricordi. The composer was skeptical about it but said that if it were going to appear, it had better be accurate; he dictated to Giulio Ricordi the account of his early years which appears in the volume. He was sent proofs and returned them "with corrections of various inaccuracies of some importance." Various striking inaccuracies of some importance remained, however, as later research has shown. Verdi's autobiographical memoir is translated in full in William Weaver's *Verdi: A Documentary Study* (London, 1977). Pougin produced a new version of the work with Folchetto's additions incorporated into the main text (Paris, 1886), and it was translated into English (London, 1887). It remained the standard biography until Carlo Gatti's two-volume *Verdi* appeared (Milan, 1931). Gatti could draw both on his own researches and on the extensive collections of correspondence that began to appear early in the twentieth century (see below). His volumes were well illustrated and copiously documented. In 1951, a one-volume edition appeared, corrected but also heavily abridged; this has been translated into English as *Verdi: The Man and his Music* (1955). Gatti, in turn, remained the standard biography until Abbiati replaced it. Two important books, one by and

one about an associate of the composer, are Antonio Ghislanzoni, *Gli Artisti da Teatro* (Milan, 1872), and Pietro
Nardi, *Vita di Arrigo Boito* (Milan, 1942).

Documents

Verdi was a prolific correspondent. Of many—but by no
means all—of his more important letters he kept copies;
these were transcribed and edited by Gaetano Cesari and
Alessandro Luzio in *I copialettere di Giuseppe Verdi* (Milan,
1913). This is the most important single volume of the
composer's correspondence. Selections from it appear in
English, translated by Charles Osborne, in *Letters of Giuseppe Verdi* (London, 1971). Other important letters were
gathered by Luzio in his four volumes of *Carteggi verdiani*
(Rome, 1935, 1947). The other major letter collections
are:

Alessandro Pascolato, *Re Lear e Ballo in maschera: lettere di
Giuseppe Verdi ad Antonio Somma* (Città di Castello, 1902).

Annibale Alberti, *Verdi intimo: carteggio di Giuseppe Verdi con
il conte Opprandino Arrivabene (1861–1886)* (Verona, 1931),
a relaxed, friendly correspondence, showing Verdi at his
most attractive.

A. Luzio, "Il carteggio di Giuseppe Verdi con la contessa
Maffei," in *Profili biografici e bozzetti storici* 2 (Milan, 1927),
505–62.

Luigi Agostino Garibaldi, *Giuseppe Verdi nelle lettere di
Emanuele Muzio ad Antonio Barezzi* (Milan, 1931), a prime
source for the years 1844–47, when young Muzio was
Verdi's companion and amanuensis and wrote chattily and
often to the composer's father-in-law.

Raffaello De Rensis, *Franco Faccio e Verdi: carteggio e documenti inediti* (Milan, 1934).

Giannetto Bongiovanni, *Dal carteggio inedito Verdi-Vigna*
(Rome, 1941).

Many other letters have been published, singly or in groups. (See the bibliography in *Grove* 6.) Some of those dealing with specific operas are noted below. There is great need for a collected edition. The Istituto di Studi Verdiani in Parma has amassed in facsimile and cataloged all the Verdi letters it can trace; there is also a very large collection on film (including many things not in Parma) in the archive of the American Institute for Verdi Studies.

An attractive "documentary biography," *Giuseppe Verdi: autobiografia dalle lettere,* was compiled by Aldo Oberdorfer (first edition, censored and pseudonymous, as by "Carlo Graziani," Verona, 1941; complete, Milan, 1951). Franz Werfel and Paul Stefan's *Das Bildnis Giuseppe Verdis* (Vienna, 1926), enlarged and translated into English as *Verdi: The Man in His Letters* (New York, 1942), is a highly recommended selection from the *Copialettere* and other sources. The chief iconographical volume was Carlo Gatti's *Verdi nelle immagini* (Milan, 1941), until William Weaver's *Verdi: A Documentary Study* appeared (London, 1977). Besides a very rich inconographical selection, this handsome volume includes (in English translation) the fullest and most balanced collection of Verdi documents, assembled from all available sources.

Musical Studies

The earliest musical study of Verdi's operas, Abramo Basevi's *Studio sulle opere di Giuseppe Verdi* (Florence, 1859), remains one of the best; it goes as far as *Aroldo.* Intelligent and revealing nineteenth-century general estimates of Verdi can be found in Henry Chorley's *Thirty Years' Musical Recollections* (London, 1862), 182 ff.; Eduard Hanslick's *Die moderne Oper* 1 (1875), 217–55; and Bernard Shaw's "A Word More about Verdi," in *Anglo-Saxon Review* (1901), reprinted in *London Music in 1888–89* (London, 1937). The opinions of an influential Italian critic appear in Filippo Filippi's *Musica e musicisti* (Milan, 1876).

The twentieth century produced several opera-by-opera commentaries as well as general studies; valuable musical observations appear in the Gerigk, Bonavia, Toye, and Hussey books mentioned above, in Massimo Mila's *Il melo-dramma di Verdi* (Bari, 1933), in several studies by Gino Roncaglia, in Andrea Della Corte's *Le sei più belle opere di Giuseppe Verdi* (Milan, 1946), and in Vincent Godefroy's *The Dramatic Genius of Verdi: Studies of Selected Operas* (London, vol. 1, 1975; vol. 2, 1978). Spike Hughes's *Famous Verdi Operas* (London, 1968) is a friendly guide that pays special attention to the scoring. Charles Osborne's *The Complete Operas of Verdi* (London, 1969) offers a light-weight popular commentary.

But the place to start is Julian Budden's *The Operas of Verdi.* Two volumes have so far appeared, the first subtitled "from *Oberto* to *Rigoletto*" (London, 1973), the second "from *Il trovatore* to *La forza del destino*" (London, 1978). Budden's chapters, built on his own careful, penetrating, enthusiastic but not uncritical observation of the works, take into account all aspects of the modern "explosion" in Verdi studies: the new attention paid to form, versification, harmony, melodic construction, sources, influences, etc. He has mastered both the old and the current literature, and in his footnotes he provides, in effect, an index to much of what is most valuable in it. Since Budden should be the starting place, in the opera-by-opera bibliography below I have usually not listed the articles to which he will in any case direct them.

On specific topics there are:

Orchestration
Francis I. Travis, *Verdi's Orchestration* (Zurich, 1956), a general survey.

Motivic Organization
Gino Roncaglia: "Il 'tema-cardine' nell'opera di Giuseppe Verdi," *Rivista Musicale Italiana* 47 (1943), 218–29; Joseph Kerman; "Verdi's Use of Recurring Themes," *Studies in Music History: Essays for Oliver Strunk* (Princeton, 1968); Frits Noske, "Verdi and the Musical Figure of Death," *Atti* 3, 349–86, reprinted in *The Signifier and the Signified* (The Hague, 1977).

Harmonic Organization
David Lawton, "Tonality and Drama in Verdi's Early Operas" (Ph.D. dissertation, University of California, Berkeley, 1973); and see below

under *Rigoletto* and *Traviata* (Chusid), *Ballo* (Levarie), *Otello* (Lawton), and *Falstaff* (Sabbeth).

Vocal Characterization
Rodolfo Celletti, "Caratteri della vocalità di Verdi," *Atti* 3, 81–88.

Versification and Melodic Structure
Friedrich Lippmann, "Der italienische Vers und die Musikalische Rhythmus . . . ," *Analecta Musicologica* 12 (1973), 253–69; 14 (1974), 324–410; and 15 (1975), 298–333.

Shakespeare Operas
Winton Dean, "Shakespeare and Opera," in *Shakespeare in Music,* ed. Phyllis Hartnoll (London, 1964) 89–175; Edward T. Cone, "The Old Man's Toys: Verdi's Last Operas," *Perspectives U.S.A.* 6 (1954), 114–33.

Individual Works

Nabucco
David Lawton, "Analytical Observations on the *Nabucco* Revisions," *Atti* 3, 208–20.

I lombardi
Quaderno 2

Ernani
Joseph Kerman, "Notes on an Early Verdi Opera," *Soundings* 3 (1973), 56.

Alzira
Massimo Mila, "Lettura dell'*Alzira*," *Rivista Italiana di Musicologia* 1 (1966), 246–67.

Attila
Michel Noiray and Roger Parker, "La Composition d'*Attila:* étude de quelques variantes," *Revue de Musicologie* 62 (1976), 104–24.

Macbeth
There is in preparation *Verdi's Macbeth: a Sourcebook,* edited by David Rosen, which will be at once the proceedings of the 1977 congress in Danville, Kentucky, devoted to the opera, and a thorough assemblage, in original language and translation, of the documents concerned with its genesis, composition, revision, and staging.

Jérusalem
Quaderno 2

Il corsaro
Quaderno 1

La battaglia di Legnano

Julian Budden, "*La battaglia di Legnano:* Its Unique Character, with Special Reference to the Finale of Act I," *Atti* 3, 71–80.

Stiffelio

Quaderno 3

Rigoletto

Bollettino 3

The sketches for this opera have been published: *L'abbozzo del Rigoletto di Giuseppe Verdi* (Milan, 1941), with an introduction by Carlo Gatti; see also Gino Roncaglia, "L'abbozzo del *Rigoletto* di Verdi," *Rivista Musicale Italiana* 48 (1946), 112–29; and Martin Chusid, "Rigoletto and Monterone: A Study in Musical Dramaturgy," *IMS Congress Report, Copenhagen 1972* 1 (1974), 325–36.

Il trovatore

Pierluigi Petrobelli, "Per un'esegisi della struttura drammatica del *Trovatore*," *Atti* 3, 387–400; David Rosen, "*Le trouvère:* Comparing Verdi's French Version with His Original," *Opera News* 41 (1977), No. 22, 16.

La traviata

Julian Budden, "The Two Traviatas," in *Proceedings of the Royal Musical Association* 99 (1972–73), 43–66 deals with the revisions Verdi effected after the first performance; Martin Chusid, "Drama and the Key of F major in *La traviata*," *Atti* 3, 89–121.

Les Vêpres siciliennes

Andrew Porter, "*Les Vêpres siciliennes:* New Letters from Verdi to Scribe," in *19th century Music* 2 (1978–79) shows how large a part Verdi played in the writing of the *Vêpres* libretto.

Simon Boccanegra

The fourth International Verdi Congress, in Chicago in 1974, was devoted to this opera. The proceedings have not been published, but most of the papers are due to appear in the *Festschrift* for Mario Medici, the first director of the Istituto di Studi Verdiani. Meanwhile, Wolfgang Osthoff's "Die beide *Boccanegra* Fassungen und der Beginn von Verdis Spätwerk," in *Analecta Musicologica* 1 (1963), 70–89, can be consulted for the revision. Frits Noske's "*Simon Boccanegra:* One Plot, Two Dramas," appears in his *The Signifier and the Signified* (The Hague, 1977) 215–40. This volume also includes the Verdi-Boito correspondence in Italian and English.

Un ballo in maschera

Bolletino 1

Siegmund Levarie, "Key Relations in Verdi's *Un ballo in maschera,*" *19th Century Music* 2 (1978–79).

La forza del destino
Bolletino 2

Don Carlos
Atti 2

Since the 1969 congress, much work has been done on the opera; see Andrew Porter, "The Making of *Don Carlos,*" *Proceedings of the Royal Musical Association* 98 (1971–72), 73–88, and Ursula Günther, "La Genèse de *Don Carlos,*" *Revue de Musicologie* 58 (1972), 16–64, and 60 (1974) 87–158. Subsequent articles by Günther and Porter are listed in the latter's "Preamble to a New *Don Carlos,*" *Opera* 25 (1974), 665–73. The Verdi–Nuitter–Du Locle correspondence about the revision is published by Günther and Gabriella Carrara Verdi in *Analecta Musicologica* 14 (1974), 1–31, and 15 (1975), 334–40. The fullest account of the opera's complicated history appears in Günther's preface to a forthcoming *edizione integrale* of the opera (published separately, Milan, 1977). Marc Clémeur proposed a new source for the libretto in "Eine neuentdeckte Quelle für das Libretto von Verdis *Don Carlos,*" *Melos/Neue Zeitschrift für Musik* 3 (1977), 496–99.

Aida
Hans Busch's *Verdi's Aida: the History of an Opera in Letters and Documents* (Minneapolis, 1978) is a very full documentation, in English translation, of the opera's genesis and first performances: 743 letters, documents including the draft librettos through stage after stage, the production notes of Verdi and of Faccio, and the *disposizione scenica* compiled by Giulio Ricordi. Original-language texts of many important letters may be found in Alessandro Luzio, "Come fu composta l'*Aida,*" in *Carteggi verdiani* 4 (Rome, 1947), 5–27; in *Quaderno* 4; and in Ursula Günther, "Zur Entstehung von Verdis *Aida,*" *Studi musicali* 2 (1973), 15–71. The first scenario Verdi received appears in Jean Humbert, "A propos de l'égyptomanie dans l'oeuvre de Verdi," *Revue de Musicologie* 62 (1976), 229–56.

Otello
Joseph Kerman, "Verdi's *Othello,* or Shakespeare Explained," *Hudson Review* 6 (1953–54), 266–77 appears in revised form in his *Opera as Drama* (New York, 1956), 129–67; Busoni, "Verdi's *Otello:* eine kritische Studie," *Neue Zeitschrift für Musik* 54 (1887), 125 is an interesting early study; Winton Dean, "Verdi's *Otello:* A Shakespearean Masterpiece," *Shakespeare Survey* 21 (1968), 87; David Lawton, "On the 'bacio' Theme in *Otello,*" *19th Century Music* 1 (1977–78), 211–20.

Falstaff

Edward T. Cone, "The Stature of *Falstaff:* Technique and Content in Verdi's Last Opera," *Center* 1 (1954), 17–23. One of Verdi's revisions of the score is discussed in Hans Gál, "A Deleted Episode in Verdi's *Falstaff*," *Music Review* 2 (1941), 266–72; Guglielmo Barblan; *Un prezioso spartito del "Falstaff"* (Milan, 1957), and Barblan, "Spunti rivelatori nella genesi del *Falstaff, Atti* 1, 16–21; Daniel Sabbeth, "Dramatic and Musical Organization in *Falstaff*," *Atti* 3, 415–42 is an extravagant example of the new tonal-psychological analysis.

Il Re Lear

Verdi's letters to Somma about this uncomposed opera, which forms a King Charles's Head through his career, are in the Pascolato volume listed under "Documents" above. See also Leo Karl Gerhartz's "Il Re Lear di Antonio Somma . . . ," *Atti* 1, 110–15, and his *Die Auseinandersetzungen des jungen Giuseppe Verdi mit dem literarischen Drama,* Berliner Studien zur Musikwissenschaft 15 (Berlin, 1968). Gerhartz reproduces the scenario Verdi sent to Cammarano, and passages of the Somma libretto; a film of the whole libretto, which is in Sant'Agata, is in the archive of the American Institute for Verdi Studies.

Requiem

David Rosen's "The Genesis of Verdi's 'Requiem' " (Ph.D. dissertation, University of California, Berkeley, 1976) summarizes previous knowledge of the piece, adds greatly to that knowledge, and contains a full bibliography.

Recordings

High Fidelity 13 (1963), October, 37–66, 146–56, and December, 90–97 has a long, careful survey by Conrad L. Osborne of six Verdi operas on disc— *Rigoletto, Il trovatore, La traviata, La forza del destino, Aida,* and *Otello*—in which it is his "aim to investigate the recorded interpretations of these six operas to see what light they may throw on the works." Verdi recordings from 1975 onward have been noted, with references to major reviews, in the *Verdi Newsletter* of the American Institute for Verdi Studies.

A Chronological Timetable of Verdi's Life and Works

Elvidio Surian

ELVIDIO SURIAN teaches music history at the Rossini Conservatory in Pesaro, Italy. He studied musicology at New York University and taught at Lehman College of the City University of New York. Among his recent publications is a survey of the literature on Verdi from 1960 to 1975 for *Rivista Italiana di Musicologia* 12/2 (1977).

1813

Oct. 9   Born (c. 3 P.M.) at Roncole near Busseto (Parma); son of Carlo (1785–1867) and Luigia Uttini (1787–1851).
(WALKER V, 1–3; MATZ, 342–45)

Oct. 11   Baptized under the name of Joseph Fortunin François at the Chiesa di San Michele Arcangelo.
(GATTI, 10–1; MATZ, 348)

1814

early Mar.   Soldiers of the Holy Alliance, fighting the French, pass through Roncole; Luigia Verdi hides with child in town's belfry.
(BARILLI, 9–10; BRAGAGNOLO-BETTAZZI, 6; MATZ, 348)

1817

Receives first formal instruction in reading and writing Italian and Latin from Don Pietro Baistrocchi, who also probably introduces Verdi to the keyboard.

(MATZ, 355)

1820

Father buys him an old spinet; Verdi begins to substitute for Don Baistorcchi as organist of San Michele at Roncole.

(MATZ, 356, 360; GATTI, 20)

1822

Engaged as organist at the church of Roncole.

(MATZ, 360; WALKERV, 4)

1823

Lives in Busseto, lodging with a certain Pugnatta; continues as organist at Roncole, returning to play for Sunday and holiday services.

(MATZ, 360–61)

Nov.   Admitted to *ginnasio* in Busseto; studies Italian grammar with Don Pietro Seletti (for 2 years), humanities and rhetoric with Carlo Carotti and Don Giacinto Volpini.

(WALKERV, 6; GATTI, 39)

1825

fall   Begins formal studies with Ferdinando Provesi, *maestro di cappella* and organist at the collegiate church of S. Bartolomeo, director of the municipal school of music of S. Bartolomeo, director of the municipal school of music and of the Società Filarmonica in Busseto.

(WALKERV, 6)

1828

Writes an overture for a performance of Rossini's *Barbiere di Siviglia* in Busseto and a cantata in eight movements for baritone and orchestra, *I deliri di Saul.*

(GATTI, 30; OSBORNE, 18, 453)

1829

Oct. 24   Applies for post as organist of Soragna (Parma); Provesi recommends him.

(WALKERV, 6; GATTI, 31; BRAGANOLA-BETTAZZI, 27)

fall (to 1832)   Becomes Provesi's assistant in Busseto.

(WALKERV, 7)

Apr.   Composes *Le lamentazioni di Geremia* and various sacred pieces for Easter services in Busseto.

(ABBIATI 1, 76)

1831

May 14   Moves to home of Antonio Barezzi, gives singing and piano lessons to Margherita Barezzi, his future wife. Carlo Verdi applies to administrators of the Monte di Pietà e d'Abbondanza of Busseto for financial assistance for his son to complete musical studies in Milan.

(WALKERV, 8)

1832

Jan. 14   Monte di Pietà grants Verdi a scholarship (300 lire annually for 4 years); payment will begin Nov. 1, 1833.

(WALKERV; GATTI, 38)

May 22   Passport to travel to Milan.

(WALKERV, 8; GATTI, 41)

June   Lodges at the home of Giuseppe Seletti in Milan.

(GATTI, 42)

June 22   Applies for admission to the Conservatory.

(GATTI, 45–46)

June 24?   Examined by registrar Francesco Basily and teachers Gaetano Piantanida (composition), Antonio Angeleri (pianoforte), and Alessandro Rolla (violin).

(GATTI, 47)

July 2   Basily reports unfavorably to director of Conservatory, Count Giuseppe Sormani-Andreani.
                                                    (TEBALDINI, 145)

July 3   Count Sormani forwards results of exam to governor. Civil clerk Giuseppe Corbari adds that Verdi is 4 years above normal age, lives outside state of Lombardy-Venetia, and did poorly on pianoforte exam.
                                        (WALKERV, 10; TEBALDINI, 145)

Aug.   Studies composition privately with Vincenzo Lavigna until summer 1835.
                                                       (WALKERV, 12)

1833

c. June 10–22   Trip to Busseto.
                                                      (ABBIATI I, 115)

July 26   Provesi dies and his post remains open in Busseto.
                                                          (GATTI, 65)

Nov. 22   Giovanni Ferrari of Guastalla (Reggio Emilia) applies for post.
                                                          (GATTI, 67)

Dec. 11   Lavigna writes to the Monte di Pietà that Verdi needs one more year of study with him.
                                                          (GATTI, 69)

Aug. 10   Verdi's sister Giuseppa Francesca, born in 1816, dies in Busseto.
                                                      (MATZ, 353–54)

1834

Apr.   Verdi *maestro al cembalo* at performance of Haydn's *Creation* at the hall of Casino de' Nobili, Milan; meets Pietro Massini, director of the Philharmonic Society, who invites him to write an opera.
                                         (WALKERV, 17; GATTI, 71)

June 18   Ferrari appointed organist in Busseto.

June 20   Verdi returns to Busseto and applies for the post; remains in town until Dec. 15, directing concerts of the Philharmonic band.
                                                  (WALKERV, 14, 19)

1835

July   Completes studies with Lavigna and returns to Busseto.

(WALKERV, 20)

fall   Lavigna recommends Verdi for post as *maestro di cappella* and organist at Monza cathedral; Verdi remains in Busseto because of public opinion.

(GATTI, 99–100)

1836

Jan.   Monte di Pietà suspends pension, after total payment of only 650 lire.

(WALKERV, 26)

Begins to write *Rocester* (libretto by Antonio Piazza).

(WALKERV, 26)

23 Jan.   Busseto announces a competition for post of *maestro di musica* and conductor of Philharmonic Society.

(GATTI, 104)

27–28 Feb.   Examined in Parma by court organist Giuseppe Alinovi for the Busseto post.

(GATTI, 105)

Feb.   In Milan for a few days to take care of some business.

(CARTEGGI IV, 73; ABBIATI I, 218)

Mar. 5   President of the Interior of Duchy of Parma names Verdi *maestro di musica* at Busseto.

(GATTI, 108)

Apr. 16   Formally engaged to Margherita Barezzi.

(ABBIATI I, 227–28; WALKERV, 22)

May 4   Weds Margherita Barezzi; honeymoon in Milan.

(ABBIATI I, 230)

May   Returns to Busseto and settles at Palazzo Tedaldi; teaches members of Philharmonic Society, conducts their concerts, writes pieces for various solo instruments, gives private lessons.

(WALKERV, 22; GATTI, 117)

c. May   Sets to music (solo voice and piano) Alessandro Manzoni's ode *Il cinque maggio*.

(ABBIATI I, 229)

Sept. 16   Completes opera *Rocester.*
                (SARTORI, 100; KIMBELL, 2)

Nov.   Composes setting of a *Tantum ergo* for voice and or-
            chestra with alternative organ accompaniment.
                (REDLICH, 235)

1837

Jan. 1   *Tantum ergo* for voice and organ performed at Bus-
            seto's Collegiate Church of S. Bartolomeo.
                (REDLICH, 235; MILA, 491)

Jan. 22   Directs concert of Busseto's Philharmonic Society;
            program includes Verdi's *Sinfonia,* two arias, a duet,
            an aria from *I deliri di Saul* (arranged for solo bas-
            soon), and a chorus.
                (REDLICH, 233–34)

Mar. 26   Margherita gives birth to Virginia.
                (GATTI, 117)

Sept. 16   Writes to Massini, hoping to stage his *Rocester* at
            Parma the next carnival season.
                (WALKERV, 26; SARTORI, 100)

Oct.   In Parma to see impresario of Teatro Ducale Granci,
            who refuses to stage new opera.
                (WALKERV, 26; GATTI, 118)

Nov. 3   Writes to Massini, asking him to intercede with Bar-
            tolomeo Merelli, impresario of La Scala, to see if
            opera could be performed in Milan
                (WALKERV, 26; GATTI, 118)

1838

Jan.–Feb.   Composes a set of *Sei romanze* for solo voice with
            piano accompaniment.
                (ABBIATI I, 244; OSBORNE, 454–55;
                MILA, 494)

Feb. 4   Directs concert of Busseto's Philharmonic Society
            that includes his new *Sinfonia.*
                (REDLICH, 234)

Feb. 18   Directs concert at Philharmonic Society that includes a new *Sinfonia,* an aria, and a *Divertimento* for keyed trumpet.
(REDLICH, 234)

Feb. 25   Directs a concert of the Philharmonic Society that includes an aria, a duet, a *Capriccio* for horn, and a solo piece for bassoon. None of these pieces survives.
(REDLICH, 234)

early May   Visits Milan for a few days.
(WALKERV, 27)

July 11   Margherita gives birth to Icilio Romano.
(GATTI, 122;

Aug. 12   Daughter Virginia dies.
(GATTI, 122)

Sept. 8–   In Milan to see if his opera can be staged at La Scala
Oct. 10   the following year.
(GATTI, 123, 127–28)

Oct. 28   Submits resignation as *maestro di musica* in Busseto.
(GATTI, 130)

1839

Feb. 6   Leaves Busseto with his family; settles in Milan, Via S. Simone (Via Cesare Correnti) near Porta Ticinese.
(WALKERV, 30; GATTI, 131, 138)

Apr.   Milanese editor Giovanni Canti publishes two songs for voice and piano (*L'esule,* text by Temistocle Solera, and *La seduzione,* text by Luigi Balestra) and a *Notturno* for soprano, tenor, and bass with flute obligato (text by Jacopo Vittorelli).
(WALKERV, 32; OSBORNE, 455–56; MILA, 493–94)

Oct. 22   Son Icilio Romano dies.
(GATTI, 138)

Nov. 17   Premiere of *Oberto* at La Scala.
(CHUSID, 128)

Nov. 17 Merelli offers Verdi a contract to compose three
operas at 8-months intervals.
(GATTI, 141; WALKERV, 33)

1840

c. beg. Mar. Begins composing *Un giorno di regno;* interrupts
work in March because of illness.
(OBERDORFER, 61; GATTI, 142)

June 18 Margherita dies of encephalitis.
(GATTI, 143)

June 22 In Busseto.
(GATTI, 143)

July Returns to Milan to complete *Un giorno di regno.*
(ABBIATI I, 349–50)

Sept. 5 Premiere of *Un giorno di regno* at La Scala; Verdi
directs.
(CHUSID, 130)

Oct. 17 *Oberto* at La Scala; Verdi directs.
(ABBIATI I, 357; CHUSID, 130)

Dec. In Genoa to direct rehearsals of *Oberto.*
(ABBIATI I, 358; RESASCO, 11–13)

1841

Jan. 9 *Oberto* (with revisions) performed at Genoa's Teatro
Carlo Felice; Verdi attends and probably directs.
(GATTI, 150–51; ABBIATI I, 358;
RESASCO, 13)

c. Jan. 15 Returns to Milan.
(GATTI, 151)

Jan. Merelli hands Verdi libretto of *Nabucco;* convinces
him to set it to music.
(ABBIATI I, 361)

Feb.–Mar. Sees librettist Solera frequently.
(ABBIATI I, 375)

Oct.   *Nabucco* completed.
(GATTI, 152; ABBIATI I, 377)

Dec. 22–23   Meets with Giuseppina Strepponi to show her part in *Nabucco* and to enlist her support in having it produced during the next season.
(WALKERV, 166–67)

1842

late Feb.   Rehearsals of *Nabucco* begun.
(GATTI, 155; ABBIATI I, 402)

Mar. 9   Premiere of *Nabucco* at La Scala; Verdi attends.
(GATTI, 156; CHUSID, 122)

Mar. 31   Piano-vocal score of *Nabucco* printed by Ricordi.
(GATTI, 165)

c. Apr.–May   Begins to frequent salons of Milanese aristocracy of Countess Clara Maffei, Sofia de' Medici, Countess Emilia Morosini, Giuseppina Appiani.
(WALKERV, 99)

c. May   Writes the song for voice and piano *Chi i bei dì m'adduce ancora* (text translated from Goethe's *Erster Verlust*), to be copied into an album for Sofia de' Medici.
(OSBORNE, 456; MILA, 495)

June   In Bologna for 5–6 days to see Rossini.
(H. WEINSTOCK, *Rossini, A Biography* [New York, 1968], 227; OBERDORFER, 76)

July   In Busseto.
(OBERDORFER, 76)

July 21   In Milan.
(OBERDORFER, 76)

c. Sept. 9–17   In Busseto.
(ABBIATI I, 430)

c. Sept. 18   In Milan.
(ABBIATI I, 430)

1843

late Jan.   In Busseto.
                                    (ABBIATI I, 431)

Feb. 11   Premiere of *I lombardi alla prima crociata* at La Scala.
                                    (ABBIATI I, 446)

c. Mar. 20–   In Vienna to stage *Nabucco* (April 4, Kärnthnertor
Apr. 8   Theater).
                                    (WALKER V, 172; ABBIATI I, 435)

Apr. 9   In Udine; writes Count Nani Mocenigo, president of
               La Fenice, Venice.
                                    (MORAZZONI, 15; LA FENICE, 13)

Apr. 10–13   In Busseto.
                                    (WALKER V, 172)

Apr. 14–   In Parma with Giuseppina Strepponi to stage *Nabuc-
May 30   co* (17 Apr.); remains for season.
                                    (WALKER V, 173)

end Apr.   In Bologna for a few days to hear Donizetti's *Linda di
               Chamounix* and *Marin Faliero*.
                                    (MILA, 122–23)

May 18–c. 21   Visits Busseto to see his mother.
                                    (ABBIATI I, 458)

May 31–   In Milan; *Re Lear* among subjects considered for La
June 6   Fenice.

July 10–   In Senigallia (Ancona) to direct rehearsals and con-
Aug. 1   duct *I lombardi* (July 29).
                                    (RADICIOTTI, 87–88; MORAZZONI, 18–19;
                                    LA FENICE 17–18)

Aug. 1   In Milan.
                                    (MORAZZONI, 19)

Sept. 5–29   Victor Hugo's *Hernani* becomes subject for Venetian
               opera.
                                    (ABBIATI I, 473–74; LA FENICE, 20)

Oct. 8   *Nabucco* at Teatro Communale, Bologna; Verdi
               attends.
                                    (WALKER V, 174)

| c. Oct. 10–15 | Vacations at Cassano d'Adda (Milan) with della Somaglia family. |
| | (ABBIATI I, 475) |

| Nov. 15 | Completes Acts I–III of *Ernani*. |
| | (GATTI, 178; ABBIATI I, 476; LA FENICE, 23–24) |

| Dec. 2 | Accepts commission *Giovanna d'Arco* for La Scala, season '44–'45. |
| | (COPIAL., 428) |

| Dec. 3 | In Venice to direct rehearsals of *I lombardi* (Dec. 26). |
| | (ABBIATI I, 478; GATTI, 180) |

1844

| early Jan. | In Verona with Giuseppina Strepponi to attend rehearsals of *Nabucco*. |
| | (WALKERV, 175; LA FENICE, 25) |

| Feb. 5 | Completes *Ernani*. |
| | (CARTEGGI I, 79; ABBIATI I, 502) |

| c. Feb. 28 | Finishes scoring *Ernani*. |
| | (LA FENICE, 27) |

| Feb. 29 | Signs contract with Teatro Argentina, Rome, for *I due Foscari*. |
| | (GARIBALDI, 70) |

| Mar. 9 | Premiere of *Ernani* at La Fenice. |
| | (CHUSID, 60) |

| Mar. 15 | In Busseto. |
| | (ABBIATI I, 502) |

| Mar. 17 | In Milan. |
| | (ABBIATI I, 499) |

| Mar. 21 | Accepts commission for *Alzira* at the Teatro San Carlo, Naples. |
| | (COPIAL., 3–4) |

| Apr. 12 | Sends libretto summary of *Attila* to F. M. Piave. |
| | (GATTI, 184; ABBIATI I, 579) |

Apr. 15   Emanuele Muzio, his only serious composition stu-
           dent, begins formal studies with Verdi.
                                              (GARIBALDI, 21)

May 14   Receives completed libretto of *I due Foscari*.
                                             (GARIBALDI, 170

Aug. 11   In Bergamo, conducts *Ernani* with Strepponi at Tea-
           tro Riccardi.
                                     (WALKERV, 176; GATTI, 188)

c. mid-Aug.   In Busseto composing *I due Foscari*.
                                     (WALKERV, 176; GATTI, 188)

Sept. 14   In Milan.
                                   (WALKERV, 176; ABBIATI I, 521)

Sept. 30   Leaves for Rome to stage *I due Foscari*.
                                     (COPIAL., 427; GATTI, 189)

Oct. 3–early   In Rome to prepare *I due Foscari*.
Nov.   (ABBIATI, 522, 527)

Nov. 3   Premiere of *I due Foscari* at Teatro Argentina, Rome.
                                   (ABBIATI I, 527; CHUSID, 56)

Nov. 12   In Milan.
                                              (GARIBALDI, 173)

Dec.   Composing *Giovanna d'Arco*.
                                              (GARIBALDI, 175)

mid-Dec.   Conducts rehearsals of *I lombardi* for performance at
           La Scala on Dec. 26.
                               (GARIBALDI, 178, 179; GATTI, 191)

1845

Jan. 12–   Scores *Giovanna d'Arco* (premiere Feb. 15, La Scala).
mid-Feb.   (GARIBALDI, 181)

Mar.–Apr.   Writes *Sei Romanze* for voice and piano to be pub-
            lished by Lucca (plate nos. 5640–5645) in Milan.
                               (ABBIATI I, 541; OSBORNE, 456–57;
                                                   MILA, 495)

c. Mar. 10–   In Venice to stage *I due Foscari*.
Apr. 1   (GARIBALDI, 187–89, 192)

Apr. 2   In Milan.
                              (GARIBALDI, 202)

May 12–   Léon Escudier in Milan to see Verdi regarding pro-
c. May 26   prietary rights for his works in France.
                              (CONATI, 553, 555)

May 26   Begins to compose *Alzira*.
                              (GARIBALDI, 202)

June 20   Leaves for Naples with an almost completed score of
          Alzira.
                              (COPIAL., 14)

July 30   In Naples, finishes scoring of *Alzira*.
                              (COPIAL., 431; ABBIATI I, 564)

Aug. 12   Premiere of *Alzira* at S. Carlo.
                              (CHUSID, 14)

Aug. 25   In Milan.
                              (GARIBALDI, 211; ABBIATI I, 567)

Sept. 3   In Busseto; begins composing *Attila*.
                  (GARIBALDI, 265, 258; ABBIATI I, 583, 587;
                              COPIAL., 439)

mid-Sept.   In Milan; sees Solera.
                              (ABBIATI I, 585)

fall   *Un giorno di regno* staged successfully at La Fenice as
       Il finto Stanislao.
                              (ABBIATI I, 590)

Oct. 6   Buys Palazzo Dordoni (now Palazzo Orlandi) from
         Contardo Cavalli in Busseto.
                              (WALKER V, 195)

Oct. 16   Signs contract with publisher Lucca to write new
          opera (*Il corsaro*).
                              (COPIAL., 47)

Oct. 17–25   Vacations at Clusone (Bergamo).
                              (GARIBALDI, 223–24, 227)

Oct. 26–29   In Milan; impresario Benjamin Lumley from Lon-
             don and Escudier from Paris see Verdi and offer

contracts for the following season; Escudier acquires rights to Verdi's works in France.
(GARIBALDI, 227–28, 234)

late Nov.– mid-Mar.
In Venice to complete scoring and direct *Attila*.
(ABBIATI I, 590; COPIAL., 439; LA FENICE, 34)

1846

Mar. 17
Premiere of *Attila* at La Fenice; Verdi directs.
(LA FENICE, 34; CHUSID, 24)

Mar. 22
In Milan; doctors order six months of rest for gastric fever.
(GARIBALDI, 236, 238; COPIAL., 19)

Apr. 10
Sends medical certificate to London explaining postponement of new work.
(GARIBALDI, 242)

May 5
In Milan, Lumley's brother unsuccessfully urges Verdi to leave for London.
(GARIBALDI, 242)

July 3
At thermal waters of Recoaro (Vicenza) for cure.
(GARIBALDI, 252)

c. mid-July
In Venice to see Piave about *Il corsaro*.
(ABBIATI I, 639–40; COPIAL., 442)

July 27
In Milan.
(GARIBALDI, 255)

mid-Aug.
Begins to consider subjects for a new opera at Florence.
(GARIBALDI, 258)

beg. Sept.
Sends libretto summary of *Macbeth* to Piave.
(ABBIATI I, 643)

Sept. 8–10
At Varese.
(GARIBALDI, 269)

late Sept.
Piave in Milan to see Verdi.
(ABBIATI I, 647)

beg. Oct.	In Como with Piave.
	(GARIBALDI, 278)
mid-Oct.	Begins to compose *Macbeth*.
	(GARIBALDI, 283, 285)
late Oct.	Completes Act I of *Macbeth*.
	(ABBIATI I, 652)
Nov. 11	Lumley in Milan to discuss *I masnadieri*, new opera for London.
	(GARIBALDI, 291; COPIAL., 31)
late Dec.–Feb. 14	*Macbeth* completed: Act II, end Dec.; Act III, c. 18 Jan.; scoring, Feb. 14.
	(GARIBALDI, 302, 307, 309; ABBIATI I, 659; COPIAL., 448)

1847

?	Composes song *Il poveretto* (text by Manfredo Maggioni) for voice and piano, published by Lucca (plate no. 6162).
	(OSBORNE, 457; MILA, 495)
Feb. 15–Mar. 25	Leaves for Florence, Feb. 15; begins rehearsing *Macbeth*.
	(ABBIATI I, 680; GARIBALDI, 311; COPIAL., 431)
Mar. 14	Premiere of *Macbeth* at the Teatro della Pergola. Verdi directs.
	(CHUSID, 108)
c. Mar. 26	In Milan.
	(ABBIATI I, 691)
May 17	Completes piano-vocal score of *I masnadieri*.
	(GARIBALDI, 318, GATTI, 231)
May 26–31	Leaves Milan with Muzio; passes through Lucerne, Basel, Strasbourg, Kehl, Karlsruhe, Mannheim, Mainz, Coblenz, Bonn, Cologne, Brussels, on his way to Paris.
	(GARIBALDI, 321)

June 1   In Paris; attends the Opéra.
                (GARIBALDI, 321, 325; COPIAL., 457;
                                  WALKERV, 183)

June 4   Leaves Paris.
                                  (WALKERV, 183)

June 7   In London for *I masnadieri:* completes scoring c.
           June 20; begins rehearsing June 30.
                (COPIAL., 456; GARIBALDI, 328, 336, 344)

July 22   Premiere of *I masnadieri* at Her Majesty's Theatre;
           Verdi conducts.
                (GARIBALDI, 344; CHUSID, 118)

July 27–   In Paris; signs contract with the Opéra and comple-
late Nov.   tes *Jérusalem,* revised French version of *I lombardi;*
           begins rehearsals Sept. 22.
             (WALKERV, 183; GARIBALDI, 350, 353, 358;
                                 COPIAL., 460, 463)

Nov. 26   Premiere of *Jérusalem* at the Académie Royale de
           Musique, Paris.
                                 (CHUSID, 92)

Dec. 26   Italian premiere of *I masnadieri* in Bergamo, Trieste,
           and Verona.
                               (CHUSID, 118)

1848

early Feb.   Signs contract for new work at the Paris Opéra in
           1849.
                (WALKERV, 184; GARIBALDI, 361)

Feb. 12   Dispatches score and libretto of *Il corsaro* to pub-
           lisher Lucca.
                   (COPIAL., 47; WALKERV, 185;
                                 ABBIATI I, 140)

Feb. 22–24   Insurrection in Paris; King Louis Philippe abdicates.
                                 (GARZANTI, 353)

Mar. 18   Milan revolts and drives out the Austrians; the Aus-
           trians return Aug. 6.
                                 (GARZANTI, 353)

Mar. 23 Piedmont declares war on Austria. First war of Independence begins.

(GARZANTI, 353)

Apr. 5 In Milan.

(WALKER V, 188; ABBIATI I, 744)

early May In Busseto; purchases estate at Sant'Agata.

(COPIAL., 48)

early June In Paris.

(WALKER V, 190; ABBIATI I, 749; COPIAL., 53)

end July– At Passy with Giuseppina Strepponi; begins compos-
end Aug. ing *La battaglia di Legnano*.

(WALKER V, 191, 193; COPIAL., 49)

early Sept. Returns to Paris.

(WALKER V, 191)

Oct. 18 Sends Giuseppe Mazzini battle hymn *Suona la tromba* (text by Goffredo Mameli) for 3-voice male chorus; it is published in the same month by Milanese editor Paolo de Giorgio (plate no. 144).

(OSBORNE, 457–58; ABBIATI I, 758–59; MILA, 493)

Oct. 25 Premiere of *Il corsaro* at Teatro Grande at Trieste. Verdi neither assists nor attends.

(CHUSID, 38)

c. mid-Dec. Completes *La battaglia di Legnano*, save for the orchestration.

(ABBIATI I, 779; WALKER V, 194)

Dec. 20 Leaves for Rome.

(WALKER V, 194)

Jan. 7 Escudier publishes Verdi's song *L'abandonnée*, dedicated to Giuseppina Strepponi, in Paris, as musical supplement to *La France Musicale*.

(WALKER V, 787; MILA, 495)

early–Jan. 27 In Rome for *La battaglia di Legnano*; rehearsals begin Jan. 18. Premiere Jan. 27. Verdi directs.

(GATTI, 207; ABBIATI I, 788)

early Feb.	In Paris.
	(ABBIATI I, 787)
Feb. 5	Roman Republic proclaimed.
	(CAPPELLI, 436)
Mar. 29	Vittorio Emanuele II becomes king of Piedmont.
	(GARZANTI, 353)
May 17	Receives libretto summary of *Luisa Miller* from Cammarano.
	(COPIAL., 78)
July 14	Pope's temporal power reestablished in Rome.
	(CAPPELLI, 436)
July 29	Leaves Paris.
	(COPIAL., 84)
Aug.–Sept.	Returns to Busseto with Giuseppina; stays at Palazzo Orlandi; composes *Luisa Miller*.
	(WALKER V, 194–95, 197)
early Oct.	Completes *Luisa Miller* (without scoring).
	(ABBIATI II, 27; COPIAL., 477)
Oct. 3	Leaves Busseto with Antonio Barezzi for Naples.
	(GARIBALDI, 378; WALKER V, 198–99)
Oct. 4–6	In Genoa.
	(GARIBALDI, 378; WALKER V, 198–99)
Oct. 14–25	In Rome; stays at Hotel de Rome owing to anticholera quarantine regulations.
	(GARIBALDI, 378; WALKER V, 198–99; ABBIATI II, 37; COPIAL., 85)
Oct. 27	Arrives in Naples.
	(GARIBALDI, 378; WALKER V, 198–99)
early Nov.	Problems receiving first payment from management of S. Carlo; threatens to cancel contract.
	(ABBIATI II, 39)
Dec. 8	Premiere of *Luisa Miller* at S. Carlo in Naples. Verdi directs.
	(CHUSID, 104)

Dec. 13	Leaves Naples.
	(WALKER V, 199)

1850

Jan 2	Proposes to Cammarano subject of Garcia Gutierrez's *El trovador* for new libretto.
	(MONALDI, 141)
Jan.–Feb.	Plans libretto for *King Lear*.
	(ABBIATI II, 49–55; COPIAL., 478)
Feb. 28	Sends Cammarano libretto summary for *King Lear*.
	(COPIAL., 478–82)
Mar. 9	Marzari of La Fenice invites Verdi to write new work (*Rigoletto*).
	(COPIAL., 96–97)
Mar. 14	Verdi accepts.
	(LA FENICE, 36)
Apr. 28	Signs contract; suggests Hugo's *Le Roi s'amuse* as possible subject to Piave; also asks Piave for libretto summary of *Stiffelio*.
	(ABBIATI II, 59–60; COPIAL., 103)
late July–Aug. 24	Piave in Busseto.
	(MARCHESI R, 873; LA FENICE, 39)
Sept. 28–Oct. 8	In Bologna to direct performance of *Macbeth*.
	(COPIAL., 116; ABBIATI II, 69–70; LA FENICE, 40)
Oct. 22	Receives text of *La maledizione* (*Rigoletto*) from Piave.
	(ABBIATI II, 71)
c. Oct. 28	In Venice.
	(ABBIATI II, 72)
Oct. 31–Nov. 20	With Piave in Trieste to direct rehearsals of *Stiffelio*.
	(STEFANI, 45)
Nov. 16	Premiere of *Stiffelio* at Teatro Grande at Trieste. Verdi directs.
	(CHUSID, 150; STEFANI, 59)
Nov. 17	Sends libretto of *La madedizione* to La Fenice.
	(LA FENICE, 40)

Nov. 20 Leaves Trieste; stops in Venice on way to Busseto to obtain formal approval from censor of libretto for *La maledizione;* does not obtain it.
(STEFANI, 64; ABBIATI II, 78–79; 83–84; LA FENICE, 40)

Dec. 9 Piave leaves *Il duca di Vendôme* (i.e., revised *La maledizione*) at Venetian censorship office.
(COPIAL., 487)

c. Dec. 20 Venetian censor approves *Il duca di Vendôme.*
(ABBIATI II, 86; La Fenice, 43)

Dec. 26 Premiere of *Gerusalemme* (Italian transl. of *Jérusalem*) at La Scala.
(CHUSID, 92)

Dec. 30 Piave and secretary of La Fenice Guglielmo Brenna in Busseto to arrive at a mutually acceptable libretto for *Rigoletto.*
(ABBIATI II, 91)

1851

Jan. 25 *Rigoletto* approved by Venetian censor.
(ABBIATI II, 103; COPIAL., 494)

Feb. 5 *Rigoletto* completed except for scoring.
(ABBIATI II, 105)

Feb. 19 In Venice for rehearsals.
(ABBIATI II, 107)

Mar. 11 Premiere of *Rigoletto* at La Fenice. Verdi directs.
(CHUSID, 138)

c. Mar. 15 In Busseto.
(ABBIATI II, 119)

late Mar.– April Sends Cammarano an outline of the libretto for *Il trovatore.*
(ABBIATI II, 122–23)

spring Verdi and Giuseppina move to farmhouse at Sant'Agata.
(WALKER V, 199; ABBIATI II, 130)

June 28	Verdi's mother, Luigia Uttini Verdi, dies at Vidalenzo (near Busseto). (ABBIATI II, 137; WALKER V, 203)
Sept. 28– Oct. 8	In Bologna to direct performances of *Macbeth* and *Luisa Miller* (Oct. 10) at Teatro Comunale.
Nov. 19	Writes the barcarole for tenor and piano *Fiorellin che sorge appena* for Giovanni Severi (text by Piave); facsimile of autograph in Stefani, 28–29 of illustrations. (RINALDI, 271; STEFANI, 67)
Nov. 20	Verdi and Piave leave Trieste. (STEFANI, 67)
Dec. 10	Verdi and Giuseppina leave Busseto for Paris. (ABBIATI II, 148)

1852

Feb.	Attends Dumas's *La Dame aux camélias* in Paris. (ABBIATI II, 163)
Feb. 28	Signs contract with director of the Opéra, Nestor Roqueplan, for new opera (*Les Vêpres*), to be performed by Dec. 1854. (ABBIATI II, 154; COPIAL., 134, 139)
Mar. 7	Leaves Paris. (ABBIATI II, 156–57; CARTEGGI I, 6)
Mar. 18	In Busseto. (ABBIATI II, 159; COPIAL., 530)
May 4	Brenna and Marzari of La Fenice in Busseto with contract for new opera (*La traviata*). (COPIAL., 147)
July 17	Cammarano dies in Naples, leaving libretto of *Il trovatore* unfinished. Neapolitan poet Leone Emanuele Bardare later completes text from Cammarano's notes. (GATTI, 295; CHUSID, 160; ABBIATI II, 169–70)

early Aug.	In Rome(?).
	(PROD'HOMME, 9)
Aug. 10	President of French Republic, Louis Bonaparte, confers title of "Chevalier de la Legion d'honneur" and sends Escudier to Italy to present it to Verdi.
	(GATTI, 298)
Sept. 29	Verdi engages Bardare to complete libretto for *Trovatore*.
	(ABBIATI II, 172)
late Oct.– early Nov.	Piave in Busseto to work on libretto for La Fenice; Verdi signs contract with Rome's Teatro Apollo to write *Il trovatore*.
	(ABBIATI II, 176–77)
Dec. 14	Has completed *Il trovatore*.
	(COPIAL., 531; CARTEGGI I, 14; ABBIATI II, 180)
Dec. 20	Leaves Sant'Agata for Rome.
	(GARIBALDI, 365–66)
Dec. 25?	In Rome.
	(COPIAL., 531; according to ABBIATI II, 188, c. Jan. 1, 1853)

1853

Jan 1.	Opera for Venice will be *La traviata*.
	(CARTEGGI I, 16–17; COPIAL., 532)
Jan. 19	Premiere of *Il trovatore* at the Teatro Apollo. Verdi directs.
	(CHUSID, 160)
Jan. 22	Leaves Rome.
	(MORAZZONI, 36; CARTEGGI I, 18)
late Jan.	In Busseto; at work on *La traviata*.
	(ABBIATI II; 216; COPIAL., 532)
early Feb.	Piave in Busseto to polish libretto of *La traviata*.
	(LA FENICE, 48)
c. Feb. 20	Completes *La traviata* (except for scoring).
	(ABBIATI II, 216; GATTI, 301)

Feb. 21	In Venice; begins scoring of *La traviata*. (ABBIATI II, 216, 218; MORAZZONI, 36)
early Mar.	Completes scoring of *La traviata*. (ABBIATI II, 216)
Mar. 6	Premiere of *La traviata* at La Fenice. Verdi directs. (CHUSID, 154)
Mar. 10	Leaves Venice. (COPIAL., 533)
Mar. 12	Arrives in Busseto. (ABBIATI II, 227)
?	Writes song *Fiorara* (text by Buvoli). (MILA, 496)
Oct. 15	Leaves for Paris. (ABBIATI II, 254)
Dec. 31	Receives completed libretto of Scribe's *Les Vêpres siciliennes,* "opéra en cinq actes." (ABBIATI II, 260; COPIAL., 152; WALKERV, 217)

1854

Feb. 16	Attends premiere of Meyerbeer's *Étoile du nord* at the Opéra-Comique. (ABBIATI II, 265; COPIAL., 540)
c. early Mar.	Begins to compose *Les Vêpres*. (COPIAL., 538–39)
Mar. ?	Trip to London to prevent performance of *Il trovatore* there without payment of royalties. (ABBIATI II, 312–13; COPIAL., 170; GATTI, 326)
May 6	Revised version of *La traviata* performed successfully at Teatro San Benedetto (Teatro Gallo), Venice. (ABBIATI II, 272)
early Sept.	Has written 4 acts of *Les Vêpres*. (CARTEGGI I, 26; ABBIATI II, 275; WALKERV, 217)

Oct. 1   Begins rehearsing *Les Vêpres* at the Opéra.
          (COPIAL., 154; WALKERV, 217)

Oct. 9   Rehearsals interrupted as soprano Cruvelli disappe-
          ars; resumed end of Nov.
          (COPIAL., 154; CARTEGGI I, 27)

Dec. 26   Conducts *Il trovatore* at the Théâtre-Italien, Paris.
          (COPIAL., 163; ABBIATI II, 282;
          CARTEGGI I, 28)

1855

early Apr.   Has completed *Les Vêpres* (except for ballets).
              (CARTEGGI I, 31)

May   *Il trovatore* at London's Covent Garden.
          (ABBIATI II, 313; GATTI, 299)

June 13   Premiere of *Les Vêpres* at the Opéra, Paris. Verdi
          directs.
          (CHUSID, 164)

Sept.   Italian translation of *Les Vêpres* completed by Ar-
          noldo Fusinato; Verdi has supervised it.
          (GATTI, 323)

c. Nov.– Supervises French translation of *Il trovatore* by Emi-
beg. Dec. lien Pacini.
          (CHUSID, 162; ABBIATI II, 310, 313, 315)

c. Dec. 20   Leaves Paris.
              (ABBIATI II, 315–16)

Dec. 21   Stops at Alessandria.
          (ABBIATI II, 316)

Dec. 23   In Busseto.
          (ABBIATI II, 316)

Dec. 26   Premieres of *Giovanna de Guzman* (Italian translation
          of *Les Vêpres*) at Teatro Ducale, Parma, and Teatro
          Regio, Turin.
          (CHUSID, 165; ABBIATI II, 316; GATTI, 324)

1856

late Jan.   In Parma to hear singers Giuglini and Cresci in Bel-
             lini's *I puritani* and to propose to the Duchy of Parma

participation in international treaty on performing royalties.

(ABBIATI II, 345)

early Feb.   In Busseto.

(CARTEGGI I, 32)

Feb. 9   Receives from King of Piedmont and Sardinia Vittorio Emanuele II title of "Cavaliere dell'Ordine di S. S. Maurizio e Lazzaro."

(ABBIATI II, 345)

Feb. 21–23   In Parma.

(ABBIATI II, 348)

Mar. 8–13   In Milan.

(ABBIATI II, 348)

Mar. 15–19   ? In Venice to stage *La traviata*.

(ABBIATI II, 351, 354)

Mar. 27   Piave at Sant'Agata to work on revision of *Stiffelio* (*Aroldo*); remains until c. mid-May.

(CARTEGGI I, 33; ABBIATI II, 354, 356)

May 2   Contract drawn up by San Carlo's impresario Luigi Alberti for new opera to be given there by Jan. 1857; Verdi will sign it—modified—on Feb. 5, 1857.

(WALKERV, 29, 39)

May 15   Signs contract with La Fenice; new opera for next season (*Simon Boccanegra*).

(WALKERV, 218; COPIAL., 191)

c. late May   Completes revision of *Stiffelio* (*Aroldo*) ?

(ABBIATI II, 356–57, but see II, 369–70, 418)

June 26   Arrives in Venice with Giuseppina for sea bathing.

(WALKERV, 218; CARTEGGI I, 36; ABBIATI II, 362)

July 19   Leaves Venice.

(CARTEGGI I, 36)

July 22   Arrives in Busseto.

(ABBIATI II, 365)

July 31   Leaves for Paris.

(WALKERV, 218; COPIAL., 194; ABBIATI II, 340, 368)

mid-Aug. Sends Piave prose version of libretto for *Simon Boc-canegra* for Venetian censors.
(ABBIATI II, 368)

Sept. ? Begins to compose *Simon*.
(GATTI, 331)

Sept. 22 Signs contract with Alphonse Royer, director of the Paris Opéra, to produce *Il trovatore* in French translation.
(GÜNTHERD, 569–69)

1857

Jan. 12. *Il trovatore* (in French translation by Emilien Pacini and with a new ballet and minor changes) at the Paris Opéra under Verdi's supervision.
(ABBIATI II, 376; GATTI, 335)

Jan. 13 Leaves for Busseto.
(ABBIATI II, 376)

Feb. 5 Signs modified contract for new opera to be performed at Teatro S. Carlo, Naples.
(WALKERL, 29–30, 40)

Feb. 19 In Venice with Giuseppina.
(ABBIATI II, 390)

Mar. 12 Premiere of the first version of *Simon Boccanegra* at La Fenice. Verdi directs.
(CHUSID, 142)

Signs contract for *Aroldo* with representatives of Teatro Nuovo, Rimini.
(ABBIATI II, 392; GATTI, 339)

Mar. 15 In Busseto.
(ABBIATI II, 393)

early Apr. Piave in Busseto to modify libretto of *Simon* for Reggio Emilia.

April 10 Signs contract with Marzi, impresario of Teatro Municipale, Reggio Emilia, to produce *Simon* there in May.
(ABBIATI II, 399)

May 10   In Reggio Emilia to direct rehearsals of *Simon.*
                                            (ABBIATI II, 414)

mid-June In Busseto.
                          (ABBIATI II, 417; COPIAL., 554)

?   Writes *La preghiera del poeta* (text by Nicola Sole).
                                  (OSBORNE, 458; MILA, 496)

early July Sends final sections of completed *Aroldo* to Ricordi.
                                            (ABBIATI II, 419)

July 23   To Rimini with Giuseppina and Piave.
                                      (ABBIATI II, 422, 425)

July 27   Rehearsals of *Aroldo* begin under Verdi's super-
          vision.
                                            (ABBIATI II, 425)

Aug. 16   Premiere of *Aroldo* at Teatro Nuovo, Rimini. Verdi
          directs and Mariani conducts.
                                                 (CHUSID, 20)

c. Aug. 20 Leaves Rimini for Busseto.
                                            (ABBIATI II, 431)

early Sept. Begins new opera for Naples.
                                                 (GATTI, 347)

late Sept. Working on libretto drawn from Scribe's *Gustavo
          III di Svezia* (*Un ballo in maschera*).
                                            (ABBIATI II, 449)

Oct. 19   Sends Vincenzo Torelli, secretary to the impresario
          of S. Carlo, libretto outline for *Gustavo III,* to be ap-
          proved by the censors.
                                  (ABBIATI II, 451; WALKERL, 30)

Early Nov. Censors in Naples refuse libretto of *Gustavo III.*
                                            (WALKERL, 30–31)

early Dec. Verdi and Somma resume libretto now entitled *Una
          vendetta in domino.*
                                            (WALKERL, 31)

c. Dec. 20 Somma at Sant'Agata to revise libretto, *Una vendetta
          in domino.*
                                            (ABBIATI II, 461)

1858

early Jan.	Completes *Una vendetta* (*Ballo*) (except for scoring).
	(ABBIATI II, 464, 466; WALKERL, 31)
c. Jan. 5	Leaves Busseto for Naples.
	(WALKERL, 31; GATTI, 351)
Jan. 7–13	In Genoa; scores *Una vendetta* (*Ballo*).
	(WALKERL, 31)
Jan. 14	In Naples; attends performance of *Batilde di Turenna* (*I vespri siciliani*) at San Carlo.
	(ABBIATI II, 466–67; GATTI, 351; COPIAL., 565; WALKERL, 32; CARTEGGI I, 39, 303)
Jan. 28	Submits libretto *Una vendetta* to censors.
	(WALKERL, 32)
Feb. 17	Censors return libretto to Verdi drastically altered and with title changed to *Adelia degli Adimari;* Verdi refuses to produce the work in Naples.
	(ABBIATI II, 474; WALKERL, 32; COPIAL., 567)
early Mar.	Agrees with impresario Vincenzo Jacovacci to have *Ballo* performed at the Apollo, Rome.
	(GATTI, 354)
mid Apr.	As a result of a lawsuit, Verdi signs contract with S. Carlo to produce another work there in Oct.–Nov. 1858 (*Simon*).
	(WALKERL, 36, 40–43; WALKERV, 219)
Apr. 23	Leaves Naples.
	(ABBIATI II, 489; WALKERL, 36; GATTI, 356)
Apr. 27	In Genoa.
	(ABBIATI II, 490; CARTEGGI I, 41)
Apr. 28–29	In Piacenza.
	(ABBIATI II, 490; CARTEGGI I, 41)
Apr. 29	In Busseto.
	(ABBIATI II, 490; CARTEGGI I, 41)
c. late June–mid-July	To Tabiano (Parma) for thermal baths.
	(ABBIATI II, 504–5)

mid-July	In Venice(?) to meet with Somma on changes in the libretto of *Una vendetta* for Roman censors. (ABBIATI II, 503, 505; PASCOLATO, 92)
early Aug.	Receives altered libretto of *Una vendetta* from Roman censors. (PASCOLATO, 93)
late Sept.	Revised libretto of *Una vendetta* sent to Rome with new title, *Un ballo in maschera*. (ABBIATI II, 508, 519; GATTI, 358)
Oct. 20	Arrives in Genoa. (PROD'HOMME, 20; GATTI, 358)
Oct. 23	Arrives in Naples to direct rehearsals of *Simon*. (ABBIATI II, 512)
Nov. 30	*Simon Boccanegra* at S. Carlo; Verdi directs. (COPIAL., 198, 555)

1859

Jan.	"Viva Verdi" first used as a political slogan to mean "Vittorio Emanuele Re d'Italia." (WALKERV, 222)
Jan. 10	Leaves Naples. (GATTI, 359)
Jan. 15	In Rome. (ABBIATI II, 515)
Feb. 17	Premiere of *Un ballo in maschera* at Teatro Apollo. Verdi directs. (CHUSID, 28)
Feb. 20	Accademia Filarmonica Romana elects Verdi its honorary member. (A. CAMETTI, *L'Accademia Filarmonica Romana del 1821 al 1860. Memorie storiche.* [Rome, 1924], 149)
Mar. 13	Leaves Rome. (CARTEGGI I, 57)
Mar. 17–18	Arrives in Genoa. (CARTEGGI, I, 58)

Mar. 20   Arrives in Busseto.
          (ABBIATI II, 534; CARTEGGI I, 58)

Apr. 29   Austria invades Piedmont. Second War of Indepen-
          dence begins.
          (WALKERV, 222)

July   To Tabiano (Parma) for thermal baths.
          (CARTEGGI I, 64)

Aug. 29   Verdi and Giuseppina marry at Collognes-sous-
          Salève (Savoie).
          (ABBIATI II, 537; WALKERV, 223;
          CARTEGGI II, 29; CARTEGGI III, 63)

early Sept.   In Busseto.
              (ABBIATI II, 550)

Sept. 4   Elected to represent Busseto in assembly of Parma
          provinces.
          (GATTI, 372)

Sept. 7–12   In Parma; vote for annexation by Kingdom of Pied-
             mont.
             (COPIAL., 581)

Sept. 15   In Turin to present petition to King Vittorio Eman-
           uele II calling for annexation of Parma to Pied-
           mont.
           (GATTI, 372; COPIAL., 581)

Sept. 17   Turin awards Verdi honorary citizenship; meets C.
           Cavour at Livorno Ferraris (Vercelli).
           (GATTI, 373; COPIAL., 581–82)

Sept. 18   Leaves Turin.
           (GATTI, 373)

Sept. 20   Arrives Busseto.
           (GATTI, 373–74)

1860

Jan. 3   In Genoa with Giuseppina to pass winter; stays at Al-
          bergo Croce di Malta.
          (GATTI, 376; WALKERV, 309;
          CARTEGGI I, 68)

Mar. 11   Leaves Genoa for Busseto.
           (GATTI, 337; WALKERV, 309;
                         CARTEGGI I, 70)

Mar. 24   Nice and Savoy annexed to France.
                         (CAPPELLI, 303)

May 11   Garibaldi lands in Sicily.
           (WALKERV, 224; GARZANTI, 359)

July   At Tabiano (Parma) for thermal baths.
                         (CARTEGGI I, 72–73)

Sept. 7   Garibaldi enters Naples.
           (WALKERV, 224; GARZANTI, 359)

early Dec. In Genoa.
           (ABBIATI II, 593–94; CARTEGGI I, 74)

mid-Dec.   In Busseto; tenor Enrico Tamberlick, acting as inter-
           mediary for St. Petersburg's Imperial Theater,
           writes Verdi asking him to compose a new work for
           that theater.
                         (ABBIATI II, 625–26)

1861

Jan. 16   In Turin to see Cavour.
           (ABBIATI II, 601; GATTI, 392;
                         COPIAL., 589)

Jan. 19   Back in Busseto.
                (GATTI, 393; COPIAL., 590)

Jan. 27   Elected as deputy for Borgo S. Donnino (Fidenza) in
           first Italian Parliament.
           (ABBIATI II, 607; GATTI, 397;
                COPIAL., 593; WALKERB, 3)

Feb. 14   In Turin to attend opening of first Italian Parlia-
           ment.
           (ABBIATI II, 617; COPIAL., 597;
           WALKERV, 316; CARTEGGI II, 17;
                         ALBERTI, 3)

mid-May   Returns to Busseto.
           (GATTI, 400, 405; MARCHESIF, 34)

June 3	Contract of a new opera for St. Petersburg drafted in Paris and sent to Verdi.
	(WALKERB, 13)
June 6	Cavour dies.
	(GARZANTI, 359)
June 17	In Turin.
	(ABBIATI II, 639–40
late June	Returns to Busseto.
	(ABBIATI II, 640)
early July	In Turin.
	(CARTEGGI III, 17)
c. mid-July	Returns to Busseto; Piave at Sant'Agata until the end of the month to work on libretto for *La forza del destino.*
	(ABBIATI II, 638–39, 645; MARCHESIF, 37)
early Sept.	Piave at Sant'Agata for 3 days.
	(ABBIATI II, 658)
c. end Sept.	Verdi begins to write *Forza;* Piave at Sant'Agata.
	(ABBIATI II, 659; MARCHESIF, 41; CARTEGGI II, 19)
Nov. 22	First version of *Forza* completed (except for scoring).
	(ABBIATI II, 667; MARCHESIF, 41)
Nov. 24	Leaves Busseto with Giuseppina for Russia.
	(MARCHESIF, 41)
Nov. 28–29	In Paris.
	(ABBIATI II, 667)
Dec. 6	In St. Petersburg; prima donna Lagrua is ill; *Forza* postponed.
	(ABBIATI II, 678–79; CARTEGGI I, 84)

1862

late Jan.	In Moscow for a few days.
	(CARTEGGI I, 84)
Feb. 24– Mar. 31	In Paris; writes cantata *Inno delle nazioni* (ten. or sop., 5-voice chorus and orch.) for London's International Exhibition; text by Arrigo Boito, whom he meets.
	(ABBIATI II, 684, 688–89; WALKERV, 447)

Apr. 1–17   In Turin; returns to Busseto for a few days.
(ABBIATI II, 694; ALBERTI, 15;
PROD'HOMME, 23; GATTI, 412;
WALKERV, 244; CARTEGGI I, 85)

Apr. 20   Arrives in London for performance of *Inno delle nazioni.*
(ABBIATI II, 695; ALBERTI, 16;
PROD'HOMME, 23)

May 24   Premier of *Inno delle nazioni* at Her Majesty's Theatre.
(ABBIATI II, 700; GATTI, 420)

May 31   Leaves London.
(ALBERTI, 20)

June 2–5   In Paris.
(ALBERTI, 20)

June 7–13   In Turin.
(ABBIATI II, 703; ALBERTI, 20)

June 13–30   In Busseto.
(ABBIATI II, 703; ALBERTI, 20)

c. June   Tito Ricordi publishes edition for voice and piano of *Inno delle nazioni.*
(MILA, 493)

June 30–
early July   In Turin.
(ABBIATI II, 704; ALBERTI, 20)

July   In Busseto.
(ALBERTI, 21)

Aug.   Scores *La forza del destino.*
(*A*BBIATI II, 707; WALKERV, 246)

late Aug.   Leaves Busseto with Giuseppina for Russia.
(GATTI, 423; COPIAL., 610)

Sept. 5   Arrives in Paris.
(ABBIATI II, 708)

Sept. 24   Arrives in St. Petersburg.
(ABBIATI II, 708; GATTI, 425)

late Sept.–
early Oct.   Visits Moscow.
(ABBIATI II, 708)

Nov. 8   Emperor awards Verdi Cross of Imperial and Royal Order of St. Stanislas.

(CARTEGG, I, 86)

Nov. 10   Premiere of the first version of *La forza del destino* at Italian Imperial Theater, St. Petersburg. Verdi directs.

(CHUSID, 76)

Dec. 9   Leaves St. Petersburg.

(ABBIATI II, 714; GATTI, 429)

c. mid-Dec.   In Paris.

(ABBIATI II, 724)

1863

Jan. 5   Leaves Paris.

(ABBIATI II, 725; ALBERTI, 23)

Jan. 11   Arrives in Madrid to direct rehearsals of *La forza del destino*.

(ABBIATI II, 725; GATTI, 431;
MARCHESIF, 1506; COPIAL., 611)

Feb. 21   *Forza* performed in Madrid. Verdi directs.

(ABBIATI II, 729; GATTI, 432;
ALBERTI, 23; MARCHESIF, 1507)

Feb. 23–
Mar. 14   Travels in Spain.

(GATTI 432–33; COPIAL., 612)

Mar. 17   Arrives Paris to rehearse *Les Vêpres* for the Opéra.

(GATTI, 433; ALBERTI, 24)

July 20   Performance of *Les Vêpres* at the Opéra.

(ABBIATI II, 739; ALBERTI, 28)

July 21   Leaves Paris.

(ABBIATI II, 739; ALBERTI, 28;
WALKERV, 322)

July 22–24   In Turin.

(ALBERTI, 28)

July 25–29   In Busseto.

(ALBERTI, 28)

July 30–31   In Turin.

(ABBIATI II, 755; ALBERTI, 29)

Aug. 1   Returns to Busseto.
                                        (ABBIATI II, 755)

c. Dec.   Composes song *Il brigidin* for soprano Isabella Gian-
          oli; performed at Parma's Teatro Regio during car-
          nival of 1864–65.
          (FURLOTTI, 84; OSBORNE, 460; MILA, 496)

1864

c. Jan. 20   In Turin with Giuseppina; then to Genoa.
                              (GATTI, 450; ALBERTI, 34, 37)

Feb.   In Genoa.
                              (ALBERTI, 35–37; MONLEONE, 4)

Feb. 25   In Turin.
                                        (ALBERTI, 37)

early Mar.   Returns to Busseto.
                              (GATTI, 450; ALBERTI, 38)

June   In Genoa; Escudier visits.
                              (ABBIATI II, 795; GATTI, 451;
                                        CARTEGGI III, 23)

July   Returns to Busseto.
                                        (ABBIATI II, 795)

late Oct.   Escudier writes inviting Verdi to revise *Macbeth* (in
          French transl.) for Paris.
          (ABBIATI II, 779, 801; COPIAL., 451)

Nov. 7   Returns to Busseto.
                                        (ABBIATI II, 779)

Early Nov.   Begins revision of *Macbeth* for Paris.
                              (ABBIATI II, 779, 803)

Dec. 11   Florence becomes the capital of Italy.
                                        (CAPPELLI, 412)

1865

Feb. 3   Has completed revision of *Macbeth;* sends Act IV to
          Ricordi.
                              (GATTI, 459; COPIAL., 455)

Feb. 5   Departs for Genoa.
                (GATTI, 459; COPIAL., 456; ALBERTI, 45)

Feb. 12–15   In Busseto to visit his ill father.
                (WALKERV, 251; CARTEGGI III, 28)

late Feb.   Again in Busseto to visit father.
                (WALKERV, 251; CARTEGGI III, 28;
                ALBERTI, 46)

mid-Mar.   In Busseto; travels frequently to Turin to attend
                meetings of Parliament.
                (ABBIATI II, 822; ALBERTI, 48, 51–53)

Apr. 21   Revised *Macbeth* (French transl. by C. L. E. Nuitter
                and A. Beaumont) at Théâtre-Lyrique, Paris.
                (WALKERV, 251; COPIAL., 456;
                CHUSID, 112)

July   Busseto's small municipal theater nearly completed;
                at first Verdi refuses to allow it to be named after
                him.
                (WALKERV, 251, 258; COPIAL., 434)

July 17   Verdi willing to revise *Forza* for the Opéra. Escudier
                at Sant'Agata; probably brings prose outline of *Don
                Carlos*.
                (GÜNTHERD, 572)

Aug.   In Genoa.
                (CARTEGGI III, 30)

mid-Aug.   Returns to Busseto.
                (ABBIATI III, 50)

Aug. 17   Permits Busseto's new theater to use his name.
                (ABBIATI III, 50)

Aug. 28   Signs contract to give a revised version of *Forza* and a
                new work in Paris.
                (GATTI, 468; GÜNTHERD, 573; GÜNTHERG, 32)

mid-Sept.   Renounces candidacy for another term in Parlia-
                ment.
                (ALBERTI, 59)

Nov. 20   Leaves Busseto for Paris via Genoa.
                (ABBIATI III, 62; ALBERTI, 60;
                CARTEGGI III, 34)

Nov. 25   Leaves Genoa.
                                    (CARTEGGI I, 96)

Dec. 1   Arrives in Paris.
                                    (ABBIATI III, 44, 62)

late Dec. Signs contract to write *Don Carlos* for the Paris
          Opéra; supervises writing of libretto by J.
          Mery and, on the latter's death, by C. Du Locle.
                   (ALBERTI, 61; CARTEGGI III, 35–36)

1866

Mar. 17   Leaves Paris after having completed Act I of *Don
          Carlos;* stops a few days in Genoa.
                        (ALBERTI, 69; ABBIATI III, 75;
                    WALKERV, 263; CARTEGGI III, 37)

Mar. 24   Arrives in Busseto; works on *Don Carlos.*
           (ALBERTI, 69; PROD'HOMME, 195; WALKERV,
                      264–65; CARTEGGI III, 37)

early Apr. Begins working on Act II of *Don Carlos.*
                                    (GÜNTHERG, 87)

c. mid-May Completes a draft of Act II of *Don Carlos.*
                                    (GÜNTHERG, 40)

early June Completes a draft of Act III of *Don Carlos.*
                                    (GÜNTHERG, 88)

June 19   Italy declares war on Austria. Third War of In-
          dependence begins.
                                    (GARZANTI, 361)

early July Completes a draft of Act IV of *Don Carlos.*
                                    (GÜNTHERG, 97)

c. July 20 Has completed the orchestration of Acts I–IV of *Don
          Carlos.*
                                    (GÜNTHERG, 99)

July 5–22 In Genoa; arranges to rent an apartment at Palazzo
          Sauli on the Carignano hill; will take formal posses-
          sion on Dec. 1, continuing to rent it until Nov. 30
          1874.
                   (ABBIATI II, 93; ALBERTI, 71; GATTI, 473;
                   CARTEGGI III, 41; WALKERV, 265, 332–33;
                                    RESASCO, 18)

July 24   Arrives in Paris; works on last act of *Don Carlos*.
(WALKERV, 265; CARTEGGI III, 41;
GÜNTHERG, 42; GÜNTHERG, 100)

Aug. 11   Begins rehearsing singers for *Don Carlos*.
(GÜNTHERG, 100)

Aug. 19–   At Cauterets (Pyrenees); completes Act V of *Don
Sept. 12   Carlos*.
(ABBIATI III, 99–100; GATTI, 477;
WALKERV, 265)

late Sept. Rehearsals of *Don Carlos*, under Verdi's direction,
begin at the Opéra.
(ALBERTI, 72)

c. early Dec. Completes scoring of *Don Carlos*.
(ALBERTI, 73)

1867

Jan. 14   Carlo Verdi dies in Busseto.
(ABBIATI III, 114; GATTI, 478;
COPIAL., 75; WALKERV, 267–68)

Mar. 11   Premiere of first version of *Don Carlos* at the Paris
Opéra. Verdi directs.
(CHUSID, 42)

Mar. 12   Leaves Paris.
(ABBIATI III, 127; CARTEGGI III, 43;
WALKERV, 268)

Mar. 14   In Genoa; takes possession of new apartment.
(WALKERV, 268, 335)

Mar. 16   In Busseto, making short trips to Genoa.
(ALBERTI, 76; WALKERV, 269)

Apr. 24   City of Genoa confers honorary citizenship on
Verdi.
(MONLEONE, 10)

late May   Decides to assume guardianship of 7-year-old Filomena (Maria) Verdi.
(ABBIATI III, 137–38; CARTEGGI I, 100)

June 1   First performance of *Don Carlos* (in Italian transla-
            tion by A. de Lauzières) at London's Covent Garden.
            (ABBIATI III, 147; GATTI, 494; CHUSID, 42)

June   In Genoa.
                                        (PROD'HOMME, 525)

June 12–15 In Busseto.
                                        (PROD'HOMME, 525)

early July In Busseto.
                                        (WALKER V, 272)

July 21   Antonio Barezzi dies in Busseto.
                        (ABBIATI III, 142; CARTEGGI I, 101;
                                            WALKER V, 273)

early Aug. In Genoa.
                                        (ALBERTI, 80)

Aug. 18   In Paris with Giuseppina and conductor Angelo
            Mariani.
                    (ABBIATI III, 138; GATTI, 497; WALKER V,
                                                    337)

Oct. 1   Leaves Paris for Busseto.
                                        (ABBIATI III, 153)

Oct. 27   First performance in Italy of *Don Carlos* (translation
            by de Lauzières) at Teatro Comunale, Bologna;
            Mariani conducts.
                            (ABBIAT III, 154; CHUSID, 42)

late Oct.   In Genoa.
                                        (ABBIATI III, 155)

early Nov. In Busseto.
                                        (CARTEGGI III, 46)

Nov. 19   In Genoa.
                                        (CARTEGGI III, 47)

1868

mid-Mar. to   Frequent visits from Genoa to Busseto
mid-Apr.   (CARTEGGI III, passim.)

May   Refuses to accept Cross of the Crown of Italy; indig-

nant at Minister E. Broglio's denigrations of music written after Rossini.
(ABBIATI III, 192, 199; ALBERTI, 88; WALKERV, 346)

June 28–30   In Genoa.
(ABBIATI III, 215)

June 30   In Milan to meet poet Alessandro Manzoni.
(ABBIATI III, 215; GATTI, 511; WALKERV, 274; PROD'HOMME, 529)

July 4   In Busseto.
(CARTEGGI III, 54)

July 14   In Genoa.
(CARTEGGI III, 55)

Aug.   In Busseto?
(ALBERTI, 96)

Aug. 22–
Sept. 15   At Tabiano (Parma) for thermal cures.
(ABBIATI III, 220; GATTI, 516)

Sept. 16   In Busseto.
(PROD'HOMME, 530)

Nov. 13   Rossini dies in Passy. Verdi conceives *Requiem* to be written by various composers.
(WEAVER, 221)

Dec. 13   In Genoa; begins revision of *La forza del destino* for La Scala.
(ABBIATI III, 234, 238–45; ALBERTI, 98; GATTI, 520; CARTEGGI III, 60–61)

1869

Jan. 24   In Milan to rehearse revised *La forza del destino* for La Scala.
(ABBIATI III, 247; WALKERV, 349)

Feb. 10   In Genoa.
(ABBIATI III, 249)

Feb. 15   Returns to Milan.
(ABBIATI III, 250)

Feb. 27   Directs revised *La Forza* at La Scala.
                    (ALBERTI, 99; CHUSID, 82)

Feb. 28   In Genoa.
                    (ABBIATI III, 252; ALBERTI, 99;
                    GATTI, 525; CARTEGGI III, 62)

Mar. 7   Briefly in Busseto.
                    (ABBIATI III, 263–64; GATTI, 528;
                    CARTEGGI I, 108)

June 6   Assigned by committee for celebration of Rossini's
                 death to compose *Libera me* for *Requiem*.
                    (ROSENM, 129)

July 5   Nominated Cavaliere dell'Ordine del Merito Civile
                 di Savoia.
                    (COPIAL., 213–14)

July 24   In Genoa.
                    (CARTEGGI I, 114)

Aug. 17   Has completed *Libera me* to be included in *Requiem*
                 for Rossini.
                    (ABBIATI III, 294; ROSENM, 129)

Aug. 22   In Busseto.
                    (ABBIATI III, 298; CARTEGGI III, 64)

Sept. 12   In Busseto.
                    (ABBIATI III, 303; CARTEGGI III, 67)

late Nov.   In Genoa.
                    (ABBIATI III, 317)

late Dec.   Du Locle in Genoa; informs Verdi that Khedive of
                 Egypt intends to have an opera written for opening
                 of Suez Canal.
                    (GÜNTHERA, 24)

late Dec.   Ricordi, at Verdi's instigation, prints album of six
                 songs for voice and piano by various composers as
                 benefit for Piave; Verdi's *stornello* "Tu dici che non
                 m'ami" included in the collection.
                    (ABBIATI III, 304, 317–18; OSBORNE, 461;
                    MILA, 496)

1870

late Jan.	Writes Du Locle in Paris to send him French translation of Richard Wagner's literary works. (ABBIATI III, 329)
Mar. 26	Leaves Genoa for Paris. (ABBIATI III, 335; ALBERTI, 117)
Mar. 31– Apr. 20	In Paris; investigates possibility of writing new work for the Opéra-Comique. (ABBIATI III, 365–66; GüNTHERA, 24–26)
Apr. 22	In Genoa. (GüNTHERA, 41)
Apr. 26	In Busseto; Du Locle, acting as intermediary for Khedive of Egypt, urges Verdi to write opera for Cairo. (ABBIATI III, 335, 340, 365; GüNTHERA, 41)
early May	In Genoa; returns to Busseto. (ABBIATI III, 343; ALBERTI, 119; CARTEGGI III, 70)
mid-May	Receives from Du Locle synopsis of libretto for *Aida* prepared by Egyptologist Auguste Mariette. (BUSCH, 17)
late May	Agrees to compose *Aida*. (GüNTHERA, 48–49)
early June	Sends Du Locle terms of contract for *Aida*. (ABBIATI III, 372)
late June	Du Locle in Busseto for a week to settle details of contract for Cairo and to complete French libretto in prose under Verdi's supervision. (ABBIATI III, 373; GüNTHERA, 18–20, 32, 56–57; GOSSETT, 296)
early July	Giulio Ricordi and A. Ghislanzoni in Busseto to plan translation and versification of libretto for *Aida*. (ABBIATI III, 374; GATTI, 543; GüNTHERA, 60; GOSSETT, 296)
July 15	Ghislanzoni sends Verdi Act I of *Aida*. (GOSSETT, 299)

Aug. 9–13	In Genoa; Verdi works on Act I of *Aida*. (ABBIATI III, 379; COPIAL., 638)
Aug. 14	In Busseto. (ABBIATI III, 381)
late Aug.– early Sept.	Ghislanzoni at Sant'Agata to work on Acts I and II of *Aida;* Verdi completes draft of Act I. (ABBIATI III, 385; COPIAL., 643; GOSSETT, 299)
Sept. 13–14	Completes draft of Act II of *Aida*. (GOSSETT, 299)
Sept. 20	Italian troops enter Rome. (CAPPELLI, 436)
Oct. 27	Has completed draft of Act III of *Aida*. (GOSSETT, 299)
c. Nov. 13	Has completed draft of Act IV of *Aida*. (GOSSETT, 299)
mid–late Nov.	Ghislanzoni at Sant'Agata for final adjustments to *Aida*. (GOSSETT, 299)
Dec. 13	Leaves Busseto for Genoa. (ABBIATI III, 405)
late Dec.	Refuses post as director of Naples Conservatory after death of Mercadante. (ABBIATI III, 354–57; GATTI, 549)

1871

c. mid-Jan.	Completes scoring of *Aida;* is appointed honorary member of Società Filarmonica of Naples. (ABBIATI III, 431; CARTEGGI I, 129)
Feb. 3	Rome becomes capital of unified Italy. (CAPPELLI, 436)
c. mid-Feb.	In Florence(?) for a few days to discuss reform of Italian conservatories with Caesare Corradi, Minister of Education. (CARTEGGI III, 75, 77)

c. early Mar.   In Florence to preside over commission for reform of conservatories.
(ABBIATI III, 427; ALBERTI, 128; WALKER V, 369)

Mar. 24   In Genoa; works on document for reform of conservatories.
(CARTEGGI I, 138; GHISI, 172–75)

Apr. 23   Leaves Genoa for Busseto.
(WALKER V, 370–71)

c. mid-May   Draneht Bey, superintendent of the Cairo Opera in Busseto, to make final arrangements for premiere of *Aida*.
(ABBIATI III, 456; GATTI, 558)

July 19   In Genoa.
(ABBIATI III, 461–62; PROD'HOMME, 536; WALKER V, 371; COPIAL., 266; ZOPPI, 227)

Aug. 13   In Busseto.
(ABBIATI III, 466, 476; CARTEGGI, 138; COPIAL., 268)

Sept., 2   Sends score of *Aida* to Ricordi.
(ABBIATI III, 477; ALBERTI, 135; COPIAL., 620)

late Sept.   In Milan for a few days to meet with designer G. Magnani regarding production of *Aida* at La Scala and to plan new seating arrangement for orchestra.
(CARTEGGI III, 84; COPIAL., 683)

Sept. 27   In Busseto.
(CARTEGGI III, 84)

Oct. 30   In Florence to hear soprano Antonietta Anastasi Pozzoni.
(ABBIATI III, 490)

Nov. 2   In Genoa.
(ABBIATI III, 490; COPIAL., 271)

c. Nov. 7–13   In Busseto.
(ABBIATI III, 503–4)

Nov. 19 — In Bologna to hear Wagner's *Lohengrin* at the Teatro Comunale; annotates Lucca piano-vocal score with comments during performance.
(CARTEGGI II, 216–20; ABBIATI III, 504–5)

Nov. 20 — In Busseto.
(ABBIATI III, 507)

c. Nov. 26 — In Genoa.
(COPIAL., 677)

late Nov.– early Dec. — Principals of *Aida* for La Scala visit Genoa to rehearse with Verdi.
(WALKER V, 407)

c. mid-Dec. — In Milan to attend rehearsals of *Forza* at La Scala.
(ABBIATI III, 523, 525)

Dec. 23 — In Genoa; principals meet to rehearse *Aida*. Verdi composes full-scale overture for *Aida;* later decides against use.
(ABBIATI III, 525; GATTI, 578–80)

Dec. 24 — Premiere of *Aida* in Cairo. Giovanni Bottesini conducts.
(CHUSID, 8)

1872

Jan. 2 — In Milan to direct rehearsals of *Aida* at La Scala.
(ABBIATI III, 541; GATTI, 579; PROD'HOMME, 537)

Feb. 8 — European premiere of *Aida* at La Scala with minor revisions; Faccio conducts; Verdi directs.
(ABBIATI III, 552; ALBERTI, 138; CHUSID, 8)

Feb. 20 — In Genoa.
(ABBIATI III, 557; CARTEGGI I, 142)

c. beg. Apr. — Du Locle begins French translation of *Aida* and (in May) of *La forza del destino.*
(GÜNTHER B, 439)

Mar. 31 — Leaves Genoa.
(ABBIATI III, 565)

Apr. 1–3   In Busseto.
(ALBERTI 143; COPIAL., 275)

Apr. 3   In Parma to direct rehearsals of *Aida*.
(PROD'HOMME, 539; GATTI, 586;
CARTEGGI I, 149; COPIAL., 275)

Apr. 20   *Aida* performed in Parma. Verdi directs.
(PROD'HOMME, 539; GATTI, 586; CARTEGGI
I, 149; CONATIC, 157)

late Apr.   In Busseto.
(ABBIATI III, 568; CARTEGGI I, 150)

July   Takes trip to Genoa.
(CARTEGGI I, 153)

c. early Aug.–   At Tabiano (Parma) for thermal cures.
Aug. 12   (CARTEGGI III, 93)

late Oct.   In Genoa.
(CARTEGGI I, 157)

early Nov.   In Naples for productions of *Don Carlos* and *Aida;*
begins rehearsals for the former.
(GATTI, 593; CARTEGGI III, 94)

Oct. 14?   Directs performance of partially revised *Don Carlos*
at S. Carlo.
(CARTEGGI III, 94; CHUSID, 42, 49;
GüntherE, 400)

1873

late Jan.   Begins rehearsals of *Aida* for Neapolitan premiere.
(ABBIATI III, 618)

Mar. 30   *Aida* at S. Carlo. Verdi directs.
(ALBERTI, 157; CARTEGGI III, 91, 96;
CONATIC, 158)

Apr. 1   *String Quartet in E minor* given private performance
at Verdi's suite in Albergo delle Crocelle.
(ABBIATI III, 624, 627; GATTI, 600;
COPIAL., 282)

Apr. 9   Leaves Naples for Busseto.
(GATTI, 600; COPIAL., 621)

late Apr.   Decides to complete *Requiem*.
                               (ROSEN M, 136–37)

mid-May   Trip to Genoa.
                               (COPIAL., 622)

May 22   Poet Alessandro Manzoni dies in Milan.

June 1–3   In Milan for funeral of Manzoni; proposes to Mayor of Milan to compose a *Requiem* in honor of poet.
                   (ABBIATI III, 643; GATTI, 605; COPIAL., 283)

June 25   Leaves Busseto for Paris.
                               (GATTI, 607)

June 28   In Paris; begins working on *Requiem*.
                          (ABBIATI III, 649–50)

late Aug.?   Leaves Paris for Busseto.
                           (ABBIATI III, 651)

Sept. 14   In Busseto.
                               (GATTI, 608)

Dec. 30   In Genoa.
            (ABBIATI III, 661; ALBERTI, 163; CARTEGGI III, 99)

1874

late Feb.   Tito Ricordi in Genoa to discuss publication of *Requiem*.
                 (ABBIATI III, 676; COPIAL., 288)

Apr. 10   Has completed *Requiem*.
                 (ABBIATI III, 673; CARTEGGI III, 101)

May 2   In Milan to begin rehearsing *Requiem*.
                          (ABBIATI III, 688)

May 22   Conducts premiere of *Requiem* at Church of San Marco, Milan.
                            (COPIAL., 287)

May 25   Conducts *Requiem* at La Scala.
                   (ABBIATI III, 690; GATTI, 615)

May 26 Leaves Milan for Paris to rehearse *Requiem*.
(ABBIATI III, 698)

June 9 Conducts *Requiem* at the Opéra-Comique.
(ABBIATI III, 699)

late June In London to investigate possibility of performing *Requiem*.
(ABBIATI III, 701)

July 1 In Paris.
(ABBIATI III, 703)

July 5 In Busseto.
(ABBIATI III, 704; ALBERTI, 176)

early Sept. Giuseppina in Genoa to arrange moving furniture from Palazzo Sauli to Palazzo Doria.
(CARTEGGI III, 103)

c. Sept. 13–17 In Genoa to accompany Giuseppina back to Busseto.
(CARTEGGI III, 103)

Nov. 15 Named senator of Kingdom of Italy.
(ABBIATI III, 721; GATTI, 616)

c. Nov. 21 In Genoa; stays at Palazzo Doria.
(ABBIATI III, 721; PROD'HOMME, 546;
ALBERTI, 179; CARTEGGI III, 106)

beg. Dec. Trip to Busseto.
(CARTEGGI III, 107)

1875

c. Feb. 22–25 In Milan.
(CARTEGGI III, 110)

Apr. 3 In Busseto.
(ABBIATI III, 747)

Apr. 10 In Milan to rehearse soloists of *Requiem* for European tour.
(ABBIATI III, 749–50)

Apr. 12 Leaves Milan.
(ABBIATI III, 750; GATTI, 618)

Apr. 14　In Paris.
(ABBIATI III, 750; GATTI, 618)

Apr. 19　Conducts *Requiem* at the Opéra-Comique.
(ABBIATI III, 750; GATTI, 618)

late Apr.　Receives Cross of Legion of Honor.
(ABBIATI III, 750; GATTI, 618)

May 13　Leaves for London.
(ABBIATI III, 750)

May 15　Conducts *Requiem* at Albert Hall.
(ABBIATI III, 751; GATTI, 618; RosenL, 152)

June 2　Leaves London.
(ABBIATI III, 751)

June 3　Arrives in Vienna.
(ABBIATI III, 751)

June 11　Conducts *Requiem* at the Hofoperntheater.
(ABBIATI III, 752; GATTI, 618; Carteggi III, 111)

June 19　Conducts *Aida* at the Hofopern theater.
(CONATIC, 161)

June 25　Leaves Vienna.
(ABBIATI III, 753)

June 26–27　In Venice.
(ABBIATI III, 754; CARTEGGI III, 111)

June 28　Returns to Busseto.
(ABBIATI III, 754; CARTEGGI III, 111)

early July　Short trip to Milan to discuss with Ricordi irregularity in his royalty payments.
(ABBIATI III, 755, 761)

Nov. 15　In Rome to be sworn in as senator.
(GATTI, 626; CARTEGGI III, 114)

1876

Jan.　In Genoa.
(ABBIATI III, 788)

Mar. 4   In Busseto.
(ABBIATI III, 793; CARTEGGI III, 117)

Mar. 20   Leaves for Paris to rehearse *Aida* at the Théâtre-Italien.
(ABBIATI III, 793; GATTI, 621)

Mar. 22   Arrives in Paris.
(GÜNTHER B, 426)

Apr. 22   Conducts *Aida,* in Italian, at the Théâtre-Italien, Paris.
(ABBIATI III, 796; GATTI, 621; COPIAL., 299)

May   Supervises Nuitter and Du Locle's French translation of *Aida.* (ABBIATI III, 795; GÜNTHER B, 437–39)

May 30   Conducts *Requiem* at the Théâtre-Italien.
(ABBIATI III, 793, 800)

June 1   *String Quartet* performed privately in Verdi's suite at the Hôtel de Bade.
(ABBIATI III, 795, 801)

June 7   Leaves Paris.
(CARTEGGI I, 182)

June 18   In Busseto.
(ABBIATI III, 802)

July 12   Sends corrected proofs of *String Quartet* to Ricordi.
(ABBIATI IV, 12)

c. Aug. 15–20   In Turin to attend graduation of Maria ("Fifao") Verdi from teachers' school; her engagement to Alberto Carrara announced.
(ABBIATI IV, 15–16; CARTEGGI III, 120)

Sept. 2–4   At Tabiano (Parma) thermal resort to fetch home Giuseppina and Maria Verdi.
(WALKER V, 435; CARTEGGI III, 120)

late Oct.–
Nov. 9   Visits Genoa.
(CARTEGGI I, 182–83)

Dec. 3   Leaves Busseto.
(CARTEGGI III, 122)

c. Dec. 11   In Genoa.

(ALBERTI, 191)

1877

Jan. 20   Ferdinand Hiller invites Verdi to conduct *Requiem* at Cologne Festival.

(CARTEGGI II, 317)

Apr. 3   Leaves Genoa for Busseto.

(ABBIATI IV, 26, 31; CARTEGGI III, 125)

c. May 10   Leaves Busseto for Cologne.

(ABBIATI IV, 26; CARTEGGI III, 125)

c. mid-May   In Cologne to conduct rehearsals of *Requiem*.

(ABBIATI IV, 26; GATTI, 627; WALKER V, 438)

May 21   Conducts performance of *Requiem* in Cologne.

(ABBIATI IV, 39; ALBERTI, 203; CARTEGGI III, 126)

late May?   In Holland.

(ABBIATI IV, 40)

early June   In Paris.

(ABBIATI IV, 41)

c. June 17   Leaves Paris.

(ABBIATI IV, 41)

c. June 20   In Busseto.

(CARTEGGI III, 127)

early Dec.   In Genoa.

(CARTEGGI I, 186)

1878

Jan. 9   Umberto I becomes king of Italy.

(CAPELLI, 287)

c. mid-Mar.   Two-day trip to Monte Carlo.

(ALBERTI, 210; CARTEGGI III, 135)

early Apr.   In Busseto.

(CARTEGGI III, 135)

Apr. 6   Leaves for Milan and Paris.
                                    (CARTEGGI III, 135)

c. Apr. 14–   In Paris.
  late Apr.   (CARTEGGI III, 135)

early May   In Genoa.
                                    (CARTEGGI III, 135)

c. May 10   Returns to Busseto.
             (ABBIATI IV, 70; ALBERTI, 219; CARTEGGI
                                         III, 135)

Oct. 11   Maria Verdi marries Alberto Carrara.
             (ABBIATI IV, 67–68; ALBERTI, 222–23;
                                    WALKER V, 440)

Oct. 18   In Genoa.
                                    (ALBERTI IV, 80)

early Nov.   Returns briefly to Busseto.
                                    (ABBIATI IV, 80)

c. mid-Nov. Back in Genoa.
                                    (ABBIATI IV, 71)

late Nov.   In Paris for eight days to visit International Exposi-
             tion.
             (ABBIATI IV, 71, 75; CARTEGGI II, 327;
                                 CARTEGGI III, 138)

early Dec.   Returns briefly to Busseto.
                                    (ABBIATI IV, 71)

c. Dec. 6   In Genoa.
                                    (CARTEGGI I, 188)

Dec. 28   Elected honorary member of Modena's Accademia
             di Scienze, Lettere e Arti
                                    (RONCAGLIA, 83)

1879

Mar. 20   In Busseto for a few days.
                                    (CARTEGGI III, 139)

c. Apr. 17   Leaves Genoa for Busseto.
                                    (CARTEGGI II, 330)

c. May 1	In Busseto.
	(ABBIATI IV, 73, 76; GATTI, 637)
early June?	In Paris?
	(ABBIATI IV, 82)
June 23	In Milan to direct rehearsals of *Requiem;* Boito presents him with plan of libretto for *Otello.*
	(ABBIATI IV, 72, 76, 83, 86; WALKER V, 473)
June 30	Conducts *Requiem* at La Scala as benefit for victims of floods.
	(ALBERTI, 237–38; WALKER V, 473)
early July	In Busseto.
	(ABBIATI IV, 86)
c. July 15– late July	In Genoa to visit Agricultural Exposition.
	(ABBIATI IV, 76, 87)
late July	In Busseto.
	(ABBIATI V, 75; CARTEGGI II, 330)
Aug. 5	Maria Carrara Verdi gives birth to daughter Giuseppina.
Sept. 17	Boito has completed sketch of libretto of *Otello* for Verdi's consideration.
	(ABBIATI IV, 94)
Nov. 18	Verdi receives completed libretto of *Otello.*
	(WALKER V, 476)
Nov. 20	In Milan for a few days; meets with Boito to discuss libretto of *Otello.*
	(ABBIATI IV, 113–14)
Dec. 8	In Genoa.
	(CARTEGGI I, 190; CARTEGGI III, 142–43)

1880

Jan. 20	Writes thanking Gesellschaft der Musikfreunde of Vienna for making him an honorary member. (Facs. of letter in Heinrich Kralik's *Das Buch der Musikfreunde* [1951], 57)

Feb. 12 Leaves for Paris to direct rehearsals of *Aida*.
(ABBIATI IV, 176)

Mar. 22 Conducts *Aida* (in French translation by Nuitter and Du Locle) at the Paris Opéra.
(ABBIATI IV, 115; GATTI, 647; CARTEGGI III, 145; CONATIC, 172)

late Mar. Nominated as Grand Officer of the Foreign Legion.
(ABBIATI IV, 116; GATTI, 648)

c. Apr. 4 Leaves Paris for Genoa.
(GATTI, 648)

Apr. 5–11 In Turin for Exposition.
(ALBERTI, 243)

Apr. 11 King of Italy confers title of Cavaliere of the Great Cross.
(COPIAL., 314)

Apr. 12 In Milan.
(Abbiati IV, 117)

Apr. 18 *Pater noster* and *Ave Maria* premiered at La Scala in benefit concert; Verdi attends.
(ABBIATI IV, 119; GATTI, 649; ALBERTI, 245)

Apr. 19 In Busseto.
(ABBIATI IV, 122; CARTEGGI III, 145)

c. Apr. 26 In Genoa.
(ABBIATI IV, 124; CARTEGGI, 145)

May 4 In Busseto.
(CARTEGGI II, 335)

early May In Turin for a few days to visit Exposition.
(ABBIATI IV, 124; GATTI, 651; CARTEGGI II, 335)

May 11 In Busseto.
(CARTEGGI III, 146)

early Aug. Receives revised libretto of *Otello* from Boito.
(WALKERV, 477)

c. mid-Oct. Boito sends Verdi text for finale of Act III of *Otello*.
(WALKERV, 478)

Nov. 18   In Genoa.

(CARTEGGI I, 194)

Dec. 12–19   In Busseto.

(CARTEGGI I, 195; CARTEGGI III, 149)

c. late Dec.   Boito begins to send Verdi material for revision of
Simon Boccanegra.

(ABBIATI IV, 138)

1881

early Jan.   Verdi begins revision of *Simon.*

(ABBIATI IV, 140; ALBERTI, 269)

early Feb.   Boito completes revised libretto for *Simon.*

(ABBIATI IV, 144)

Feb. 21   Verdi has completed revision of *Simon.*

(ABBIATI IV, 144)

Feb. 24   Leaves Genoa for Milan to direct rehearsals of revised *Simon.*

(CARTEGGI II, 338)

Mar. 24   Premiere of revised *Simon Boccanegra* at La Scala;
Verdi directs.

(CHUSID, 146; ABBIATI IV, 148)

Mar. 28   In Genoa.

(ABBIATI IV, 150; ALBERTI, 283; GATTI,
660)

Apr. 6   Visits Busseto for a few days.

(CARTEGGI III, 150)

early May   Returns to Busseto.

(ABBIATI IV, 150; ALBERTI, 286)

early July   Giulio Ricordi and Boito at Sant'Agata to discuss
Otello.

(ABBIATI IV, 180; WALKER V, 485)

c. late July   Boito sends Verdi revised text for finale of Act III of
Otello.

(WALKER V, 486)

late Aug.   In Milan for Industrial Exposition.
              (ABBIATI IV, 182; GATTI, 663; CARTEGGI
              III, 151)

Sept. 2   In Busseto.
              (GATTI, 663; COPIAL., 695; CARTEGGI III,
              151)

late Nov.   Accompanies Giuseppina to Genoa; returns to Busseto.
              (CARTEGGI I, 197)

early Dec.   In Genoa.
              (GATTI, 666; ALBERTI, 291)

c. mid-Dec.   In Milan.
              (ALBERTI, 292)

Dec. 20–22   Briefly in Busseto.
              (ALBERTI, 294; CARTEGGI III, 152)

Dec. 22   In Genoa.
              (ALBERTI, 294)

1882

May 2   In Paris to ensure his copyright interests after death
              of Léon Escudier; begins work with librettist Nuitter
              on 4-act version of *Don Carlos*.
              (ABBIATI IV, 194, 198, 200; CARTEGGI II,
              340; CARTEGGI III, 154)

May 18   Leaves Paris with Nuitter's revised libretto for *Don
              Carlos;* stops in Turin.
              (ABBIATI IV, 200)

May 21   In Busseto.
              (ABBIATI IV, 200; CARTEGGI II, 340)

June 18–   At Montecatini Terme.
c. July 5   (CARTEGGI I, 197; CARTEGGI III, 155–56)

mid-Sept.   Begins revising *Don Carlos*.
              (GÜNTHER E., 398)

Dec.   Continues revision of *Don Carlos*.
              (ABBIATI IV, 204; CARTEGGI III, 158)

c. Dec. 18–21   In Busseto.
                                    (CARTEGGI III, 159)

1883

c. Feb. 25–   In Busseto.
  c. Mar. 3   (CARTEGGI III, 163)

mid-Mar.   Completes revision of *Don Carlos*.
                 (GATTI, 676; ALBERTI, 300; COPIAL., 698)

c. Apr. 3   In Busseto.
                                    (ABBIATI IV, 215)

June 26–   At Montecatini Terme.
  July 15   (ABBIATI IV, 217, 220; CARTEGGI III,
                                                164–65)

July 16   In Busseto.
                                    (CARTEGGI III, 165)

early Dec.   In Genoa.
                 (ABBIATI IV, 224; CARTEGGI II, 342;
                                    CARTEGGI III, 165)

late Dec.   In Milan to direct rehearsals of revised *Don Carlos*.
                                    (GATTI, 678)

1884

Jan. 10   Conducts premiere of revised *Don Carlos* in 4 acts
                 (revised Italian translation by A. Zanardini) at La
                 Scala.
                                    (CHUSID, 42, 52)

mid-Jan.   In Genoa.
                                    (GATTI, 681)

Feb. 17–19   In Busseto.
                                    (CARTEGGI III, 166)

c. mid-Mar.   Begins *Otello*.
                                    (WALKER V, 488)

May 6   Leaves Genoa for Busseto.
                                    (ABBIATI IV, 244)

c. mid-June– June 28	In Turin for Exposition. (GATTI, 684; CARTEGGI III, 168)
June 29– c. mid-July	At Montecatini Terme. (GATTI, 685; CARTEGGI I, 200; CARTEGGI III, 168)
late Sept.– early Oct.	Boito in Busseto to discuss changes in libretto for *Otello*. (ABBIATI IV, 249; WALKER V, 491)
Nov. 23	Accompanies Giuseppina to Genoa; returns to Busseto. (CARTEGGI III, 169)
Nov. 30	In Genoa; resumes composition of *Otello*. (CARTEGGI III, 170; WALKER V, 493)
c. Dec. 20–23	In Busseto. (ALBERTI, 317; CARTEGGI III, 170)

1885

c. mid-Feb.	Visits Busseto briefly. (CARTEGGI III, 171)
c. May 1–3	In Milan for dental work. (ALBERTI, 319)
May 4	In Busseto. (ALBERTI, 320)
July	At Montecatini Terme. (WALKER V, 492)
Aug.?	At Tabiano (Parma) for thermal cures. (WALKER V, 492)
c. mid-Sept.	Resumes composition of *Otello* (except for scoring). (ABBIATI IV, 265; WALKER V, 493)
Oct. 5	Has completed Act IV of *Otello* (except for scoring). (ABBIATI IV, 265; WALKER V, 493)
Oct. 16–18	Boito and Giulio Ricordi at Sant'Agata for further revisions of *Otello*; discussions of interpreters, scenes, costumes for premiere performance. (ABBIATI IV, 266)

Nov. 21   In Milan to purchase dentures.
> (ALBERTI, 326; CARTEGGI III, 172)

Dec. 4   In Genoa.
> (ABBIATI IV, 271; ALBERTI, 329)

Dec. 20–22   Trip to Busseto.
> (CARTEGGI III, 172)

1886

mid-Jan.   Boito and Giulio Ricordi in Genoa.
> (ABBIATI IV, 272)

early Mar.   Boito in Genoa.
> (ABBIATI IV, 272)

Mar. 19   Leaves for Paris to engage Victor Maurel as Iago for premiere of *Otello*.
> (ABBIATI IV, 280; ALBERTI, 331–32)

Apr. 11   Leaves Paris.
> (CARTEGGI III, 176)

Apr. 13–15   Briefly in Milan.
> (CARTEGGI III, 177)

Apr. 15   In Genoa.
> (ABBIATI IV, 282; CARTEGGI III, 177)

Apr. 29   In Busseto.
> (ALBERTI, 332; CARTEGGI III, 177)

June 24–July 14   In Montecatini Terme.
> (ABBIATI IV, 285; GATTI, 692; CARTEGGI III, 178)

July 15   In Busseto.
> (CARTEGGI III, 178)

Sept. 28–Oct. 1   Giulio Ricordi at Sant'Agata.
> (CARTEGGI III, 178)

Nov. 1   Has completed *Otello*.
> (ABBIATI IV, 293–94; GATTI, 693; WALKER V, 493; CARTEGGI I, 203; COPIAL., 700)

Nov. 22   In Milan to see Boito about French translation of *Otello*.
> (ABBIATI IV, 300)

Dec. 10   In Genoa.
                    (ABBIATI IV, 301; GATTI, 693)

Dec. 26   *Don Carlos* (revised version with original Act I re-
                stored) at Modena's Teatro Municipale.
                    (ROSENQ, 370–71; GUALERZI, 499;
                    GÜNTHERG, 18)

1887

Jan. 4   In Milan to direct rehearsals of *Otello*.
                    (ABBIATI IV, 309; GATTI, 694)

Jan. 17   Rehearsals of *Otello* begin.
                    (GATTI, 694)

Jan. 27   Receives the Great Cross of the Order of SS. Mauri-
                zio e Lazzaro from King Umberto I.

Feb. 5   Premiere of *Otello* at La Scala.
                    (CHUSID, 132)

Feb. 8   Mayor of Milan awards honorary citizenship to
                Verdi.
                    (GATTI, 699)

c. Feb. 10 In Busseto.
                    (GATTI, 699)

Mar. 11   In Genoa.
                    (CARTEGGI III, 181)

Mar. 30–   In Busseto.
Apr. 1   (CARTEGGI III, 181)

early May   In Busseto.
                    (ABBIATI IV, 335)

c. May 11   In Genoa.
                    (ABBIATI IV, 336)

May 16   In Busseto.
                    (ABBIATI IV, 337; CARTEGGI III, 182)

late June   In Milan.
                    (ABBIATI IV, 341)

June 29   At Montecatini Terme.
                    (ABBIATI IV, 342; CARTEGGI III, 183)

(July?) Aug.	In Busseto.
	(ABBIATI IV, 343; CARTEGGI III, 184)
early Sept.	Boito at Sant'Agata with completed French translation of *Otello*.
	(GATTI, 701)
Sept. 11–13	In Milan.
	(CARTEGGI III, 185)
Nov. 17	Accompanies Giuseppina to Genoa.
	(ABBIATI IV, 348; GATTI, 703; CARTEGGI III, 185)
Nov. 19–21	In Busseto.
	(CARTEGGI III, 185)
Nov. 21–23	In Milan to settle business with new firm Ricordi-Erba.
	(CARTEGGI III, 186)
Nov. 23	In Genoa.
	(CARTEGGI III, 186)
Nov. 30–Dec. 3	In Busseto.
	(ABBIATI IV, 349; CARTEGGI III, 186; COPIAL., 346)
Dec. 3	In Genoa.
	(ABBIATI IV, 349; CARTEGGI III, 186)

1888

c. May 5	In Busseto.
	(CARTEGGI III, 188)
June 27–July 11	At Montecatini Terme.
	(CARTEGGI III, 188–89)
July 11	In Busseto.
	(CARTEGGI III, 189)
Nov. 6	Inauguration of hospital funded by Verdi at Villanova sull'Arda Piacenza.
	(GATTI, 703; WALKER V, 494)
late Dec.	In Genoa.
	(CARTEGGI III, 190)

1889

c. late Feb.	In Milan; returns to Genoa. (ABBIATI IV, 374–75)
Mar. 30– Apr. 2	Trip to Busseto. (CARTEGGI III, 192)
c. mid-Apr.	In Busseto. (CARTEGGI III, 192)
July 4–21	At Montecatini Terme; Boito sends Verdi libretto synopsis for *Falstaff*. (ABBIATI IV, 382, 384; GATTI, 711; CARTEGGI III, 194; WALKER V, 495)
July 10	Verdi decides to set *Falstaff* to music. (ABBIATI IV, WALKER V, 496)
July 23	Returns to Busseto. (GATTI, 712; CARTEGGI III, 195)
Aug.	Begins composition of *Falstaff*. (GATTI, 712)
Oct. 18	Signs contract acquiring land near Porta Garibaldi in Milan, future site of Casa di Riposo per Musicisti. (ABBIATI IV, 392; GATTI, 710)
Nov. 4–11	Boito at Sant'Agata with libretto of Acts I and II of *Falstaff* completed. (ABBIATI IV, 392; WALKER V, 498)
Nov. 23– Dec. 6	In Milan. (CARTEGGI III, 196–97)
Dec. 6	In Genoa. (CARTEGGI III, 197)

1890

Mar. 8	Receives from Boito completed libretto of Act III of *Falstaff*. (ABBIATI IV, 396; WALKER V, 498)
Mar. 17	Has completed Act I of *Falstaff*. (ABBIATI IV, 397; WALKER V, 498)

c. Apr. 28– c. May 3	Visits Milan.
	(CARTEGGI III, 197)
c. May 3	In Busseto.
	(GATTI, 717; CARTEGGI III, 197)
July 1–c. mid-July	At Montecatini Terme.
	(CARTEGGI III, 198; COPIAL., 705)
c. mid-July	In Busseto.
	(CARTEGGI III, 198)
early Dec.	In Genoa.
	(GATTI, 720; COPIAL., 712)

1891

c. mid-Apr.	Brief visit to Busseto.
	(COPIAL., 367, 370)
c. Apr. 28	In Busseto.
	(GATTI, 720; COPIAL., 368)
July	At Montecatini Terme.
	(ABBIATI IV, 423)
Aug.	In Busseto.
	(ABBIATI IV, 424)
c. mid-Sept.	Has completed Acts I, II, and part of Act III of *Falstaff*; begins scoring.
	(WALKER V, 500)
Dec. 8	In Genoa.
	(COPIAL., 374)

1892

Apr.	Completes scoring of Act I of *Falstaff*.
	(WALKER V, 500)
Apr. 7	In Milan to participate in Rossini centennial celebrations.
	(ABBIATI IV, 437; GATTI, 724)

Apr. 10	Conducts the "Preghiera" from Rossini's *Mosè* at La Scala.
	(ABBIATI IV, 436)
Apr. 11	In Genoa.
	(ABBIATI IV, 439; GATTI, 725)
June 18–20	At Tabiano (Parma) for thermal cures.
	(ABBIATI IV, 445)
June 20–c.23	In Busseto.
	(ABBIATI IV, 445)
c. June 24	At Tabiano (Parma).
	(ABBIATI IV, 445)
early July	At Montecatini Terme.
	(ABBIATI IV, 446–47)
c. July 20	Leaves Montecatini Terme.
	(ABBIATI IV, 447)
Aug. 1	In Busseto.
	(ABBIATI IV, 450)
late Sept.	Has completed scoring of Act III of *Falstaff*. (All scoring now completed except the first part of Act II.)
	(ABBIATI IV, 461; WALKER V, 501)
early Oct.	Giulio Ricordi and Boito at Sant'Agata to discuss staging of *Falstaff*.
	(ABBIATI IV, 459, 462; WALKER V, 501)
Oct. 13–16	In Milan to make some changes in printed libretto and to decide details of *Falstaff* premiere.
	(ABBIATI IV, 463–64)
Oct. 24	In Genoa.
	(ABBIATI IV, 464)
Dec. 25	Has completed scoring of *Falstaff*.
	(ABBIATI IV, 469)

1893

| Jan. 2 | In Milan to direct rehearsals of *Falstaff*. |
| | (ABBIATI IV, 469; CARTEGGI I, 213) |

Jan. 3   Rehearsals of *Falstaff* begin.
                                    (ABBIATI IV, 469, 471)

Feb. 9   Premiere of *Falstaff* at La Scala; Verdi directs.
                                    (WEAVER, 248; CHUSID, 66)

Mar. 2   In Genoa.
                                    (ABBIATI IV, 478)

Apr. 13   In Rome for performance of *Falstaff*.
                                    (ABBIATI IV, 478, 503)

Apr. 14   Rome's mayor confers honorary citizenship on
           Verdi.
                                    (ABBIATI IV, 503; GATTI, 742)

Apr. 15   Attends performance of *Falstaff* at Teatro Costanzi.
                                    (ABBIATI IV, 503; GATTI, 742)

Apr. 20   Leaves Rome for Genoa.
                                    (ABBIATI IV, 504; GATTI, 743)

May 4   Returns to Busseto.
                                    (ABBIATI IV, 506; GATTI, 744)

July?   At Montecatini Terme.
                                    (ABBIATI IV, 516)

early Aug. In Genoa.
                                    (ABBIATI IV, 516)

Aug. 6   In Busseto.
                                    (ABBIATI IV, 517)

Sept.   Boito at Sant'Agata to complete French translation
           of *Falstaff*.
                                    (GATTI, 745; COPIAL., 721)

Nov.   In Genoa.
                                    (GATTI, 745)

1894

early Mar. Visits Milan for 4–5 days.
                                    (COPIAL., 393)

Apr. 4   In Paris for production of *Falstaff*.
                                    (ABBIATI IV, 540)

Apr. 18	Attends performance of *Falstaff* at the Opéra-Comique.
	(ABBIATI IV, 540)
c. Apr. 20	Leaves Paris for Genoa.
	(ABBIATI IV, 540)
c. mid-May	Boito at Sant'Agata to discuss production of French *Otello* in Paris.
	(ABBIATI IV, 543)
July	At Montecatini Terme; receives old Greek, Turkish, and Venetian dance melodies in preparation for ballet music of Parisian *Otello*.
	(ABBIATI IV, 549)
late July	In Busseto.
	(ABBIATI IV, 550)
Aug. 21	Sends ballet music of *Otello* to Ricordi.
	(ABBIATI IV, 551)
c. Sept. 18	In Genoa.
	(ABBIATI IV, 555)
Sept. 26	In Paris to attend rehearsals of French *Otello*.
	(ABBIATI IV, 556)
Oct. 12	Attends Performance of *Otello* (in French) at the Paris Opéra; receives Grand Cross of Legion of Honor.
	(ABBIATI IV, 559; GATTI, 754)
Oct. 22	Leaves Paris.
	(ABBIATI IV, 557)
Oct. 23	In Genoa.
	(ABBIATI IV, 557)
c. Nov.	Verdi's song *Pietà Signor* (text adapted by Boito from the *Agnus Dei*) published in *Fata Morgana* for the benefit of victims of an earthquake in Sicily and Calabria.
	(OSBORNE, 463; MILA, 496)

1895

Jan. 29– early *Feb.*	In Milan to arrange for construction of the Casa di Riposo. (ABBIATI IV, 568; GATTI, 756; COPIAL., 411)
c. late Mar.– early Apr.	Returns to Busseto. (COPIAL., 396, 399)
Apr.	Begins writing *Te Deum*. (ABBIATI IV, 570, 572)
early July	At Montecatini Terme. (ABBIATI IV, 575)
July 21	Returns to Busseto. (ABBIATI IV, 575)
Dec.	In Genoa. (GATTI, 760)

1896

late Mar.	Brief stay in Milan to settle performing rights with Ricordi; deposits sum of money for construction at Casa di Riposo. (COPIAL., 406–7)
early May	In Busseto. (ABBIATI IV, 592)
Oct.	In Genoa. (GATTI, 762)

1897

May	In Busseto. (ABBIATI IV, 609)
July	At Montecatini Terme. (ABBIATI IV, 611–12; GATTI, 764)
Aug.	In Busseto. (GATTI, 765)

late Oct.	Sends the *Quattro pezzi sacri* to Ricordi for publication.
	(ABBIATI IV, 616; WALKER V, 504)
Nov. 14	Giuseppina dies at Sant'Agata.
	(ABBIATI IV, 618; COPIAL., 130)

1898

early Jan.	In Milan to supervise publication of the *Pezzi sacri*.
	(GATTI, 768)
late Feb.	In Genoa.
	(GATTI, 768; COPIAL., 722)
Apr. 7	*Stabat, Laudi,* and *Te Deum* premiered at the Paris Opéra.
	(ABBIATI IV, 625; COPIAL., 411, 414)
early May	In Milan for consultation on last will.
	(ABBIATI IV, 629)
May 28	In Busseto.
	(ABBIATI IV, 628)
July	At Montecatini Terme.
	(ABBIATI IV, 631; GATTI, 772)
Aug.	In Busseto.
	(ABBIATI IV, 632; GATTI, 772)

1899

Feb. 9	In Genoa.
	(ABBIATI IV, 637)
early June	In Milan.
	(ABBIATI IV, 643)
July	At Montecatini Terme.
	(ABBIATI IV, 648; GATTI, 778)
Aug.	In Busseto.
	(GATTI, 778)

Dec. 16   Signs document that establishes foundation of Casa
            di Riposo.
                      (ABBIATI IV, 651; GATTI, 779; GATTI, 779
                                          [says Dec. 20]

1900

Mar. 1   In Genoa.
                                  (ABBIATI IV, 651)

May   In Busseto.
                                  (ABBIATI IV, 652)

May 14   In Milan; signs last will and sends it to notary Angelo
             Carrara.
                        (ABBIATI IV, 653; GATTI, 782)

late May   In Busseto.
                                  (ABBIATI IV, 657)

c. mid-Dec.   Leaves Busseto for Milan after having arranged to
             collect and burn his early compositions; stays at
             Hotel Milan.
                                  (ABBIATI IV, 666)

1901

Jan. 21   Has fatal stroke.
                                  (WALKER V, 508)

Jan. 27   Dies at 2:50 A.M.
                                  (ABBIATI IV, 668)

Appendix A

Dramatis personae: People Associated with Verdi during His Lifetime

ABBADIA, LUIGIA (1821–96). Italian mezzo-soprano. Debut in 1836 in Sardinia. Created role of Giulietta di Kelbar in *Un giorno di regno*, Scala, and sang in revival of *Oberto*, Scala, 1840, both directed by Verdi, who wrote new music for her. Repertory included *Ernani, Nabucco, Attila, Luisa Miller, Traviata, Trovatore* and *Ballo*.

ALIZARD, ADOLPHE-JOSEPH-LOUIS (1814–50). French bass, later baritone. Created role of Roger in *Jérusalem*, at the Paris Opéra. Sang in Brussels (1842–44), Marseilles (1845–46), Paris (1847–49).

ANGELINI, GIAN FRANCESCO. Italian bass-baritone. Created Padre Guardiano in *Forza*, Imperial Theater, St. Petersburg, 1862. Also sang in *Nabucco, Lombardi, Ernani, Luisa Miller, Rigoletto, Trovatore*, and *Don Carlos*.

APPIANI, GIUSEPPINA (c. 1797–?). Born Countess Strigelli. Maintained salon in Borgo Monforte, Milan. Close friend of Bellini, Donizetti, and the young Verdi.

ARATI, MARCO. Italian bass. Debut in 1838–39, Pisa. Created role of Alvaro in *Alzira*, San Carlo, Naples, and Wurm in *Luisa Miller*, San Carlo, Naples, 1849.

ARDITI, LUIGI (1822–1903). Italian conductor, composer, and violinist. Friend of Verdi. Conducted premiere of *Inno delle nazioni*, Her Majesty's Theatre, London, 1862, and numerous U.S. and British Verdi premieres.

ARPINO, FERDINANDO. Italian lawyer. Verdi's attorney in court proceedings in Naples regarding *Un ballo in maschera*'s aborted premiere there (1858). Prepared and published *La difesa del Maestro Cavaliere Giuseppe Verdi*.

ARRIVABENE, COUNT OPPRANDINO (1805–87). Italian writer and patriot. Frequented Countess Maffei's salon. Close friend of Verdi. Their rich correspondence has been published.

BAGIER. French impressario, manager of Théâtre-Italien, Paris after Calzado (*q.v.*). Verdi, unenthusiastic about Bagier's and the theater's qualities, was unwilling to have his works mounted there.

BALDERI, ARCANGELO. Italian bass. Created Ferrando in *Trovatore,* Teatro Apollo, Rome, 1853. Also sang in *Nabucco* and *Masnadieri.*

BALESTRA, LUIGI (1808–63). Italian lawyer and poet from Busseto. Provided text for a duet Verdi intended to add to *Oberto* for Genoa revival, 1841. Verdi set two Balestra translations of Goethe, included in the *Sei romanze,* 1838, his first published work.

BARBIERI-NINI, MARIANNA (1820–87). Italian soprano. Debut 1840, Scala. Created role of Lucrezia in *I due Foscari,* Teatro Argentina, Rome, 1844; Lady Macbeth in *Macbeth,* Teatro della Pergola, Florence, 1847; Gulnara in *Il corsaro,* Gran Teatro, Trieste, 1848. Also sang in *Nabucco, Attila, Battaglia,* and *Trovatore.*

BARBOT, CAROLINE DOUVRY (c. 1830–?). French soprano. Created Leonora in *Forza,* Imperial Theater, St. Petersburg, 1862. Wife of the tenor Joseph-Théodore-Désiré Barbot. At the Paris Opéra, 1859, then active in Italy. Repertory included *Ballo, Vêpres, Trovatore,* and *Simon.*

BARDARE, LEONE EMANUELE (1820–after 1874). Neapolitan librettist. Director of Scuole magistrali (teacher-training schools) for the Reale Albergo dei poveri, Naples. Completed libretto of *Il trovatore* after Cammarano's death. Altered text of *Rigoletto,* on instructions from censor, for performance in Naples, December 1857, with the title *Clara di Perth.*

BAREZZI, ANTONIO (1798–1867). Busseto merchant and music lover. Verdi's patron, father of Verdi's first wife, Margherita. In Verdi's own words, Barezzi was his "secondo padre." *Macbeth* dedicated to him.

BARTOLINI, LUIGI (1777–1850). Italian sculptor, follower of Canova. Prominent in Florentine artistic circles during Verdi's stay in the city. Giuseppina Strepponi's son Camillo studied with him briefly.

BARTOLINI, OTTAVIO (1821–94). Italian baritone, specialist in Verdi repertory. First emerged in *Ernani,* later a popular interpreter of *Ballo,* as well as *Lombardi, Vespri, Rigoletto, Trovatore, Nabucco, Foscari, Attila, Macbeth, Luisa Miller,* and *Traviata.*

BASEVI, ABRAMO (1818–95). Italian author, music critic. Wrote first serious work on Verdi's music: *Studio sulle opere di Giuseppe Verdi,* Florence, 1859, which covers Verdi's career from *Nabucco* (1842) to *Aroldo* (1857).

BASILY (or BASILJ or BASILI), FRANCESCO (1766–1850). Italian musician and educator. Headed the examining board of Milan Conservatory, 1832, when Verdi was rejected. Recognized Verdi's gifts as a composer.

BASSI, CALISTO (c. 1800–?). Italian librettist and translator. Wrote text of aria "Io la vidi," set by Verdi during student days (c. 1834). Translated *Jérusalem* into Italian.

BAUCARDÈ (or BOUCARDE or BEAUCARDE), CARLO (1825–83). Italian tenor, created role of Manrico in *Il trovatore*, Teatro Apollo, Rome, 1853. At a later performance, in Florence, he inserted the high C in "Di quella pira." Verdi maintained silence, but three years later rejected the tenor for *Aroldo*, writing to Piave that he wanted nothing more to do with "lunatics." Also sang in *Lombardi, Masnadieri, Luisa Miller,* and *Vespri.*

BAZZINI, ANTONIO (1818–97). Italian violinist and composer, professor of composition at Milan Conservatory, 1873, director after 1882.

BEAUMONT (pseud. for BEAUME), ALEXANDRE (1827–1909). French librettist. With Charles Nuitter, revised and translated into French the second version of *Macbeth,* Théâtre-Lyrique Impérial, Paris, 1865.

BELLAIGUE, CAMILLE (1858–1930). French critic, author. Wrote for *Correspondant, Revue des deux mondes, Figaro.* Defended Verdi while opposing Debussy. Some correspondence with Verdi. Friend of Boito. Published a book, *Verdi,* in 1912.

BELLINI, ANDREA. Italian baritone. Created Pietro in *Simon,* Fenice, Venice, 1857. Also sang in *Corsaro.*

BELLINZAGHI, GIOVANNINA. Italian soprano. Created Fenena in *Nabucco,* Scala, Milan, 1842. Only role at La Scala.

BENDAZZI, LUIGIA (1833–1901). Italian soprano. Debut in *Ernani,* San Benedetto, Venice, 1850. Created Amelia in *Simon Boccanegra,* Fenice, Venice, 1857. Also sang in *Vespri, Ballo, Lombardi, Trovatore, Nabucco, Due Foscari, Luisa Miller, Gerusalemme, Aroldo;* especially successful as Lady Macbeth in *Macbeth,* as Gilda in *Rigoletto,* and as Violetta in *Traviata.*

BENEDETTI, NICOLA. Italian bass. Created Banquo in *Macbeth,* Teatro della Pergola, Florence, 1847. Also sang in *Lombardi, Ernani, Attila,* and *Masnadieri.*

BENZA (-NAGY), IDA. Mezzo-soprano. Sang Preziosilla in revised *Forza,* Scala, Milan, 1869. Repertory also included *Ernani, Macbeth, Trovatore, Traviata, Ballo,* and *Don Carlos.*

BIANCO, GIOVANNI. Italian baritone. Sang Pietro in revised *Simon,* Scala, Milan, 1881.

BOCCABADATI, VIRGINIA (1828–1922). Italian soprano, particularly admired as Violetta in *Traviata*. Also sang in *Luisa Miller, Rigoletto, Trovatore*, and *Aroldo*. Not to be confused with Augusta Boccabadati (?–1875), her sister, or her mother, Luigia.

BOITO, ARRIGO (born Enrico) (1842–1918). Italian poet, composer, librettist, translator. Provided Verdi with text for *Inno delle Nazioni*, 1862; revised Piave's libretto of *Simon Boccanegra*, 1881; wrote librettos of *Otello*, 1887, and *Falstaff*, 1893. His own operas are *Mefistofele* (1868) and *Nerone* (1924, posthumous). Valuable correspondence with Verdi.

BOITO, CAMILLO (1836–1914), brother of Arrigo. Architect, responsible for the construction of the Casa di Riposo G. Verdi, Milan.

BOLDINI, GIOVANNI (1845–1931). Italian painter. Painted two famous portraits of Verdi and made several drawings of him.

BONNEHÉE, MARC (1828–86). French baritone. Debut 1853. At the Paris Opéra, created Guy de Montfort in *Les Vêpres siciliennes*, 1855, and Di Luna in *Le Trouvère*, 1857. Also sang in *Rigoletto* and *Ballo*.

BORGHI-MAMO, ADELAIDE (1829–1901). Italian contralto. First Paris Azucena in both Italian and French versions of *Trovatore*. Debut Urbino, 1846. Mother of soprano Erminia Borghi-Mamo, who made her debut in Nice as Leonore in French premiere of *Forza* (1873) with her mother singing Preziosilla.

BOTTESINI, GIOVANNI (1821–89). Italian composer, conductor, and outstanding double-bass player. Conducted premiere of *Aida*, Khedival Theatre, Cairo, December 24, 1871. Verdi wrote the double bass solo in Act IV of *Otello* for him and was instrumental in having Bottesini named director of the Parma Conservatory shortly before his death. Early in his career, he was active in the U.S. Correspondence with Verdi.

BOUCHÉ, STEFANO LUCIEN, French bass. Created role of Moser in *I masnadieri*, Her Majesty's Theatre, London, 1847. Also sang in *Ernani, Luisa Miller, Trovatore, Vêpres*, and *Simon*.

BRAMBILLA, TERESA (1813–95). Italian soprano of a family of singers. Debut 1831, Teatro Carcano, Milan. Created role of Gilda in *Rigoletto*, Teatro La Fenice, Venice, 1851. Also sang in *Nabucco, Ernani, Attila, Masnadieri, Luisa Miller*, and *Trovatore*. Not to be confused with her niece and namesake, also a soprano, wife of Amilcare Ponchielli.

BRENNA, GUGLIELMO. Italian theater administrator. Secretary of La Fenice, Venice. Friend of Piave and instrumental in his being engaged as Verdi's librettist for *Ernani*. At the time of *Rigoletto*, Brenna accompanied Piave to Busseto to work out libretto modifications with Verdi.

BRUNACCI, ANGELO (?–1850). Italian tenor. Created Macduff in *Macbeth*, Teatro della Pergola, Florence, 1847. Died of yellow fever in Brazil.

BRUSCHI-CHIATTI, ABIGAILLE. Italian soprano. Sang the role of Elisabeth in *Don Carlos* at La Scala in 1884. Repertory also including *Trovatore, Ballo, Forza,* and *Aida.*

BÜLOW, HANS GUIDO, Baron von (1830–94). German conductor, pianist, critic. Closely associated with Wagner and, later, Brahms. Attacked Verdi's *Requiem* at the time of its premiere. Wrote Verdi a repentant letter in 1892.

CALZADO, TORRIVRO (1805–?). Spanish-born (??) impresario, manager of Théâtre-Italien. Presented *Trovatore* there in carnival season 1854–55. Sued by Verdi for refusal to pay rights on *Rigoletto* and *Traviata.* Verdi lost the case. In 1863 Calzado produced *Lombardi* without permission. Forced to resign his post in 1863 because of financial scandal.

CAMMARANO, SALVATORE (1801–52). Italian librettist. Member of a large artistic Neapolitan family. Wrote librettos of *Alzira, Luisa Miller, Battaglia di Legnano, Trovatore* (completed by Bardare). Also liberttist of many operas by other composers, including Donizetti's *Lucia,* Mercadante's *Vestale,* and Pacini's *Saffo.* Important correspondence with Verdi, who greatly admired him.

CANTI, GIOVANNI. Italian music publisher, Milan. Brought out Verdi's first published work, *Sei romanze,* in 1838. The following year published other works, including the *Notturno* for three voices, flute, and piano.

CAPPONI, Marchese GINO (1792–1876). Italian statesman and writer, member of distinguished Florentine family. Verdi met the blind patriot at the time of *Macbeth* in 1847.

CAPPONI, GIUSEPPE (1832–89). Italian tenor. Debut 1860, Pesaro. Sang in premiere of *Requiem,* San Marco, Milan, 1874. Sang in Italian premiere of *Don Carlos,* Teatro Comunale, Bologna, 1867, and in Trieste *Aida,* 1873. Repertory also included *Ernani, Trovatore, Traviata,* and *Forza.*

CARCANO, GIULIO (1812–84). Italian author, dramatist, translator of Shakespeare. Friend of Verdi. Suggested a libretto on *Hamlet,* which Verdi rejected.

CARARA, ALBERTO (1854–1925). Italian lawyer. Son of Angiolo Carrara of Busseto, for many years Verdi's administrator. In 1878, married Verdi's heiress, Filomena Maria Verdi. Descendants still live in Verdi villa at Sant'Agata.

CARVALHO(CARVAILLE), LÉON (1825–97). French baritone and impresario, manager of Théâtre-Lyrique (1856–60; 1862–68). Presented *Rigoletto, Traviata,* and the revised *Macbeth* (1865). From 1868–72, managed the Cairo Theater, which opened its doors with *Rigoletto* (1869), conducted by Muzio and presented the premiere of *Aida* in 1871. Married to singer Caroline-Marie-Felix Miolan.

CASALONI, ANNETTA. Italian mezzo-soprano. Created Maddalena in *Rigoletto,* Fenice, Venice, 1851. Also sang in *Luisa Miller* and *Trovatore.*

CENCETTI, GIUSEPPE. Italian director. Staged first productions of *Ballo,* Teatro Apollo, Rome, 1859, and first Italian *Forza* as *Don Alvaro,* Teatro Apollo, 1863. Staging manuals based on these productions published by Ricordi shortly after the performances.

CHAPERON, PHILIPPE-MARIE (1823–1906). French scene painter. Designed first production of *Don Carlos* for the Paris Opéra, 1867, and, with Rubé, Acts I and IV of *Aida* for Cairo.

COLETTI, FILIPPO (1811–94). Italian baritone. Debut 1834 or 1835. Verdi specialist. Created roles of Gusmano in *Alzira,* San Carlo, Naples, 1845; Francesco in *I masnadieri,* Her Majesty's Theatre, London, 1847; and Germont in the revised *Traviata,* Treatro San Benedetto, Venice, May 1854. His repertory also included *Nabucco, Ernani, Foscari, Giovanna d'Arco, Attila, Luisa Miller, Stiffelio, Rigoletto, Trovatore, Vespri, Boccanegra,* and *Ballo.*

COLINI, FILIPPO (1811–63). Italian baritone, debut 1835. Created role of Giacomo in *Giovanna d'Arco,* Scala, Milan, 1845; Rolando in *Battaglia di Legnano,* Argentina, Rome, 1849; and Stankar in *Stiffelio,* Teatro Grande, Trieste, 1850. Also sang in *Oberto, Nabucco, Lombardi, Ernani, Macbeth,* and *Luisa Miller.*

COLONNESE, LUIGI (c. 1833–?). Italian baritone. Sang Don Carlo in revised *Forza,* Scala, Milan, 1869. Also sang Fra Melitone in *Forza* and *Aida.* Reputation as a better singer than actor. Father of soprano Elvira Colonnese.

CORTICELLI, MAURO. Italian theatrical agent. Presumably born in Bologna, where he was active for some years. Managed international tours of actress Adelaide Ristori, and was with her in Russia when Verdi arrived for *Forza.* From 1867–79 lived at Sant'Agata and managed the Verdi estate, until his womanizing and financial unreliability led Verdi to discharge him. A stout man, he is supposed to have served as a model for Falstaff.

COSTA, MICHELE ANDREA ANGELO (later SIR MICHAEL) (1810–84). Italian tenor, composer, conductor, from Naples. After 1833, conductor at Her Majesty's Theatre, London; 1846–54, conductor of the Philharmonic Society, then conductor at Covent Garden. Conducted *Ernani* (1845), *Rigoletto* (1853), *Trovatore* (1855), and *Don Carlos* (1867), among other Verdi operas. Composed an earlier setting of *Don Carlos*, London (1844).

COSTANTINI, NATALE. Italian bass-baritone. Created the role of Ezio in *Attila*, La Fenice, Venice, 1846.

COTOGNI, ANTONIO (1831–1918). Italian baritone. First Posa (*Don Carlos*) in Italy. Had a repertory of 157 operas, including *Ernani, Foscari, Attila, Macbeth, Rigoletto, Trovatore, Traviata, Vespri, Ballo,* and *Aida*.

CRUVELLI, SOFIA (SOPHIE CRÜWELL) (1826–1907). German soprano. Debut 1847, Venice in *Ernani*. Created the role of Hélène in *Les Vêpres siciliennes*, at the Paris Opéra, 1855. Also sang in *Nabucco, Attila,* and *Luisa Miller*. Considered a fine singer, but an eccentric, unreliable person.

DAMINI, PAOLO Italian bass. Created Monterone in *Rigoletto*, Fenice, Venice, 1851.

D'ANGERI (ANGERMAYER DE REDENBURG), ANNA (1853–1907). Austrian soprano, pupil of Marchesi. Sang Amelia in revised *Simon*, Scala, Milan, 1881. Also sang in *Ernani, Trovatore, Vespri, Ballo, Don Carlos, Aida.* Verdi invited her to sing Desdemona, but she had retired to marry (1881) and refused.

DAVID, JOSEPH (c. 1838–?). French bass. Created the Inquisitor in *Don Carlos* at the Paris Opéra, 1867. Repertory included *Aida*.

DE AMICIS, EDMONDO (1846–1908). Italian writer. Author of best-selling children's book *Cuore* and various travel books. Friend of the Verdis. Wrote a perceptive essay on Giuseppina Verdi in her old age (published in 1908).

DE AMICIS, GIUSEPPE. Italian engineer, cousin of the above. One of the Verdis' circle of friends in Genoa.

DE BASSINI, ACHILLE (1819–81). Italian baritone. Debut c. 1837. Created roles of Francesco in *Foscari*, Argentina, Rome, 1844; Seid in *Corsaro*, Teatro Grande, Trieste, 1848; Miller in *Luisa Miller*, San Carlo, Naples, 1849; Melitone in *Forza*, Imperial Theater, St. Petersburg, 1862. Repertory included *Nabucco, Lombardi, Ernani, Alzira, Macbeth, Masnadieri* (Italian premiere), *Trovatore, Vespri,* and *Simon*.

DE GIULI-BORSI, TERESA (stage name of MARIA TERESA PIPPEO) (1817–77). Italian soprano. Debut 1839, Milan. Created the role of Lida in *La battaglia di Legnano*, Argentina, Rome, 1849. Repertory included

Nabucco (revival of 1842, Scala) *Lombardi, Ernani, Foscari, Macbeth, Luisa Miller, Rigoletto, Traviata, Vespri,* and *Ballo.* Regarded by Verdi with affection and esteem.

DELFICO, MELCHIORRE (DE FILIPPIS DEI CONTI DI LANGANO) (1825–95). Italian caricaturist, painter, composer, and poet. Important member of Verdi's Neapolitan circle of friends. Left many caricatures of this group—especially of Verdi—from the 1850s. His work also appeared in foreign magazines, including *Punch.*

DEL SIGNORE, CARLO (or CARLINO). Italian businessman. Member of the Genoa circle, close friend of Verdi and of the conductor Angelo Mariani. After their breach, Del Signore attempted a reconciliation, but failed. Later tried unsuccessfully to persuade Mariani to conduct *Aida* in Cairo.

DEMALDÈ, GIUSEPPE ("Finola") (1795–?). Italian writer. From Busseto, close friend of Verdi's. Collected material for and wrote some of a biographical work, *Cenni biografici,* which was never published during his lifetime. Generous excerpts have been published, with translation in *Verdi Newsletters* Nos. 1, 2, and 3. A rich source of information on Verdi's early life (until about 1841). Ancestor of the present Verdi line, the Carrara-Verdi family.

DE RESZKE, EDOUARD (EDOARDO) (1855–1917). Polish-born bass. Debut 1876, Paris (King in *Aida*). Sang Fiesco in revised *Simon,* Scala, Milan, 1881; also *Ernani, Rigoletto, Ballo, Aida.*

DE RESZKE, JEAN (1850–1925). Tenor. Brother of above. They often appeared together. Repertory included *Forza, Ballo.*

DÉRIVIS, PROSPER (or Prospero) (1808–1880). French bass of a family of singers. Debut 1831, Paris. Created roles of Zaccaria in *Nabucco,* Scala, Milan, 1842 and of Pagano in *Lombardi,* Scala, Milan, 1843. Sang Fernand (Ferrando) in Paris premiere of *Le Trouvère,* 1857; also in *Ernani, Attila, Masnadieri, Rigoletto,* and *Vespri.*

DE SANCTIS, CESARE (?–1881). Italian businessman, member of the Verdis' Neapolitan circle and a good friend of Cammarano. Important correspondence with Verdi, largely published.

DONIZETTI, GAETANO (1797–1848). Italian composer. Admired and supported the young Verdi, on whom he exerted a strong musical influence. Directed the Vienna premiere of *Ernani.* Wrote, in a letter of 1844; "I am all the happier to have given place to a man of talent like Verdi."

D'ORMEVILLE, CARLO (1840–1924). Italian dramatist, librettist, director, critic, theatrical agent. Staged premiere of *Aida* in Cairo. Friend of Emanuele Muzio.

DRANEHT, PAUL BEY (born PAVLOS PAVLIDIS) (1815–94). Greek Cypriot. Settled in Egypt in 1827, entered the service of the country's ruler, whose minister he became. Active in the negotiations for the construction of the Suez Canal, Draneht was also superintendant of the Egyptian railways and intendant of the Khedival theater, thus primarily responsible for the commissioning and production of *Aida*.

DU LOCLE (DU COMMUN), CAMILLE (1832–1903). French librettist and opera director. Son-in-law of Emile Perrin (*q.v.*). Manager of the Opéra-Comique from July 1870 until January 1874 in collaboration with Adolphe de Leuven, then alone until March 1876. Completed the libretto of *Don Carlos* (1865–67) after the death of Joseph Méry. Translator, with Nuitter, of *Forza* and *Aida*, also translated *Boccanegra*, and— with Boito—*Otello*. Friend of Mariette (*q.v.*), he played a vital role in the creation of *Aida*. While at the Opéra-Comique, he produced *Carmen* and sponsored performances of Verdi *Requiem* with the composer conducting.

DUPONCHEL, CHARLES (c.1795–1868). French impresario, manager of the Paris Opéra from 1835 to 1849. With his colleague Roqueplan, presented *Jérusalem*, 1847.

DUPRÉ, GIOVANNI (1817–82). Italian sculptor. Knew Verdi in Florence in 1847 and made a cast of his right hand (later carved in marble). Wrote *Memoirs* with amusing Verdi anecdotes.

DUPREZ, GILBERT LOUIS (1806–96). French tenor. Created role of Gaston in *Jérusalem* at the Paris Opéra, 1847. His brother, Édouard, translated *Aroldo, Ballo, Rigoletto, Traviata*.

DUVEYRIER, CHARLES (1803–66). French writer and librettist. With Eugène Scribe, wrote libretto of *Il duca d'Alba* for Donizetti, later revised as *Les Vêpres siciliennes* for Verdi, 1855.

ECHEVERRIA, JOSÉ (or GIUSEPPE) (1825–60). Spanish bass. Created role of Fiesco in *Boccanegra*, Fenice, Venice, 1857. Also sang in *Ernani, Foscari, Luisa Miller, Nabucco, Lombardi, Masnadieri, Trovatore, Giovanna de Guzman* (*Les Vepres siciliennes*), *Rigoletto*.

EDEL, ALFREDO (1859–1912). Italian painter, illustrator, and designer. Designed costumes for Scala *Don Carlos* and for premiere of *Otello*. After 1890, worked extensively in London and in Paris (for Sarah Bernhardt, among others).

ESCUDIER, LÉON (1821–81). French publisher, author, impresario and agent, for many years in collaboration with his brother MARIE (1819–80). Published most of Verdi's operas in France, first at the Bureau Central de Musique, later under his own name. Important correspondence with Verdi. With his brother, founded *La France musicale* in 1837. Manager of the Théâtre-Italien after 1874, where he mounted the French premiere of *Aida*. Published *Memoirs* with many interesting pages about Verdi.

FACCIO, FRANCO (born FRANCESCO) 1840–91). Italian composer and conductor. His opera *Amleto*, libretto by his close friend Boito, was produced in Genoa in 1865, then in Milan in 1871. The cool reception of the Milanese virtually marked the end of Faccio's career as a composer. At La Scala, he conducted the Italian premiere of *Aida* (1872), and the premieres of the revised *Simon* (1881) and *Otello* (1887). He was the outstanding Italian conductor of his day and Verdi came to admire and respect him immensely, mourning his untimely death.

FANCELLI, GIUSEPPE (1833–88). Italian tenor. First sang as comprimario in major Italian opera houses, then promoted to leading roles. Sang Radamès in Italian premiere of *Aida*, Milan, 1872. Repertory included *Lombardi, Trovatore, Ballo,* and *Don Carlos*.

FAURE, JEAN-BAPTISTE (1830–1914). French baritone. Debut 1852, Paris. Created role of Posa in *Don Carlos* at the Paris Opéra, 1867. One of the few French singers Verdi admired.

FERLOTTI, RAFFAELE. Italian baritone from Bologna. Created Belfiore in *Giorno di regno*, Scala, Milan, 1840. Sang title role in the revival of *Oberto*, Scala, Milan, 1840, for which Verdi authorized transposition of some of the music a step higher to accommodate his voice. Also sang in *Nabucco, Lombardi, Ernani, Foscari,* and *Giovanna d'Arco*.

FERRARINI, CESARE (1807–91). Italian conductor and violinist. Conductor at Teatro Regio in Parma in 1850s. Conducted there the first Italian performance of *Giovanna de Guzman* (*Vêpres*) and an early *Don Carlos*. Correspondence with Verdi.

FERRARIO, CARLO (1833–1907). Italian scene designer and painter. Especially active at La Scala, where he designed sets for *Macbeth, Masnadieri, Trovatore, Forza, Don Carlos, Aida* (Italian premiere), *Otello* (premiere), *Falstaff* (premiere). Also designed sets for premiere of *Mefistofele*, Scala 1867–68.

FERRETTI, JACOPO (1784–1852). Italian librettist. Active in literary circle in Rome. Wrote text of Rossini's *Cenerentola*. Met Verdi at time of *Alzira*.

FERRI, GAETANO NICOLA (1819–?) Italian baritone. Debut 1839, Piacenza. Created Egberto in *Aroldo*, Teatro Nuovo, Rimini, 1857. Sang in *Nabucco* at Scala, 1842, and in U.S. premieres of *Vespri* (1859) and *Ballo* (1861), both in New York. Also sang in *Lombardi, Ernani, Giovanna d'Arco, Alzira, Attila, Rigoletto, Trovatore,* and *Traviata*.

FÉTIS, FRANÇOIS JOSEPH (1784–1871). Belgian composer and writer, active in Paris. Founded the *Revue Musicale*. His persistent hostility toward Verdi was profoundly reciprocated.

FILIPPI, FILIPPO (1830–87). Italian critic. Wrote for *La Gazzetta Musicale di Milano*, 1858–62, and for *La Perseveranza*, 1859–87. A supporter of Wagner and the Italian Wagnerians, he did not enjoy Verdi's sympathies. Attended Cairo premiere of *Aida* and published an extended account of the event in his *Musica e Musicisti*, 1876.

FIORENTINO, PIER ANGELO (1816–64). Italian-born critic, naturalized French citizen. Collaborated with Dumas *père*. Music critic of *La Presse*. Hostile to Verdi.

FLORIMO, FRANCESCO (1800–88). Italian writer and librarian. Friend and fellow student of Bellini at Naples Conservatory. Remained there and reorganized the library. Author of books on Bellini and on music in Naples. Edited collections of vocal music. The Verdis saw him regularly when they were in that city (and privately called him "Lord Palmerston"). Correspondence with Verdi.

FORNARI, VINCENZO. Italian tenor. Created Rodrigo in *Otello,* Scala, Milan, 1887.

FRASCHINI, GAETANO (1816–87). Italian tenor. Created Zamoro in *Alzira,* San Carlo, Naples, 1845; Corrado in *Il corsaro,* Teatro Grande, Trieste, 1848; Arrigo in *La battaglia di Legnano,* Argentina, Rome, 1849; title role in *Stiffelio,* Teatro Grande, Trieste, 1850; and Riccardo in *Un ballo in maschera,* Teatro Apollo, Rome, 1859. Also sang in *Traviata* (Théâtre-Italien, 1863) with great success. Verdi began *Masnadieri* with Fraschini in mind and thought of the tenor as late as 1870 for Radamès in *Aida*. Sang nearly all of Verdi's tenor roles and was much admired by the composer. He was known as the "tenore della maledizione" for his effective delivery of the curse in *Lucia*.

FREZZOLINI-POGGI, ERMINIA (1818–84). Italian soprano. Debut Florence 1837. Created, at Scala, Milan, Giselda in *Lombardi,* 1843, and title role in *Giovanna d'Arco,* 1845. Repertory included *Ernani, Rigoletto, Trovatore, Traviata.* Contributed to the popularity of Verdi's operas in Paris. Married to tenor Antonio Poggi (*q.v.*).

FRICCI (FRIETSCHE), ANTONIETTA (1840–1912). Austrian soprano/mezzo-soprano. One of a school of new singers that emerged in the mid-1850s. Debut Pisa, 1858, as Violetta. First London Eboli, a role she also sang in Bologna. Repertory included. *Ernani, Macbeth, Rigoletto, Trovatore, Traviata, Ballo, Forza, Don Carlos,* and *Aida* (in which she sang both the title role and Amneris).

GAILHARD, PIERRE (1848–1918). French singer, and, from 1884 to 1894, artistic director (with M. Ritt) of the Paris Opéra. Obsessed with idea of presenting *Otello* at the Opéra.

GALLO, ANTONIO. Italian impresario, violinist, and bookseller. One of Verdi's Venetian supporters. Kept a music shop in Piazza San Marco, where Verdi frequently met friends like Antonio Somma, lawyer and librettist of *Ballo*, and Cesare Vigna, distinguished alienist.

GARBIN, EDOARDO (1865–1943). Italian tenor. Debut 1891 in *Forza*. Created Fenton in *Falstaff*, Scala, Milan, 1893. Also sang in *Lombardi*, *Rigoletto*, and *Traviata*. Some recordings. Married to soprano A. Stehle (*q.v.*).

GARDONI, ITALO SEVERO (1821–82). Italian tenor. Created role of Carlo in *Masnadieri*, Her Majesty's Theatre, London, 1847. Also sang in *Ernani*, *Foscari*, *Giovanna d'Arco*, *Attila*, *Traviata*, and *Don Carlos*.

GAZZANIGA MALASPINA, MARIETTA (1824–84). Italian soprano. Debut 1841, Venice. Created title rôle in *Luisa Miller*, San Carlo, Naples, 1849;) Lina in *Stiffelio*, Teatro Grande, Trieste, 1850; Elena in *Gerusalemme* (premiere of Italian version of *Jérusalem*), Scala, Milan, 1850. Repertory included *Nabucco*, *Lombardi*, *Foscari*, *Giovanna d'Arco*, *Traviata*, *Vespri*, *Aroldo*, and *Ballo*.

GEMITO, VINCENZO (1852–1929). Italian sculptor. As a very young man, threatened with induction into the army, he was introduced to Verdi by Domenico Morelli (*q.v.*). Verdi gave Gemito the sum necessary to buy his exemption from military service, in return for two busts, of Verdi and Giuseppina. Verdi did not like the latter's bust, nor did he like Gemito. In old age, the sculptor published some highly unreliable memoirs.

GHISLANZONI, ANTONIO (1824–93). Italian writer, baritone, patriot. Debut 1846 (the career was patchy and not distinguished). Forced to flee Italy for political reasons in 1851. Supplied several composers with librettos and turned the French prose draft of *Aida* into Italian verse. Provided second verse of Verdi's song, *Stornello*. Edited various journals. Wrote many humorous and informative articles, including a description of Verdi at Sant'Agata. Novel *Gli artisti da teatro* describes theatrical and operatic atmosphere of the 1840s. Sang Carlo in *Ernani*.

GIRALDONI, LEONE (1826?–97). Italian baritone. Created title role in *Simon*, Fenice, Venice, 1857; and Renato in *Ballo*, Apollo, Rome, 1859. Repertory included *Lombardi*, *Ernani*, *Foscari*, *Attila*, *Macbeth*, *Masnadieri*, *Corsaro*, *Luisa Miller*, *Trovatore*, *Traviata*, *Giovanna de Guzman* (*Vespri*), *Forza*.

GIUGLINI, ANTONIO (1827–65). Italian tenor. Contributed to the popularity of Verdi's operas in London where he sang in *Luisa Miller* and *Trovatore*.

GIUSTI, GIUSEPPE (1809–50). Italian (Florentine) poet. Verdi was given a letter of introduction to him in 1847, and through him met prominent Florentines such as Gino Capponi (*q.v.*) and Baron Bettino Ricasoli. Giusti referred to Verdi in one of his most famous poems and wrote the composer a well-known letter, after the premiere of *Macbeth,* advising him to stick to Italian themes.

GOGGI, EMILIA. Italian soprano/mezzo-soprano. Created role of Azucena in *Trovatore,* Apollo, Rome, 1853.

GRAZIANI, FRANCESCO (1828?–1901). Italian baritone. Debut 1851. Created role of Don Carlo in *Forza,* Imperial Theater, St. Petersburg, and sang first Macbeth in British Isles, Dublin, 1859. Repertory included *Ernani, Masnadieri, Luisa Miller, Rigoletto, Trovatore, Traviata, Ballo,* and *Don Carlos* (first performance in Italian, London, 1867). Fervent patriot and friend of Mazzini.

GRAZIANI, LODOVICO (1820–85). Italian tenor, brother of the above. Created role of Alfredo in *Traviata,* Fenice, Venice, 1853. Repertory included *Lombardi, Ernani, Masnadieri, Corsaro, Stiffelio, Rigoletto, Giovanna de Guzman* (*Vespri*), *Simon, Ballo, Forza* (Italian premiere, Rome, 1863).

GROSSI, ELEONORA (c. 1840–79). Italian mezzo-soprano. Studied under Mercadante at Naples Conservatory. Debut c. 1858, Messina. Created role of Amneris in *Aida,* Cairo, 1871. Also sang in *Rigoletto, Trovatore,* and *Ballo.*

GUASCO, CARLO (1813–76). Italian tenor. Debut c. 1839. Created roles of Oronte in *Lombardi,* Scala, Milan, 1843, title role in *Ernani,* Fenice, Venice, 1844 (Verdi reported Guasco was hoarse all evening), and Foresto in *Attila,* Fenice, Venice, 1846. Also sang in *Foscari.*

GUERRINI, VIRGINIA (1872–?). Italian mezzo-soprano. Created role of Meg in *Falstaff,* Scala, Milan, 1893. Also sang the *Requiem* frequently. Repertory included *Aida.*

GUEYMARD, LOUIS (1822–80). French tenor. Debut, Paris Opéra, 1848. Was the original Henri in *Vêpres* at the Paris Opéra, 1855. Also sang Manrique in Paris premiere of *Trouvère,* and created roles in many French operas of the period, including *Le Prophète* and *Sapho.*

GUEYMARD, PAULINE LAUTERS (1834–?). Belgian soprano/mezzo-soprano, wife of the above. Created the role of Eboli in *Don Carlos,* Paris Opéra, 1867. Sang Leonore in Paris premiere of *Trouvère,* 1857 with her husband.

GUICCIARDI, GIOVANNI (1882–?). Italian baritone. Debut, Reggio Emilia, 1847. Created Di Luna in *Trovatore*, Apollo, Rome, 1853. Probably the Guicciardi who sang Michele in *Giovanna de Guzman* (*Vespri*), Scala, 1857–58. Also sang in *Nabucco, Ernani, Giovanna d'Arco, Attila, Luisa Miller, Rigoletto, Traviata, Simon,* and *Ballo.*

HAYEZ, FRANCESCO (1791–1882). Italian painter. Member of the Scala's supervisory committee on set and costume designs. Gave Verdi advice on *Macbeth* production for Florence.

HILLER, FERDINAND (1811–85). German composer, writer, and pianist. Directed Lower Rhine Festival at Cologne 1853–83 and invited Verdi to conduct the *Requiem* there in 1877. Important correspondence with Verdi.

HOHENSTEIN, ADOLFO (1854–?). Russian-born painter and designer. Designed sets and costumes for first production of *Falstaff* and did a series of deathbed drawings of Verdi.

HUDSON, SIR JAMES (1810–85). British diplomat. Minister plenipotentiary to the Court of Sardinia, in Turin, for much of the Risorgimento period. Intimate with Cavour, arranged for Verdi to meet him. Urged Verdi to represent Busseto in the Parma Provincial Assembly.

HUGO, VICTOR MARIE (1802–85). French poet and dramatist. Verdi used Hugo plays as the basis of *Ernani* and *Rigoletto* (drama entitled *Le Roi s'amuse*). Hugo was annoyed at this use of his work, for which no permission had been asked.

ISMAEL (ISMAËL, ISMAIEL) JAMMES (JEAN-VITAL) (1827–?). North African baritone of Jewish descent. Sang title roles in French-language opening of *Rigoletto*, 1864, and *Macbeth,* 1865. Also sang in *Ernani, Jérusalem, Trouvère,* and *Vêpres.*

ISMAIL, PASHA, Vicerory of Egypt (1830–95). Autocratic modernizing ruler of Egypt, 1863–79. His reign marked the opening of the Suez Canal, the Cairo Opera, the first Egyptian archaeological museum (founded and directed by Mariette Bey, *q.v.*). His interest in Italian music led to the commissioning of *Aida.*

IVANOFF, NICOLA (1810–77). Russian tenor. Rossini commissioned Verdi to write two substitute arias for Ivanoff, a close friend: the first for *Ernani,* Parma, 1844, the other for Foresto in *Attila* (Act III), probably for Trieste, autumn, 1846. Repertory included *Masnadieri, Lombardi.*

JACOVACCI, VINCENZO ("CENCIO") (1811–81). Italian impresario, manager at one time or another of the principal theaters of Rome in his day, notably the Apollo (from 1840 to the end of his life), but also the Argentina, Alibert, Anfiteatro, and Costanzi. Presented premieres of *Trovatore* (1853) and *Ballo* (1859), as well as the Italian premiere of

Forza, as *Don Alvaro* (1863). Giuseppina Strepponi sang for him in the 1840–41 Carnival season at the Apollo and was godmother to his daughter.

JULIAN VAN GELDER. Soprano. Created Hélène in *Jérusalem* at the Paris Opéra, 1847. Probably the Julian who studied with Giuseppina Strepponi at that time. Sang at Her Majesty's in London, 1849–51, under the name of Giuliani. Repertory included *Lombardi, Nabucco* (Fenena), *Ernani,* and *Foscari.*

JULIENNE-DEJEAN, EUGENIE. French soprano. Created the role of Amelia in *Ballo,* Teatro Apollo, Rome, 1859. Also sang in *Lombardi, Ernani, Foscari, Luisa Miller, Jérusalem, Trovatore, Traviata, Vespri,* and *Aroldo.*

JUNCA, MARCEL (MARCELLO) (1818–78). French bass. Studied at the conservatories of Toulouse and Paris. Sang Padre Guardiano in revised *Forza,* Scala, Milan, 1869. Also sang in *Nabucco, Ernani* (Silva), *Rigoletto, Ballo, Don Carlos* (Philip), *Aida,* and U.S. premiere of *Vespri* (Procida), Academy of Music, New York, 1859.

KRAUSS, GABRIELLE (1842–1906). Austrian soprano. Debut 1858, Vienna. Repertory included *Trovatore, Ballo, Ernani, Rigoletto.* Sang French premiere of *Aida,* Paris Opéra, 1880.

LABLACHE, LUIGI (1794–1858). Italian bass. Debut 1820. Major figure in nineteenth-century opera, created several Bellini and Donizetti roles, as well as the role of Massimiliano in *Masnadieri,* Her Majesty's Theatre, London, 1847. Had sung (1837) in Mercadante's setting of the same story, *I briganti.*

LAGRUA, EMMA (1831–?). Italian soprano born in Palermo, but educated in Germany and France. Debut Dresden, c.1851; Italian debut, 1855, Turin. Repertory included *Nabucco, Attila, Trovatore, Ernani, Traviata.* Was to have created role of Leonora in *Forza* in St. Petersburg, but was indisposed, and the production was postponed for a year, when another soprano sang the role.

LAMPUGNANI, GIOVANNI BATTISTA (1813–73). Italian theatrical agent, personal representative of Draneht (*q.v.*) in Milan, friend of conductor Angelo Mariani (*q.v.*). Participated in the negotiations for the premiere of *Aida.* Married to Katinka Evers, a former soprano, who continued his business after her husband's death.

LANARI, ALESSANDRO (1790–1862). Italian impresario, a key figure in Italian operatic history. Close friend of Giuseppina Strepponi during her active career in the theater. Impresario at Senigallia 1837–43 (where he met Strepponi). Manager of Teatro alla Pergola, Florence, from 1823–28, 1830–35, 1839–48 (when he commissioned *Macbeth*), and later in the 1860s. Extensive correspondence with Verdi, Strepponi, and others (largely unpublished).

LANDI, GIOVANNI (1821–?). Debut Vercelli, 1843–44. Italian tenor. Sang Alfredo in the revised *Traviata*, Teatro San Benedetto, Venice, 1854. Also sang in *Lombardi, Ernani, Masnadieri* and *Rigoletto*. One of the few tenors to sing both *Stiffelio* and *Aroldo*.

LAVIGNA, VINCENZO (1776–1836). Italian composer, musician, and teacher. Author of several operas. *Maestro al cembalo* at La Scala early nineteenth century. Verdi studied with him, 1832–35. Took active interest in Verdi's early, preoperatic career.

LHERIE, PAUL. French baritone. Created role of Posa in *Don Carlos* at the Paris Opéra, 1867.

LIND, JENNY (1820–87). Swedish soprano. Debut 1838, Stockholm. At height of her popularity, especially in England, created role of Amelia in *Masnadieri*, Her Majesty's Theatre, London, 1847.

LOEWE, SOFIA (SOPHIE JOHANNA) (1816?–66). German soprano from a family of actors. Scala debut in 1841, after success in Germany and London. Created role of Elvira in *Ernani*, Fenice, Venice, 1844, and Odabella in *Attila*, Fenice, Venice, 1846. Was to have sung Lady Macbeth, but cancelled and was replaced by Barbieri-Nini (*q.v.*). Repertory included *Lombardi* and *Alzira* (Verdi wrote an aria for her in this opera, performed in Venice, 1845).

LOTTI DELLA SANTA, MARCELLINA (1831–1901). Italian soprano. Debut 1850–51, Constantinople. Created role of Mina in *Aroldo*, Teatro Nuovo, Rimini, 1857. Repertory included *Nabucco, Lombardi, Ernani, Foscari, Giovanna d'Arco, Attila, Macbeth, Stiffelio, Rigoletto, Trovatore, Vespri, Ballo*. Sang in St. Petersburg, London, Lisbon.

LUCCA, FRANCESCO (1802–72) and his wife GIOVANNINA STRAZZA (1814–94). Italian music publishers. The firm shared rights with Ricordi for *Nabucco*, obtained rights for *Attila, Masnadieri*, and *Corsaro*. Verdi did not enjoy dealing with the firm. After her husband's death, Giovannina continued the business vigorously, sparking further Verdian wrath by her introduction of new French opera composers into Italy and by encouraging Italian productions of Wagner, whom she also published.

LUCCARDI, VINCENZO (1811–76). Italian sculptor, professor at the Accademia di San Luca, Rome. Close friend of Verdi from about 1844, helped with practical arrangements for Verdi's visits to Rome. Important correspondence with Verdi.

LUMLEY, BENJAMIN (1811–75). English impresario. Managed Her Majesty's Theatre, London, off and on, 1841–59. Commissioned *Mas-*

nadieri and persuaded Verdi to come to London and conduct it. Also produced *Nabucco, Lombardi, Ernani, Foscari, Attila, Luisa Miller, Trovatore, Traviata* in England. Lucca dedicated the piano-vocal vocal score of *Attila* to him. Left a valuable volume of memoirs.

MAFFEI, ANDREA (1798–1885). Italian poet, translator. Close friend of Verdi from the 1840s. Verdi set several Maffei poems as songs. Made revisions of *Macbeth* libretto and wrote some scenes at Verdi's request. Provided libretto for *Masnadieri*. Husband of Clara Maffei *(q.v.)*.

MAFFEI, Countess CLARA (born CARRARA SPINELLI) (1814–86). Italian patriot and intellectual. Close friend of Verdi from the early 1840s. Friend of Mazzini and Cavour, as well as of many writers and musicians whom she entertained in her Milanese salon. Introduced Verdi to Manzoni (1868). After legal separation from Maffei, she was the lifelong friend of the patriot-statesman-writer Carlo Tenca. Their correspondence has been published.

MAGNANI, GEROLAMO (GIROLAMO) (1815–89). Italian painter and designer from Parma. He designed many Verdi productions for the Teatro Regio there, including *Ernani, Foscari*. Much admired by Verdi, he designed the Italian premiere of *Aida*. Also worked in London, Paris, Philadelphia, and New York. Mentioned in Verdi's correspondence.

MALVEZZI, SETTIMIO (1817–87). Italian tenor from Rome. Debut 1840–41, Perugia. Created Rodolfo in *Luisa Miller*, San Carlo, Naples, 1849. Also sang the role at La Scala, 1851–52. Was the first Paris Ernani (1846). Repertory included *Foscari, Rigoletto, Trovatore*, and *Traviata*.

MAMELI, GOFFREDO (1827–49). Italian patriot. At Mazzini's request, Verdi set Mameli's patriotic poem, "Fratelli d'Italia" or "Suona la tromba," in 1848.

MANZONI, ALESSANDRO (1785–1873). Italian writer. Author of *I promessi sposi*, most famous Italian novel. Verdi first met Manzoni June 30, 1868. Moved profoundly by the author's death in 1873, the composer completed the *Messa da Requiem* begun some years earlier at the death of Rossini.

MARIANI, ANGELO (1822–73). Italian conductor, violinist, composer. Close, but sometimes strained friendship with Verdi from 1857. Conducted premieres of *Aroldo*, Rimini, 1857, and (Italian premiere) *Don Carlos*, Bologna, 1867. Lover of Teresa Stolz *(q.v.)*, who broke off with him after meeting Verdi. Outstanding Italian conductor of this time, responsible for the first Italian performance of a Wagner opera (*Lohengrin*, Bologna, 1871).

MARIA LUIGIA (MARIE LOUISE) (1791–1847). Austrian-born ruler. Second wife of Napoleon I; after his downfall, Duchess of Parma, Pia-

cenza, and Guastalla. Patroness of the arts, responsible for founding of
Parma conservatory and construction of Teatro Regio. Granted Verdi a
scholarship. *Lombardi* dedicated to her. First edition of the piano score
of *Oberto* dedicated to her consort, Count Neipperg.

MARIETTE, AUGUSTE-ÉDOUARD (1821–81). French Egyptologist.
First saw Egypt in 1850. His excavations revealed the Serapis Temple
and Apis tomb near Memphis. Later he unearthed the temple of the
sphinx and other important monuments and treasures. Made Bey in
1858 and Pasha in 1879. Established Boulaq Museum of Egyptian an-
tiquities in 1863. Wrote the original outline of *Aida.*

MARINI, IGNAZIO (1811–73). Italian bass. Debut 1832. Created title
role in *Oberto,* Scala, Milan, 1839, and title role in *Attila,* Fenice, Venice,
1846 (also sang the role in the American premiere of the opera, New
York, 1850). Verdi wrote Silva's cabaletta "Infin che un brando vindice" in *Ernani* for Marini.

MARIO, GIOVANNI MATTEO DI CANDIA (1810–83). Italian tenor.
Debut Paris, 1838. Married the soprano Giulia Grisi. Outstanding
Verdi interpreter: first Duca (*Rigoletto*) in London; Paris premieres of
Foscari, Trovatore, Traviata, and *Ballo;* also sang in *Lombardi.*

MARTINELLI, AMILCARE. Italian lawyer and writer. Drafted Giuseppina Strepponi's will and left a moving account of her last days.

MASINI, ANGELO (1844–1926). Italian tenor. Debut 1867, Finale di
Modena. First Radamès (*Aida*) in Florence, Paris, and Vienna. Had important international career. Repertory included *Ernani, Rigoletto, Traviata, Forza.*

MASSINI or MASINI, PIETRO. Italian musicophile. Director of group
of amateurs who performed Haydn's *Creation* at the Teatro dei Filo-
drammatici, April 1834. Verdi replaced the conductor and became a
friend of Massini, who helped the composer at the start of his career.

MAUREL, VICTOR (1848–1923). French baritone. Debut Marseilles,
1867. Sang title role in revised *Simon,* Scala, Milan, 1881. Created role of
Iago in *Otello,* Scala, 1887, and title role in *Falstaff,* Scala, 1893. While
still a student at the Paris Conservatory, sang in the chorus at the premiere of *Don Carlos,* 1867. Also sang in *Ernani, Rigoletto, Trovatore, Ballo,*
and *Aida.*

MAZZUCATO, ALBERTO (1813–77). Italian violinist, composer, writer,
teacher. From 1839 taught at Milan Conservatory; Boito was one of his
students. Named its director in 1872 and remained in this post until his
death. Wrote an *Ernani* (1833) eclipsed by Verdi's. Contributed to *La
Gazzetta musicale di Milano* (1845–56) and was its editor 1856–58. Conductor at La Scala 1858–68. Member of the committee for the abortive

collective Requiem for Rossini, admired Verdi's contribution ("Libera me"). Conducted the Milanese premiere of *Don Carlos* (1868). Correspondence with Verdi.

MERCADANTE, GIUSEPPE SAVERIO RAFFAELE (1795–1870). Italian composer. Head of Naples conservatory 1840–70. Wrote sixty operas, widely performed in Italy and abroad. Verdi respected the older composer, and also set some of the same subjects, such as *Ballo* (Mercadante's *Il reggente*) and *Masnadieri* (*I briganti*).

MERELLI, BARTOLOMEO (1793–1879). Italian impresario, at La Scala 1836–50, and also in Vienna (where he commissioned a work from Weber). Responsible for the premieres of *Oberto, Un giorno di regno, Nabucco, Lombardi, Giovanna d'Arco*. Verdi quarreled with him at the time of *Giovanna* and had nothing to do with La Scala for twenty-five years afterward. Verdi objected to the impresario's parsimony in producing works and his poor choice of singers.

MERMILLOD, GASPARD (1824–92). Swiss priest who performed marriage ceremony for Giuseppina Strepponi and Verdi at Collonges-sous-Salève, 1859. Later elevated to cardinal; a distinguished if controversial church figure, writer, and diplomat.

MÉRY, FRANCOIS JOSEPH (pseudonym of JOSEPH PIERRE AGNES) (1797–1865). French librettist and writer. Wrote most of the libretto of *Don Carlos*, but died before its completion.

METLICOWITZ, LEOPOLDO (1868–1944). German graphic artist and painter. Did posters and frontispieces for Ricordi at the turn of the century. Left some lovely watercolors of Verdi at Sant'Agata, where the painter was occasionally a guest.

MIRAGLIA, CORRADO. Italian tenor. Created Ismaele in *Nabucco*, Scala, Milan, 1842. Also sang in *Ernani, Foscari, Giovanna d'Arco, Alzira, Macbeth, Luisa Miler, Trovatore,* and *Vespri.*

MIRATE, RAFFAELE (1815–85). Italian tenor. Debut Naples, 1837. Created Duca in *Rigoletto*, Fenice, Venice, 1851. Also sang in *Lombardi, Ernani, Giovanna d'Arco, Masnadieri, Battaglia, Gerusalemme, Stiffelio,* and *Aroldo.*

MOCENIGO, Count NANI. Italian aristocrat and musicophile. President of the Fenice, Venice. During his presidency, premieres of *Ernani* (1844) and *Attila* (1846). First edition of *Ernani* dedicated to Mocenigo's wife.

MONALDI, Marchese GINO (1847–1932). Italian author and journalist. Wrote for leading musical magazines. Manager of Teatro Morlacchi, Perugia, and later of the Teatro Costanzi and the Teatro Argentina, Rome. Wrote an early biographical study of Verdi entitled *Verdi*

1838–1898, frequently revised and reissued, despite unreliability. Also wrote popular book on singers of the day.

MONGINI, PIETRO (1830–74). Italian tenor. Debut Genoa, 1852–53. Created role of Radamès in *Aida,* Cairo, 1871. Repertory also included *Lombardi, Ernani, Masnadieri, Luisa Miller, Rigoletto, Trovatore, Vespri, Ballo, Forza,* and *Carlos.*

MONJAUZE (1825–77). Italian tenor. Debut Paris, 1855. Sang the Duke in first French-language performances of *Rigoletto,* in Paris (1863). Created the role of Macduff in revised *Macbeth,* Théâtre-Lyrique, Paris, 1865. Repertory included *Traviata* (entitled in French, *Violetta*).

MONPLAISIR, HIPPOLYTE-GEORGE (pseudonym of HIPPOLYTE-GEORGE SORNET) (1821–77). French dancer and choreographer, active in Italy. Solo dancer at La Scala, 1844. Toured U.S. extensively in late 1840s. Choreographer at La Scala from 1861 until his death. Presented his epic ballet *Le figlie di Cheope* on December 31, 1871, shortly before premiere of *Aida,* thus initiating Verdi. Choreographed *Aida,* Paris *Macbeth,* 1865, and *Don Carlos* at La Scala, 1868.

MONTARIO, ENRICO (1816–86). Italian journalist. Editor of *Rivista di Firenze.* Adversely criticized Maffei's libretto of *Masnadieri.*

MORCHIO, DANIELE. Italian lawyer and amateur poet, from Genoa. He and his wife Ernesta were close friends of the Verdis.

MORELLI, DOMENICO (1826–1901). Italian painter, from Naples. One of the outstanding artists of his day. Close friend of Verdi, whose portrait he painted; and important member of the Verdis' Neapolitan circle. Verdi and Morelli exchanged letters on the characters in *Otello,* also discussing the possible costumes and settings for that opera.

MORÈRE, A. French tenor. Created title role in *Don Carlos* at the Paris Opéra, 1867. Repertory also included *Trovatore* and *Ballo.*

MORIANI, NAPOLEONE (1806 or 1808–1878). Italian tenor. Debut Pavia, 1833. Popular singer throughout the 1840s, known as the "tenore della bella morte" for his moving death-scene in *Lucia.* Repertory included *Ernani, Lombardi, Attila* (Verdi wrote a new aria for Foresto in Act III of this work, sung by Moriani, Carnival season, Milan, 1846–47). Believed by Frank Walker to be the father of Giuseppina Strepponi's illegitimate children.

MOROSINI, Countess EMILIA (*d. c.* 1848). Italian noblewoman of Swiss origin. Intellectual hostess in Milan during early years of Verdi's career. Verdi was a friend of the countess and her family.

MUZIO, EMANUELE (1825–90). Italian composer and conductor. Verdi's principal pupil, whose studies were also aided by Antonio

Barezzi. A fellow native of Busseto, Muzio remained with Verdi for some years, acting as his amanuensis and companion. Later conducted Verdi's operas throughout Europe and in America (including U.S. premieres of *Vespri,* New York, 1859, and *Aida,* New York, 1873). Conducted the production of *Rigoletto* for the opening of the Cairo Opera House, 1869.

NANTIER-DIDIÉE, CONSTANCE (MARIE) (1832–65). French mezzo-soprano. Debut Turin, 1849. Created Preziosilla in *Forza,* Imperial Theater, St. Petersburg, 1862. Sang *Luisa Miller* at Théâtre-Italien, 1851. Repertory included *Rigoletto* and *Ballo.*

NAVARINI (NAVARRINI), FRANCESCO (1855–1923). Italian bass. Sang Inquisitor at premiere of revised *Don Carlo,* Scala, Milan, 1884, and created Lodovico in *Otello,* Scala, Milan, 1887. Also sang in *Ernani* (Silva), *Trovatore, Simon, Ballo* (Samuele), and *Aida.*

NEGRINI (pseudonym of CARLO VILLA) (1826–65). Italian tenor. Created Gabriele in *Simon,* Fenice, Venice, 1857. Also sang in *Giovanna d'Arco, Attila, Gerusalemme, Rigoletto, Trovatore, Traviata, Giovanna de Guzman (Vespri),* and *Ballo.*

NUITTER, CHARLES-LOUIS-ETIENNE (anagram of C.-L.-E. Truinet) (1828–99). French librettist and translator. Translated with Alexandre Beaumont, Verdi's *Macbeth* into French, 1865; *Aida,* with Du Locle, 1872, and with Verdi in 1876; *Forza* with Du Locle in 1882; and *Boccanegra* in 1883. After 1866, Nuitter was archivist of the Paris Opéra for some years; in 1875 he replaced his friend Du Locle temporarily as director of the Opéra-Comique.

OBIN, LOUIS-HENRI. French bass. Created Procida in *Vêpres,* 1855, and Philip in *Don Carlos,* 1867, both at the Paris Opéra.

PACINI, EMILIANO (or Emilien) (1810–98). Italo-French translator. Translated *Trovatore* into French, 1857.

PALIANTI, LOUIS. Stage director in Paris. Published a series of staging manuals based on production at the Paris Opéra, including many of Verdi's operas, e.g. *Vêpres* and *Trouvère.*

PALIZZI, FILIPPO (1818–99). Italian painter, one of a family of Neapolitan painters. Member of the Naples circle of Verdi's friends. Specialized in animal subjects and painted portrait of the Verdi's Maltese spaniel Lulù. Verdi bought other paintings by Palizzi.

PANCANI, EMILIO (1830–98). Italian tenor. Sang in chorus in his native Florence, then studied and made debut as Macduff (*Macbeth*) in 1848, Reggio Emilia. Created title role in *Aroldo,* Teatro Nuovo, Rimini, 1857. Repertory also included *Ernani, Foscari, Giovanna d'Arco, Attila, Corsaro, Trovatore, Traviata.*

PANDOLFINI, FRANCESCO (1836–1916). Italian baritone, popular at La Scala during later years of Verdi's life. Repertory included *Nabucco*, *Ernani*, *Macbeth* (Italian premiere of revised version), *Rigoletto*, *Trovatore*, *Traviata*, *Vespri*, *Aroldo*, *Ballo*, *Forza*, *Don Carlo*, and *Aida* (Italian premiere). His daughter, the soprano ANGELICA (1871–1959) was also a noted Verdi interpreter; she sang in *Traviata*, 1897–98, and *Falstaff*, 1898–99.

PANTALEONI, ROMILDA (1847–1917). Italian soprano. Debut Milan, 1868. Created role of Desdemona in *Otello*, Scala, Milan, 1887, under conductor Faccio, who was her lover. Verdi liked her personally but did not find her interpretation satisfactory. Repertory included *Trovatore*, *Ballo*, *Forza*, *Don Carlo*, *Aida*. She also sang Desdemona in the Rossini *Otello* (Malta, 1871–72) and created the role of Tigrana in Puccini's *Edgar*, 1889.

PAROLI, GIOVANNI. Italian tenor. Created Cassio in *Otello*, Scala, Milan, 1887, and D. Caius in *Falstaff*, Scala, Milan, 1893.

PASETTI, FRANCESCO. Italian music lover; friend and supporter of Verdi at the outset of his career. Ricordi dedicated piano-vocal score of *Oberto* to Pasetti.

PASQUA, GIUSEPPINA (1855–1930). Italian mezzo-soprano. Debut as soprano Palermo, 1869, as Oscar in *Ballo*. Sang Eboli in revised *Don Carlos*, Scala, Milan, 1884, and created role of Quickly in *Falstaff*, Scala, 1893. Also sang in *Trovatore* (Leonora and Azucena), *Forza* and *Aida*.

PATTI, ADELINA (1843–1919). Spanish-born soprano of Italian origin. Raised in U.S., where she made her early career. Sang in *Ernani*, *Giovanna d'Arco*, *Rigoletto*, *Trovatore*, *Traviata*, and especially famous for her *Aida*.

PENCO, ROSINA (1830?–94). Italian soprano. Debut 1847, Copenhagen. Created role of Leonora in *Trovatore*, Apollo, Rome, 1853. Repertory included *Lombardi*, *Ernani*, *Giovanna d'Arco*, *Luisa Miller*, *Traviata*, *Vespri*, and *Ballo*. Verdi admired her but considered her a better actress than singer.

PERRIN, EMILE-CESAR-VICTOR (1814–85). French painter and administrator. Director of Opéra-Comique, 1848. In 1854 also assumed management of Théâtre-Lyrique (until 1855). Left Comique in a prosperous state in 1857. Director of the Paris Opéra in 1862; there commissioned *Don Carlos* (1867). Director of the Théâtre-Français, 1873–85.

PIATTI, GIULIO (1816–72). Italian painter, specializing in historical subjects. Active in Florence, where he became friends with Verdi at the time of *Macbeth* (1847).

PIAVE, FRANCESCO MARIA (1810–76). Italian librettist. Joined staff of La Fenice as librettist and stage manager in 1844. Wrote his first libretto, *Ernani*, for Verdi, and soon became his friend, collaborator, and "errand boy." In 1859 moved to Milan to stage productions at La Scala and teach. Paralyzed in 1869. Verdi contributed to his family's support. Wrote librettos of *Ernani, Foscari, Macbeth, Corsaro, Stiffelio, Rigoletto, Traviata, Boccanegra, Aroldo, Forza,* and completed Solera's *Attila.* Important correspondence with Verdi.

PIAZZA, ANTONIO. Italian journalist. Presumably wrote original libretto of *Oberto*, subsequently refashioned by Solera, and perhaps by Verdi himself.

PICCOLOMINI, MARIA (1834–99). Italian soprano. Debut Florence, 1852. Repertory included *Lombardi, Giovanna d'Arco, Luisa Miller* (London premiere), *Rigoletto, Trovatore,* and *Traviata.* Verdi intended her to sing Cordelia in the *King Lear* he thought to write—but did not—for Naples, 1857–58. He also admired her Violetta very much.

PILLET, LEON. French impresario. Director of the Paris Opéra. Late 1845 or early 1846, he tried, unsuccessfully, to induce Verdi to write an opera for him.

PINI-CORSI, ANTONIO (1858–1918). Italian baritone. Debut Cremona, 1878. Created role of Ford in *Falstaff,* Scala, Milan, 1893. Admired as a buffo, he also sang Rigoletto and Germont (*Traviata*). Was Schaunard in first performance of Puccini's *Boheme.*

PINTO Brothers. Italian violinists. Verdi asked them to take part in the private first performance of his *Quartet* in a Naples hotel. One of the brothers was also a first violinist in the premiere of the *Requiem,* Chiesa di San Marco, Milan, 1874.

PIROLI, GIUSEPPE (1815–90). Italian lawyer and statesman. Came from Busseto, childhood friend of Verdi. Professor of law at University of Parma. Member of Cavour's Liberal Party. Senator, 1884. Long and invaluable correspondence with Verdi, largely published.

PIZZI, ITALO (1849–1920). Italian orientalist and writer. Friend of Verdi's and author of a useful volume of memoirs. Published in 1884 a lyric drama, *Bisero.*

POGGI, ANTONIO (1808–75). Italian tenor from Bologna. Debut Bologna, 1827–28. Created role of Carlo in *Giovanna d'Arco,* Scala, Milan, 1845. Verdi directed him in Senigallia performance of *Lombardi* (July 1843) and wrote the new cabaletta "La mia letizia infondere" for that production. Husband of soprano Ermina Frezzolini-Poggi.

PONIATOWSKI, Prince JOSEPH (1816–73). Italian composer of Polish origin. Leading figure in Milanese society, wrote several French and

Italian operas including *Giovanni da Procida*, in which Giuseppina Strepponi sang.

PONZ (PONS), FELICIANO. Italian bass. Created Sparafucile in *Rigoletto*, Fenice, Venice, 1857. Repertory included *Nabucco, Ernani, Macbeth,* and *Luisa Miller.*

POUGIN, ARTHUR (FRANÇOIS ARTHUR PAROISSE-POUGIN) (1834–1921). French musicologist and author. One of his most important works was his life of Verdi (1881), which was translated and considerably amplified by Folchetto (Jacopo Caponi) and published by Ricordi, with the tacit legitimization by Verdi of the book's facts—many of them subsequently revealed to be fictitious.

POZZONI (ANASTASI-POZZONI), ANTONIETTA (1846–1914). Italian soprano, later mezzo. Sang in *Vespri* and *Macbeth* in Rome, 1866–67, and in *Traviata* in Florence, 1871, where Verdi heard her and approved her for the role of Aida, which she created in Cairo in 1871. In 1874 she sang Amneris. Included in her repertory were *Ernani, Ballo,* and *Forza.*

PROVESI, FERDINANDO (1770?–1833). Italian musician and teacher. *Maestro di cappella* and organist at the Church of San Bartolomeo, Busseto, he was Verdi's first serious music teacher. Wrote words and music for several comic operas performed in Busseto, 1825–29. Also conducted Busseto's Società Filarmonica. Verdi served as his assistant and, after his death, replaced him, though not without considerable local opposition.

RANIERI-MARINI, ANTONIETTA. Italian soprano. Debut Milan, 1839. Created role of Leonora in *Oberto*, Scala, Milan, 1839, and role of Marchesa del Poggio in *Giorno di regno*, Scala, 1840. Wife of Ignazio Marini (*q.v.*).

RAPAZZINI, CAROLINA (Carlotta?) Italian soprano. Created Medora in *Corsaro,* Teatro Grande, Trieste, 1848. Also sang in *Foscari, Giovanna d'Arco, Rigoletto,* and *Trovatore* (Azucena).

REY-BALLA (?–1889). French soprano. Sang Lady Macbeth, Théâtre-Lyrique, Paris, 1865. Sang at La Scala, 1870. Retired in 1872. Wife of composer Jean Rey. Repertory included *Nabucco, Lombardi, Ernani, Luisa Miller, Rigoletto, Trovatore,* and *Ballo.*

RICORDI FAMILY. Italian music publishers.

GIOVANNI (1785–1853) established the Stamperia di Musica in Milan, 1808, and began publishing piano-vocal scores of successful operas. By 1844 the firm had published works of Verdi, as well as operas of Rossini, Bellini, and Donizetti. In 1842 Giovanni founded *La Gazzetta musicale di Milano,* which continued publication until 1902.

TITO (1811–88), son of Giovanni, worked for his father from 1825 until his death. In 1864 he established the Clausetti firm in Naples, and in 1887 took over the catalogs of Guidi of Florence and Del Monaco of Naples. Was an accomplished amateur pianist.

GIULIO (1840–1912), son of Tito, entered the family firm in 1863, took over the *Gazzetta* in 1866, and gradually supplanted his father in the handling of the firm's never easy relations with Verdi. In 1888, Ricordi took over the firm of Lucca, their chief Italian rival, and Giulio assumed the management. Giulio was also a writer, painter, and (under the name of J. Burgmein) composer. He wrote the production manuals, published by Ricordi, for *Aida*, the revised *Boccanegra*, and *Otello*. He recognized the talent of the young Puccini and persuaded the firm to support the composer until he was successfully launched.

Verdi wrote about 1500 letters, not all published as yet, to the firm of Ricordi from 1843 to his death.

RISTORI, ADELAIDE (1822–1906). Italian actress, famous and admired also outside Italy, thanks to her numerous international tours. Compared, by the French, to Rachel. Verdi knew and admired her and considered her a glorious goodwill ambassador of the new Italy.

RIVAS, ÁNGEL DE SAAVEDRA Y RAMIREZ DE SAN BANQUEDANO, DUQUE DE (1791–1865). Spanish dramatist. Wrote the play *Don Álvaro (o la fuerza del sino)*, which Verdi used as the basis of *Forza*.

ROMANI, FELICE (1788–1865). Italian poet, critic, librettist. Wrote approximately 100 librettos. His comic text *Il finto Stanislao*, originally set by Adalbert Gyrowetz in Milan, 1816, later became *Un giorno di regno*, set by Verdi in 1840.

RONCONI, GIORGIO (1810–90). Italian baritone. Debut Parma, 1830–31. Donizetti specialist, then the prototype of the Verdi baritone. Created title role in *Nabucco*, Scala, Milan, 1842. Also sang Doge Francesco in London premiere of *Foscari* and Don Carlo in Paris premiere of *Ernani*. His repertory also included *Rigoletto* and *Trovatore*. A great favorite of Verdi's.

ROOSEVELT, BLANCHE (pseudonym of MACCHETTA, BLANCHE ROOSEVELT TUCKER) (1853–98). American journalist and novelist. Enterprising reporter, she met Verdi several times and attended premiere of *Otello*. Left vivid accounts of Verdi, Boito, and the gala opening in her book *Verdi: Milan and "Othello,"* 1887. Also wrote books on Gustave Doré and Victorien Sardou.

ROPPA, GIACOMO. Italian tenor. Created role of Jacopo in *Foscari*, Argentina, Rome, 1844. Also sang in *Ernani, Alzira, Luisa Miller,* and *Trovatore*.

ROQUEPLAN, NESTOR (1804–70). French theater director. Managed Paris Opéra, 1847–54, then Opéra-Comique, 1857–60. The Opéra reopened with the lavish premiere of *Jérusalem*, 1847, initiating his management.

ROTA, GIACOMO (1836–98). Italian baritone. Debut in *Ernani* 1865, Asti. Sang Melitone in revised *Forza*, Scala, Milan, 1869. Also sang in *Trovatore* and *Ballo*.

ROYER, ALPHONSE (1803–75). French librettist and theater director. Joint director, with the librettist Vaez (*q.v.*), of the Paris Opéra. Had previously provided, also with Vaez, the libretto of *Jérusalem*.

SALVATI, FEDERICO. Italian tenor. Sang Paolo in revised *Simon*, Scala, Milan, 1881.

SALVI, LORENZO (1810–79). Italian tenor. Debut in 1830, Zara. Created role of Riccardo in *Oberto*, Scala, Milan, 1839, and Edoardo in *Giorno di regno*, Scala, 1840. Repertory also included *Lombardi*. Sang in New York, 1850–53.

SALVINI-DONATELLI, FANNY (1815–91). Italian soprano and actress. Stepmother of the actor Tommaso Salvini. Created role of Violetta in *Traviata*, Fenice, Venice, 1853, and was the most successful of the three principals on that not entirely happy first night. Repertory included *Lombardi, Ernani, Foscari, Alzira, Macbeth, Masnadieri, Corsaro*, and *Aroldo*.

SANTLEY, Sir CHARLES (1838–1922). British baritone. Repertory included *Rigoletto, Trovatore, Traviata, Ballo, Forza*. Left several volumes of memoirs with interesting accounts of Piave and Verdi.

SASSAROLI, VINCENZO. Italian composer. After success of *Aida*, he persuaded Verdi and Ricordi to allow him to set the libretto again. Also composed a Requiem, saying the competition(?) with Verdi's would determine the true inheritor of Italian musical tradition. (Challenge published in the joke column of *La Gazetta musicale di Milano*.)

SASSE (SASS, SAX, SAXE), MARIE-COSTANCE (1838–1907). Belgian soprano. Debut Paris, 1859. Created role of Elisabeth in *Don Carlos*, Paris Opéra, 1867. Repertory included *Trouvère, Vêpres, Ballo*. Married the singer M. Castan (Castelmary). Was the first Selika in Meyerbeer's *L'Africaine* and the first Elisabeth in the Paris version of *Tannhäuser*.

SBRISCIA, ZELINDA. Italian contralto. Created Ulrica in *Ballo*, Teatro Apollo, Rome, 1859.

SCOTTI, PAMELA. Italian soprano. Created Oscar in *Ballo*, Teatro Apollo, Rome, 1859.

SCRIBE, AUGUSTIN EUGÈNE (1791–1861). French librettist and dramatist. Prolific author of plays, melodramas, vaudevilles, and librettos for opera and ballet. For Auber he wrote *Gustave III,* 1833, on which Somma based his *Ballo* libretto, 1857. With Charles Duveyrier he wrote the libretto of *Le Duc d'Albe,* which Donizetti left unfinished; Scribe transformed the libretto, with Verdi's consent, into the text of *Les Vêpres siciliennes.*

SCUDO, PAUL (1806–64). French music critic of Italian origin. Wrote regularly for *La Revue des Deux Mondes.* Hostile to Verdi.

SELETTI, PIETRO (1770–1853). Italian priest and teacher. Verdi was his pupil at the Busseto Ginnasio (1827) and later lived with Don Pietro's nephew Giuseppe, in Milan, though the landlord was not fond of the composer. Giuseppe's son Emilio became an important lawyer, historian, and public figure in Milan; he was a friend of Verdi in his later years.

SELVA, ANTONIO (1820?–89). Italian bass. Debut 1842, Padua, in *Nabucco.* Created roles of Silva in *Ernani,* Fenice, Venice, 1844, and Walter in *Luisa Miller,* San Carlo, Naples, 1849. Also sang in *Attila* and *Ballo.*

SEVERI, GIOVANNI. Italian tenor. Created role of the Prior in *Lombardi,* Scala, Milan, 1843. Sang Ismaele in Vienna *Nabucco.* Later retired from the stage to manage his father-in-law's business in Trieste. Verdi and Piave stayed with his family at the time of *Stiffelio* and wrote a barcarole, "Fiorellin che sorgi appena," for Severi's infant son.

SHAW, MARY (née POSTANS) (1814–76). British contralto. Sang role of Cuniza in premiere of *Oberto,* Scala, Milan, 1839, and thus was Verdi's first foreign interpreter.

SILVESTRI, ALESSANDRO. Italian baritone. Sang Philip in premiere of the revised *Don Carlos* at Scala, 1884. Also sang in *Otello* (Lodovico).

SOLANGES, PAUL (1847–1914). French poet and translator. With Boito, translated *Falstaff* into French.

SOLE, NICOLA (1827–59). Italian lawyer, member of Verdi's Neapolitan circle. A dilettante poet, he wrote poems on such subjects as religion, patriotism, high morals, family life.

SOLERA, TEMISTOCLE (1815–78). Italian librettist, composer, police official. Led a checkered career, including a period as court advisor to Isabella of Spain and secret envoy between Cavour and Napoleon III. Provided librettos for *Nabucco, Lombardi, Giovanna d'Arco,* and *Attila* (except for the last act, written by Piave). His failure to complete this last assignment caused a break with Verdi. He also lent a hand in revising Piazza's libretto for *Oberto.*

SOMMA, ANTONIO (1809–65). Italian lawyer, patriot, writer. Wrote several tragedies, well received. From 1840–47 director of the Teatro Grande, Trieste. Commissioned by Verdi to write libretto of *Re Lear*, never set, and *Ballo*, later revised for censorship reasons. Valuable correspondence with Verdi, largely published.

SORMANI-ANDREANI, Count GIUSEPPE. Italian musician. Director of Milan Conservatory when Verdi's application for admission was turned down.

SOUVESTRE, EMILE (1806–54). French writer, author of the play *Stiffelius* on which Verdi's opera *Stiffelio* was based.

SPEZIA-ALDIGHIERI, MARIA (1828–1907). Italian soprano. Debut 1849. Much favored by Verdi, she sang Violetta in the highly successful revised version of *Traviata*, Teatro San Benedetto, Venice, 1854. Repertory included *Nabucco, Ernani, Attila, Macbeth, Luisa Miller, Rigoletto, Trovatore, Aroldo* and *Ballo*.

STEHLE-GARBIN, ADELINA (c. 1865–1945). Austrian-born soprano. Created Nannetta in *Falstaff*, Scala, Milan, 1893. Also sang Gilda (*Rigoletto*) and Violetta (*Traviata*). Wife of tenor Edoardo Garbin (*q.v.*).

STELLER, FRANCESCO (1826–81). Italian baritone. Created role of Amonasro in *Aida*, Cairo, 1871. His career lasted at least thirty years; he was particulalry active in Russia. His repertory included *Nabucco, Lombardi, Ernani, Giovanna d'Arco, Masnadieri, Luisa Miller, Rigoletto, Trovatore, Traviata,* and *Ballo*.

STOLZ, TERESA (1834–1902). Bohemian soprano. Debut 1857, Tiflis (Elvira in *Ernani*). Sang Leonora in premiere of the revised *Forza*, Scala, Milan, 1869; the first performance of the *Requiem*, Chiesa di San Marco, Milan, 1874; and the Italian premiere of *Aida*, Scala, Milan, 1872. Repertory also included *Foscari, Giovanna d'Arco, Macbeth, Luisa Miller, Trovatore, Traviata, Vespri,* and *Don Carlo*. Rumored to be mistress of Verdi, though no real evidence of such a relationship has been found. Close friend of both Verdis in their late years.

STREPPONI, GIUSEPPINA (CLELIA MARIA JOSEPHA) (1815–97). Italian soprano. Verdi's second wife. Debut 1834. Immediately successful, a leading singer for the next decade, after which her voice declined sharply. Created role of Abigaille in *Nabucco*, Scala, Milan, 1842. Also sang Elvira in *Ernani*. After her retirement from the stage, she moved to Paris, where she sang in concert (mostly Verdi), taught, and probably began living with Verdi there in 1847. They were married in 1859. Left voluminous correspondence and important notebooks (only partially published).

SUPERCHI, ANTONIO (1817–1893). Italian baritone. Debut 1836. Created role of Don Carlo in *Ernani*, Fenice, Venice, 1844. Repertory included *Nabucco, Attila, Luisa Miller, Rigoletto,* and *Trovatore.*

TADOLINI, EUGENIA (1810?–?). Italian soprano. Debut c. 1828. Created title role of *Alzira*, San Carlo, Naples, 1845. Repertory included *Ernani* (Vienna premiere, 1844), *Attila,* and *Macbeth.*

TAMAGNO, FRANCESCO (1850–1905). Italian tenor. Debut 1870, Turin as comprimario. Debut as primo tenore, 1874, in *Ballo* (Palermo). Sang Gabriele Adorno in premiere of revised *Boccanegra*, Scala, Milan, 1881, and title role in revised *Don Carlos*, Scala, 1884. Created title role in *Otello*, Scala, Milan, 1887. Repertory included *Ernani, Trovatore, Aida, Ballo,* and *Rigoletto.*

TAMBERLICK, ENRICO (1820–89). Italian tenor. Debut Naples, 1841. Created role of Don Alvaro in *Forza*, Imperial Theater, St. Petersburg, 1862. Had been instrumental in arranging the commission for this opera and in persuading Verdi to accept it. Renowned for his high notes. Repertory of almost one hundred operas included *Nabucco, Lombardi, Ernani, Giovanna d'Arco, Attila, Luisa Miller, Rigoletto, Trovatore, Aroldo, Ballo,* and *Aida.*

TENCA, CARLO (1816–83). Italian patriot and writer. Editor of *Rivista Europea*. Lover of Countess Maffei after her separation. Friend of Verdi.

TERZIANI, EUGENIO (1824–89). Italian violinist, conductor, and composer. Chief conductor first in Rome and later at La Scala, where Faccio was his assistant. Under Verdi's supervision, conducted premiere of revised *Forza*, Scala, Milan, 1869. Returned to Rome, 1871.

TIBERINI, MARIO (1826–80). Italian tenor. Debut 1851. Sang Don Alvaro in premiere of revised *Forza*, Scala, Milan, 1869. Repertory included *Trovatore, Ballo,* and *Don Carlos*. Admired by Verdi.

TIETJENS, THERESE CATHLINE JOHANNA ALEXANDRA (1831–77). German-born Hungarian soprano. Popular in London, where she sang in British premieres of *Vespri*, 1859; *Ballo*, 1861; and *Forza*, 1867. Also sang in premiere of *Inno delle nazioni*, Her Majesty's Theatre, 1862. Was quite proud to have sung four Leonores: *Fidelio, Favorita, Trovatore,* and *Forza.*

TORELLI, ARCHILLE (1844?–1922). Italian dramatist from Naples. Sometime manager of Teatro San Carlo. His plays much enjoyed by the Verdis.

TORELLI, VINCENZO (1806?–84). Father of the above. Italian critic and journalist, in Naples. Editor of *Omnibus*, Neapolitan theatrical and literary paper. Often acted as Verdi's representative. Important member of Verdi's Neapolitan circle. Secretary of the San Carlo for some years. Correspondence with Verdi survives, largely published.

TORNAGHI, EUGENIO (1844?–1915). Italian publisher. Milanese agent for Ricordi, in frequent contact with Verdi. Ricordis tried to blame him for certain irregularities in Verdi's contracts and royalty statements, which had led to a rift between the composer and the firm (c. 1874). Verdi not convinced.

TOSCANINI, ARTURO (1867–1957). Italian conductor. Played second cello in orchestra at premiere of *Otello*, 1887, having come specially from Paris to see and work under the composer. Conducted at La Scala during Verdi's last months. Responsible for important revival of *Falstaff* there in 1921. Left numerous Verdi recordings.

VAEZ, GUSTAVE (pseud. of JEAN NICOLAS GUSTAVE VAN NIEU-WENHUYSEN) (1812–62). Belgian librettist, translator, and administrator. Prepared libretto for *Jérusalem*, with Royer (*q.v.*). Also had administrative positions at the Odéon (from 1853) and the Paris Opéra (from 1856).

VARESI, FELICE (1813–89). Italian baritone. Debut 1834. Created title role in *Macbeth*, Pergola, Florence, 1847; title role in *Rigoletto*, Fenice, Venice, 1851; created role of Germont in *Traviata*, Fenice, 1853. Repertory also included *Ernani, Foscari, Masnadieri, Corsaro, Luisa Miller*. Artist of unusual intelligence (which Verdi respected) and—though not handsome—a convincing and versatile actor.

VASSELLI, ANTONIO (c. 1795–1870). Italian lawyer, from Rome. Brother-in-law of Donizetti (who called him "Toto" and corresponded with him regularly). Friend of Verdi. First editions of *Rigoletto* and *Trovatore* dedicated to him by Ricordi.

VAUCORBEIL, AUGUSTE EMANUEL (1821–84). Director of the Paris Opéra, 1879 until his death. Made a special trip to Sant' Agata in 1879 to persuade Verdi to permit the production of *Aida* at the Opéra. The mission was successful. Some correspondence with Verdi.

VELA, VINCENZO (1822–91). Italian sculptor. Much admired by Verdi, who saw his *Spartacus* at the Paris Exposition, 1855. Sculptor of Donizetti's tomb, Bergamo.

VERCELLINI, GIACOMO. Italian baritone. Created Paolo in *Simon*, Fenice, Venice, 1857.

VIARDOT-GARCIA, PAULINE (1821–1910). French singer and composer of Spanish origin. Member of the celebrated Garcia family, sister of Maria Malibran. Sang in *Trovatore* at Covent Garden, 1855. Was first

Lady Macbeth in British Isles (Dublin, 1859). She lowered or omitted much of her part.

VIGNA, CESARE (1814–1912). Italian alienist. A pioneering specialist in mental disorders, Vigna directed the Women's Asylum of San Clemente (after 1874) and brought about important reforms. One of Verdi's close friends and strong champions in Venice, along with Gallo and Somma. Ricordi dedicated *Traviata* to Vigna. Correspondence with Verdi published.

WALDMANN, MARIA (1844–1920). Austrian mezzo-soprano. Debut Trieste, 1869 (*Don Carlos*). Sang Amneris in Italian première of *Aida* at La Scala, Milan, 1872. Sang in the first performance of the *Requiem*, Chiesa di San Marco, Milan, 1874. Also sang in *Rigoletto* and *Trovatore*. Retired early from the stage, on marrying into an aristocratic family of Ferrara. Verdi admired her both as an artist and as a person, and remained friendly after her retirement. Long correspondence, largely published.

WERNER, ZACHARIAS (1768–1813). German author and dramatist. Colorful, romantic figure. Wrote, in 1808, *Attila, King of the Huns,* which served as the basis for the libretto of Verdi's *Attila*.

ZILLI, EMMA (1864–1901). Italian soprano. Created role of Alice in *Falstaff*, Scala, Milan, 1895.

Appendix B

A List of Verdi's Major Works by Date of First Performance[1]

Oberto, Conte di San Bonifacio	Nov. 17, 1839	La Scala, Milan
Il finto Stanislao, as *Un giorno di regno*	Sept. 5, 1840	La Scala, Milan
Nabucodonosor	Mar. 9, 1842	La Scala, Milan
I lombardi alla prima crociata	Feb. 11, 1843	La Scala, Milan
Ernani	Mar. 9, 1844	La Fenice, Venice
I due Foscari	Nov. 3, 1844	Teatro Argentina, Rome
Giovanna d'Arco	Feb. 15, 1845	La Scala, Milan
Alzira	Aug. 12, 1845	San Carlo, Naples
Attila	Mar. 17, 1846	La Fenice, Venice
Macbeth I	Mar. 14, 1847	La Pergola, Florence
I masnadieri	July 22, 1847	Her Majesty's Theatre, London
Jérusalem, revision of *I lombardi*	Nov. 26. 1847	L'Opéra, Paris
Il corsaro	Oct. 25, 1848	Teatro Grande, Trieste
La battaglia di Legnano	Jan. 27, 1849	Teatro Argentina, Rome
Luisa Miller	Dec. 8, 1849	San Carlo, Naples
Stiffelio	Nov. 16, 1850	Teatro Grande, Trieste
Rigoletto	Mar. 11, 1851	La Fenice, Venice
Il trovatore	Jan. 19, 1853	Teatro Apollo, Rome
La traviata	Mar. 6, 1853	La Fenice, Venice

1. Adapted from "A Listing of the Operas by Date of First Performance" in Martin Chusid's *A Catalog of Verdi's Operas* (1974), 173.

Les Vêpres siciliennes [2]	June 13, 1855	L'Opéra, Paris
Simon Boccanegra I	Mar. 12, 1857	La Fenice, Venice
Aroldo, revision of *Stiffelio*	Aug. 16, 1857	Teatro Nuovo, Rimini
Un ballo in maschera	Feb. 17, 1859	Teatro Apollo, Rome
La forza del destino I [3]	Nov. 10, 1862	Imperial Theatre, St. Petersburg
Macbeth II	Apr. 21, 1865	Théâtre-Lyrique, Paris
Don Carlos (Don Carlo I)	Mar. 11, 1867	L'Opéra, Paris
La forza del destino II	Feb. 27, 1869	La Scala, Milan
Aida	Dec. 24, 1871	The Opera, Cairo
Requiem	May 22, 1874	Church of San Marco, Milan
Simon Boccanegra II	Mar. 24, 1881	La Scala, Milan
Don Carlo II (*4-act* version)	Jan. 10, 1884	La Scala, Milan
Otello	Feb. 5, 1887	La Scala, Milan
Falstaff	Feb. 9, 1893	La Scala, Milan

2. First Italian performances simultaneously in Parma and Turin, December 26, 1855, with a censored text and entitled *Giovanna de Guzman.* All Italian performances of *Vêpres* to 1860 were of censored versions: *Giovanna de Guzman* in northern and central Italy; variously in Naples and Sicily as *Batilde di Turenna, Giovanna di Sicilia* and *Il vespro siciliano.* See Chusid, appendix entitled "Alternate Titles for the Operas." After 1860, only as *I vespri siciliani* in an Italian translation of the original.

3. First Italian performance with a censored libretto as *Don Alvaro* (Rome 1863). Subsequent Roman performances to 1871 used this title and libretto and a piano-vocal score of this version was published by Ricordi, Plate nos. 34681–34715. (Ibid.)

Index of
Verdi's Works

General Index

Abbadia, Luigia, 84
acting, emphasis on, 148–49, 167–69, 179, 189, 191
acts, structure of, 147
adaptations, unauthorized, 83–84, 147, 175–76, 183
L'Africaine (Meyerbeer), 101
aggressive characters, writing for, 219, 222
Alberti, Luigi, 279
American Institute for Verdi Studies, vii, 149, 242, 249
Appiani, Giuseppina, 263
archetypes, 161, 166, 217*ff.*
arias, conventions and performance of, 69*ff.*, 81*ff.*, 98, 199–208, 218*ff.*, 222*ff.*, 233
Ariosto, 2, 134
Arrivabene, Count Opprandino, 175, 248, 326
artisti da teatro, Gli (Ghislanzoni), 128
Auber, Daniel François, 8
audiences, 69, 88, 107, 129, 132, 142–43, 194, 198
auditions, 179
Aurelio in Palmiro (Rossini), 81
Austrian influence in Italy, 17*ff.*, 96, 194, 270*ff.*
autographs of opera, 109–10

Bach, Johann Sebastian, 4, 6, 7, 10, 13, 40, 67, 88
Baistrocchi, Don Pietro, 256
Balakirev, Mily, 8
Balestra, Luigi, 116, 261
Balfe, Michael William, 67
Barbaja, Domenico, 111
barbiere di Siviglia, Il (Rossini), 44, 69, 114, 256

"Una voce poco fa," 69, 81
Barbieri-Nini, Mariana, 57, 185
Barblan, Guglielmo, 136
Bardare, Leone, 275, 276
Barezzi, Antonio, 43, 50, 248, 257, 293
Barezzi, Margherita, 16, 50, 66, 257, 259, 262
baritone, Verdi's writing for, 77, 225–29
Basevi, Abramo, 94, 249
Basily, Francesco, 43, 257
bass, Verdi's writing for, 77, 82–83, 227, 229–30
Baudelaire, Charles Pierre, 10, 97, 204, 205
Beethoven, Ludwig van, 5, 6, 206
bel canto, 232, 233
Bellini, Gentile, 165
Bellini, Vincenzo, 8, 9, 52, 75–79, 83, 86, 91, 93, 100, 109, 111, 203, 218, 221, 222, 226, 228, 278
Berg, Alban, 206
Berganza, Teresa, 238
Bergonzi, Carlo, 235
Berini, 183
Berlioz, Hector, 74, 88, 152
Bizet, Georges, 68, 231
bohème, La (Puccini), 104
Boieldieu, François, 8
Boito, Arrigo, 8, 9, 10, 11, 54, 63, 97–98, 102, 120, 128–30, 139, 162, 165–67, 170, 172, 203, 286, 307*ff.*
Boito, Camillo, 64, 99
Borodin, Alexander, 8
Bottesini, Giovanni, 163, 299
Bourbons of Naples, 15, 83
Brahms, Johannes, 40
bravo, Il (Pacini), 90
breathing rhythms, 236–38
Brenna, Guglielmo, 124, 274

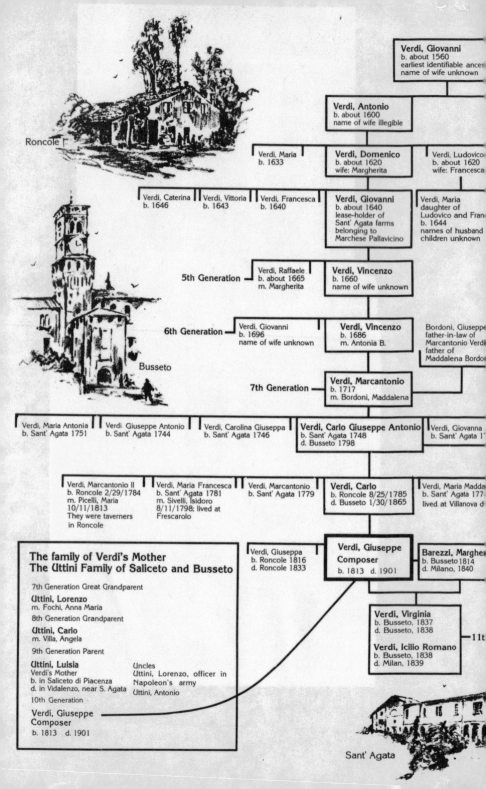

Roncole

Busseto

Sant' Agata

Verdi, Giovanni
b. about 1560
earliest identifiable ances[tor]
name of wife unknown

Verdi, Antonio
b. about 1600
name of wife illegible

Verdi, Maria
b. 1633

Verdi, Domenico
b. about 1620
wife: Margherita

Verdi, Ludovico
b. about 1620
wife: Francesca

Verdi, Caterina
b. 1646

Verdi, Vittoria
b. 1643

Verdi, Francesca
b. 1640

Verdi, Giovanni
b. about 1640
lease-holder of
Sant' Agata farms
belonging to
Marchese Pallavicino

Verdi, Maria
daughter of
Ludovico and Fran[cesca]
b. 1644
names of husband
children unknown

5th Generation —

Verdi, Raffaele
b. about 1665
m. Margherita

Verdi, Vincenzo
b. 1660
name of wife unknown

6th Generation —

Verdi, Giovanni
b. 1696
name of wife unknown

Verdi, Vincenzo
b. 1686
m. Antonia B.

Bordoni, Giuseppe
father-in-law of
Marcantonio Verdi
father of
Maddalena Bordo[ni]

7th Generation —

Verdi, Marcantonio
b. 1717
m. Bordoni, Maddalena

Verdi, Maria Antonia
b. Sant' Agata 1751

Verdi, Giuseppe Antonio
b. Sant' Agata 1744

Verdi, Carolina Giuseppa
b. Sant' Agata 1746

Verdi, Carlo Giuseppe Antonio
b. Sant' Agata 1748
d. Busseto 1798

Verdi, Giovanna
b. Sant' Agata 1[...]

Verdi, Marcantonio II
b. Roncole 2/29/1784
m. Picelli, Maria
10/11/1813
They were taverners
in Roncole

Verdi, Maria Francesca
b. Sant' Agata 1781
m. Sivelli, Isidoro
8/11/1798; lived at
Frescarolo

Verdi, Marcantonio
b. Sant' Agata 1779

Verdi, Carlo
b. Roncole 8/25/1785
d. Busseto 1/30/1865

Verdi, Maria Madda[lena]
b. Sant' Agata 177[...]
lived at Villanova d[...]

The family of Verdi's Mother
The Uttini Family of Saliceto and Busseto

7th Generation Great Grandparent

Uttini, Lorenzo
m. Fochi, Anna Maria

8th Generation Grandparent

Uttini, Carlo
m. Villa, Angela

9th Generation Parent

Uttini, Luisia
Verdi's Mother
b. in Saliceto di Piacenza
d. in Vidalenzo, near S. Agata

Uncles
Uttini, Lorenzo, officer in
Napoleon's army
Uttini, Antonio

10th Generation

Verdi, Giuseppe
Composer
b. 1813   d. 1901

Verdi, Giuseppa
b. Roncole 1816
d. Roncole 1833

Verdi, Giuseppe
Composer
b. 1813   d. 1901

Barezzi, Margher[ita]
b. Busseto 1814
d. Milano, 1840

Verdi, Virginia
b. Busseto, 1837
d. Busseto, 1838

Verdi, Icilio Romano
b. Busseto, 1838
d. Milan, 1839

—11t[h]